BloodFeud

THE STEWARTS & GORDONS AT WAR
IN THE AGE OF MARY QUEEN OF SCOTS

BLOODFEUD

THE STEWARTS & GORDONS AT WAR
IN THE AGE OF MARY QUEEN OF SCOTS

The gool, the Gordon, and the hoodie craw
Are the three worst faes that Moray ever saw.
From the *Gordon Ballads*

HARRY POTTER

TEMPUS

First published 2002

PUBLISHED IN THE UNITED KINGDOM BY:

Tempus Publishing Ltd
The Mill, Brimscombe Port
Stroud, Gloucestershire GL5 2QG
www.tempus-publishing.com

PUBLISHED IN THE UNITED STATES BY:

Tempus Publishing Inc.
2 Cumberland Streeet
Charleston, SC 29401
1-888-313-2665
www.tempuspublishing.com

British Library Cataloguing in Publication Data.
A catalogue record for this book is available from the British Library.

COPY EDITED AND PAGED BY:
Joanna de Vries

ISBN 0 7524 2330 4

CONTENTS

List of Plates   7
Preface   9
Map of Scotland Showing the Principal Places in Our Narrative   14

1.   The People of the North   15

PART I: THE 4th EARL OF HUNTLY AND THE 1st EARL OF
           MORAY, 1524 – 1563

2.   Cock o' the North   1524–1553/4   25
3.   The Bastard Lord James   1553/4–1561   49
4.   Corrichie   1561–1563   57

PART II: THE 5th EARL OF HUNTLY AND THE 1st EARL OF
           MORAY, 1563–1576

5.   The Slave of Passion   1563–1567   79
6.   The Twigs of Ambition   1567–1576   89

PART III: THE 6th EARL OF HUNTLY AND THE 2nd EARL OF
           MORAY 1567–1591/2

7.   St Colme's Son   1567–1582   107
8.   Tua Housis in the North   1576–1584   123
9.   Banging it out Bravely   1584–1588   131
10. A Particular Friend and a
     General Christian King   1587–1589   141
11. Disdain and Envy   1589–1591/2   155
12. Fashion among the Best Sort   7 February 1591/2   173
13. Execution done on Cawdor   4 February 1591/2   181

PART IV: THE 6th EARL AND 1st MARQUIS OF HUNTLY AND
           THE 3rd EARL OF MORAY 1591/2-1638

14. 'The Horror of Dinnibirsall'   February–March 1592   189
15. The First Puff of a Haggis   1592–1594   201
16. A Gowk's Storm   September – October 1594   213

17. The Brightest Jewel   1595–1597   223
18. Bequest of Hatred   1598–1638   229
19. Pacificus   239

APPENDICES

1.   Chronology   245
2.   The Ballad of the Battle of Corrichie   255
3.   The Birth-date of the second Earl of Moray   257
4.   The Succession to the Earldom of Moray   259
5.   The Moray Memorial   261
6.   The Ballad of the Bonnie Earl of Moray   265
7.   The Ballad Annotated   269
8.   The Moray Vault   271
9.   Genealogies of the Earls of Huntly, Moray, Argyll, Atholl, Bothwell,
     Errol and Arran, and the Lords Ochiltree   273
10   Glossary   277

Abbreviations   281
Notes   285
Bibliography   317
Biographical Index   331
General Index   347

LIST OF PLATES

1.   The Siblings. Lord James Stewart, first Earl of Moray by Hans Eworth. In a private Scottish collection. Photograph by Antonia Reeve.

2.   Mary Queen of Scots (The Deuil Blanc Portrait). The Scottish National Portrait Gallery. Photograph by Antonia Reeve.

3.   Approach to Linlithgow Palace, where the mortally wounded Moray went to die. Author's photograph.

4.   Commemorative Plaque near the scene of Moray's assassination. Author's photograph.

5.   St Giles Edinburgh, tomb of the Regent Moray. Author's photograph.

6.   Double portrait of Mary Queen of Scots and James VI, sixteenth century, from the Blair Castle, Perthshire, Collection.

7.   James VI aged 29, attributed to Adrian Vansen. The Scottish National Portrait Gallery.

8.   Queen Anne aged 19, attributed to Adrian Vansen. The Scottish National Portrait Gallery.

9.   Edinburgh c.1582 from Braun and Hogenberg's *Civitates, Orbis Terrarum*, vol. iii. By kind permission of the National Library of Scotland.

10. Moravia – Morayland – by Timothy Pont, published in Blaeu's Atlas Novus, vol. 5, 1654. By kind permission of the National Library of Scotland.

11. Doune Castle. Author's photograph.

12. Kilmadock cemetery, burial place of the second Earl of Moray. Author's photograph.

13. Donnibristle Bay, near Aberdour and Inverkeithing, showing Inchcolm in the background and the horseshoe curve of the beach where the second Earl of Moray was killed. Author's photograph.

14. Aberdour castle, showing the east end, very probably similar to Donnibristle House at the time of the murder of the second Earl of Moray. Author's photograph

15. The Darnley Murder sheet, sixteenth century. The Public Record Office.

16. The Carberry Banner, sixteenth century. The Public Record Office.

17. The Darnley Memorial by Livinus de Vogelaare, The Royal Collection © 2001, Her Majesty Queen Elizabeth II.

18. The second Earl of Moray after his murder, by an unknown artist ('The Moray Memorial'). In a private Scottish collection. Photograph by Antonia Reeve.

19. The doubtful portrait of the second Earl of Moray. In a private
     Scottish collection. Photograph by Antonia Reeve.
20. The Marquis and Marchioness of Huntly. The Scottish National
     Portrait Gallery.
21. Huntly Castle from the south, showing the great oriel windows, the
     inscriptions above 'George Gordon, First Marquis of Huntly,' and
     below 'Henriette Stewart, Marquisse of Huntly, and the great tower.
22. Huntly Castle from north-west. Author's photograph.
23.- Illustration of the funeral cortege of the Marquis of Huntly, 1636. The
-32. Trustees of the National Museums of Scotland.
33. Blackness Castle, the royal prison where Huntly was confined.
     Author's photograph.
34. Archibald seventh Earl of Argyll by an unknown artist, in a private
     Scottish Collection. Photograph by Antonia Reeve.

PREFACE

I went to school in Glasgow in the sixties and read history at Cambridge University in the early seventies. At neither institution did Scottish history figure very much; other than when reference was made to a Scottish defeat, invariably and monotonously at the hands of the 'Auld Enemy', the English. When the Scottish kings came on the scene their theatre was in England and their performance amateurish. The Stewart dynasty seemed to emerge from obscurity in 1603 and to last less than a century. It began with James I (not VI) succeeding the Virgin Queen, drooling over his male favourites, and eventually losing his marbles. It continued with his son losing the Civil War and his head. It ended with one of his grandsons losing a warship named after him to the Dutch and another losing his kingdom to the same insignificant foe. There was a romantic twilight of royal pretenders fighting lost causes, and then an exotic extinction. With it Scotland became 'North Britain'.

Scottish schools in the days of my youth taught a completely Anglo-centric curriculum in both history and literature. It was not until the sixth form that we were encouraged to read Scott, MacDiarmed or even Burns. I do not recall ever seriously studying the history of my homeland. Few books on Scottish history were in the shops, and those which were tended to be rather dull if worthy narratives by Mackie or Dickinson, too general to be interesting let alone arresting. The magnificent *History of Scotland* by Patrick Tytler had been out of print for a century or more and was unknown to me until I began my research for this book. Although written almost two centuries ago it remains by far and away the best political history of Scotland. Only Walter Scott with his *Tales of a Grandfather*, or Nigel Tranter with his historical novels of the Wallace and the Bruce, or John Prebble with his novelistic accounts of Glencoe or Culloden could bring to life the vivid past that lay around us. Scotland is a land that aches with its violent past. Round every bend, in every bay, on every hill, in every town is a castle, or a monastery, or a battlefield. Edinburgh itself, or Stirling, could be Hollywood sets. Yet largely these ruins were the bones of an unknown dinosaur, these places were unmapped in the geography of my mind. I could muse in the ruins of St Andrews Cathedral as Gibbon did in the Roman forum, but I, a Scot, knew far less of my own past, than did he, an Englishman, of Rome's.

The fault now is largely my own. I have lived many years in the south and could easily have made up for the deficiencies of my youth.

This book is my first attempt. It arises out of, and offers an apology for, my ignorance. In 1993 I bought a cheap second-hand CD called 'The Songs of Scotland.' The first track was the 'Ballad of the Bonny Earl of Moray.' I had never heard of him and I could not make out the words. But I was moved by the lament and wondered about the tale that lay behind it. I soon realised that its genesis was in a fascinating story of intrigue and betrayal in sixteenth-century Scotland. I determined to find out more.

When in 1994 I began my researches on the feud between the Earls of Moray and Huntly, there had been nothing written on it in 400 years other than Keith Brown's 1986 study *Bloodfeud in Scotland* which had a chapter devoted to it. I sensed a book in the waiting. A year or so later when I approached the present Earl of Moray with a view to seeing Darnaway House and the Moray Memorial which still hangs there in the great hall he mentioned that an American was pursuing a similar project. I carried on regardless. He beat me to it. Edward Ives published *The Bonny Earl of Moray* in 1997.

How can I justify a second book on the feud within a few years of the first when centuries have happily rolled by without one? As follows: given the background of wide academic research into the nature of the bloodfeud in sixteenth-century Scotland, detailed study of the most prolonged, dramatic and important feud of the time can never be otiose.[1] There is always something more to say. Further, Ives' ends and mine are rather different. His interest in the history of the feud is a prelude to his study of the ballad, while my interest in the ballad is incidental to my narrative. Finally, his work centres on the 'Bonny Earl of Moray.' Apart from the fact that my sympathies are less with Moray than with the sixth Earl of Huntly, a far more significant and interesting figure than the man he murdered, equally important in my account is the fourth Earl of Huntly and his destruction by Mary and her brother Lord James Stewart, the first Earl of Moray. This is more than a mere prelude to the later feud; it is vital for understanding the succeeding generations. Lord James deposed Huntly from his unique position of intimacy with the monarch, snatched the earldom of Moray from his grasp, and finally defeated and destroyed both him and his house.

This same Moray dethroned the Queen, seized the kingdom, and outmanoeuvred the fifth Earl of Huntly, her champion. The Reformation, the passion and violence it unleashed, and the instability and lawlessness it engendered, provided a backdrop that merely magnified enmities. It is against this history of bitterness and resentment, exacerbated by religion, that the personal detestation that the sixth Earl of Huntly felt for the second Earl of Moray and the numerous clashes between them must be seen. It did not take much to ignite their inherited enmity into deadly feud. And the feud, of course, merely intensified with the demise of one of the major participants. First Moray's brother, then his son, continued in their efforts to bring the killer of their near kin to account. They were aided in this by a coalition of family and friends and by the foes of the Earl of Huntly. It took the passing of much time and a belated marriage alliance to bury the feud for good. All this forms a substantial part of my work.

Both Brown and Ives utilised many of the estate documents in the Moray Muniments, and the latter 'translated' or modernised them, another beneficial service for those not accustomed to reading sixteenth-century Scottish secretary hand. I have made extensive use of the same treasure trove.

There is another issue relating to sixteenth-century documents. To the less well educated of us the spelling adopted in early modern Scotland comes as a great consolation. Phonetic variations are the norm. Two different spellings of the same word can occur in the same passage and by the same hand. Names are the worst: Hume or Home, Dunbar or Dumbar, Melvil, Melvill, or Melville. To avoid confusion and inconsistency I have always referred to the Morays and Stewarts in those spellings and not in the alternative of Murray and Stuart. Donnibristle and Darnaway are so spelt and not in their many variants such as Dunnibrissel and Tarnaway. In my text they are always thus. In the original documents I have usually amended them to those standard forms, and generally modernised spellings, but occasionally, to allow the full flavour of the original to be savoured, I have kept some deviations. I too can be inconsistent.

The Earl of Moray in person most kindly showed me around Darnaway some years ago. He also without complaint conveyed to Edinburgh the documents in his archives I wished to read. The staff of the Scottish National Record of Archives were unstinting in their assistance. In addition my thanks are due to the staff of the libraries of St Andrews and Cambridge universities and of the British Library for their books and facilities. The virtues of my work are often attributable to others, the vices are all my own.

My prejudices I trust are at least informed. I have little time for Mary Queen of Scots, an impetuous and inadequate monarch at any time, even if she did not have the misfortune to be on the Scottish throne at the same time as her cousin Elizabeth reigned majestically in England. The fourth Earl of Huntly was a man of many parts, some of them virtuous. But he went into decline, lost his political acumen, and finally his reputation for double-dealing and self-aggrandisement caught up with him. The first Earl of Moray, on the other hand, was a striking figure, cool, clever, a man of principle and talent, whom an ill fate doomed never to be king. Our loss as much as his. Fortunately the young prince he nurtured took little after his mother and more after his uncle. My admiration reflects that of Jenny Wormald for James VI and his extraordinary deftness when dealing with the difficult task of ruling Scotland with its inaccessible regions and its wayward barons. The sixth Earl of Huntly is a huge figure, the second Earl of Moray a pygmy.

I offer no new interpretations of Scottish history, no fresh analysis of the relationship between king and nobility, except in one respect. In my view events often took the turn they did because of the personalities, and personal relationship between, the participants. Mary herself acted often along lines of personal dependence: upon her brother or upon her husbands. James' indulgence towards the sixth Earl of Huntly was less to do with grand policy than with his liking for him. At times he seems besotted by his intelligent, witty, cavalier contemporary. His extraordinary affection for Huntly crosses the line of love. Huntly was a great friend and more. Moray was not. A young, silly, spendthrift was not likely to endear himself to a subtle and discerning king. One other factor in the makeup of the King is very important: the considerable emphasis James put on reconciliation and forgiveness, an aspect of his character which sorely tried the patience of his loving cousin, Elizabeth. James was a forbearing and a genuinely Christian monarch at a time when Christian monarchs were sorely lacking in the concomitant virtues. His motto was *Beati Sunt Pacifici* – 'Blessed are the Peacemakers' – a motto he lived by. These are perhaps obvious points but are strangely ignored by most historians who seem reluctant to attribute to historical figures the personal motivations, convictions and emotions that influence us all.

What I have tried to achieve is a coherent narrative, drawing together all the threads and details of the saga between these two grand families and their monarchs during the latter half of the sixteenth century. I hope that my work will be sufficiently strong in story line and explanation for the general reader and may even engage the scholar looking for an accurate and detailed account. I trust that my work will be authoritative. Thus I have tried to be comprehensive and meticulous in giving details and dates, and extensive in annotating. To that end I have compiled a chronology, appendices on such matters as the birth-date of the second Earl, the ballad, and the Memorial, a glossary, maps, and a full bibliography.

Names and designations are a fruitful source of chaos, even in the most meticulous works on early modern Scottish history. It often seems that almost every man in sixteenth-century Scotland is called Adam, Alexander or James, and every woman Elizabeth or Mary. Fathers frequently named their first sons after themselves. Thus, for example, a succession of Earls of Huntly go by the name of George. In the literature landed gentry are often referred to by their surname and the place with which they are associated or even just by the latter, for instance

'Gordon of Auchindoun,' or simply 'Auchindoun.' Further, there is disagreement among genealogists, upon occasion, as to whether so-and-so is the ninth or tenth Earl of such-and-such, as a result of titles being attainted or a potential heir living only a few weeks longer than his predecessor. In what I can claim to be a unique attempt to minimise confusion in otherwise potentially very confusing narratives I have provided genealogies of the major, and short biographies of all, the actors in the drama. Where I have been able I have specified the dates of their birth and death and of other significant events.

It will be for others to judge how much and how well I have achieved. Although no novice to the study of history I was a complete neophyte to Scottish history. Being largely self-taught in this field I have no one and nothing to hide behind other than my own ignorance. Where I have fallen into error the fault is my own and not that of the scholarly works which I have plundered so happily and extensively. However convincing or lasting an account I may have produced or however superficial or transitory, my exertions have been a labour of love and a means of expiating my ignorance of my own country's past. At least to me they have not been in vain.

HARRY POTTER
Christmas 2001

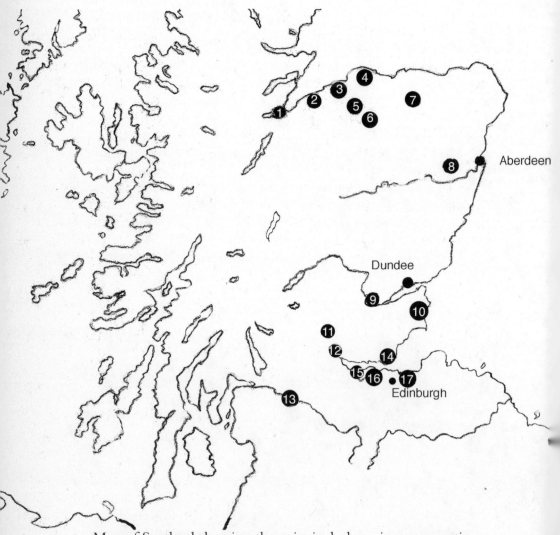

Map of Scotland showing the principal places in our narrative

1. Inverness	10. St. Andrews
2. Cawdor	11. Doune
3. Darnaway	12. Stirling
4. Spynie	13. Langslide
5. Ballindalloch	14. Donnibristle
6. Glenlivet	15. Linlithgow
7. Strathbogie	16. Blackness
8. Corrichie	17. Pinkie
9. Perth	

1

THE PEOPLE OF THE NORTH

To the people of the North God gave less intelligence than to those of the South, but greater strength of body, a more courageous spirit, greater comeliness.

John Major [1]

Moray land ... is a country alane by all the rest commendet with us for baith plenty and pleasure, for it is even and plane, without dubis [pools] and mires, marvellous delectable in fair forests, in thick woods, in sueit sairing [savouring] flouris, weil smelling herbs, pleasant meadows, fyne quheit, and all kind of stuff orchards and fruitful gairdings [gardens], and than sa neir the coast. Thair is the air maist hailsum, uncorrupt, temperate, their cludis and rain mekle less than in ony other place, and therefore sa gret incresse and plenty of corns amang the nobility of the country.

Bishop John Leslie [2]

Scotland in the sixteenth century was an interesting country. Small, poor, sparsely populated it may have been, but it was vibrant nonetheless. On the furthest north-western corner of Europe, it was a strange blend of continental culture — made manifest in the great Renaissance hall at Stirling Castle — and barbarous behaviour largely untrammelled by the veneer of civilisation. The Lowlands, poor as they were, had towns and trade, civic society and a legal framework for the conduct of affairs. Ports were vital to the commerce of goods and ideas. The latter could be cheaply imported even if luxuries could not. Education was at least as important as in its more prosperous neighbour to the south, and Scotland could boast four universities to England's two, a disparity not rectified until the nineteenth century.

The kingdom was divided both by religion and by geography. The Lowlands were soon penetrated by, and receptive of, the reformed teachings of Geneva. The Highlands were largely inaccessible both to new ideas and reformed faiths, and even to ordinary travellers. It is hard for us to appreciate the way in which the country was bisected by its geological formations and isolated by its terrain. High mountains and thick forests were serious barriers. Roads, where they existed, were muddy and rutted, inns infrequent, and travel arduous. In particular, royal control weakened the further from Edinburgh one went. The Highland chiefs and earls were largely autonomous and were left to their quarrels by the central authority. The king in council could legislate and reprimand but he had no way, short of punitive and punitively expensive military expeditions, of ultimately enforcing his decrees. Local lairds and noblemen fought their own battles in their own localities, keeping an uneasy equilibrium.

Much of the trouble lay in the poverty of the land. There were few sources of income and even fewer lucrative ones. Farming was a small scale and harsh occupation, the expending of hours of hard labour being rewarded with a small crop of basic foodstuffs, oats and barley. Industry was unknown apart from weaving, smelting and weapon making, although most swords and shields were imported from the Lowlands. There were, however, two sources of rich rewards – fishing and the Church – and where these were concerned rivalries easily boiled over into violence and feud.

In fish stocks, if in nothing else, Scotland was said to exceed England. Her rivers abounded in salmon, trout, turbot and pike, her shores in crabs and oysters, and the surrounding seas in herring and haddock. Fishing was a dangerous business. Offshore, there was the risk of storms encountered in the bleak North Sea. On the rivers there were the equally dangerous disputes – frequent and frequently violent – over fishing rights. Rivers marking the boundaries between territories were a hazardous meeting place, and their rich stock, particularly of valuable salmon, were often fought over. Nets were cut, stocks were plundered, and fishermen were attacked, sometimes fatally. No river had a richer supply of salmon than the Spey, the main artery of the north-east, and the river near which the Earls of Huntly, Moray and Athol, and the laird of Grant built their castles and staked their claims.[3]

Another source of dispute was over the rich revenues to be had from the possession of Church benefices. In a lean country the Roman Catholic Church possessed 'prebends many and fat,' but subject to predation.[4] As a result of royal patronage, laymen in sixteenth century Scotland had been increasingly appointed as commendators, or lay administrators, of abbeys. Such grants were a reliable source of valuable income, squeezing the local population in the name of God. Control of such positions could alter the balance power and influence in the area. They were also a stepping stone to further elevation.

Loyalties were to the clan and the family, rather than to the king or the country. Clan and family were often considered coterminous. The name of the clan was taken by its adherents: Macleod, Mackintosh, and Campbell. Other families, not real clans, such as the Gordons, spread their name promiscuously amongst their adherents. The cognomen Gordon spread all over the north-east. Newcomers were viewed with suspicion, especially if they came with an authority granted by the King. They were men of the moment and must not unsettle the established ways to which they owed no fealty. The King had no choice but largely to leave his northern subjects to themselves. Deference to royal authority was not a predominant virtue in Stewart Scotland. This is perfectly illustrated in an anecdote concerning George Buchanan, the tutor of James VI. When the Countess of Mar reproached him for disciplining the Lord's anointed, Buchanan retorted, 'Madam, I have whipped his backside and you may kiss it if you please.'[5] The best the monarch could hope for was to have powerful men whom, if a law unto themselves in their own domains were loyal to him. No family better fitted the bill than that of Gordon.

Although they were to become the predominant power in the north-east of Scotland the Gordons were not natives to that part or indeed to Scotland, and had a feudal rather than a Gaelic origin. Of Norman descent, they were one of many families welcomed into his kingdom by David I. By the early twelfth century they had settled in the village and estates of Gordon, near Kelso in the Scottish Borders under the protection of their kinsman, the Earl of Dunbar. For the next two centuries or so they loyally carried out their responsibilities in that turbulent region. They did so only as minor magnates, acting at the behest of their feudal superiors, but gradually increasing their land-holdings, one accession being the lands of Huntly on the western border of Gordon parish where two farms are still known as Huntly and Huntly-wood.

It was their migration north that was the making of them. It came about in this manner. The Sir Adam Gordon who first appears on record in 1296 pledging homage to Edward I had the foresight to back Robert the Bruce against his rivals, Balliol and Comyn, in his struggle for the throne. When the Bruce triumphed, Adam could expect his reward and the King would use his benefaction to ensure he had a most loyal supporter as the power in the far north-east. The pro-Balliol Earl of Athol duly forfeited Strathbogie, one of the five ancient lordships or thanages that comprised Aberdeenshire and it was granted to Sir Adam. The 120 square miles of prime land that Strathbogie consisted of was enough to lure the aspiring Gordons north. In the north they proved to be, as was expected of them, a bastion of loyalty. When danger threatened the King elsewhere his loyal Gordons would rush to his defence. Whenever rash royal ambition propelled the King to attack the English, his steadfast Gordons would be at the fore of battle. Thus the steady increase of their power over the fourteenth century was punctuated at regular intervals by the bloody demise of their chief. In 1333 Sir Adam was killed at the battle of Halidon Hill. His son, Sir Alexander, died in the battle of Neville's Cross near Durham in 1346. Sir John,

Alexander's son, fell at Otterburn in 1388. His son, Adam Gordon, by
a very canny marriage to Elizabeth, the only child of William, Lord
Keith, Marischal of Scotland, acquired the Fraser lands of Aboyne,
Glentanar and Glenmuick on Dee-side. The King elevated him to the
nobility as first Baron Gordon. Lord Gordon had provided well for
future of his name. But it was to be blotted out when he too was killed
in royal service, at Homildon Hill in 1402, leaving only a daughter as
his heir. The male Gordon line, loyal to the last, was extinct: its blood
poured out over the battlefields of the Borders.

Redemption came through a woman. In 1408 Lord Adam's
daughter, Elizabeth, the last remnant of the Gordon name, married Sir
Alexander Seton. He was the second son of Sir William Seton, and a
scion of another Norman family planted in Scotland by King David I.
The Duke of Albany, governor of Scotland during the imprisonment
of James I in England from 1406 to 1424, confirmed Alexander's title
to the land and baronies of Gordon, Huntly, and Strathbogie. Blessed
with spouses who died young, his son, another Alexander, increased
his holdings with every new match, and there were three in all. With
this constant acquisition of lands the lords of Gordon and Huntly
could have made enemies, but perhaps surprisingly they remained on
good terms with other Aberdeenshire magnates, and in particular
with their neighbours at Slains, the Hays. This was an important and
useful association. The Hays were another Norman import, and had
been rewarded for their service to the Bruce not merely with the
earldom of Errol but with the hereditary office of Lord High
Constable of Scotland.

In recognition of his pre-eminent position in the north-east and his
loyalty to the crown, Alexander Seton was created the first Earl of
Huntly in 1445. Six years later King James II increased his power and
status still further by granting him the old Comyn lordship of
Badenoch. In 1454, or thereabouts, Seton changed the family name to
Gordon, thus continuing the line of the Gordon chiefs. At the same
time James II offered his sister, Annabella, in marriage, further
securing Huntly's loyalty to the Stewart dynasty by his entry into the
royal family.

In the civil war occasioned by the murder of William, eighth Earl of
Douglas, by James II, the new Earl of Huntly rapidly repaid his liege by
routing the Earl of Crawford at Brechin Moor. Huntly, however, was
unable to join his forces with that of the King to press home this
victory over the rebel earls. His own territories in the north, denuded
of fighting men, were under threat from the predatory Archibald
Douglas, Earl of Moray, and brother of the murdered Earl of Douglas.
Taking full advantage of Huntly's absence Moray had invaded his
neighbour's lands and burnt the 'Peil of Strathbogie,' Huntly Castle.

Huntly returned north to exact punishment. Half of Elgin had sided with Moray. That half was burnt to the ground. But Huntly's horsemen were slaughtered or drowned in a savage little skirmish with Moray's infantry in a quagmire called the Bog of Dunkinty. It was the first murderous encounter between the two rival earldoms in the north-east. Many more were to come.

The earldom of Moray had lands adjoining those of the Gordons. It had an even more ancient history dating back to before the Norman Conquest. It ceased to be a Celtic earldom in the twelfth century and became the gift of the king, in effect a royal peculiar. Robert the Bruce bestowed the earldom on his nephew, Thomas Randolph, in thanks for which, the latter seized Edinburgh Castle from the English. On the failure of male heirs with the death of the third Earl at Neville's Cross 1346, it again reverted to the crown. Robert II granted it to his son-in-law, Patrick Dunbar. The last of the Dunbar earls, James, was murdered in 1429. Dunbar's daughter and her husband, Archibald Douglas styled themselves Countess and Earl of Moray until the earldom was forfeited to the crown on the final defeat of the Black Douglases and the death of the then Earl of Moray at the battle of Arkinholme in 1455. In 1501 James Stewart, the bastard of James IV, was created Earl of Moray by his father. On his death in 1544 the earldom again reverted to the crown. Thus there was no hereditary tradition, no dynasty, no clan Moray. The earl of Moray was a feudal magnate pure and simple, a creation of the king. The earldom was given and taken at royal will. So very different from the earls of Huntly with their local roots, long lineage and huge Gordon kindred.

The lands of the large and profitable neighbouring earldom had long been coveted by the Gordons. 'Moray Land' was a veritable cornucopia – at least by Scottish standards. Its gentle hills were coated with a rich covering of valuable deciduous forest. Its land was low lying and fertile. Its rivers – the Findhorn, Ness, Nairn, Lossie and above all the Spey – were full of fish. The loch of Spynie was rich in both salmon and swans, and was the perfect place for the Bishop of Moray to build his 'honourable castle and pleasant palace.'[6] Even its climate was temperate and the sea air wholesome. George Buchanan pronounced it 'the first county in Scotland.'[7] For the greatest men in the north to look over their borders and see better lands than their own was galling. To see them in the hands of their only potential rivals was worse. Incorporating this rich appendage into their already extensive domains had obvious advantages. It would consolidate their possessions into one large coherent block covering the whole of the north-east of Scotland. It would mark them out as the permanent and paramount force in that region, and as the premier earl in the nation. It would leave nowhere for any potential rival to take root. Finally, its acquisition would double their income, and ensure a stable return year on year, since this was a land naturally blessed with vast renewable resources of livestock, grain, fruit and fish, easily harvested and readily marketable.

In 1455 the first opportunity arose for dynastic enlargement: the untimely demise of the then Earl of Moray. The first Earl of Huntly acted with the determination that marked his family. He arranged that his son George, the master of Huntly, should marry Elizabeth Dunbar who was not only the widow of one Earl of Moray – Archibald Douglas – but also the daughter of another, James Dunbar. As part of the marriage settlement the Moray seat, Darnaway Castle, 'celebrat, famous and of gret renowne' was to pass to Huntly.[8] The marriage was not made in heaven, lasted but a year, ended in divorce, and more significantly, without issue. The appropriation by Huntly of the rich province of Moray and of the imposing edifice at Darnaway was frustrated.

Twenty years later, in 1470, Master George Gordon succeeded his father as the second Earl of Huntly. He proved signally more effective in furthering his ends than his father had been on his behalf. Not only did he make a very good match in marrying Elizabeth Hay, daughter of William, Earl of Errol, further cementing that important alliance, but she bore him that priceless gift, four sturdy sons. In 1476 James III appointed him royal Lieutenant in the North, giving public recognition to the reality that the Gordons by then not only ranked among the most powerful families in Scotland but also were unchallenged in their hegemony of the north-east. The head of the family, the Earl of Huntly, was 'Cock of the North.'

With regal authority Huntly used his own retainers to keep order among the unruly Highlanders who lived far beyond the limits of royal control. His own interests and those of his master were closely identified. The Gordons continued to thrive on loyalty. In January 1488 Huntly, along with the Earl of Crawford, was appointed a justiciar north of the Forth. His son and heir, Alexander, as master of Huntly, was made keeper of the castles of Inverness and Kildrummy and granted other lands. While his father stood neutral in the final crisis of the reign, Alexander raised troops for his King. Almost alone of all the nobility, he was hurrying to join him when James III confronted the rebel forces, led by his own son and heir, which would end both his reign and his life, at the 'Field of Stirling,' later known as the Battle of Sauchieburn, on St Barnabas Day, 11 June 1488. The King, bearing the sword of the Bruce, was routed and murdered by unknown assassins as he fled. James IV succeeded to his father's throne.

Alexander did not ultimately suffer for his enduring loyalty to the deposed monarch nor even for his initiating rebellion against the new regime in 1489. His father's studied neutrality and reputation undoubtedly helped. The second Earl so rose in favour that he replaced the Earl of Angus as Chancellor in 1497. Alexander used this opportunity of his father's frequent absences at court to assert his authority in his family's lands in the north, and beyond. When in June 1501 he succeeded his father as third Earl of Huntly he was the obvious candidate to bring order in the Highlands and islands. Almost immediately he was given a commission of lieutenancy in the north, one that was for longer duration and with more extensive powers than that of his great rival in the north-west, Archibald Campbell, the second Earl of Argyll. He used this commission ruthlessly but to good effect, and soon proved the King's most reliable liege and most successful general. By royal reward Huntly increased his already extensive land-holdings, and by royal favour continued his inexorable rise, peaking in his appointment in 1509 as hereditary sheriff of Inverness, and keeper of the King's castle.[9] By the end of James IV's reign Huntly had been elevated to perfect dominance in the north, controlling by himself or by proxy almost all the land beyond the Great Glen in addition to his patrimony of Lochaber, Badenoch and most of Aberdeenshire. He could even despoil the Castle of Darnaway, an insult that the Earl of Moray was powerless to punish.[10]

Despite their status and aspirations, the Gordons remained firmly loyal. In 1513, at Flodden Field this loyalty was exemplified. It was Huntly alone, while Lord Home hesitated, who urged the men of the reserve to aid their King when the battle was already lost and the ground dyed crimson with the blood of 10,000 Scots.[11] He urged in vain. James IV was hacked down among his troops, yards from the English centre. Huntly was the only Earl who fought that day and escaped with his life. His own brother William, ancestor of Lord Byron, was amongst the fallen, sacrificing himself on the altar of royal service that was the hallmark of his family.

Dynastic matches both assisted in securing the Gordons' position of pre-eminence and testified to that reality. Huntly's younger brother, Adam, in right of his wife, Elizabeth, Countess of Sutherland, whom he married in 1500, became Earl of Sutherland in 1515. But the high-point was the match Alexander engineered between his first son, John, and Margaret Stewart, the natural daughter of King James IV. Once again the Gordons had moved from being courtiers in the royal bedchamber onto the royal bed itself, even if this time on the wrong side of the sheets. John died in 1517 seven years before his father but not before he had done his duty, siring a brood of sons by Lady Margaret, the first of whom, born in 1514, was George Gordon, heir apparent to the earldom of Huntly. George was of tainted blood perhaps but of royal blood nonetheless.

PART I

THE 4TH EARL OF HUNTLY

AND

THE 1ST EARL OF MORAY

1524–1563

2
COCK O' THE NORTH
1524-1553/4

The wylyest lad that lyved.
> Sir George Douglas on the fourth Earl of Huntly.[1]

In man's opinion, under a prince, there was not such a one
these three hundred years in this realm produced.
> John Knox on the same subject.[2]

Ten years later, upon the death of his grandfather in 1524, Lord George Gordon became the fourth Earl of Huntly. George was a precocious lad, and one blessed, both in estate and in person. Family tradition later extolled him as 'a child of so lovely a countenance and carriage, so quick and witty in jests and discourses that the Earl of Angus...(unto whom Huntly's education was entrusted), could hardly ever want him from his presence and conversation.'[3] Exaggerated as this description may be, the young Earl's prospects were rosy indeed. He was the inheritor of one of the greatest earldoms in the land, the lord of vast estates, and the head of the great clan Gordon. Over the previous two centuries his forebears had made many and remarkable advances in the family's fortunes. He was to continue in this tradition. But first he had to survive.

After the death of the third Earl, Margaret Tudor, the Queen Mother was granted the wardship of her ten-year-old stepgrandson. It was only befitting that a child of his lineage be adopted into the royal family and educated at court, a semi-princeling, and a virtual captive. His playmates were his younger brother, Alexander, and the young King, James V. James was two years older than George and more like an elder brother than the uncle he was. Living at the heart of things during a critical phase in a royal minority the young Earl witnessed at first hand the ceaseless court intrigue and the bitter squabbling between various factions vying for power. He was himself a pawn between them.

In the immediate aftermath of Flodden, Margaret Tudor had assumed the regency. For those wishing to revenge themselves on England, having the sister of Henry VIII in charge of Scotland was an affront. Within a year she had disqualified herself from the post by marrying Archibald Douglas, the sixth Earl of Angus. The dead King's cousin, John, Duke of Albany, was summoned from France to replace her. Margaret had taken herself off to England. She was eventually allowed home on condition that she behaved like a good Scotswoman, a tall order for an English princess. Shortly after her return in 1517, Albany had visited France in an attempt to renew the Auld Alliance. Times had changed. A delicate *rapprochement* had broken out between the old enemies, France and England. Far from finding succour, Albany had found himself detained for what would ultimately prove to be four years.

In Albany's absence a regency council, consisting of the two Scottish archbishops, along with the Earls of Angus, Arran, Argyll, and Huntly, and Albany's French agent, Anthony Darcy, had purported to rule Scotland. Distrust, suspicion and rivalry between its members had plunged the country once more into anarchy. Angus and Arran were the main culprits and their clashes had occurred as much in the streets as in the council chamber. James Hamilton, first Earl of Arran, had had the initial advantage since Margaret by this time had wanted to divorce Angus and marry him, while the Chancellor, Archbishop Beaton, was his kinsman.

But in 1520 he had overplayed his hand, leading a large force against 400 Douglas spearmen in the High Street of Edinburgh. Initially outnumbered Angus had been hard-pressed until Sir David Home and his Borderers had intervened to assist him and forced the Hamiltons to flee down the 'wynds' of the city, thus 'Cleansing the Causeway,' as the aristocratic fracas was disparagingly called. Angus's reprieve had been short-lived. France, reverting to type in its relations with England in 1521, had sent Albany home. Three years later Albany's wife had died, and Margaret had transferred her fickle affections to her husband's leading rival. By divorcing Angus and marrying Albany she would rid herself of a feckless encumbrance and effectively regain her position as Queen-Regent. In addition to being governor, Albany was a grandson of James II and thus heir to the throne should James V die young and childless. Albany, however, did not seem to share the old Queen's enthusiasm for this alliance, and in any case was becoming increasingly disgruntled with his fellow countrymen. When the Scots refused to try their military hand against the English again, Albany had taken his final leave and returned to France, taking his French troops with him, but leaving his importunate admirer behind.

Margaret, thwarted once more in her marital assignations, turned from the men who had disappointed her to the boy she had ignored. She prevailed on her young son James to take up his kingly functions in 1524 at the tender age of twelve. With a king regnant on the throne Albany was formally removed from his governorship and she had enhanced status and influence as Queen Mother. In this stratagem she was backed by Arran. In the same year the young Huntly came under her control. Not surprisingly Angus leagued against her – more surprisingly in 1526 he outmanoeuvred her, seized Edinburgh and took control of his fourteen-year-old stepson, the King, and of his protégé, the twelve-year-old George Gordon. George was the apple of Angus' eye. The young man had been festering under female tutelage, and saw in this usurpation by Angus an escape and adventure both for himself and for his friend the King.

The older boy looked at it very differently. He had found not an escape from his mother but an ensnarement by his stepfather. For two years he was held in thrall, for two years he was a cypher, for two years his bitterness towards his captor grew, for two years he plotted escape and revenge. Finally, in 1528, the young King achieved both. He eluded Angus and took refuge with his mother. The retribution of mother and son was swift and severe. The Douglas stronghold of Tantallon fell after a three week siege, the Douglases were attainted, their lands seized, and their Earl forced into exile in England. The teenage Huntly went with him. He had played his first hand in the poker game of politics and had been thoroughly fleeced. For many years his play would improve until that final hand when once again a queen would trounce his knave.

At least in exile he at last escaped the trammels of the court.[4] Having asserted his independence, within months he returned home and made his peace with his erstwhile playmate and lifelong friend. The childhood bond between them created a trust and affection that James had for no other of his nobles. Trust and favour flowed together. The following year, 1529, Huntly was awarded the lordship of Braemar, Strathdee and Cromar – all lands in the temporally defunct earldom of Mar – along with the forest of Cluny.[5] James in turn borrowed 2,000 merks from his friend when the royal coffers ran dry. The reconciliation was complete.

Despite his close associations and favoured status at court, George Gordon was astute enough to know that his power base was not primarily there but in his ancestral lands in the north. They had made his forefathers great and would be neglected at his peril. For many years, however, as an absentee, under-age heir he was subject to the same irksome female dominance at home as he had been at court. This constraint was compounded three-fold by the longevity of strong-willed Huntly widows: his great-grandmother, Elizabeth Hay; his step-grandmother, Elizabeth Gray, widow of the third Earl; and his mother, Margaret Stewart. Running his lands and curtailing his allowances they kept him dependent upon their will. Two years after he had inherited his title he had taken them before the Lords of Council, complaining that his 'haile leving is in the hands of the saidis ladies by reason of terce,' that he had nothing, and praying 'for a competent leving for his sustentation.'[6] It was not until he was nineteen, however, and under the tutelage of Lord Erskine and Sir John Campbell of Lundy, that he finally persuaded the Lords of Council to compel his mother to renounce – in return for a life rent of the lands – the lordship of Badenoch and the forest of Enzie and Boyne together with the tower of Bog of Gight.[7]

The pre-eminence of the Gordons in the north was enhanced and ensured by an extensive network of alliances built round the nucleus of a powerful and united kin group. Over 150 families of the Gordon name were established in the counties of Aberdeen and Banff. Not all were blood kin or old feudal retainers. Many of them had adopted the name in order to demonstrate a spurious affinity and so elicit kin protection in an area where the King was rarely present but the Gordon chief frequently was. The Earl of Huntly was only too ready to welcome them into his expanding fold, and expended much of his prodigious energy towards extending his 'affinity' by the creation of bonds of manrent with the small lairds and knights in his area.[8] They were bound to aid him in any actions, causes and 'deadly feuds.' In return they kept their identities and gained protection both from their own enemies and from Huntly's displeasure. They needed the Earl of Huntly, as he did them, for mutual security and influence. One of the first to sign a bond of manrent with Huntly was Hector Mackintosh, leader of the Clan Chattan.

The 'tribe' of Chattan was a confederacy of clans, 'the children of St Catan:' Mackintosh, MacPherson, MacBean, and others, claiming descent from Gilliechattan their traditional ancestor. In all probability they first occupied that part of Lochaber which extends westwards from Loch Lochy to Knoydart and Morar, and which became known as the lands of Glen Loy and Loch Arkaig. By the end of the fourteenth century, however, the Camerons were encroaching on these so success-fully that the Clan Chattan moved into Badenoch. It meant bad blood between them for generations. The chieftainship of Clan Chattan was held by the head of the Mackintoshes but in none of the Chattan areas were the Mackintoshes exclusive occupiers;[9] in none had they compact territories, in none did they hold directly from the crown. In Badenoch all branches of the clan were tenants of the Earl of Huntly as lord of Badenoch; the other districts were mainly in the earldom of Moray. Hector was thus squeezed between two powerful members of the aris-tocracy and wanted his own space. He tried to get it by playing one off against the other.

He had first turned his predatory designs on the lands of weaker of the two, Moray. Hector's men had ravaged his estates, stolen his cattle and even besieged his prestigious seat, Darnaway Castle itself. Such bravado would not go long unpunished. Moray's weakness on the ground was more than made up for by his influence at court. He was, after all, the bastard son of James IV. On 10 November 1528 he had been issued with letters of fire and sword authorising him, as Royal Lieutenant, to extirpate Clan Chattan once and for all, by putting all the men to the sword or noose, and by packing all their women and children off to Norway. In this noble endeavour he was to be assisted by the Earls of Sutherland and of Caithness and the Lords Fraser and Forbes. All was sound and fury signifying nothing. The military police action had failed to materialise; the threats were never put into effect. Clansmen had the habit of vanishing when retribution drew near and recouping when it withdrew again. Nonetheless Hector had thought it wise to pacify the Royal Lieutenant by making a bond of manrent with him in 1530.

Within a year he had changed allegiance. Hector wanted to align himself with the more successful and powerful magnate. Huntly was in the ascendant while Moray was waning. Secure in their new bond, Clan Chattan began again to encroach on the lands of the bishopric of Moray. In their depredations, assisted by James Grant of Freuchy, they killed some twenty men, women, and children, and caused £12,000 worth of damage. Moray was once more instructed to proceed against the adder he had not scotched. So too was Huntly, who found himself, aligned against his erstwhile retainer. Hector had overstretched the mark. He was a brigand who could not be trusted. His actions were destabilising the north. His known association with Huntly was doing the latter's reputation no good. Knowing where his ultimate loyalty lay, the young Earl acted decisively, putting Mackintosh in ward, and restoring the north to uneasy tranquillity. In so doing he had sacrificed those in bond to him. It was a sacrifice worth making.

Where Huntly could not command he could subdue. He had long been at odds with the sixth Lord Forbes over the profits of lands in the barony of Strathbogie. A civil case begun in 1533 concluded three years later with Forbes being ordered to hand over all the profits – £200 – for the period from 1528 to 1531. During the currency of that case Huntly had taken out criminal charges against John, the master of Forbes, for 'fire-raising and destruction, under silence of night, of poynding falds and other crimes in the forest of Corennie.'[10] These charges were a mere prelude to the accusations he was to make in 1537 when he accused Lord Forbes and his son of plotting the assassination of the King in Aberdeen, and the restoration of the Douglases. Despite being tried before a jury heavily under the influence of Huntly, Lord Forbes was acquitted. His son was convicted. The master of Forbes, whether or not he was guilty of this crime, was guilty of many others, and went to the scaffold unmourned by the people.[11] The feud with the Forbes would erupt every so often over the following sixty years. This was inevitable, as the Forbes, with their principal seat at Drumminor, felt ever more hemmed in by the all-enveloping power and presence of the Gordons.

In the north the hegemony of Huntly was unassailable, and his ability to gather adherents to serve his power and share in his success, unrivalled. He was even granted wardship of the Sutherland earldom after the death of his kinsman, Alexander Gordon, master of Sutherland whose heir was only ten years old. In 1535 Huntly was made a privy councillor, and the following year warden of the Marches and a Vice-Regent while the King was away in France marrying Princess Magdalene. In the north Huntly's estate was regal; at court he could deputise for the King himself; in the south he was defender of the kingdom from the 'auld enemy', England. Master of all he surveyed – save the Moray lands – George Gordon, fourth Earl of Huntly was magnificent in his pretensions, and vaunting in his ambitions: the very Cock o' the North!

His endeavours to secure the future of his dynasty were equally successful. On 2 February 1535, at the age of twenty-one, he married Lady Elizabeth Keith. She was the daughter of the late Robert, Lord Keith, sister of William, fourth Earl of Marischal, and – incidentally – aunt of Lord James Stewart's future wife, Lady Agnes Keith. Lady Elizabeth and Huntly had been betrothed since 1530, and the delay before marriage was partly occasioned by the need to get a dispensation from the Pope from the impediments of consanguinity.[12] Over the years of their happy union they would produce nine sons and three daughters.[13] The Gordon dynasty seemed secure, unrivalled in power, rich in progeny.

Two siblings sired by King James V, but on different sides of the sheet, were to stay this quasi-regal progression of the fourth Earl of Huntly: James Stewart, the future Regent, and Mary Stewart, the as yet unborn Queen. George Gordon was first cousin to both. Together, when full-grown, they were to be his nemesis, and his fall was to be all the more titanic because of the veneer of invincibility surrounding him.

Those were the actors, but the backdrop to his downfall was that massive deluge which threatened the dissolution of the State itself: the Reformation. It began in Scotland as a trickle but soon became a flood. James V had allowed satirical attacks on clerical abuses by his literati, Sir David Lindsay of the Mount and George Buchanan, but he never anticipated the full-blown revolution that was so rapidly to take place. He could laugh at the excesses of the Roman Church but he would not countenance its destruction. The King of Scots would not lead from the front as his contemporary did in England, but defend from the rear. He was happily married to a French Catholic, Mary of Guise, his first friend was France, and his chief advisors were clerics – James Beaton, Archbishop of St Andrews, and his nephew David, the future cardinal.

James' refusal to march in step with an England already in schism provoked Henry VIII to abjure his former peaceful relations with his northern neighbour and recommence the more normal state of hostilities between the two countries.

In August 1542 Henry instructed the Earl of Rutland, his warden of the Marches, to provoke trouble. Sir Robert Bowes, the warden of the East March, led 3,000 men to raid Teviotdale. In this enterprise he was accompanied by Huntly's erstwhile guardian, the Earl of Angus, and Angus' brother, George Douglas. Bowes set up his main base at Hadden-Rig near Kelso, and sent out two large raiding parties – the Redesdale and Tynedale reivers – to burn and despoil the surrounding countryside. It was a mistake to separate his forces when faced with determined opposition. That opposition the Earl of Huntly was to provide. He had been recently appointed Lieutenant of the Marches in lieu of the Earl of Moray who was sick.[14] In that capacity Huntly encountered the raiders before they could rejoin the main force at Hadden-Rig. They were laden with spoil, and intent on driving cattle and sheep before them, when Huntly launched his surprise attack. His riders severed the forays from their base, throwing them into confusion when they realised their line of retreat was cut. The Borderers were the first to make off, saving their own lives and as much of the spoil as they could, but leaving their compatriots to their fate. The English were routed, perhaps 1,000 were slain, and 600 taken prisoner, including Bowes.[15] Huntly's veneer of invincibility was polished by that rarest of Scottish achievements, a military victory over the English. With a degree of exaggerated pomposity that could only emanate from a country whose success rate against the English was so low, it was claimed by a later family apologist that 'the English historians term him the valiant Gordon, and the French ambassador call'd him the Wisdom of Scotland, and the Terror of England.'[16] Contemporary Scottish historians on the other hand declined to attribute this victory to a Catholic earl at all. Huntly is written out of the Protestant script.[17]

Though only twenty-eight, 'the wisdom of Scotland' was experienced and mature enough to know the limitation of the Scots. They could, if fighting as guerillas on their own soil, worry and wound the English; they could not, on English ground and in pitched battle, destroy them. He feared that Hadden-rig would be the skirmish that provoked full-scale war. Henry, smarting at his humiliation, wanted the Scots chastened and subdued. In the ensuing peace negotiations at York in September, 'the terror of England' tried to mollify the Earl of Rutland and ensure that there were no reprisals.[18] As Huntly was being given bland reassurances, the English mustered under the Duke of Norfolk.

In October Norfolk with a force of between 10,000 and 20,000 men crossed the Tweed, raided Border towns, and sacked Kelso Abbey. He wanted to confront the Scots in pitched battle or, exploiting their habitual rashness, lure them over the border where they could be anni-hilated on safe ground. Scotland mobilised. Moray, then restored to health, had 'great dissensions' with Huntly over who should have the vanguard.[19] They ended up splitting their forces. Huntly probably commanded no more than 4,000 light horse and 3,000 infantry, a mobile skirmishing detail rather than a battle-ready army. With these resources he harassed Norfolk as he could, but inflicted no signal defeat. When Norfolk re-crossed the Tweed on 27 October the wise general, having had 'gret wordes' with the Earl of Moray declined to follow the English over the border. This was a prudent move consid-ering the time of year and the relative strength of the forces, but oppro-brium was heaped unfairly upon him. His failure to engage the English rearguard gained Huntly the sobriquet 'cowarde captaine' and cost him the lieutenancy, an office that reverted to his old rival, Moray.[20] The loss of his lieutenancy possibly saved him his life or at least his liberty. He had returned to the north by the time Henry exacted his revenge at the battle of Solway Moss on 24 November 1542. As a result of the Scots engaging in the sort of tactics that the wise Huntly had disdained, an English force of perhaps 3,000 Borderers trounced an army six times its size.

It was all so unnecessary. The campaign began well with the King himself leading some 18,000 men towards Cumberland. Norfolk was in the East March and unable to intercept him. James, however, fell ill and retired to Lochmaben Castle near Dumfries. He relinquished his army to Lord Maxwell, an elderly but normally competent general, but bifurcated the command by giving a commission to his favourite Oliver Sinclair to take charge once they had passed the border. Only a small force mustered at Carlisle under Thomas Wharton, the Warden, was there to oppose the Scots' ingress. Surprisingly, it was more than enough. The Scottish Army, with that silly bravura that so often typified it, failed to send out scouts or a screen of cavalry. The van was caught in the crook between the Rivers Esk and Line when Wharton's nimble Border light horse – aptly named 'prickers' – darted in and out of their opponent's ranks causing confusion and consternation. An able and unified leadership could have kept the men in order and saved the day, but that leadership was divided when Sinclair claimed the command. The dissension among their leaders increased the chaos in the ranks, and the army broke. Trapped on the Esk ford, with the great moss of the Solway to the rear, it came apart at the seams. It was a disintegration rather than a defeat. The Scots panicked and fled. Only some twenty were killed in the fighting, but large numbers drowned in the morass of Solway and 1,200 were taken prisoner. Five or six men at a time were seen to surrender to single English riders. 3,000 horse and twenty-four cannon were taken. Of Wharton's men seven had been killed and one taken prisoner. 'Solemn Moss' as Godscroft called it, was a disaster and disgrace for Scotland from which not a crumb of comfort could be taken. At least Flodden had been heroic with James IV fighting to the last in the midst of his men and spawning an immortal lament worthy of its great tragic theme. This debacle was pathetic and is best passed over in silence.

Perhaps not surprisingly James V never recovered from this disgrace. He retired to the safety of Falkland Palace and took to his bed for the three weeks it took him to die, bemoaning in his last words that other triple misfortune which was about to befall his dynasty. The heir to his throne was not a man, nor a boy – his two sons had predeceased him – but a sickly wee baby, seven days old, a daughter, a girl whose nearest male relative was a great uncle, none other than Henry VIII himself. James Stewart's army was destroyed, his reputation ruined and his dynasty, which had come with a lass, would, he feared, go with one too.[21] He was very nearly right. And so, on the death of her father, whom she never knew, the infant Mary became Queen of Scots. Huntly had lost a singular friend and had inherited a dual responsibility – his share and interest in the upbringing of his cousin and Queen, and the running of Scotland during her minority.

A council of regency had to be appointed for that purpose and controversy inevitably dogged the formation of so influential a body. The great lords were as united in their desire for personal power and aggrandisement as they were divided over the perennial problem of England. James Hamilton, the second Earl of Arran, a weak man but a hairs-breadth from the throne, wanted rapprochement and the marriage of Mary to King Henry's son, Edward. Cardinal Beaton, along with Huntly, Argyll and Lennox, favoured France as the key to Scotland's continuing independence. So too of course did that other force in the land, the Queen Mother, Mary of Guise. Rumour had it that on his death-bed the King had signed a sheet of paper – blank and later filled in by Beaton – which named the cardinal as governor, and the Earls of Moray, Huntly and Argyll as the council of regency.[22] Arran, the heir presumptive, was excluded. He successfully contested the appointment and was confirmed as governor in December 1542. The following month at the convention of the Scottish lords – many captured at Solway Moss and recently released under pledge to promote the interests of England and the royal marriage compact – he completely vanquished his opponents. Foremost among these returnees were Archibald Douglas, Earl of Angus and his brother George Douglas of Pittendriech. As champions of Arran they would walk close to the throne. As agents of England the Catholic party held them in contempt. More secure in his tenure of office, Arran felt able to depose his great rival, Cardinal Beaton, from the chancellorship and have him incarcerated.

Huntly, Moray and the third Earl of Bothwell offered themselves as sureties for Beaton's appearance to answer the charges against him. Their offer was dismissed. A bolder move was needed. Shortly before Parliament was to meet in March 1542/3 the same triumvirate with the addition of Argyll, supported by a multitude of lesser barons and gentry, bishops and abbots, assembled at Perth, demanding that Beaton be released and that they be consulted in all high matters of state. Against this powerful phalanx of noble opinion Arran acted with unusual resolution and called their bluff. On pain of treason they were ordered to disperse. Faced down by the governor and his supporters, and lacking popular support, this they did. Huntly sent in his adherence to the governor the day before parliament sat. His colleagues followed suit. The parliament assembled on 12 March, and under Arran's guidance soon showed a determination to resist the English demands. The infant Queen would not be surrendered until she was ten years old, nor would any fortresses be handed over to King Henry. It seemed that the fears of the Catholic party were unfounded.

Huntly tried a different tack. He was seen by an English agent to 'doff his cap to George Douglas and bid him good morrow with a low reverence.' Douglas was not fooled but others may have been. Turning to the Englishman Huntly took him in his arms and declared with all sincerity that 'there is never an earl in Scotland but I may be hail fellow with him at this day, I thank God and the King my master.'[23] He employed his charm and skill at intrigue. He ingratiated himself with his rivals. He outmanoeuvred the Douglas faction, persuading Arran to place the cardinal in the custody of Lord Seton, a faithful supporter of the Queen Mother, one of whose French ladies he had married. Seton was also, of course, a relative of Huntly. Beaton's release was now only a matter of time. The Douglas brothers were furious with the Regent, deriding Arran as 'the most wavering and unstable person in the world.' A great schemer himself, frustrated by Huntly's machinations, Sir George Douglas had met his match and showed his pique. He openly admitted to being at his wits' end. The moment his back was turned Huntly would be forever 'in the governor's ear with fayre wordes and flatterie' and within two hours would persuade him to change allegiance. He warned Sir Ralph Sadler, the English ambassador, not to be taken in by Huntly's protestations of goodwill towards the designs of England. The Earl was 'the wyliest lad that lyved,' and the 'falsest and wiliest young man alive.'[24] A singular example of the pot calling the kettle black!

Sadler, an experienced judge of character, could recognise and admire an enemy's qualities and could distinguish the relative merits of one against another. He found Huntly 'far more frank' than the Earl of Moray, that 'good Papist, wholly given to the old ceremonies and traditions of Rome'. In contrast to that 'dour beadsman,' Huntly was considered 'a jolly young man and of a right good wit'.[25] Undoubtedly he was an engaging character, well liked for the most part by those not currently frustrated by his twists and turns, or bettered by him. Douglas' assessment of him, shrewish at it was, was also shrewd. Even Cecil, no mean practitioner of the arts of political chicanery, was later to 'feare his dooblying.'[26] In the context of the time and from an aficionado such as this, this was more a compliment than a criticism. Skelton's later verdict is simplistic as well as harsh: that though the fourth Earl was 'a man of vast possessions as well as of vast experience his instability was notorious and the suspicion of dishonesty tainted his career.' Until its last days his career was spectacular and successful, and the Earl of Huntly was a masterful player of a difficult game. He could use both sides in a dispute to his own best purpose to ensure that, however the game went, he would be on the winning side. His early promise was more than fulfilled: 'his rare spirit became so well polished,' recorded a family chronicler, 'that coming to riper years ... he bred in all an admiration of his virtues and so much good liking of his person, as he gained both honour and esteem to himself and to his country which had given him such education at home and brought him to such a degree of humanity, modesty, affability, valour and prudence'.[27] To what extent he had these higher virtues is arguable but in the months and years ahead it was the more rugged ones of which he had aplenty – determination, cunning and good fortune – that would see him through.

By the summer of 1543 Cardinal Beaton was free, just in time to thwart English plans to gain control of the infant Queen's person prior to the promised marriage. On 1 July 1543 the Treaty of Greenwich had been signed, an agreement whereby Mary Queen of Scots and Edward Prince of Wales were to marry as soon as the former was ten. Meanwhile she should continue to live in Scotland, but with an English nobleman being part of her household. It further purported to guarantee Scotland's freedom, and to create an inviolable peace between their two kingdoms. Beaton, however, proclaimed that behind this facade there was a secret clause to the treaty binding those noblemen taken at Solway to the English cause at the expense of their native allegiance. It was not a treaty between independent nations but a treasonable compact. Huntly and Beaton mustered troops in the north, Argyll and Lennox in the west, while Bothwell and Home guarded the borders. With Scotland betrayed and Arran her Judas, his opponents could this time expect popular support to ensure their success. They must first secure the infant Queen. Mary was resident at Linlithgow, vulnerable to kidnap. On 21 July the cardinal along with Huntly, Lennox, Argyll and Bothwell assembled 7,000 men to escort her back to the safety and security of Stirling Castle, her impregnable home for the next five years. Sir George Douglas 'said his mind at large to [Huntly],' but he had been bested yet again.[28]

As a result of increasing resentment at their arrogant inroads into the independence of Scotland, the tide began to turn against the English. Arran turned with it. On 8 September he abjured his Protestant religion and the English faction. The marriage of two nations was off. The following day Mary was crowned Queen in the royal chapel at Stirling Castle. Arran remained Regent. Beaton again became Chancellor. No immediate attempt was made to alienate England but in December 1543 the Scots parliament ratified a treaty with France reviving the Auld Alliance, thereby effectively severing the connection with England and repudiating the English marriage. The birth of a son to the future Henry II of France in January 1544 opened the prospect of an alternative union.

Henry VIII embarked on a new strategy, the 'Rough Wooing' as it was later known,[29] a series of plundering invasions which punctuated the next few years, and which were designed to terrorise the Scots into authorising the marriage of Mary to Edward. The first took place in May 1544 when Edward Seymour, Earl of Hertford, was ordered to cross the borders with his army and devastate everything from there to Edinburgh which in turn was to be 'defaced' as a memorial and warning to future generations. He was, in short, to 'torment' the Scots. Torment them he did. The prosperous but vulnerable abbeys of Jedburgh and Melrose were desecrated. The feeble Scots muster led by Beaton and the Earls of Huntly, Moray and Bothwell beat a rather undignified retreat from before Leith at the first sight of the English, leaving Edinburgh to be burnt and the Abbey and Palace of Holyrood to be sacked.[30] As the English withdrew, the same fate befell Leith. The English marched back to England, despoiling the country as they went, and scattering the feeble attempts to impede them. One result was that a loose coalition of disgruntled nobles from both sides determined to replace Arran with Mary of Guise. Angus joined with Huntly, Moray and Argyll in proclaiming Mary as Regent, Angus as her lieutenant, and Arran deprived.[31] Yet Arran, backed by Beaton, clung to office, and the strength of his opponents was soon to be weakened by the need for Huntly and Argyll to return to the Highlands to repress a clan rebellion fostered by England. The best the dissidents could achieve was a council presided over by Cardinal Beaton but on which both Mary and Arran sat.

In the winter months of 1544-5, the English renewed their raids under Sir Ralph Eure, Sir Brian Layton and Sir George Bowes. These manoeuvres had the adverse effect of managing to alienate the leader of the pro-English faction, Archibald Douglas, Earl of Angus. His ancestors were buried at Melrose Abbey. When Melrose was again pillaged the graves of the Douglases were deliberately despoiled. The outraged Angus mustered his troops and catching the English over-confident and unawares roundly defeated them at Ancrum Moor in February 1544/5.[32] Eure and Layton were among the dead. Thus Angus avenged the disturbed shades of his ancestors. The respite was short-lived. The English returned in September led this time by Hertford in person, to plunder the Marches and burn Melrose and Dryburgh Abbeys yet again.

Deeply embroiled in palace politics and the defence of the realm as he was, Huntly also had to see to the north. In the aftermath of Solway Moss, there had been a breakdown of law and order in the Highlands: 'The Scotis that duelt in the mountainis and Iles of Irland [the Hebrides], now began to schaw taikens of their inconstancie and gret wildnes.'[33] This 'gret wildnes' had been exploited by Donald Dubh, the pretender to the defunct Lordship of the Isles. The government was quite incapable of maintaining permanent executive forces that could keep order in the Highlands and was obliged to delegate its powers to local nobles such as Argyll and Huntly. The latter was made Lieutenant in the North when the incumbent Moray, riddled with gout and gravel stones, finally died at Darnaway in 1544. As lieutenant he could make such statutes and ordinances for the administration of justice and the preservation of peace, as he thought necessary, and, where those measures failed, he was authorised to raise armies under the royal banner and compel his lieges to join them. Under commissions of fire and sword he could invade the territories of those who rebelled against him; imprison or execute them, seize their castles, and appoint constables for them; or he might treat with them and receive them back into obedience. In this viceregal capacity he engaged in various police actions against two of the most turbulent clans of his region the MacDonalds of Clanranald – one branch of Clan Donald – and Clan Cameron of Lochaber.

In the spring of 1544 Huntly summoned Fraser, the third Lord Lovat, William Mackintosh, the young chief of Clan Chattan, and the laird of Grant, to assist in the reinstatement of Ranald Galda – as chief of Clanranald. Ranald had gained the sobriquet 'Galda' -'the stranger' – because his own clan saw him as an alien importation. He was the grandson of the third Lord Lovat, had been brought up by his mother's family, the Frasers, and imposed on Clanranald with their help. Despite this, Clanranald, assisted by the MacDonalds of Keppoch and the Clan Cameron, laid waste to lands belonging to Lovat and Grant. When the Frasers aligned themselves with the Earl of Huntly against the Macdonalds, the suspect Galda was deposed from the chieftainship and replaced by an illegitimate but popular claimant, John Moydertach (or John of Moidart). It would take a concerted effort under a Royal Lieutenant to bring them to heel. Huntly's campaign seemed surprisingly easy and successful, the Macdonalds having dispersed at the first approach of the royal army, which penetrated as far as Inverlochy in Lochaber. But in the Highlands to be dispersed is not to have been defeated, as the Frasers were to discover. On their homeward journey they separated from the main force, and were stalked, and then ambushed at Kinloch Lochy, by the reconstituted Macdonalds. The bloody battle that took place there came to be known as the 'Field of Shirts' because in the summer heat the belligerents had fought in their shirt sleeves. Sweat, blood and tears flowed together.

Both Lord Lovat and his heir perished, together with the hapless Ranald Galda. The MacDonalds had triumphed, and the usurper Moydertach remained the clan chief after all. In December Huntly again raised a force to invade Lochaber and punish Clan Cameron for assisting the Macdonalds. Mackintosh as deputy Lieutenant of the North accompanied him, and captured the two chiefs, Cameron of Lochiel and Macdonald of Keppoch. He sent them to Huntly, who beheaded them and cowed their followers 'with severity of the law.'[34] Moydertach fled to the Isles, lying low for some time. Huntly was very much the man of the moment, with whom all wished to be friends. On 25 March 1545 Grant, Mackintosh, Mackenzie, Ross of Balnagown and Munro of Foulis all attended the Earl at Inverness, where he had quartered his army, and entered into a contract whereby they were to defend and obey him while he would defend and reward them. Huntly's empire was growing.

By the middle of the sixteenth century Huntly controlled one of the greatest earldoms of the kingdom. In the south he held Gordon and Huntly in Berwickshire. In the north-east his lands stretched from the Grampian Mountains to the Lowlands of Glentanner and Glenmuick in Aberdeenshire, and Enzie in Banffshire. Despite his Highland acquisitions, it was these Lowland areas that remained the real source of his wealth and manpower. In the 'Low Countries' the name of Huntly was 'very considerable and powerful.' He could with ease muster 'a great posse of gentlemen on horse back in Enzie and Strathbogie.' Families sharing his patronymic of Gordon were widespread and dominant in the shires constituting a strong and warlike clan who could bring out powerful numbers of their vassals and tenants into the field. By contrast his following of Highlanders in Strathavon and Glenlivet was said to be only 300, while Badenoch and Lochaber were not thought to provide him with any followers since these areas followed their natural chieftains. Men were just one component in the control of the north-east; castles were the other. Huntly was well aware of the strategic and psychological importance of imposing his presence in stone and mortar. In his own right he held the fastnesses of Strathbogie, Bog of Gight, Aboyne, Ruthven in Badenoch and Drummin in Glenlivet. As the King's lieutenant he added the captaincy of the royal fortresses of

Inverness and Inverlochy.[35] This formidable array of castles studded across the north-east of Scotland made his power unrivalled in the region. His magnificence reached such an apogee that an Act of Parliament bestowed the noble name of Huntly upon Strathbogie itself.

His status was such that he was the natural successor to Cardinal Beaton as Chancellor when the latter was coerced into relinquishing this office by his untimely demise at St Andrews Castle on 29 May 1546. The cardinal had been murdered in retaliation for the 'burnt-offering' he had made of the Protestant evangelist George Wishart a few days before. Disguised, his sixteen assassins killed the gatekeeper, slipped into the castle, and forced the door of the cardinal's bedchamber. While Kirkaldy of Grange barred the exit, one of Wishart's friends, James Melville, gave Beaton a final opportunity to repent of the martyr's death, an opportunity of which he did not avail himself. Melville ran him through. It was, he said, 'the work and judgment of God.'[36] With echoes of his English counterpart, Wolsey, the Scottish cardinal expired, murmuring 'Fie, all is gone.' He was right. His dignity fled with his spirit. The corpse of their 'God' was displayed before the townsfolk, his trousers were undone exposing his genitalia while one of the assassins 'pishit' into his open mouth. The body was them 'buried' in a cask of salt at the bottom of the sea-tower, like so much dead meat. This assassination presaged troubled times to come. The good and the great were falling victim to the torrents of the times. Many more would follow.

Meanwhile Huntly's appointment went some way to reconciling him with Arran, the head of the government. Arran was not over-disposed to make the appointment but he needed both Huntly and his ally the Queen-dowager to broaden the base of his support in the trying times ahead. That support was immediately in evidence when the new Chancellor accompanied the Regent in his siege of Dumbarton Castle. Both Dumbarton and St Andrews had to be secured as quickly as possible in the face of the ever-present threat from England. Dumbarton was talked into surrender and in December Huntly argued in council that peaceful resolution be made to the ineffectual siege of St Andrews Castle. The siege had already lasted five months, costly both to the governor and the whole realm. Hunger would eventually force the defenders to yield but this would not be 'hastily done; and the King of England prepares all his power to come upon this realm hastily.' Huntly had returned to office just in time to confront a renewed assault by the 'Auld Enemy.' It was expected in February 1546/7.[37]

The threat from the south was delayed but not diminished by the death of Henry VIII in January 1546/7 and the succession of his nine-year-old son, Edward VI. As Scott put it, Henry's 'impatient and angry spirit continued to influence the counsels of the nation.'[38] It was embodied in Edward Seymour, the young King's uncle, who had

recently been elevated from his earldom of Hertford to become Duke of
Somerset and Lord Protector. He determined on out and out attack to
reduce the French party in Scotland, secure his nephew's marriage with
Mary, and even establish an English pale. Although initially caught
unawares by a French fleet, which forced the surrender of St Andrews
Castle on 30 July 1547, Somerset was soon ready to recommence hostilities against the Scots. On Sunday 28 August he mustered at Newcastle.
His army consisted of between 15,000 and 19,000 men, a third of whom
were mounted. These latter included a rapid deployment force of 200
Spanish mercenaries armed with arquebuses. He had a powerful heavy
artillery train, and a naval force under Lord Clinton. With this well
armed and mobile body he purposed to defeat the Scots, erect artillery
strong points and leave permanent garrisons. Somerset and his lieutenants, Warwick and Thomas Dacre, were all very experienced
commanders. They wanted to strike hard and fast. They headed for
Edinburgh with their main contingent, bypassing the near impregnable
castles of Dunbar and Tantallon, to strike at the heart of the country.

The Scots had mobilised against him well in advance. In July Huntly
promised and delivered 8,000 men, which comprised over a third,
according to his own estimate, of the Scottish Army.[39] With a fighting
force of more than 20,000 men the Regent ought to have been able to
withstand the invader. Yet his army was top-heavy in infantry –
pikemen traditionally equipped 'with jack, spear, steel bonnet, sword
and whinger'- good in defence especially if against cavalry in the right
terrain, but poor at manoeuvre, cumbersome in pursuit and vulnerable
to enfilading fire. He had precious few horse – some 1,500 light armed
Borderers – and only twenty-five to thirty pieces of artillery. The limi-
tations of his army would not be so marked if he took a strong defensive
position out of range of cannon fire and preserved his cavalry and
bowmen to protect his wings and harry the enemy in retreat.

Well informed by his spies, Arran marched his army from Edinburgh
to block the English progress. He took up position a few miles outside
the city on the high ground behind Musselborough, ready to contest
any attempt at crossing the River Esk. It was a wise move. The Scots
had the initial advantage, both in numbers and terrain. The sea was on
their left, an impassable bog on their right, and the river before them,
its only bridge covered by the Scots artillery. Huntly commanded the
left flank next to the sea, Arran the centre where the artillery was, and
Angus the right. The invaders were forced to rein in their advance and
were at a loss how to proceed. For two long days the Scottish and
English stood facing each other. Time was with the Scots if they would
but bide it. But the Scots seemed not to know the common proverb:
'It is better to sit still, than to rise up and fall.'[40] If they did know it,
they ignored it.

The Scots, a short-service army fired with adrenalin, anxious to fight and go home, could not be held in check by their own commanders for long. The first skirmish originated with the Scots and ended in defeat. A cavalry sortie across the Esk on 8 September by the light horse, supported by 500 infantry, was a rash gambit which led to their speedy annihilation at Fawside Brae by Sir Francis Bryan's Border cavalry. 1,300 Scots were killed within sight of their own camp, and Lord Home's son was taken. Somerset, however, realising the difficulties he still faced against the main Scots forces entrenched in such a position, was willing to parley: ten years of peace for a promise to keep Mary in Scotland and not marry her off to a foreigner. Arran would have none of it, but sent a herald to Somerset's camp with a counter proposal: that they exchange prisoners and arrange for safe conduct for the English. In the event of this not being accepted, Huntly, in a rather ridiculous act of bravura, issued a challenge that the matter be settled personally between him and Somerset with twenty men apiece or even one to one. Both offers were rejected by the Lord Protector of England, Huntly's challenge being contemptuously dismissed as coming from a person of insufficient rank. Nor would Somerset allow such hotheads as his lieutenant, the Earl of Warwick, to take it up instead since Huntly was 'not equal in rank to the English Earl.' The only battle was to be between armies – if the Scots would take up that challenge and meet the English force in a plain field. Somerset noted that his adversaries were of the proud sort, and that Huntly was 'a glorious young gentleman,' but trusted 'to see their pride abated shortly, and the Earl of Huntly's too.'[41]

On Black Saturday, 10 September 1547, the English advanced in battle order. By eight o'clock some of their artillery and attendant troops had moved from the main force and gone in the direction of the harbour. The English were hoping to set up gun positions by St Michael's church on the low hill of Pinkie Cleugh on the east bank of the Esk, overlooking the Scottish lines. Arran interpreted this manoeuvre as either a withdrawal on their part or a desperate attempt to get supplies from the ships at anchor off shore. He had succumbed to astonishing wishful thinking. The Scottish horse had been thrashed the day before and Somerset had been contemptuous in the face of their peace overtures. It was inconceivable that he would now retreat. Moreover the English had been entrenched for some time with their supply routes protected. They had no need to cross the Scots line to reach their ships. Rashly, Arran sent word to his commanders to leave their ground on Edmonston Edge, ford the Esk, and take the English marching columns in the flank. Angus demurred and was peremptorily told by the Lyon King of Arms to obey orders on pain of treason. William Patten, an English participant, wondered at these 'marvellous men' who 'would not believe there were any bees in the hive, till they came out and stang them by the nose.'[42]

Reluctantly, Angus moved forward across the Esk. As Huntly's rearguard began crossing the river over the bridge of Musselburgh between the Church-Knoll of Inveresk and the sea, it came within range of the English gun ships moored just offshore. They opened fire. The lucky first shot brought down the master of Graham and twenty-five of his pikemen who were tightly packed in marching formation. The cannonade so panicked Argyll's Highland archers forming the wing that they refused to advance any further. Huntly began to move his column inland out of range of the ships. In doing so he edged towards Arran's main battle where the two forces coalesced into one mass. Angus's right wing was forced south and behind the rest of the army. Nonetheless the troops moved forward and up the high ground of Fawside Brae towards the English. The whole Scots Army had become a massed line of pikes whose flanks were unprotected since the bowmen had withdrawn and the remaining cavalry lingered far in the rear out of reach of the more formidable English forces which had trounced them earlier.

Encumbered with pulling cannon through steep and marshy ground, their order broken, their clothes heavy with water, the disordered forces of the Scots were a tempting prey for an English cavalry charge. Lord Grey de Wilton's forces were ordered to attack down the slope of Fawside Brae and into the ranks of Angus' wing. Just in time however, the formidable Scottish spearmen managed to form a phalanx that held off the heavy armoured horsemen who were floundering in the mud of the Pinkie Cleugh. Their eighteen-foot pikes impaled or repelled all those who came within reach as easily as a bare finger piercing 'through the skin of an angry hedgehog,' as an English participant observed.[43] Lord Grey himself was speared in the mouth and neck. The front ranks of horse turned on those behind them, throwing the English cavalry, and the infantry behind it, into confusion. They began to withdraw in disorder. A Scottish cavalry charge at this point might have been decisive but the Scottish horse was virtually no more. Under the leadership of Sir Ralph Sadler, the English ambassador, the cavalry and infantry were allowed to rally and reform.

The Scots had lost the momentum and their advance had been checked. Their ranks had been compressed by the English cavalry charges and the bodies of horses and the dead and wounded of both sides formed a further obstacle to their uphill advance. In the time gained by their cavalry the English had commandeered the crest of Fawside Brae for their artillery. They opened fire on Huntly's wing at 200-300 yards to devastating effect. Pikemen could repel cavalry but having done so, were left exposed to gunfire. The noise of the cannon had almost as much effect as the shot, Argyll's Highland archers, inexperienced in the means of modern warfare and already shaken, began to flee, throwing down their arms. The remaining horse made off for Dalkeith. Men in the rear followed, any qualms they may have had at deserting their comrades calmed by the enfilading fire of the English hackbutters and bowmen and their mercenary force of mounted Spanish arquebusiers. The latter could ride up to within range, discharge their weapons and gallop off again before any retaliation was possible.[44]

Choking dust rising from the dry stubble fields where the battle raged further added to the confusion of the Scots. Arran broke and ran. Angus decided to withdraw out of cannon-range and to seek succour from Huntly's forces, but they mistook his men for the English and engaged. Set upon by Scots in front and English infantry behind, the right wing of the broken army threw down their pikes and fled, only to be mown down as they did so by the reformed and reinvigorated English cavalry. Huntly is reputed to have stood his ground until the chase passed him and only then did he withdraw. As he and 100 of his men held the crossing of the Esk to cover the retreat of their comrades, he was unhorsed and taken prisoner by Sir Ralph Vane. Splendidly clad in gilt and enamelled armour, Huntly was a rich and obvious prize, thus ensuring his survival amidst the carnage. It was a carnage he was to immortalise in a phrase taken to typify the whole campaign. Sitting on a tree stump surrounded by the dead and dying, he was taunted by his captors. Since God himself seemed to approve the match by the outcome of the battle, he was asked how he viewed the union between the two princes. Wiping sweat and grim from his brow he expressed himself favourable to the marriage but 'lyke[d] not this wooing.'[45]

The pursuit lasted from one o'clock until six over bare hillsides ideal for cavalry. Scottish losses were very high as their English pursuers cut them down without mercy. Patten puts the number of the slain at 13,000, but Huntly estimated them more modestly and probably more accurately at 6,000. Of these Patten claimed 4,000 were gentlemen. Most died in flight. Only 1,500 were taken prisoner. The English lost less than 1,000, perhaps as few as a quarter of that, almost all being cavalry.[46]

Now unopposed, Somerset proceeded to ravage the Lowlands and install English garrisons at strategic spots, including the island of Inchcolm. But any higher aims were frustrated. The Scots united against him. He did not even attempt to besiege Edinburgh Castle, fortify the city or garrison Leith, and the little Queen eluded him. Mary was whisked away from Stirling to safety in Inchmahone. It was a prelude to her departure for the ultimate security of France in August of the following year, after Arran had arranged her marriage to Francis, the Dauphin, and received the French dukedom of Chatelherault as reward.[47] French troops were later to be sent to assist in defence of the realm to which it was supposed France would be irrevocably linked by marriage and procreation. This union between Mary Queen of Scots and the French Dauphin marked the ultimate defeat of all the English endeavours in the 'rough wooing.' The English had failed to unite the two island kingdoms, and by so attempting had opened to the door to their own old enemy, France. But these were the future consequences of Pinkie. In the more immediate aftermath Scotland was as usual deprived of some of its senior nobility, by death on the field or incarceration in England.

Huntly was the most prominent Scottish captive taken at the battle of Pinkie. He was an important prisoner indeed. This 'terror of England' was now confined far in the south, a second Wallace in English captivity. His fate was rather different from that of his martyred forebear. The French Ambassador, Odet de Selve, to whom Huntly became a frequent visitor and constant source of information on Scottish affairs, was surprised to observe that 'he is neither lodged in the Tower nor any other prison but on the contrary he is treated graciously and humanely, even fêted, able to come and go as he pleases though always accompanied by a young English knight of whom he is the prisoner.'[48] The ambassador became ever more concerned about Huntly's reliability and over the months of the Earl's captivity distrust began to displace respect in his dealings with him.[49] The English looked on Huntly as their most promising northern agent to secure the longed for marriage of their King and the Scottish Queen. They went out of their way to flatter and seduce him. By way of a test, they even let their prisoner travel on a long leash to Newcastle, on an information-gathering mission. Their liberality seemed to work. From the north Huntly wrote to Somerset, pledging his 'service in furthering the King's purpose ... for the weal of both realms so long at discord' and thanking the Protector for his 'great goodness and humanity shown to me.' He even despatched to Somerset a letter that Arran had sent to him.[50] But the negotiations between Huntly and the English, thus begun, took a long time to come to fruition.[51]

Huntly's 'double dealing' or 'principled obduracy' (depending on the perspective) was largely to blame. He was prepared to offer his wife and children as hostages but a promise of service and fealty to the English King was a demand too high. The English were equally reluctant to release the best Scottish general before the Scots had been fully cowed and his loyalty assured. They needed so influential a man as Huntly, but they would not trust him. He was a man who played 'double parts.'[52] In a report by one of their Scottish agents the English were warned that so desperate were Arran and Mary of Guise to secure the return of their 'Pope and God, Huntly' that they were urging him to say and sign anything. Simultaneously, it was reported, there was a plan to spirit Huntly to France or Flanders: 'so watch him and keep this from him like fire from gunpowder.'[53] There was substance to their disquiet. The

Queen-Regent was certainly prepared to pay his ransom to secure his return, and, to secure his support for the proposed marriage of the Queen and the Dauphin, to reward him with a substantial French pension and the promise of lands in Orkney, Ross of Moray.[54] The English could not make up their minds whether it was more in their interests to keep Huntly captive, or to let him home where he could either work to their will, or at least, by his presence, divide the Scottish leadership. The Earls of Angus and Argyll in particular were both by this time enemies and rivals of Huntly and were both in the pay of England. Argyll had been humiliated by his failure at Pinkie and the contrast frequently and publicly made between his shortcomings and Huntly's generalship was insupportable. On one occasion when the possibility of the latter's return was mentioned by the English agent, Argyll started, beat his fist on the table, and exclaimed 'If ye let him home, ye mar all.'[55] In the event they kept him awhile. Finally, after months of procrastination, Huntly procured his release the following December and on his own terms, by signing an indenture with Somerset to pursue the cause of Edward VI in Scotland and to seek the union of the two kingdoms by the union of the two monarchs.[56] He did not swear fealty to a foreign power. When he was heading north, however, Somerset seemed to realise that Huntly's word was not his bond, and sent officers in pursuit. Huntly eluded them and made his escape. He had become a man around whom legends grew. According to one story, while imprisoned at Morpeth, he cunningly duped his captors into the distraction of card playing while he made a bold dash across the nearby border. It may even be true, although he was certainly assisted in getting out of England by a George Kerr.[57] Somerset with impotent fury railed against 'the false and subtle departure of the Earl of Huntly who so much did dissemble with us.'[58] This was an unfair judgement by a gaoler who had been outwitted by his captive. Huntly was a loyal Scot who used the arts of guile and diplomacy to serve both himself and his country, and he used them well.

After more than a year's absence, Huntly was warmly welcomed back in Scotland, and was soon rewarded for his privations, or at least bought back into loyalty. He was reappointed as Chancellor by Arran and on 13 February 1548/9 the Queen Mother, 'for services done to the child queen's father,' and for his support of the marriage of Mary Queen of Scots to the Dauphin awarded Huntly the long coveted earldom of Moray. Mary of Guise even contemplated making him a Duke – a novelty introduced into Scotland by Arran's recent assumption of the title – for his good services to her. To this suggestion the affronted Angus had retorted, 'If he be a duke [pronounced 'duck'], I will be a drake.'[59] His opposition put paid to any such preferment.

Thus from 1549 Huntly held the earldom of Moray together with the lordships of Abernethy, Petty, Brachley and Strathdearn under the

crown in whose gift they lay. With the wars with England drawing to
their close,[60] he was able to devote more time to his northern territories. It was just as well. His acquisition of the rich and fair 'Morayland'
was the source of much contention. Good land and rich fishings were
jealously guarded or enviously coveted, and none were better than
those in Moray. Since 1544 John, Earl of Sutherland, had the government of the earldom of Moray, a benefit that had bred a jealousy and
discontent between him and his near kinsman, Huntly. But they were
quickly reconciled and he renounced the earldom to Huntly in return
for a fixed annual revenue out of the rent. Sutherland was to support
Huntly in the 'peaceable brouking and joising of the said earldom of
Moray, and shall assist, fortify and concur at his power that the said Earl
of Huntly obtain all further richt that may be obtenit of the said
earldom of Moray,' receiving 500 merks in return.[61] Such support was
welcome. Many powerful men had claims on the lands: in addition to
Huntly the Earls of Rothes and Athol had property in the area. Lesser
men lived there: the Grants in Strathspey; Clan Chattan in Badenoch.
Yet, such was Huntly's power that his neighbours presently acquiesced
in his authority, but for the independence of one, his own deputy, the
fifteenth chief of Clan Chattan, William Mackintosh.

   Although nominally head of the clan since 1524 when his father had
died, his minority had seen Hector in charge while William was
'liberally educated' by the Earl of Moray. William had become chief in
1540 when he was nineteen. Although he had loyally supported
Huntly in the past, he may have proved susceptible to the wiles of the
English who wanted to disturb the peace of the north in order to
induce Huntly more readily to acquiesce with Somerset.[62] At any rate
Mackintosh refused to sign a further bond of manrent. This was not
just insolence, it was disloyalty, since Huntly, as well as being his
commanding officer, was feudal superior of the Mackintosh lands in
Nairnshire and in Badenoch. Huntly deprived William of his deputy
lieutenant-ship. Word reached Huntly from Lachlan Mackintosh,
William's own cousin, that William was plotting the Earl's
murder.[63] This was not the most reliable source since Lachlan was hardly
disinterested, aspiring as he did to the chieftainship of the clan.
Nonetheless, it served as sufficient justification for Huntly to act. In
1550 William was arrested and tried in Aberdeen for treason against
the Queen's lieutenant. The trial itself took place before a 'packed'
court, and the convicted felon was then sentenced to death. The
provost of Aberdeen protested against this and appealed to parliament.
Deprived of the public display of his power of life and death in
Aberdeen, Huntly secreted the young Mackintosh either to Strathbogie
or Gight. According to Buchanan's partisan account he was duped into
throwing himself on Huntly's mercy. He received none. Huntly

avoided personal responsibility by persuading his wife to shoulder it when the young chief bowed his head in submission. 'This the unfeeling woman undertook, and in the absence of her husband, she beheaded the wretched man, doomed though affirming his innocence.'[64] With his wife playing the Lady Macbeth of Strathbogie Huntly seemed secure and supreme. William Mackintosh's lands were granted to Huntly's son, Alexander, Lord Gordon,[65] thus compounding Clan Chattan's bitter resentment.

The north settled, Huntly was able to concentrate on further ingratiating himself with the Queen Mother. When he and the third Earl of Cassilis quarrelled openly in the Privy Council over the fate of Mackintosh, they willingly submitted to the intercession of Mary of Guise, each holding the outstretched hand of the 'Queen's Grace.'[66] They both also agreed to form part of her entourage on her imminent trip to France, ostensibly to visit her daughter but in reality to secure the support of the French King for her political designs. Mary of Guise welcomed the presence of such an important nobleman as Huntly since she needed his help in her ambition to supplant Chatelherault when her daughter reached the age of twelve or even before. Huntly was duly fêted by the French. They flattered his ego with the Order of St Michael, and bought his support with gold.

On his return to Scotland the Earl and his wife proceeded in the years 1551 to 1554 to rebuild the keep and great tower of the newly named Huntly Castle in sumptuous and ostentatious fashion. Ever since the early thirteenth century a castle has stood on this elevated and strategic site overlooking and dominating the confluence of the River Deveron and the Bogie, a stream from which it derives its name. The stone castle dated from about 1452 when it was erected by Alexander, the first Earl of Huntly. The walls of the circular keep are ten feet thick with a staircase reaching the roof where an elegant crestellated wall afforded superb views over the surrounding countryside. Adjacent were the new apartments, the ground floor sheer and with few windows, the upper hall itself sporting three semi-circular double-floored dormers and at the far end from the keep a square corner tower. The internal decor has all but gone, but the splendour of the exterior would have been matched within, with elaborately painted walls and gilded ornamentation. Strathbogie had been transformed in three years from a medieval fortress into a Renaissance palace.[67]

The existence of a fine house was indispensable for any magnate who wished to maintain any significant regional connection.[68] Huntly was no ordinary magnate, but the Lord Lieutenant of the North, counsellor to kings, a pillar of state. Perhaps to magnify the significance of his downfall his old enemy John Knox conceded he was 'the wisest, the richest, and a man of greatest power' in Scotland, for 'in man's opinion,

under a prince, there was not such a one these three hundred years in
this realm produced.' The English opined that 'whosoever should be
King of the south, Huntly would be king of the north.'[69] David
Calderwood, the historian of the Kirk, concurred: 'he bare himself like
a king in the north.' The grandeur of his household was for Huntly not
merely an acknowledgement of his status but also of his loyalty. He was
the Queen's viceroy, her presence in the north. As such he had to live
up to that station. His ordinary living expenses were estimated at £660
per annum. Certainly his princely apartments impressed even Mary of
Guise's French court when in 1556 they visited. Every modern luxury
was provided and the harshness of Scots winters ameliorated. Silk,
velvet and gold-embroidered coverings adorned the beds, with table
clothes to match. The windows were hung with richly coloured and
heavy curtains. Huge fires, constantly tended, heated, and flaming
torches lit, the rooms. The great hall had the proportions and decor of
a presence chamber, with a great crimson 'claith of state' embroidered
with gold. Sumptuous cushions festooned the furniture and tapestries
and other hangings covered the walls.[70] The reception afforded the
Queen-Regent was royal, 1,000 men forming the guard of honour, and
the splendour of the entertainment was such that after a few days his
guest offered to leave to spare Huntly further expense. He assured her
that the display was within his means and showed her his vaults
crammed with provisions. Astonished at their magnificent reception in
this outpost in the north the French insinuated that 'the wings of the
Cock of the North should be clipped.'[71]

3

THE BASTARD LORD JAMES
1553/4-1561

Surely the Lord James is a gentleman of great worthiness!

William Cecil[1]

Huntly ... was a crafty and turbulent man who made but a cloak of religion to attain his own ambitious ends and designs... [Lord James] by the contrary was sincere, upright, trusty and faithful in all his actions.

Hume of Godscroft[2]

On 19 February 1553/4 the Duke of Chatelherault finally yielded to the tempting financial inducements and continual political pressure and resigned the governorship, handing over the regency to Mary of Guise. The Scotland the new Queen-Regent inherited was rapidly falling further into turmoil, riven by the forces of the Reformation, forces she never understood and always underestimated. Her eyes were more fixed on the traditional 'big power' rivalries of England and France than on domestic disharmony. She appointed her own men to positions of influence. These appointees included Frenchmen, constituting the first step towards integrated government and a permanent Franco-Scots axis against the English. This was a controversial departure and immediately aroused the hostility and suspicions of the Scottish lords, Protestant and Catholic. The prospect of their country being submerged by France and the loss of their prerogatives at home were the two things that could unite them in opposition to the Crown.

Mary rapidly became suspicious of these sulky Scottish noblemen who had never really accepted her in her own right; and she quickly became enraged by the increasing signs of discontent and disobedience, especially on the part of erstwhile friends and allies. Her greatest ally, Huntly, fell foul of this paranoia in late 1554 when he failed to put down the continuing depredations of John Moydertach, the leader of the Clanranald of whom Huntly had failed to dispose a decade before. Huntly proceeded against him as far as Abertarff in Inverness-shire, but when it came to pursuing him into the mountains, his forces declined to follow. The Lowland troops refused to go into a terrain unsuited to cavalry and his Highland foot, many of who were Mackintoshes, were disaffected, still angry at the fate of their chief in 1550. It was too dangerous to proceed and Huntly was forced to retire. Those, such as the Earl of Cassilis, who disliked his arrogance and mistrusted his power, were quick to poison the Queen-Regent against him. She saw Huntly's atypical inaction as a deliberate flouting of her authority. As a result he was imprisoned in Edinburgh Castle, deprived of both the chancellorship and the earldom of Moray, and sentenced to five years exile in France.[3] He bought his way out of the last measure, and, on his release in March 1555, he retired to his estates in the north, a great loss to the Regent. Loyal to the crown, but cognisant that he was invaluable to it, he acquiesced in his treatment, biding his time. The family motto of the Gordons was, after all, precisely that: 'Bydand.' He did not have to bide long.

Desperate for support among the nobility for her planned campaigns against England, on behalf of France, the Queen-Regent implored Huntly's backing. He refused. Perhaps this was to repay her for humbling him, but it was a sensible restraint given Scotland's past calamities when confronting the English. It was the same policy as he had pursued before Solway Moss. On the former occasion he had been abused, his advice ignored, and the invasion had taken place with disastrous consequences. On this occasion Huntly's opposition – backed as it was by the Catholic Duke of Chatelherault and the Protestant fourth Earl of Argyll – was decisive. Mary was angry at this frustration of her will and she determined to bridle the power of these turncoat lords who had dared oppose the councils of France. In this she received support from her stepson, Lord James Stewart, prior of St Andrews, 'one of the wisest of the late King's base sons,'[4] who thus makes his first entry on the national stage.

Born in 1531 to James V and his mistress Margaret Erskine, the wife of Robert Douglas of Lochleven, Lord James was frustrated by his illegitimacy from ascending to a throne he would have more than graced. A complex and highly intelligent man, he was as politically ambitious as he was able, an ambition which daily festered with the reproach that he was precluded from his father's throne by the carelessness of his birth. 'The Twigs of his Ambition,' the contemporary historian, William Camden, remarked, 'daily sprung forth more and more in his Words and Deeds.'[5] Admittedly Camden was a writer not fond of his subject, but ambition was an obvious and natural trait in one so endowed by nature and birth. Some would say he was unscrupulous but that would be wrong. He had scruples aplenty. His ambition was married to his principles and, like many at the time, he saw himself as the instrument of the will of the Almighty. This, and his blood and his breeding made him formidable. His portraits show a strong man but hardly a kindly one. He was capable of a forgivingness unusual in that age, but this was the condescension of power not the effect of a generous spirit. The stern dictates of a triumphant Calvinism, and its disregard for the prerogatives of birth, had obvious appeal to such a man, intellectually secure but blighted by bastardy. Thus, although born a Catholic, and a nominal prior of a lucrative benefice from the age of eight, it is hardly surprising that he was to become in time the champion of Protestantism. He first came into pervasive contact with the intellectual ferment occasioned by the Reformation when a student at St Andrews University in the mid 1540s. The university was run down but it was also on the east coast. The Chancellor was Cardinal Beaton, but his inept oversight could not suppress the new ideas emanating from the Continent.[6] Lord James would have been resident in the city when three of the most dramatic events of the early Scottish Reformation took place: the burning of George Wishart on the orders of a corrupt and vindictive cardinal, that cardinal's own brutal but bold assassination, and the long ensuing siege of St Andrews Castle, a siege prolonged by the obduracy and courage of Beaton's killers within. This martyrdom proved an 'ignorant means ...to outlaw question.' The fact that Wishart had not 'flinched from the flame of the burning' leant credence to the doctrine he taught.[7] Doubts were doubtless fuelled, seeds were surely sown in the mind of the young Lord James, but it was not until a meeting with John Knox in 1555 that he was finally 'rescued from the puddle of papistry,' and became the genuine and sincere Protestant that even his enemies acknowledged him to be. Unlike some others who crossed the same personal Rubicon, this convert was to remain firm in his adherence to the Reformed Faith until his dying day.

He was equally certain of the necessity of strong government, civil order, and friendship with England. Mary was the Regent and centre of all legitimate government. He was her kinsman. She was tolerant of Protestants. She was antagonistic to Archbishop Hamilton, and the erstwhile Hamilton ascendancy had done nothing to advance Lord James. His father's widow and her husband's bastard were obvious allies. So they became. In the long run her Catholic and Francophile policies would have the double effect of antagonising England and provoking major disruption at home. In this maelstrom James' convictions stood firm but his loyalties wavered, depending on where the emphasis had to be placed at any particular moment. In these circumstances Mary could not entirely rely on a heretic stepson, but once more needed the active support of the most powerful Catholic Earl in her kingdom. In August 1557, although his forfeiture of Mackintosh's lands was annulled, Huntly was restored to favour to become once again Lieutenant General of Scotland.

To counter Mary's plans for her daughter to marry the Dauphin and other hellish plots of 'the Congregation of Satan', as the Roman Catholic Church was fondly characterised, on 3 December 1557 Argyll, Morton and other lesser members of the aristocracy formed the first bond of 'Lords of the Congregation of Christ'. This was a hard-line Protestant association, which would grow rapidly, unify the opposition to the Regent, and have a major influence on the politics of the succeeding years. Lord James would ultimately become their *de facto* leader. The sectarian divide was on the brink of civil war.

It soon came, starting in the central Lowlands and moving north. Although Mary of Guise sent Lord James to France as one of the commissioners to negotiate the terms of the nuptial settlement, after the marriage of her daughter and the Dauphin on 24 April 1558, the Regent no longer needed the support of the Protestants, and could begin overtly to favour the Catholics and the French. In early 1559, outraged by the wanton destruction of the beautiful priory of the Carthusians at Perth, she determined to restore order there by force. The Reformers reacted with another orgy of destruction, vandalism and looting, sacking the monasteries of the friars in Edinburgh and other towns, and setting fire to Scone Abbey. With his viceregal authority Huntly did what he could to meliorate their worst excesses in the north. The Bishop of Aberdeen called on him to save the Church, and while that was beyond even Huntly's capacity; he could preserve her fabric. The treasures of St Machar's Cathedral in Aberdeen were packed up and handed over to him for safekeeping. Robes and hangings made from the English tents at Bannockburn and 843oz of cathedral plate were stored securely in Strathbogie.[8]Lord James, likewise horrified by the chaos engendered by the zealots, rejoined the Marian camp. The Queen-Regent's forces, including these supporters, marched on Perth. Order was soon restored, and the Protestants, deserted by their leaders, were in the mood to parley. On 29 May 1559, as her proxies, Lord James, Argyll and Huntly signed a peace treaty with the Lords of Congregation.

Within hours Mary reneged on the treaty of Perth. Within days Argyll and Lord James announced that as a result of this betrayal they would join with the Congregation. They had promised so to do if she went back on the agreement. She had done so in spirit if not in letter. Troops in French pay if not French troops themselves were still in occupation in the town and French influence was unchecked. The combination of a French female Regent and a French occupying force played into the hands of a party which could claim patriotism as well as Protestantism.

In rapid succession, Perth fell to the Lords of the Congregation on 25 June, and Edinburgh on 29 June, although the latter's vital stronghold, the castle, remained tantalisingly beyond the grasp of the occupying

forces. Despite the fact that its governor, Lord Erskine, was Lord James'
maternal uncle, he refused to open its gates to his nephew's entreaties.
The Queen-Regent had evacuated the capital as Lord James approached
with his army, and retreated to Dunbar. Mary of Guise tried to procure
delay, reckoning on the arrival of a large auxiliary force from France.
She tried to sow division by spreading rumours that Lord James aspired
to the throne.[9] She arranged for a proclamation in the name of Francis
and Mary to be published accusing the lords of sedition, of treasonable
associations with England and of seeking to overthrow the existing
government under guise of religious reformation. She had some success.
Chatelherault deserted the Congregation, others grew lukewarm, and
England itself began to have misgivings about how this reformation
might turn into revolution. Fortified by the knowledge that daily deser-
tions were haemorrhaging the ranks of the Congregation, the Queen-
Regent advanced from Dunbar to Edinburgh.

The lords doubted they could defend the capital. She doubted she
could take it. Chatelherault and Huntly were delegated to agree a
compromise. In return for evacuating the town, refraining from further
desecrations, and obeying the Queen-Regent, the Protestants were
assured that they had liberty of religion, their preachers had freedom of
speech, and no one would be persecuted for religion's sake. A truce was
signed between the two parties, which was intended to last until 10
January. It survived a lot less long than that.

At the end of August more French troops disembarked in Leith where
they were employed by the Queen-Regent in fortifying the port. Leith
was much easier to defend than Edinburgh and was strategically of
immense importance. It was the lifeline with France. The Lords of the
Congregation matched this threat by reiterating their aims in another
band at Stirling on 1 August: to subvert Popery, to overthrow the
Queen-Regent, and to expel the French. The following month
Chatelherault rejoined the Congregation and signed the band. At the
same time Lord James, Argyll and Athol agreed on a perpetual league
against the Earl of Huntly, whose power in the north had to be checked
in all their interests. In October the Lords were strong enough to
mobilise an army of 12,000 men and on the 16 October they re-
occupied an Edinburgh deserted by the Queen-Regent for the new
fortifications of Leith. Triumphantly they announced the deposition of
Mary of Guise from the regency and set up a council to govern in her
stead on behalf of the young Queen and her husband. Lord James,
Chatelherault, and the new Earl of Arran all held key positions. It was
one thing to say, another to do. Shortly thereafter, by a number of
military actions, Mary of Guise forced them to withdraw and the capital
once again passed into her hands. So long as she could command well-
trained and well-equipped French troops she could withstand the Lords

of the Congregation. The only way to counter this superiority was to gain foreign support themselves.

They looked to England. Alarmed by increasing French infiltration in Scotland, Elizabeth intervened, but, reluctant to commit herself too far, she first of all sent a fleet of fourteen ships under Admiral Winter to the Firth of Forth to cut off the French from their supplies. This soon proved too little, too late. They forestalled an attack on St Andrews, but the French troops merely returned to the security of Leith. Elizabeth resolved to give more determined encouragement to the Congregation. The Duke of Norfolk was dispatched to Berwick to confer with the Scottish secretary, William Maitland of Lethington, Lord Ruthven and other Scots emissaries. The Treaty of Berwick, a mutual defence pact against France, was then signed in February 1559/60. In response to this Lord Grey with an English army of between 2,000 and 6,000 foot was sent north to buttress the forces of the Congregation. He entered Scotland on 2 April 1560, joined up with the Scots and laid siege to Leith.

Huntly still held back, prevaricating from day to day, watching the progress of events and calculating how best to serve his interests and those of his country. He feared the Queen-Regent's tendency to try to render the crown independent of the nobility, and build up an absolutist monarchy on the French model. The number and permanence of French troops on Scottish soil and the influence of the French especially in the north increased his concern. They were infringing on his 'principality.' He tried to secure his own position by associating himself with, if not allying himself to, the stronger party. He secretly engaged to make common cause with the Congregation; he treated with Chatelherault (whose daughter Anne, Huntly's son George had recently married) to ensure that his power base was preserved from attack by the Queen's party in the north – a league of dissident noblemen, clansmen, islesmen and the French;[10] and he wrote to Queen Elizabeth promising assistance in the unification of the isle. Yet in the last resort he was reluctant to take up arms against the Queen-Regent. He played a waiting game and would neither oppose her nor come to her aid.

Finally at the end of April 1560, after some deft persuasion by Lord James himself, Huntly publicly threw in his lot with the Congregation, signed a covenant drawn up by them, and joined his voice to those of the other lords calling for the expulsion of the French troops, the reduction of Leith, the storming of Edinburgh Castle,[11] as well as for the reformation of religion. To add his name to this last call is inexplicable, unless it was driven by necessity. His religion was both orthodox and sincere. He had no truck with heretics, and yet here he is appending his signature to a heretic band. His transfer of allegiance was based on both principle and expediency, and proved a temporary deviation.

The debilitating siege of Leith continued, and although an English assault in May was repulsed with considerable loss, the Queen-Regent, worn-out, isolated and desperate for peace, offered to negotiate with Huntly and Glencairn. In the event her offer was taken up by her less-malleable stepson Lord James Stewart attended by Maitland, Lord Ruthven and the Master of Maxwell instead. If the French were removed from the kingdom, they would submit to her authority. This was the sticking point that Mary was unable to move. Before the stalled negotiations could be progressed further, Mary fell ill. In widowhood she had sacrificed herself for her adopted country, foregoing a leisurely retirement in her native France for the thankless task of sustaining her cold kingdom through the turmoil of religious discord, faction, and foreign incursion, to hand over to the daughter she hardly knew. In so doing she became the tool of France and seemed to be prepared to submerge Scotland under a Continental shelf. Throughout its history Scotland had seen the French as allies against the menace of English ambitions. Under the regency of Mary of Guise, and the revolution in allegiances brought about by the Reformation, the poison and the antidote were reversed. Now two embattled semi-Protestant states on one small island needed to stand shoulder to shoulder against the Catholic Continental powers. Thus the harder Mary strived, the more intransigent the opposition to her policies became. Sensing this, and being a reconciler at heart, in her last hours she was magnificent, and tragic. To her deathbed she summoned the Lords of the Congregation. Argyll, Marischal, and Glencairn came with Lord James and Chatelherault. Dying and defeated, she graciously and generously praised their efforts and enjoined them to further exertion in the cause of peace. She urged them to remove both French and English troops from the kingdom. Her only reproach – but it was a bitter one – was for the absent Huntly for what she perceived were his 'pernicious counsels' and his betrayal of her personally and of the Catholic cause. She died on 10 June 1560. Her last reproaches were to be made known to her daughter, briefly reigning in France.[12]

Within six months of the death of her mother, peace had been concluded with the treaty of Edinburgh, the French had left Scotland, and Mary was herself a widow, Queen-dowager in France, but Queen of Scots. The time was ripe and she was ready to return home to her rightful throne. Young, inexperienced, Catholic-born and French-educated, effectively a foreigner in her own kingdom, Mary would look to her older cousin, the most experienced councillor, and the foremost Catholic nobleman – the 'Cock o' the North,' and 'the Pope of the North-East' – for succour, counsel and support. Or so he hoped and others expected.[13]

4

CORRICHIE
1561–1563

Now they think Lord James grows cold; he aspires to great matters; he is lieutenant and all but commander of the queen, like soon to be Earl of Moray and Treasurer of Scotland.

Thomas Randolph.[1]

Murn, ye heighlands, and murn ye leighlands!
I trow ye ha'e meikle need;
For the bonnie burn of Corrichie
Has run this day wi' bleid.
The Ballad of the Battle of Corrichie.[2]

In April 1561, while still in mourning in France, Mary received two rival emissaries, John Leslie, parson of Oyne, later Bishop of Ross, and Lord James Stewart, her half-brother. Leslie got there first. Representing the Scottish Catholics, he acted in full conjunction with Huntly. He warned Mary of the ambitions of Lord James, and urged her to detain him in France. He urged her to land at Aberdeen, where 20,000 men under Huntly could be guaranteed to meet her. She could then take Scotland by storm and restore the true faith. The following day Lord James tried to persuade her to let the Protestant party alone. He told her that she could count on her subjects' obedience and on her freedom to exercise her religion provided that she did not come to spearhead renewed French domination or Catholic reaction. Relations with England she should strengthen. For himself he pledged his support, loyalty and obedience as her prime advisor, a position that would be strengthened, he hinted, if she were to grant him the earldom of Moray.[3]

Mary was realistic enough to know that she could not undo the Reformation even if – with persistence – she could have undermined it. Her mother had exhausted herself, and died in the attempt, and within months of her death the treaty of Edinburgh, the adoption of Knox's Book of Discipline by Lord James and many of the leading nobility, and the enactments of the 'Reformation Parliament', had extinguished her hopes of an indelibly Francophile and Catholic Scotland. Huntly was an archaic apostle of a losing cause. Mary's mother was French, so was her late husband, but despite her birth and breeding, the young Queen's eyes were turned to England where Elizabeth, a woman older than she – and unmarried and childless – had been on the throne for the past three years. Mary was next in line and a whole new prospect for Scottish diplomacy and ambition was opening, a union of crowns. England was Protestant – Protestants were dominant in Scotland. While Mary's ambitions lay in succeeding Elizabeth she could not risk alienating her own Protestant subjects and so Protestant England. Further, to achieve anything in furtherance of her dynastic ambitions Mary would need the active support of her Protestant lords; lords recently allied to the English in their opposition to her mother. She was prepared to accept the inevitable, and declined to attempt the impossible, in return for their loyalty and help. In the person of her own brother they were now offering both.

Mary was persuaded by his argument, as much for personal reasons as for political. Lord James came in person. Huntly sent an emissary. Lord James was her brother, Huntly her cousin. Lord James, as a youth, had accompanied her on her flight to France, had visited her thereafter, and had been one the commissioners appointed to help negotiate her marriage to the Dauphin. Huntly she neither knew nor remembered. Lord James was twelve years her senior, a vigorous father figure upon whose trusty shoulder the young widow in a strange land could at long last lean. Huntly was old enough to be her grandfather. Lord James was able, intelligent, and with a rare political acumen. He was adept at portraying himself as a man of stern principle, loyal to his sister, influential with her nobility. In contrast Huntly was tainted in the young Queen's eyes. Although he had long supported Mary of Guise, he had ultimately let her down, or even betrayed her. Lord James would have told Mary that her mother on her deathbed had mistrusted the old Earl and so should she. Mary became 'well acquainted with [Huntly's] perfidiousness against her father first and next to her mother.' Sowing these subtle seeds of mistrust, Lord James had accomplished his mission and 'fully grope[d] her mind.'[4] He then, in secret interview with the English ambassador, disclosed all that had passed between himself and his sister.

On 19 August 1561 the young Queen, absent from Scotland since her infancy, landed at Leith. Huntly had been rebuffed in the shape of his messenger. He was to be no more successful in person. He was now approaching the age of fifty, and life as the premier Earl had taken its toll. Bulky, dour, short of breath, 'grizzled like a great northern bear,' grown corpulent with age, Huntly was the very pattern of the Highland patriarch.[5] Still finding her feet in what was in all respects a foreign country, Mary initially confirmed him as Chancellor. In the new political climate Huntly soon proved to be an outspoken and indiscreet advocate of the conservative cause. He was one of only four Catholics –

the others being Errol, Athol and Montrose – on a Privy Council dominated by the leading Protestants of the regency. They comprised the majority; they predominated in attendance. First among them were Lord James and his increasingly close ally, Maitland of Lethington. Accustomed to being an indispensable part of government for so long, Huntly felt much put out by the rising star of Lord James, royal bastard though he was. The leading representatives, as they were, of the two sides in the Reformation and of different generations, growing personal hostility was an important factor when allied to political and religious disagreement. When closely tied to the crown Huntly had been able to outmanoeuvre all his rivals or win the support of those eager to be allied to an Earl so much in royal favour. For the first time in his life he found himself ranged against the monarch. He made no secret of his disapproval of the Queen's cool policy towards the Catholics, while her appeasement of the Protestant ruling party left him isolated, angry, and surprised. Religion added the glue that would enable a coalition of enemies to grow up around Lord James in his vendetta against Huntly. Vendetta it became. The royal visit to St Andrews was marred by a violent quarrel between the two about the Mass, with Mary present, when Huntly declared that if the Queen commanded it he would set up the Mass in three shires. Living up to his reputation for dealing 'rudely, homely and bluntly,' Lord James told him to his face that 'it was past his power.'[6]

That assertion was soon to be tested. In the north Huntly had been a law unto himself and it was vital to both James and Mary that his power should be curbed. Mary of Guise had been warned to clip his wings; Mary Stewart would do it. Huntly was the past. By contrast Lord James was the future. He had so far been instrumental in holding the more extreme Protestants in check and could be relied on to secure more of the Church's wealth for the crown. It was prudent that he be rewarded with a dignity commensurate to his status as the Queen's chief counsellor. A convenient and plausible method of doing so, and creating a counterweight to Huntly in the north, was by transferring the earldom of Moray – a royal gift – to him. The stumbling block was Huntly who was, as sheriff of Aberdeen, the *de facto* holder of the vacant earldoms of both Mar and Moray. Under her brother's guidance, the Queen acted circumspectly. Lord James was granted the earldom of Moray on 30 January 1561/2 but the charter creating him such was kept *in retentis* [held back] and Huntly was not forfeited, continuing to hold the earldom informally under the crown. He was further reassured by being restored to the chancellorship. He suspected nothing. Camouflage helped. In February Lord James was married to Agnes Keith, eldest daughter of William, Earl Marischal, and niece of Huntly's wife. At the magnificent wedding banquet he was invested Earl of Mar – not Moray – and publicly assumed that title. The revival of this earldom and the assumption of lands in Braemar, Strathdee, and Cromar – long coveted by Huntly – were bad enough. If Huntly had known he was about to lose the Moray lands his disgruntlement would have been even greater. The dissembling continued for some time, even after Lord James was forced to resign his new title when Lord Erskine protested that the earldom of Mar was an Erskine perquisite. Despite holding the Moray title he reverted to being mere Lord James.

Mary was increasingly eager to meet Elizabeth; France looked to Huntly, that inveterate English baiter, to prevent such an encounter.[7] Mary would not listen. She had her back to France and face towards England. Her back was also turned on Huntly. Obsessed with the English succession, nothing – not her faith, let alone a subject like Huntly – would be allowed to get in her way. Since his views were largely ignored he would cease to give expression to them. Having regularly attended the Privy Council in the early months of 1562, Huntly failed to appear at the 19 May meeting (or any thereafter), excusing himself on the ground that he had a sore leg, a touch of the gout no doubt. It was a feeble excuse. Another Scottish nobleman, equally discontented with the way the wind was blowing, was the Duke of Chatelherault, head of the Hamiltons, and with unrivalled power in the south-west. Protestant though he now again was, he adhered to the French interest. His motives were more selfish than those of Huntly, who at least had religious and political objections to moves towards England; Chatelherault had lands in France and a claim to the throne in Scotland. Neither did he wish to jeopardise. In his case it was a sore arm that prevented his attendance at court. In the absence of these two infirm old malcontents the council agreed in principle to a meeting between the two Queens, and the following month Elizabeth gave her consent to such a rendezvous. In June the English ambassador, Thomas Randolph, could gleefully report that Huntly held no credit with the Queen and that France was very disturbed at developments.[8] Huntly took a dangerous step in sending his oldest son and heir, Lord George Gordon, to sound out Chatelherault. In his partisan *History*, John Knox was to interpret these overtures – and those he alleged were made simultaneously to the Earl of Bothwell who had just escaped from imprisonment in Edinburgh Castle – as an attempt by the young Gordon to co-ordinate a rising in the south against the Queen's advisors that would coincide with a rebellion instigated by his father in the north.[9] He may have been right. The circumstances were suspicious. At the time contemporaries did not seem to have construed it thus, but the prospect of a closer association between Huntly and Chatelherault worried Mary and the Protestants. Huntly was suspect.

It was a typical brawl so common among the hot-tempered and easily slighted nobility that finally brought Huntly and nearly his whole family down. Women and land were at the root of it. Huntly's third son, Sir

John Gordon, was the instigator. In 1535 Elizabeth Gordon, a niece of the second Earl of Huntly, became the second wife of Alexander Ogilvie of Deskford and Findlater. Rumour had it that shortly thereafter she alleged that her husband's son and heir, James Ogilvie of Cardell, had tried to seduce her. Just in case this was not affront enough to make the old man act, his wife told him that his son was plotting to imprison him, and when he went mad, assume control of his estates. Whatever the reason, the old Lear disinherited his son, and, on his own death in 1554, left his lands, including Findlater Castle, to Sir John Gordon, reserving his wife's life-rent. Sir John was to assume the name and arms of Ogilvie. As was all along intended, Elizabeth now became the mistress or 'pretended spouse' of Sir John who was 'in the very flower of youth' and good-looking. This scandalous alliance which merged into marriage did her little good for within months of their wedding, when John realised that he could not secure from her all the lands he wanted, he immured her within her room, discarded her as a mistress, and disowned her as a wife.[10] Issues of land, however, were not so easily disposed of. It was quite inconceivable that a feud would not erupt between this usurper of the title and the natural claimant, James Ogilvie. He had been a loyal champion of Mary of Guise, and attempts were made by the Queen-Regent to resolve this awkward dispute between a staunch supporter of the crown and the son of a wavering one. Compromise proved impossible, and John Gordon and James Ogilvie were still at loggerheads when Mary Queen of Scots landed in Scotland.

In June 1562 both men were in Edinburgh to seek legal resolution on their differences. Before others could adjudicate on their dispute, matters were settled out of court. Whether by accident or design, they met in the street between nine and ten at night on 27 June. A fight ensued and John severely wounded Ogilvie, severing his right arm. Buchanan, ever ready to read what he wanted into an incident, maintains that this brawl was set up by Huntly in the hope that Lord James would sally forth to quell the disturbance and be overcome in the commotion being unarmed and unsuspecting. If lure it was, it failed. John was thrown into prison in the Tolbooth by Mar but a month later on 25 July he escaped, 'Scotch prisons [being] ever notorious for their unretentiveness of prisoners of his rank,' as Burton remarked.[11] With his father's connivance, or so it was rumoured,[12] John fled north to his familial domains. Queen Mary was not amused. The root of her antagonism towards the House of Huntly lay in her determination to see justice done to so faithful a servant of the House of Stewart as Ogilvie of Cardell.[13]

As a result of the religious crisis in France, Elizabeth cancelled the longed-for meeting in July, and so Mary had time on her hands. She would tour her northern shires, humble Huntly, and thus reaffirm her good intentions towards England. Under armed escort on 11 August the Queen rode north accompanied by two men determined to pluck the 'Cock o' the North:' Lord James and James Ogilvie, now recovered from his wounds. Maitland was in attendance and Randolph was invited along as well. His presence would ensure that Queen Elizabeth received a detailed first-hand account of her cousin's strong action.[14] Mary was 'utterly determined to bring [Huntly] to utter confusion,' was the ambassador's early favourable opinion. Certainly she wanted him to recognise that she was Queen and he her subject, to accept that Lord James was first in her favour – Protestant or no – and that no one, no lord be he ever so mighty, no lieutenant however accustomed to supremacy in the north, no peer albeit the leading Catholic in the kingdom, should presume to associate his will with her own.

Travelling slowly via Stirling, Glamis, and Edzell, to the urbane and urban Randolph the journey northwards had been 'terrible both for horse and man, ... cumbersome, painful and marvellous long, the weather extreme foul and cold, all victual marvellous dear, and the corn that never like to come to ripeness.'[15] It was little surprising that the north was usually left entirely alone by the Scottish monarchs. On 27 August Mary finally arrived in Old Aberdeen. Tired and dirty, she was greeted at the city gates by the Countess Elizabeth and her splendid train of attendants. This vigorous woman, sister of the Earl Marischal and aunt to James Stewart's wife, was, according to Buchanan, possessed of 'the passions and purposes of a man.' She used every device to probe the Queen's mind and bend her to her will. She pleaded with Mary to pardon her son. Mary was prepared to give the young ruffian another chance. She appointed a court of justiciary to be held in the Aberdeen tolbooth. Gordon surrendered to the court and was ordered to ward himself in the provost's lodging until the Queen's decision was known. The sincerity of his acquiescence in the royal will was thrown into doubt when he arrived accompanied by over 1,000 men when he had been ordered to bring no more than 100. Mary insisted he must return to ward at Stirling Castle within seven days before a pardon could be contemplated but not promised. Stirling was under the charge of John, Lord Erskine, the uncle of Lord James. Gordon, understandably refused to entrust himself to the keeping of so partisan a gaoler and sought refuge in one of his own castles.[16] Another reason for his reluctance to surrender, surmised Randolph, was that he feared if he handed himself in he would be forced to set his wife at liberty and forego her lands as long as she lived. His shameless treatment of his wife further incensed Mary against him, especially when rumours were circulating that he had planned to harry the royal party and abduct the Queen, thinking she would accede to his charms. Mary was furious with Sir John's insubordination and no doubt blamed his father as well.

The Earl and Countess of Huntly invited Mary to visit Strathbogie on her way to Inverness. As great preparations had been made to receive her as had been done for her late mother. The 'Pope of the North-East' even invited her to attend a flagrantly illegal private mass at his chapel. The mass was a privilege restricted to Mary's own household; it was not for subjects, however elevated, to offer it to the Queen. Huntly was trying hard to please and with every attempt confirmed the Queen's view of him as an over-mighty subject. Despite the privations of the journey, Randolph reported, Mary would not be allured by the comforts of Strathbogie 'though it be within 11 miles of her way, and the fairest in the country' since 'the Earl of Huntly is not well in his princess's favour.' Although she refused to go herself she allowed Randolph and Argyll to visit Strathbogie. Randolph, despite himself, was as impressed as those courtiers who visited in Mary of Guise's time: 'His house is fayer best furnished of any house I have seen in this country, his cheer is marvellous great, his mind then such as it appeared to us as ought to be in any subject to his sovereign.' Later it was rumoured that had she gone there Huntly would have killed Moray, Maitland and Morton, and married her off to his son.[17] Of this there is no evidence at all. Nor had Randolph reported any suspicious activity in Strathbogie. Nonetheless he thought it a possibility that Moray could be in danger since Huntly wanted, 'either to get Mary into his hands or else cut off Moray whose credit is so great with her that he could not prevail in anything he aspired to, as chiefly to have been Earl of Moray.'[18]

Pointedly skirting Strathbogie, Mary spent one night about twelve miles from Aberdeen, at Balquhain, the house of William Leslie, one of Huntly's friends. The following night she stayed at Rothiemay, a village in the Abernethys, five miles north-east of Strathbogie, at the house of Lord Saltoun. Huntly again pressed her to stay but again she refused and would not come unless Sir John returned to obedience. On 3 September she passed from Rothiemay towards Grange. She stayed in 'the fair and famous merchant town' of Elgin[19] from 6 to 8 September, and spent a further two days at the Abbey of Kinloss.

Most significantly, in bypassing Strathbogie, she visited Darnaway Castle, the Moray stronghold a few miles from the sea in the west of Morayshire. This 'castle of the kings, celebrated, famous and of great renown'[20] had largely been built by Thomas Randolph, the Regent during the minority of David II, but the ancient hall (still extant) was begun by Archibald Douglas about 1450. A century later neglect had done its work. The English ambassador opined that while 'the country is pleasant, the place called Ternawe [is] very ruinous saving the hall, very fair and large builded,' able to house a 1,000 armed men.[21] Its situation remained impressive: on rising ground in the midst of an extensive forest not far from the River Findhorn: 'Darnaway green/Is bonnie to be seen/In the midst of Morayland.'[22]

There, on 10 September Mary held a meeting of her Privy Council in the great hall. Although it was not minuted, she publicly announced that Lord James, presently Earl of Mar, had been granted the greater earldom of

Moray in its stead and invested him with the honour. Randolph was pleased: 'Men greatly hope that Moray will do much good in this country: his power in men is great and the revenue esteemed to 1,000 merks by year.'[23] One man who had no such hope was his new neighbour, Huntly, who 'since the time of the last Moray has had government of the country, and being given away from him, he has lost great commodity and profit, making him much offended.' Although Lord James was not literally the first Earl of Moray, as we have seen, it was with him that the hereditary principle began, forever removing the earldom from the aspirations of others such as Huntly. The council went on to proclaim that Sir John was not to be helped by anyone and that the property in dispute with Ogilvie – Findlater and Auchindoun – was to be surrendered to the crown.

The following day[24] Mary reached Inverness and was denied entry into the castle by its captain, Alexander Gordon of Bothrom.[25] Inverness Castle had been built by Malcolm Canmore and had always retained its status as a royal castle. This 'large and stark' edifice had latterly been more of less ceded into the hands of the Earls of Huntly, as sheriffs of Inverness. In 1509 the third Earl had first been appointed to that post with power to garrison and further fortify the castle.[26] He had built a stone hall, kitchen and chapel within the ramparts at his own expense. Thus the enhancement, maintenance, and control of the citadel for the past fifty years had been assumed by the Gordons.[27] The captain refused to open the gates until ordered to do by Lord George Gordon, its hereditary keeper or by Huntly himself. George Gordon was in the south with the Duke of Chatelherault, and, assuming that the Queen would have visited Strathbogie and been accompanied to Inverness by his father, had neglected to authorise her admission. The refusal to admit the Queen was merely a mistake in administration rather than an act of rebellion. The fact that the garrison numbered only twelve men lends substance to this contention! Rumourmongers saw the matter in a more lurid light. Having failed on the way, the Gordons were reputed to be plotting to seize the royal person at Inverness. The Queen was disposed to believe the worst. Her mood was not mollified by being forced to spend the night in a private lodging in Bridge Street, long known as the wine shop. Local chieftains rallied to her cause. William, tutor of Lovat, arrived with 400 men, including Lord Hugh who at seventeen was making his first appearance on the public stage. The Queen was impressed, the boy flattered. The castle doors were soon opened – on Huntly's orders – forestalling a siege, but not appeasing the irate Queen.[28] Her annoyance with Huntly had curdled into mistrust of an over-mighty subject whose minions could ban the monarch from her own keep. The keeper of the castle and his garrison were condemned, their hands bound on the scaffold, but at the last moment reprieved apart from Alexander Gordon himself. For his lèse majesté his body was hanged over the battlements and thereafter his severed head was exhibited there.[29]

Rumours abounded as to what was afoot at Strathbogie. According to Randolph, when Huntly heard that Mary had executed his keeper, fearing for his own safety, he assembled his forces and committed 1,000 Gordon horsemen to his son John to forestall the Queen at the Spey. According to one historian – partisan to Huntly but probably on the right track – it was Moray's own spies who alarmed the Queen with intelligence of the massing at dangerous points of great bodies of men with the intention of attacking her. When other scouts were sent out, they reported back that neither man nor horse was to be seen. Another apologist for Huntly, conceding that a muster had taken place, asserts disingenuously that 'it is most certain that the Earl of Huntly gathered these forces at her Majesty's own desire, to free her from the Earl of Moray's power.' Taking no chances, Lovat and his men accompanied her to the Spey. Whatever the truth of the matter, no attack came there or anywhere else and her force of 3,000 went unscathed. Her composure did not. One further act of defiance on her journey worsened her mood. Passing the former Ogilvie stronghold of Findlater, now in Gordon hands, she called on it to surrender. It declined. Since she had no cannon to take the sea-girt castle, she passed on, leaving some of her guard to prevent the garrison breaking out. Huntly was still not resolved on out and out rebellion, but he was being forced to the brink.

On 22 September Mary was welcomed back to New Aberdeen with a variety of entertainments. While the Queen waited to see if Huntly would submit and hand over John, she sent for cannon, 120 harquebuses,[30] and her most experienced generals: Lord Lindsay, Sir William Kirkaldy, the laird of Grange, and Sir John Cockburn of Ormiston, all keen Protestants. She further demanded that Huntly surrender within forty-eight hours the formidable cannon and two 'falcons' [light ordnance] which he had hidden in his cellar. This was the cannon which, in order to intimidate his Highland subjects, he as lieutenant had obtained 'to lie in Strathbogie, ... a terrible sight to those who entered the house or offended the Earl.' It remained royal property nonetheless. Huntly received Hay, the royal messenger, with protestations of loyalty, saying that not only the cannon but also his body and goods were at the Queen's disposal, and even offering to besiege Findlater and Auchindoun if she so commanded him. He was not a party to the offence of his son and even offered to join Mary in pursuing him provided he could bring his own troops with him. The cannon, however, could not be moved in time to assist the Queen. 'These and other like words, mingled with many tears and sobs, he desired to be reported to his dear mistress from her most obedient subject.' The Countess of Huntly took Hay aside to see the chapel 'fair and trimly hanged, all ornaments and mass robes ready lying upon the altar with cross and candles standing upon it.' Here was a haven of the true faith in the house of the Queen's true servant. Tell the Queen of this sanctuary, she begged, and tell her that had her husband forsaken the Faith as the Queen's other advisors had done, he

would not be set upon in this way. 'God and He that is upon this holy altar
... will save us and let our true meaning hearts be known. My husband was
ever obedient unto her, and so will die her faithful subject.' Mary was as
unmoved by Huntly's tears as she was by his wife's sermon. She laughed at
them. Randolph wryly observed, 'She knows so many of their conceits that
she does not believe a word of either, and so declared the same herself unto
her council, whereat there has been much good pastime.'[31] Maitland – an
avowed enemy of Huntly – wrote more fairly:

> How it will fall out is yet uncertain and her majesty doth not
> intend to burden any innocent if the fault be his. It maybe
> thought to have proceeded from too great simplicity, rather
> than any craft, or malice, specially by so many as have experi-
> ence how playnely, sincerely and uprightly he has always been
> accustomed to deal.[32]

Lady Gordon was not done. Deputising for her husband once more, she
made her way to present herself to Mary, to give Huntly's reply and to
offer profuse apologies for any slight. Mary believed not a word of the
Countess's protestations. Next a boy arrived at Aberdeen bearing the keys
of the houses of Findlater and Auchindoun, 'left woide.' She refused to
receive them off a stable lad and said she had other means of opening
doors.[33] She now determined to take the two houses and to apprehend
Huntly, 'the chief deviser of the whole mischief.' She was resolute beyond
expectation. The English ambassador had 'nere seen her merrier, never
dismayed.' She had resources that he had not previously appreciated.

Mary learnt that, fearing capture, Huntly never spent a night in his own
house or two nights in any one place, but he always returned home by
day. It should have been a simple matter to take him there. Kirkaldy of
Grange, accompanied by only twelve men, took horse one morning
intending to reach Strathbogie by noon, twenty-four miles off, and seize
the obese Huntly at his dinner. They were also to arrest John Gordon, if
he were there, and secure the house until reinforcements arrived. An hour
after Grange, John of Cowdingham was to follow with his forty men and
after him Lindsay and Fife. Grange and his party got there on time, raising
no suspicions because of their small number. They questioned the
doorman, while sending horse around the house to prevent escape. Before
they had gained ingress, however, a watchman in the tower sighted
Cowdingham and his larger party a mile off, and alerted Huntly. Leaving
his meal half finished and without either boot or sword, he escaped out
of a back gate and over a low rear wall. He rode off, and although he was
chased for a couple of miles, knowing the area and being fresh horsed, he
eluded his pursuers who returned dejected to Strathbogie. Life on the
run, however, cannot have appealed to the elderly and ailing Huntly.

Mary had already sent Alexander Stewart with 120 soldiers to besiege Findlater. They lodged in the little village of Cullen. During the night of 11 October John Gordon with 150 horse came upon a detachment of these soldiers. The captain was taken, some soldiers killed, and fifty-six harquebuses were seized. The Queen was furious. The urgent question was how to deal with an earl whose hold in the north was so dangerous that one son could refuse the Queen her own castle and another could harry her troops with impunity. Total submission was required. Huntly was commanded to present himself – with John – before the council within the week, or face being outlawed. The Earl refused to put himself into the power of his enemies assembled in Aberdeen, but offered to surrender himself for trial by his peers in parliament. Meanwhile 'confessions' seemed to confirm Mary's worst fears. One Thomas Kerr and his brother, retainers of Huntly, admitted under torture that they knew of his plots to kill Moray and Maitland. Letters were found which purported to confirm that John Gordon's reprobate actions were 'by his father's advice and counsel.' As a result, on the orders of the Privy Council, Huntly and John Gordon were both 'put to the horn'. With three blasts of the horn at the Mercat Cross of Edinburgh, Linlithgow, Stirling and Glasgow Huntly and his son were proclaimed rebels. Royal messengers were dispatched throughout the kingdom to denounce the renegades. Summonses were sent to Kynneil, Stirling, Glasgow, Hamilton and Paisley, charging Lord George Gordon to surrender to the Queen in Aberdeen. The last two places were included because it was known he had gone to consult Chatelherault. A general roundup of potentially dissident Gordons was ordered. Huntly strengthened himself in his Highland retreat, Badenoch, which in winter was considered impenetrable by men or guns. He sought to weary his Queen by weather and dearth. Had he remained there he might well have succeeded.[34]

A third and final attempt to speak woman to woman was made by Huntly's wife. Setting out to see the Queen, she had come to within two miles of Aberdeen when she was intercepted by a royal messenger – Leslie says sent by Moray[35] – informing her that the Queen would not speak with her and commanding her to return to Strathbogie. This she did, but she was much put out. There, it was said, she communed with witches and encouraged by their prophecy that by nightfall her husband would be lying in the tolbooth at Aberdeen without any wound in his body, she urged Huntly to relinquish his fastness and attack.

Whether spurred on by his scorned and militant wife or not, on 27 October Huntly finally decided to make one last desperate gambit to redeem his position or die in the attempt. He assembled 700-800 men at the Hill of Noth in Strathbogie and marched towards Aberdeen to seize the Queen before she got back to the Lowlands and no doubt 'liberate' her from 'evil counsellors.' This number of retainers compared ill with the

1,000 Huntly was supposed to have mustered only weeks before at the Spey. He had boasted that he could raise three shires and 20,000 men on behalf of the Queen; he certainly could not raise them against her. Far less important men than he could muster 300 men. Huntly went via Keig to the Lochsken. By the time he encamped a short distance west of Garlogie in an area sometimes still called Gordon's Moss, some twelve miles from Aberdeen, desertion had reduced his force to a rump consisting of 500 of his nearest family and loyalist friends.[36]

The composition of the royalist forces confirms the view that the campaign was not undertaken out of political or religious principle but out of loyalty to the throne. No member of the nobility sided with Huntly though his cousin Sutherland was in treasonable correspondence with him. Athol, Errol and Montrose, Catholics all, were with Mary. His support was almost entirely familial and local, Gordon lairds or lairds in Aberdeenshire and the adjacent north-eastern counties. Some Frasers fought with him. But not even all of his retainers rallied to his side. Two or three Gordon lairds took up arms against him. Others stayed at home. One reason for the failure of many lairds to support him was the clause in the bonds of manrent entered into since 1534, which excepted their service against the Crown. In the last resort the Queen could command a loyalty higher than that to her lieutenant. Mackintosh tenants on the Gordon estates, on their way to join Huntly's rebellion, rallied to the royal cause after being waylaid on the route by the chief of Clan Mackintosh who overrode their loyalty to Huntly by that to himself as their clan superior. Personal dislike and jealousy motivated some. The Forbes, for instance, at last scenting revenge for the execution of their young Master in 1537, eagerly marched against him. Fear dissuaded others. Erstwhile dependants began to notice the holes in the boots they had polished. His status had been further diminished by the way in which over the weeks he had been treated by the Queen.[37]

Moray was commissioned to march against the dissident Earl, and to pursue him and his supporters to the uttermost. They were to be put to the sword, their houses burned, those who gave them succour punished.[38] The royal army entrusted to the eager Moray was estimated at some 2,000 seasoned Lowland troops, including trained Lothian pikemen and the harquebusiers sent from Edinburgh. This in addition to the local levies pouring in. Morton and Athol each commanded a division. The Queen's banner flew above this force lest any should think this was a quarrel between rival earls and not an assault on the monarchy itself. Huntly, faced with such odds, had decided to beat a retreat before the battle could begin the following morning. But at daybreak on Wednesday 28 October Moray's vanguard led by Lord Forbes engaged Huntly's pickets and skirmishing began. According to the inventions of Knox and Calderwood, being in ill health and corpulent, Huntly could not rise before ten o'clock, by which time it was almost too late.

When he arose, his speech failed him, neither could he doeanything right, by reason of his corpulency. Some of his friends left him. There remained only 300 men. He said to them, 'This great company which approacheth will do us no harm: I only fear the other small company which standeth upon the hill side. But we are a sufficient number, if God be with us.'

Then upon his knees he uttered these forlorn words,

'O lord, I have been a bloodthirsty man, and by my moyen much innocent blood hath been spilt: if thou will give me victory this day, I shall serve thee all the days of my life.' He confessed he was guilty of the shedding of much innocent blood, and yet begged power and strength to shed more; thinking, belike, he would satisfy God for all together.

The contrasting account provided by Leslie is equally implausible. The noble Earl beset all around encouraged his followers in terms of stirring nobility:

To yield would be disgraceful, and death against the odds opposed to you were most glorious ...Meet boldly the enemy's attack and doubt not God will give us strength. It is His cause and the cause of Justice, which we defend against the oppressor of our country and of the true Faith. We are but few, but God can preserve the lives of his servants whether they be many or few. ... We have one friend a match for all – the justice of the cause for which we fight.[39]

In Moray's camp Maitland passionately charged the Queen's troops to remember their duty and fear not the enemy.

Old though he might have been, Huntly had not lost the military acumen of his youth when he had worsted the English and known the right time to withdraw. He drew off westward and sought safety on the high ground of the Hill o' Fare in Banchory Ternan parish, on the border of Kincardinshire and Aberdeenshire. His retreat of about six miles via Garlogie and Cullerlie was harassed by the royal vanguard consisting of less than 100 cavalry. He took up a commanding position on the hill, a granite outcrop fringed by birch and pine woods above the burn and field of Corrichie. The burn descends from the saddleback of the hill formed by the summits of Criagroth (1,429ft) and Blackyduds (1,422ft), a position impregnable to horse because of the surrounding bogs.[40]

But northern retainers were now to be met by the full force of modern warfare as the royal army arrived in hot pursuit. Moray deployed his guns.

They raked the hillside. Snipers harried the higher summits to the west.
Huntly's men were forced ever lower. They were harassed but they could
still fight. Seeking to use such high ground as they could retain to launch
fierce charges at the pursuing troops, they turned on the local levies of
Forbes and Leslie, which had been sent in first. Such units, cajoled into
service against their neighbour, lacked heart and resolution and the royal
vanguard yielded many casting away their spears ready to run some placing
sprigs of heather in their bonnets so that they might be known by the
pursuing Gordons. Huntly's hope that ultimately more local loyalties would
come into play and that many of the Queen's troops would desert to his side
seemed not misplaced.

Seeing his vanguard falter, Moray sent in his more resolute Lowland
companies of Angus and Fife. They owed no divided loyalties as was
suspected of the northerners. The Lothian troops 'stuid fermlie still' and
with levelled pikes broke the Gordon charge. The attackers were 'put upon
their backs with spears.' The steadfastness of the pikeman was later attributed to the spirited action of William Douglas, the laird of Kemnay (later
Earl of Angus). When his companies were looking for mounts with which
to escape the Gordons, he cried out 'No horses my Lords, no horses, we
are strong enough for Huntly!'[41] And strong enough they were. The
Lowland troops formed phalanx and Huntly's men armed only with swords
could not get at them or break their ranks. They were forced back. Huntly's
troops were driven by harquebus shot into a low mossy ground where the
horse could attack them, forcing them into the Howe of Corrichie, a
corner between the hill and the marshland where they could not escape.
Seeing them falter, the local levies turned yet again and set upon them. The
battle turned into a rout. According to Knox some two dozen men were
slain in the front, but in the fleeing there fell nigh 100. By four in the
afternoon 220 of Huntly's men lay dead, a further 120 had been captured.
Many of Moray's men had been hurt but the dead consisted entirely of
horses.[42] Small were the losses but great the consequences of this 'skirmish
in a remote bog, late one autumn afternoon.' It changed the balance of
power in the north-east, set the seal on the Reformation, and effectively
prevented a Catholic resurgence from taking place.[43]

Legend has it that, on conceding defeat, Huntly asked what ground it
was and being told, cried out the name Corrichie three times. A
Highland witch had told him that he should die at Corrichie, but he had
taken this to be Crichie, near Inverurie, a place he regularly passed by, but
shunned, on his way from Strathbogie to Aberdeen.[44] Yet Corrichie was
to be the humiliation and death of him. After being taken prisoner by
Andrew Redpath, one of the Queen's guard who had mounted him on
his horse to bring him to Mary, he fell down dead seemingly of an
apoplectic fit or heart attack, an event testified to in a despatch by
Randolph. Buchanan suggests that he was choked in the crowd. The

Diurnal put it most graphically: 'He brisit and swelled, sua that he spak not ane word, bot deceissit.' The Catholics believed that he had been murdered on Moray's orders either by being stabbed by David Stewart of Inchbreck, by strangulation, or by means of a flintlock being discharged close to his ears, the shock killing him without leaving a mark. The variety of the means of his murder gives the lie to this suggestion. Moray would have wanted to bring him to public trial and condemnation, and Randolph is the most measured and reliable eyewitness of the events. Hume of Godscroft discounts the suggestion that he was pistol-whipped. Age, infirmity and armour were to blame: 'The Earl being an aged and corpulent pursie man, was stifled with his armour, and was choked for want of breath, in the taking.'[45]

Immediately after the battle his unmarked body was thrown roughly over a pair of 'crealles' (fish baskets) and taken to the Aberdeen tolbooth to lie there for the night – as the witches had predicted. According to Knox's 'infamous invectives'[46] Huntly's widow blamed the chief witch, Janet. The day after the battle, a wise and religious woman, Lady Forbes, beholding the corpse of Huntly lying upon the cold stones, 'having upon him only a doublet of canvass, a pair of Scottish grey hose and covered with arras work,' said:

> What stability shall we judge to be in this world! There lyeth
> he that yesterday in the morning was hodin the wisest, richest,
> and man of greatest power in Scotland.[47]

His two younger sons – John and Adam – were brought prisoner to Aberdeen. As traitors they were nonetheless treated extravagantly: £350 was paid to Alexander Sauchie, tailor, for expenses made in furnishing clothing, meat and drink to the young men imprisoned in the tolbooth.[48] On 30 October the lords sat in judgement on the prisoners. On 2 November, John, the 'author of all these troubles,' after supposedly making a full confession that 'at iv divers times he and his company took purpose to have slain the Earls of Moray and Morton, Lethington and the Justice Clerk,' and that had Aberdeen fallen his father would have 'burned the Queen and as many as were in the house with her,' was to be beheaded by a precursor of the guillotine, the Maiden.[49]

The execution took place in the Castlegate with Mary herself watching from the tolbooth. Gordon propaganda has it, that seeing her, Sir John cried out that he was solaced by the presence of his Queen. She was hardly to be solaced by what next befell. It was an appalling spectacle. The executioner botched the job, the blade was blunt and, according to some biased sources, including Buchanan, Mary was reduced to weeping and broke down completely, having to be carried from the scene and remaining in her chamber for the whole of the following day. This display of emotion gave rise to speculation. The Gordons suggested that Moray's evil hand may have been behind the cruelty and that Mary had been almost won over by the young man's attainment.

> Buchanan says 'Regina mortem ejus cum multis lachrymis spectavit.' And indeed it was no wonder: he was in the prime of his age, adorned in body and mind with all the gifts of nature; and that which excited in all the beholders no less indignation against Moray, than compassion towards him, was his being cruelly mangled by the executioner. [Moray] had even the cruelty to force her to the window to see young Gordon pass by, tied with ropes as a common malefactor. This spectacle produced the desired effect; the sudden change of fortune; the handsomest man of Scotland in fetters, and the deplorable state the person was in, who had once raised his thoughts to her bed, brought tears from her eyes.... when he was to be beheaded, either by chance, or by Moray's instigation, the executioner was so awkward as to wound him several times before he struck off his head.[50]

Moray, so this line of apologetic continues, had him executed 'to the Queen's grief who, out of love and compassion shed abundance of tears for him.'[51]Apologists on the Catholic side depicted John as a St Sebastian. For he was 'a youth of most brave and manlike countenance, of a valorous spirit, and one who by his noble behaviour had raised great expectations of himself.' This may refer to the recurring rumour that he aspired to marriage with the Queen, and that his desires were reciprocated. Protestants enlarged this into a Machiavellian conspiracy to destroy both Moray and Huntly. Godscroft related that the 'Guisards' had written to the Queen to feed Huntly with 'large promises,' including the hope of her marrying his son, in order to enlist him as the instrument for the doing away of Moray and Morton. Then she could rid herself of Huntly whom she hated more than Moray. The Pope had written to the same effect. To lull Moray and Morton 'asleep in security' she is then said to have shown this correspondence to them. Sadly but unsurprisingly, none of these missives survives, though the silly tale they spun has outlived the vellum they were allegedly written on. Buchanan, while repeating the canard, spoke warmly of John's physical attributes: he was 'generally pitied and lamented, for he was a manly youth, very beautiful and just entering on the prime of his age, not so much designed for the royal bed as deceived by the false prospect of it.'[52]

His death does seem to have been widely lamented by friends, and even by strangers. Balladeers, with as little sense of metre as of history, bemoaned his passing:

But now this day maist waefu' cam'
That day the quine did greit hir fill;
For Huntly's gallant stalwart son
Wis headit on this heidin hill.
Five noble Gordones wi' him hangit were
Upon this samen fatal playne;
Cruel Murray gart thi waeful' quine luke out,
And see her lover and liges slayne.

John was the first 'bonnie' victim of the feud between the Morays and the Gordons, the first to call 'Highlands and Lowlands' to mourn, the first to be said to have had designs on a Queen. He was buried at St Nicholas church, Aberdeen. In contrast to the money lavished on him in his lifetime, a paltry twenty shillings was spent on his funeral.[53]

His siblings fared better. His youngest brother, Adam, who was aged only seventeen, was spared to become one of the most ferocious and turbulent of all the Gordons. At the end of November George Gordon, the heir, was brought to Edinburgh and warded in the castle. On 8 February 1562/3 he was put to an assize, condemned for treason and sentenced to be executed, drawn and quartered 'at our souverain's plesor.' A few days later he was transported and put into free ward at Dunbar Castle until the fate of his dead father's corpse be decided.[54]

The intimacies and economics of its disposal are detailed in the *Inventory* and *Diurnal*: the bowels were removed and filled with spices by a French physician who received £21 15s for his pains. The embalmed body was carried to Edinburgh in Patrick Hume's boat for £10 14s. There it lay in the Abbey of Holyrood without burial. The ancient law of high treason against the monarch, reaffirmed in 1540, made provision for the presence of the offender, dead or alive, for trial before the three estates of parliament. Even in death the Cock o' the North could not escape his public disgrace. It took a long time to bring a corpse to justice. Thus the body had to be well preserved, possibly for months. On arrival in Edinburgh a sum of £28 3s 4d was paid to a barber-surgeon Robert Henderson 'for expenses made by him upon spices vinagre aquavitie pulderis odouris and hardis with sundry uthiris necessaris and for his labouris in handling of the said Earl of Huntly's body that it should not putrefy.'[55] His pickled and embalmed corpse was confined to a chest at Holyrood to await its fate. On the 28 May 1563 it was carried through the streets first to be displayed at the tolbooth, and then into the council chamber for trial. There the macabre scarecrow was propped up in front of the full session of parliament, with Mary sitting on her throne, and his eldest son George brought from prison to watch.

The coffin was set upright, as if the Earl stood upon his feet and upon it a piece of good black cloth with his arms fast

pinned. His accusation being read his proctor answering for
him, as if he had been alive, the inquest was impaneled.

The mummified relic was then declared guilty of treason, the sentence of
forfeiture was passed on it and its erstwhile belongings, and the title of the
Earl of Huntly was attainted. The ceremonial stripping of the regalia then
took place.

> Immediately hereupon the good cloth that hung over the
> coffin was taken away, and in its place a worce hanged on, the
> arms torn in pieces in sight of the people, and likewise stroken
> out of the herald's book.

The convicted corpse was then deposited in Blackfriars priory in
Edinburgh. It was not until 21 April 1566 that he was finally buried
alongside his ancestors in the family vault in Elgin Cathedral.[56]

His son, traumatised by being made spectator to this macabre proceeding,
and with the knife only inches from his own neck, was returned to Dunbar
where every day could be his last. According to one biased account Moray
tried to get Mary to kill Lord Gordon. He sent a secret warrant to Robert
Preston of Craigmiller, captain of Dunbar Castle, commanding to execute
Lord Gordon. Preston informed the Queen who refused and disclaimed the
warrant. According to another equally partisan account, the saintly Moray
is said to have interceded for him with Mary.[57]

Huntly's house was despoiled. The list of his goods forfeited included:
elaborate tapestries, nine beds covered with velvet and hung with fringes of
gold and silver-work, vessels of gilded and coloured glass, and figures of
animals. The spoils of Strathbogie were either given to Moray for his new
castle at Darnaway or taken to the Queen by boat to Edinburgh. It is said
that the tapestries of Strathbogie were employed to deck the house of Kirk
o' Fields while the rich vestments were removed to Holyrood and put to
secular use, which included a bed covering for Darnley and a doublet for
Bothwell. This was the first forfeiture that the Huntlys had ever suffered,
but the demise of their House seemed certain and complete, 'reduced in a
moment to insignificance and beggary.'[58] In contrast to Huntly's fate, James
was 'belted' Earl, probably under the title of Moray, Lord Abernethy and
Strathearn. He also received the sheriffdoms of Elgin, Forres, and Inverness.
He was made keeper of Inverness Castle along with lands and fishing rights,
which were forfeited from George Lord Gordon.[59]

The Protestant apologists, so distrustful of Mary's every action as they
were, could not believe that she would willingly act against her senior
Catholic nobleman and in favour of a bastion of Protestantism. Knox
concedes that she was angry with Huntly when she refused to visit
Strathbogie, and that she was 'inflamed' when Sir John cut off one of her

patrols. Nonetheless she had fought him half-heartedly, and was 'gloomed' when word of Moray's victory at Corrichie reached her. Though she had executed John Gordon, 'it was the destruction of others that she sought.' This is the most perverse judgement and demonstrable rubbish. Calderwood was scarcely more reasoned or less partisan. His Mary hated Huntly 'for his perfidy to her father and mother, and feared his great power in the north.' But the real object of her spite was Moray whose 'innocency and uprightness of life, and prosperity was as venom to her venomed heart.' There was no convincing some Protestants.[60]

Catholics, on the other hand, have found it hard to believe that a Catholic monarch would wantonly destroy a loyal Catholic subject and have ascribed the fall of Huntly to the machinations of the evil bastard half-brother of the Queen, James Stewart. While undoubtedly benefiting from the destruction of his rival in the north, there is no evidence that James conspired to bring it about. Randolph, a more objective observer and a perceptive eyewitness, leaves no doubt that it was Mary herself who was intent on the expedition and that during it she became ever more hostile to Huntly. This hostility may have been aggravated by Moray, but was not created by him. Patrick Tytler, who was the first historian properly to research this incident by reference to the original documents, concluded that while it was true that Moray 'availed himself of Huntly's offences to strengthen his own power', the accusation that 'prior to the rebellion, he had laid a base design to entrap him into treason, is ... founded on conjecture, and contradicted by fact'.[61] Despite their later falling out, Mary never accused her brother of misleading her over Huntly. She had reason enough of her own to overthrow the mighty Earl. In a conversation with Randolph the Queen thanked God for having delivered her enemy into her hand. She declared: 'many a shameful and detestable part that [Huntly] thought to have used against her, as to have married her where he would, to have slain her brother, and whom others he liked; the places, the times where it should have been done; and how easy a matter it was, if God had not preserved her'.[62] That about sums it up. She did not much care for the old Earl, or his ways.

Policy buttressed prejudice, since Huntly's destruction rid her of a powerful obstacle to her English plans. In November 1562 Maitland wrote to William Cecil, claiming that he and Queen Elizabeth should have no fear of Mary showing favour to Catholics should she be accepted as the heir to the throne of England, for her behaviour in the north and her distancing herself from her Catholic subjects had proved her to be free of any such partiality. The tone of a letter Mary wrote to her uncle, the cardinal of Lorraine, asking him to 'make any excuses if I have failed in any part of my duty towards religion,' betrays 'no regret that circumstances had compelled her to lay low her greatest Catholic subject.'[63] It merely reflects her concern at the Continental reaction.

Her actions had disastrous consequences for her own position in the short-term, for the peace of the north-east in the mid-term, and for the survival of Catholicism in the long-term. In the short-term her destruction of Huntly and her later attempt to find love and secure her position by marriage to Darnley would prove a double calamity. The latter would alienate Moray and isolate the Queen. As a result she would have to reinstate George Gordon to his attainted earldom. He would prove far less a stalwart of the crown than his predecessors, and his inaction on her behalf, born of the psychological scars of her treatment of his father, and of himself, would ultimately seal the fate of the Queen who had so recklessly inflicted them. In the long-term by destroying Huntly she had removed the most powerful and effective opposition to the hegemony of the Protestant nobility and so she ensured the triumph of the Reformed Faith. In the mid-term her northern polity demonstrated that Mary failed to understand that peace, good government and the long-preserved security of the Stewart dynasty itself, depended on a partnership between the crown and its lieu-tenants in the far-flung reaches of the kingdom, and on a fine balance between the most powerful of the nobility. By imposing her brother in Moray she had planted a tree with no roots in the north and set him against a long line of earls whose record of loyalty to the crown over two centuries was impressive and unflagging. In place of the traditional reliance of the crown on the Gordons, she had created a Stewart-Gordon rivalry, which would flare up again and violently disrupt the north-east in the late 1580s and 1590s.[64]

As harbinger of this, shortly before his death the fourth Earl of Huntly had become a grandfather. His grandson was also named George, as custom demanded. He would be the sixth Earl of Huntly and would in his time slay another James Stewart, another Earl of Moray.

PART II

THE 5TH EARL OF HUNTLY

AND

THE 1ST EARL OF MORAY

1563–1576

5

THE SLAVE OF PASSION
1563-1567

Moray promised to me, Huntly, that my ancient inheritance should be restored unto me, and that I should be in eternal favour with the exiles, if I would favour the divorce.... Hereupon, seeing the King was murthered by wicked hand within a few days after, we, out of the inward testimony of our conscience, do hold it most certain that Moray and Liddington [Lethington] were the authors, contrivers, and persuaders of this Regicide, whosoever were the Actors.[1]

Maitland and Moray had played their hand well. The Jesuits despaired: Moray 'holds all the heretics, except the Earl of Hamilton [*sic*] so completely under control by interest and all the Catholics by fear and by use of the royal authority that no one ventures to oppose his will.'[2] Control of the Queen would ensure a smooth transition to a Protestant Scotland without risk of war. Mary, now firmly under their control and direction as they supposed, would inevitably marry and that important event had also to be put to their advantage. No Scottish nobleman could be allowed to usurp their control. Spain was distant and provided a useful counterweight to the influence of France. Thus Lethington, with Moray's tacit support, conducted negotiations for a possible marriage with Don Carlos, the son of Philip II, despite the danger to the position of the Protestant party in Scotland. These moves further estranged them from Knox. In 1563 Moray refused to press Mary to get parliament to put the seal on the Protestant ascendancy. This refusal, Knox suggested with a rare degree of acumen, was owing to the Earl's desire to get royal confirmation of his Moray title and lands. But there was another motive to be found in the proposed Spanish match. If Mary had to leave the country then Moray would enjoy a viceregality he had hoped for before the death of her first husband brought his sister precipitously home.[3] This would put the de iure stamp on his de facto governance.

The proposed Spanish match aroused Elizabeth's concern as much as Knox's. She suggested an English marriage with her own lover Leicester, an improbable suggestion and intended to delay her rival's ultimate marriage. Mary, however, refused to be dictated to either by her cousin or by her brother and soon made her own choice: Henry Stewart, Lord

Darnley. Their union would soon prove disastrous but it was not on the face of it a misalliance. He was the son of the Earl of Lennox by his wife Margaret Douglas who was herself the daughter of Margaret Tudor. After Mary and his own mother, Darnley was next in line to the English throne. Uniting two claims would make her irresistible. Her Catholic subjects would also approve since Darnley's mother was regarded by English Catholics as their leader and had brought her son up in the Old Faith. Pleasure would not be universal. Elizabeth was bitterly opposed, her own security threatened by this congress of claimants. Moray was alienated, his hegemony undermined. His influence as the power behind a throne he could never occupy himself would ineluctably ebb.

In April 1565 Moray, pretending to be offended with the Catholic ceremonies practised in Holyrood, withdrew from court and entered the political wilderness for the one and only time. He proceeded to indulge in a whole series of hostile manoeuvres in league with Chatelherault and Argyll, the intention of which was to demonstrate his opposition to Darnley and the House of Lennox, without breaking into open rebellion until he could be assured of English support. In May he pointedly refused to sign a written declaration of support for the marriage, put into his hands by the Queen in private consultation with him. In June he refused to attend the convention of nobles called at Perth on the ostensible grounds of a plot by Darnley to assassinate him. He could not substantiate this accusation, although given his outspoken opposition to the proposed marriage there was motive, and Darnley was a young hothead capable of such murderous machinations. Darnley and Lennox vehemently professed their goodwill towards him and disclaimed any treacherous design. Moray next purposed to kidnap the father and son as they rode with the Queen from Perth to Callander, and send them as prisoners to Elizabeth, but that plot too came to nothing.[4] Moray then turned to England for help. He asked Randolph for a subsidy of £3,000 to support the Protestant cause. His actions seemed to verge on treason; his correspondence with Elizabeth certainly did.[5] Undeterred by her brother's petulance, perhaps made more determined, on 29 July 1565 Mary, Queen of Scots, married Henry Stewart, recently elevated to Duke of Albany, in a Catholic ceremony in the chapel of Holyrood House.[6] Three days later Moray, having refused to put in any appearance before Mary, was put to the horn, and his properties, along with those of his supporters, the Earl of Rothes and Kirkaldy of Grange, were seized. Two weeks after that Moray, and other insurgents, took up arms in rebellion.

The breach between siblings was implacable and bitter. Now for the first time the Queen urgently needed allies against the man she had elevated so high. The north-east, where his own earldom lay, was secured against him. The earldom of Mar, so recently bestowed on Moray, was given to John, sixth Lord Erskine, whose family had long had claims to it, and would keep it thereafter. The Earl of Sutherland was recalled from banishment. But no counterweight could be more effective than a revived House of Huntly, no ally better than George Gordon, Moray's sworn enemy. On 3 August she pardoned him, released him from ward, and three weeks later restored him 'to his fame, honour, and dignity and to the lordship of Gordon.' On 8 of October he was finally restored amidst great solemnity to all his father's estates and made the fifth Earl of Huntly. It was an astonishing resurrection. The new Earl rapidly fitted back into the traditional role of his forebears as the chief conservative nobleman in the north. Like his predecessors he was soon to be adjudged 'an Earl of great power, and of the most revenue of any Earl in the land.'[7] But he was never to be a man of such stature as either his predecessor or successor to the title. Although tolerant of Catholicism, he had no personal commitment to it. Where his father had been an idio-syncratic Catholic he was a dubious Protestant.[8] He attended Presbyterian sermons at St Giles and was later to decline the Queen's invitation to take part in her Candlemas celebrations. But he was beholden to the Queen even though she had been responsible for his father's death and his own attainder and confinement. And more, he needed her support in reasserting his status. He still had some way to go. He was not made Lieutenant in the North. That position went to Athol, the man who – with Moray and Morton – had destroyed his father at Corrichie.

As once she had marched with Moray against an earl of Huntly now Mary declared she would march against the rebel Moray. She swore that she would rather lose her crown than her revenge on her brother. Randolph reported that she was now so offended that she could not 'abide any man that wishes concord' between her and the insurgents. It was a splendid opportunity for Huntly not only to take revenge on the man he blamed for the destruction of his father, but to re-secure his family's position of pre-eminence in the north.[9] Mary and Moray now tried farcically to come to blows in a fruitless escapade referred to dismis-sively as the 'Chaseabout Raid.' For once the latter misjudged his position. When the Queen left Edinburgh for the west, he slipped into the capital hoping for both local and English support, but finding little of either. With the exception of Chatelherault and Argyll none of the leading nobility had joined the rebellion. Edinburgh Castle was held for the Queen by the newly elevated Earl of Mar, and under threat of its guns Moray was forced to withdraw. Mary waited in Glasgow for her northern levies to meet her at Stirling before engaging with the rebels. Denied English support other than for an offer of asylum, and confronted with a determined Queen, Moray could make no headway. The country was not ready to rise against a sovereign in favour of a bastard. It would take terrible errors on her part to change that position. On 8 October Moray fled to England as Mary prepared to attack him. Mary had vanquished. In fact it was her penultimate triumph.

Her avowed aim, by this time, was to restore Catholicism to its rightful place in the heart of Scotland. The concomitant of this would be the eventual demise of Protestantism. The crucial moment would be at the parliament in March 1565/6 when Moray was to be forfeited and Catholicism restored at least as an equal of the Reformed Faith. Perhaps of equal significance it was suspected that an inquiry was to be made into the rights of the lay commendators to retain their benefices. At the eleventh hour Fate or God intervened. Mary's marriage had been going disastrously wrong. Other than his looks and his proximity to the English throne, Darnley had nothing to commend him. Vain, spoilt and immature he was reduced to petulant sulking. He resented not receiving the crown matrimonial. When he drank – and he drank often and much – he would insult and degrade his wife, reducing her to tears. When he was sober, he would ignore her. He was jealous of the Queen's secretary, David Ricchio, both for his influence with the Queen and her fondness for him, a fondness rumoured to be carnal. Fatally Darnley entered into negotiations with men of an acumen and ruthlessness far greater than his own: Chancellor Morton and Secretary Maitland. They too wanted rid of Ricchio who continually poisoned the Queen against both the restoration of Moray and toleration of Protestantism. They were also anxious to disrupt the forthcoming parliament and its Catholic agenda. In return for their support for his claim to the crown matrimonial, which would give him rights of succession if Mary were to die childless, Darnley promised to procure Moray and the other rebels' pardon, and uphold the religious settlement. Moray and the other exiles were informed of, and assented to, the conspiracy. A necessary adjunct to this agreement was a plot between Darnley, Morton, the Lords Ruthven and Lindsay and others – including James Stewart of Doune – to murder Ricchio and imprison the Queen. This they did on 9 March 1565/6. Erupting into the royal apartments in Holyrood, they seized the terrified secretary and butchered him in the very presence of their pregnant Queen. Huntly and Bothwell, hearing that the Queen was in danger, arrived at the palace. They were outnumbered and agreed to parley with Ruthven. He tried to reassure them over a drink, but they took the wise precaution of leaving the palace as soon as his attention was distracted. Their route was via a window and the menagerie. The day after the murder Moray, with a heavy escort, returned to Edinburgh, his alibi foolproof.

The Queen retaliated, first ingratiating herself with her long-lost brother by throwing herself under his protection, and then winning back the feckless Darnley by empty assurances of forgiveness. She escaped Edinburgh on 12 March, and joined forces at Dunbar with Huntly and James Hepburn, the fourth Earl of Bothwell. Her escape had been aided by the dowager Lady Huntly, widow of the fourth Earl and mother of the fifth. She had blamed her husband's sorry end on Moray and like the rest of the family was grateful to the Queen for their restoration to favour and estates.

Lady Huntly, still a formidable figure whom none would search, proved an ideal conduit of communication between the Queen and her supporters. Recent exiles, Argyll and Glencairn, had seized the opportunity of making their peace with their monarch and joined the more consistently loyal Earl of Athol, and the Lords Fleming, Livingstone and Seton. As a result Mary returned to Edinburgh in triumph on 18 March, the assassins fleeing to England. Huntly replaced Morton as Chancellor. Mary felt able to make her peace with Moray and his chief adherents, Argyll and Glencairn on condition that they disassociated themselves from the murderers of Ricchio. If Darnley had the face to deny any involvement in the plot, so could they. Lesser men such as Doune were also pardoned for their part in the murder.[10]

Moray had returned from England at the invitation of her husband and against her wishes, but with Darnley now despicable in her eyes, Mary's old reliance on her older brother resurfaced. He was, as Randolph noted, in 'good credit' with the Queen, reconciled to Bothwell, Huntly and Athol and reinstated to the Privy Council. The Queen celebrated this rapprochement with a banquet to which they were all invited.[11] Together with the other beneficiaries of Darnley's disfavour Moray formed the coalition that would rule Scotland for the rest of Mary's reign. His star was again in the ascendant and would shine brightest in the heavens until its sudden eclipse.

The birth of Prince James on 19 June 1566 secured the succession and finally dashed Darnley's hopes of becoming king. He had fathered a child, given a son to his Queen. He was dispensable and Mary wanted rid of him. Distrust walked hand in hand with distaste. She held in her arms the union of the Scottish and English thrones. Nothing could be allowed to endanger that. But if her marriage were annulled – as it probably could have been since it was solemnised before the Papal dispensation from the degrees of consanguinity was signed – her son would be rendered illegitimate. That was inconceivable. The alternative was divorce but for a Catholic monarch this was well nigh impossible. Recovering from a gastric ulcer brought on by worry, she despairingly confessed to Moray and Huntly that 'unless she might by some means or other be despatched of the King, she should never have a good day [and] rather than she would abide to live in such sorrow, she would slay herself.'[12] How could the Queen cut this Gordian knot? Who would rid her of this troublesome spouse?

She was not alone in her distaste for her husband. He had no friends left among the nobility, but the Protestant lords in particular had 'such a misliking for their King as never was more of man.'[13] This was to prove a fatal marriage of minds. Darnley increasingly felt marginalised by the renewed influence of the senior nobility and in particular by the superior character and unique position of the Queen's brother. In a drunken boast he rashly threatened to kill Moray who, he complained, bore the Queen too much company. Mary, concerned that no one should be 'unfriend to my Lord of Moray,' told him of the threat. Moray confronted his traducer who immediately broke down and confessed 'that reports were made to him that my Lord of Moray was not his friend, which made him speak the thing he repented.' Repentance may have been too little too late for the silly and petulant drunk. Darnley may have signed his own death-warrant.[14]

On 20 November 1566 Mary, suffering a nervous collapse, went to Craigmiller Castle, some three miles south of Edinburgh, to convalesce. Sometime before her departure on 5 December the 'Craigmiller Conference' took place. The 'Protestation,' written by Bishop Leslie in order to exculpate Huntly and Argyll and rehabilitate Mary, provides the main but tainted source of what transpired. It was effectively a cabinet meeting. The great councillors of the kingdom, Moray, Lethington, Bothwell, Huntly and Argyll gathered in seclusion to discuss a double agenda: the reinstatement of the exiles and the disposal of the King. Moray and Lethington wanted the murderers to be allowed home to swell the Reformers ranks, and they wanted the Queen divorced, or otherwise freed from her marriage, to make her ever more dependant on her Privy Council. They won Huntly to their side by telling him that Morton, Lindsay and Ruthven had slain Ricchio in order to save Moray who was about to be proscribed. The Queen agreed to pardon the three main conspirators and seventy-four of their accomplices. It seems that she also gave her advisors *carte blanche* to solve the problem of her feckless husband, providing that no spot be laid to her honour. Maitland assured her that they would find the means to rid her of her husband without prejudicing her son. He would not promise more. Moray, he continued, who was as scrupulous a Protestant as she was a Catholic, 'would look through his fingers' at their doings, and say nothing. The Queen likewise should see nothing but good. Mary, depressed and weary, sighing for death or at least for retirement in France, and yearning to be rid of Darnley, was prepared to entrust the distasteful task of ensuring it to her counsellors. The imprimatur having been given, Maitland, Bothwell, Huntly, Argyll and James Balfour, clerk register to the Privy Council, drew up a bond for Darnley's elimination.[15] Moray, cannily, was not among the signatories. If Moray could stand back and look through his fingers as events unfolded, the Queen, by entrusting the resolution of her problem to these senior members of her nobility, was shutting her eyes to the obvious immediate consequences, and must also have been oblivious to the long term ones. With Darnley finally disposed of, she too would be dispensable. She would have but titular power while the great men of her kingdom ruled for a generation until James came of age. The crown would be in hock for her infant son. In the event, the ultimate resolution of her marital problems had an even worse denouement, involving as it did the eradication of both the parents of the future James VI.

Charles James Stewart was baptised at Stirling Castle, according to Catholic rites, on Tuesday 17 December 1566. The sumptuous ceremony was presided over by John Hamilton, Archbishop of St Andrews, assisted by the Bishops of Dunkeld and Dunblane. The disgruntled Darnley did not attend, thus casting doubt on his own son's legitimacy. It was another rash and reckless decision making his removal all the more necessary. The fastidious Moray would not cross the threshold of the chapel royal, but stood at the door watching, this time not through his fingers. Queen Elizabeth was James' godmother, two kingdoms his inheritance. To this happy future prospect the baby prince was oblivious as he was to the less happy fate of his father and mother. His uncle James could see future events much more clearly, while striving to keep his hands clean.[16]

Darnley was murdered at Kirk o' Fields in the early hours of 10 February 1566/7. The house blew up, but in the garden the King's body was found, unscathed by the explosion. He had been strangled. The following morning Bothwell and Huntly went to inform the Queen of her husband's death. The actual assassin is unknown, but virtually all contemporaries considered Bothwell the prime suspect.[17] He was put on trial for the murder, a prosecution launched not by the Queen but by the dead Darnley's father, the Earl of Lennox. The trial, however, was held in Edinburgh where 4,000 Hepburns and other followers of Bothwell were present. Lennox was ordered to bring but six retainers. He dared not go. For want of prosecution the charge failed and Bothwell was acquitted. Huntly was one of his judges. The verdict of his contemporaries was 'Guilty;' that of history is 'Not Proven.' Mary's reputation was dirt.

The murder of her consort precipitated the Queen's destruction. She was not content to be a puppet. She sought to fracture the ruling alliance by marrying one of its component parts. Bothwell, her husband's reputed killer, was the inappropriate object of her desire, as she was of his. Once again he tried to ensure the active support of his fellow-nobles. On 19 April, the day of Huntly's final restoration from forfeiture,[18] Bothwell provided a lavish entertainment at Ainslie's Tavern in Edinburgh at the end of which he persuaded eight bishops, nine earls and seven barons, none too sober, to support and encourage his prospects should the Queen be so disposed. The presence of 200 hackbutters in Bothwell's pay may have helped anaesthetise their better judgement. Moray was happily absent, having conveniently taken himself off to France and out of harm's way. The signatories to the compact included Morton, Maitland, Argyll, Seton, Sutherland and even Huntly, Bothwell's present brother-in-law, forgetting for a moment that the man he bonded with was married to his sister. It seems that the return of his estates had come at a price. What the nobility and episcopacy consented to in their cups they did not necessarily affirm in their sobriety, as their later actions showed. This applied in particular to Huntly who soon had leisure to repent of his disgraceful acquiescence in his sister's humiliation. Nor had they anticipated the brutal means by which Bothwell would bring his suit to fruition.

Armed with the seeming approval of his peers Bothwell abducted and seduced Mary. To bed her was easy; to wed her he would need to free himself of an encumbrance. Just a year before, with the Queen's active blessing, he had married Lady Jean Gordon.[19] She brought a dowry to ease his desperate finances and an even more valuable connection to the premier Earl in the north, and another prominent Protestant supporter of the Queen. It was no love match, nor was the husband faithful. Yet Bothwell sought release through nullification not divorce, a nullification casually pronounced by Archbishop Hamilton whose consistorial jurisdiction was restored by Mary for just this purpose.[20] Bothwell may have had his marriage cynically annulled by a Catholic prelate who had given the dispensation for their union in the first place, but the redoubtable Lady Jean took her husband to the Protestant commissary court where a divorce was granted on the genuine grounds of his undoubted adultery. Lady Jean was a woman of intellect and strength of character. She had been married to the benefit of Mary. Now her marriage was dissolved for the benefit of her erstwhile husband and Mary. She had been manipulated in and out of a loveless union. Her high dudgeon at her treatment would quickly have had an effect on her brother, who despite his hasty acceptance of the Ainslie Bond, must have felt that his loyalty and the person of his sister were being abused. Huntly had been captured with the Queen when she was seized by Bothwell. On 6 May he was in the royal entourage as it entered Edinburgh. The day after, his sister's marriage was annulled.

On 15 May the Queen again deferred to her subject and married James Hepburn, newly made Duke of Orkney, according to Protestant rites. There could be no clearer indication of her utter domination by him. It was as pathetic as it was unseemly. The Pope gave her up as a lost cause, dismissively commenting that 'one cannot expect much from persons who are the slaves of their passions.' By so hasty an alliance with the man suspected of being the murderer of her previous husband she enraged the country and, despite the bond, offended most of the nobility, including Huntly.[21] Despite being a witness at the wedding and making a few desultory appearances at the Privy Council in May,[22] he was curiously absent from that decisive engagement at Carberry which was to determine her fate. Thereafter, when Bothwell was gone for good, he would return to champion her cause in the north, even if that was more to protect his own position, and that of his co-religionists, than a serious attempt to have her re-instated. At the end, as at the beginning,[23] of her short personal reign this foolish Queen alienated the support of the traditional stalwart of the throne, the dominant family in the north, the chief conservative magnate in the realm, the one man who might have saved her. This time Huntly's alienation would be to her ruin not his own. She had acted in such a way that usurpation could now be countenanced and even welcomed.

The troops mutinied. Mary met with a blank refusal when she tried to summon her nobles to attend her with their forces for an expedition into Liddesdale. Instead on 6 June 1567 twelve earls and fourteen lords led by Glencairn banded together in a group soon known as the Confederate Lords with the avowed aim of rescuing the Queen from her 'captivity'. Huntly entered into correspondence with them while Lethington betrayed to them all her plans. Home, one of the most powerful Border lords, was active in his opposition to her.[24] The expedition was abandoned.

Sensing a need for a safe lodging, Mary and Bothwell tried to gain entry into Edinburgh Castle, but its gates were closed against them by its new keeper, Sir James Balfour. Eluding capture at Borthwick Castle, ten miles south of the capital, they then withdrew to the greater security of Dunbar to weather the storm. The Queen and her husband were soon tempted to take the initiative and attempt to seize the capital. They assumed others would rally to their monarch. The Lords Seton, Yester and Borthwick did so, with 2,000 men, but they were the only ones. Huntly remained with the Hamiltons inside Edinburgh Castle. He did not take arms against her but by his abstention he secured her fate. The avenging forces of the Confederate Lords ranged against the Queen and her consort proved too great. Bearing banners depicting the slaughter of Darnley and crying for vengeance they blocked her way south of Edinburgh at Carberry Hill on 15 June 1567. Her troops deserting in droves, naively she surrendered herself to Kirkaldy of Grange while Bothwell was allowed to make off. The fact that he was allowed to go when the Confederate Lords had him within their grasp indicates that he was less of problem on the run than in captivity where he could implicate others in the murder of Darnley, others such as Lethington, Argyll and Huntly.

Mary and Bothwell had been four weeks married, and would never see each other again. Bothwell had some initial success in trying to rally support. The Hamiltons and Lord Fleming stayed loyal and Argyll and Lord Boyd actually rejoined the royal cause. But Huntly continued to be elusive. His sister, Lady Jean, returned to the north and on the way informed her cousin, the Countess of Moray, that she would have no more to do with her outlawed former husband. Huntly, belatedly rediscovering family loyalty, followed suit. Despite a visit from Bothwell to Strathbogie he would not raise the Highlands. Reinstated to his inheritance, Huntly had lost any incentive to assist the friendless fugitive, and was content that Bothwell 'should miscarry, to rid the Queen and his sister of so wicked a husband.'[25] Without Huntly's aid, Bothwell was doomed. Hemmed in the north by Kirkaldy of Grange, and in danger of imminent capture, he fled first to the Orkney Islands, and from there to Norway, and a life of exile, imprisonment, and death abroad, in a prison in Denmark in 1578. His fate was to parallel that of his wife.

Riding between Morton and Athol, Mary, Queen of Scots, was brought captive through the streets of her capital. The crowds who had so rapturously received her six years before then subjected her to taunts and insults. She was called whore and murderess to her face, her hands like those of Lady Macbeth, were stained in a king's blood. 'The soldiers, unrestrained by their officers, kept constantly waving before her eyes the banner on which was painted the murdered King, and the prince crying for vengeance.'[26] Mary was shut up in the house of Fleming of Craigmiller, the provost of Edinburgh, from which she awoke to see the macabre banner hung up opposite her window. More secure accommodation was needed and that evening she was removed to the little island castle of Lochleven, a Douglas stronghold. She was a liability and a danger as well as an embarrassment.

Just as the birth of her son had made her first husband disposable so the royal baby's healthy survival had rendered his mother dispensable. Abandoned by all and in the midst of miscarrying twins, she was forced to abdicate on 24 July 1567, in favour of her son. The infant James was crowned King five days later by Adam Bothwell of Orkney, the same bishop who had recently presided over his mother's third marriage.

6

THE TWIGS OF AMBITION
1567–1576

I wis' our quine had better frinds
I wis' our countrie better peice;
I wis' our lords wid na discord
I wis' our weirs at hame may ceisse!

Ballad of the Battle of Corrichie

Promises are commonly trodden under foot, when they lie in the way either to honour or revenge.

George Gordon, fifth Earl of Huntly[1]

THE REGENT MORAY 1567–1569/70

Most significantly, Moray was the natural choice and only conceivable contender as Regent for his infant nephew James. Mary had been willing to resign the government to him. He had kept his hands clean. He was not implicated in the killing of Darnley, he was not in the country when the Queen was deposed, and as late as July was professing his loyalty to his sister, professions we have to take seriously. The Confederate Lords undoubtedly informed him of their plans and equally undoubtedly wanted him on their side. Yet no correspondence from him to them survives but for one oral message in which he repudiated their designs. He had even turned down some splendid French bribes 'lest he should be bound where he is now free.'[2]

On receiving news of his election, Moray returned home from France via England. He was appraised of the accusations and evidence against the Queen. He sought her out, upbraided her like 'a ghostly father,'[3] and, without promising anything in return, secured her agreement to him assuming the regency. Promising to serve God, maintain the true faith, and root out heresies, he was duly declared Regent on 22 August 1567 to widespread acclamation. Edinburgh Castle was surrendered to him two days later and with it the Queen's jewels. Dunbar was reduced. On 15 September Moray informed his friend Cecil that the whole realm was quiet. All the nobility, even Argyll, Hamilton and Huntly, gave their adherence to the new government. When Mary heard that the last had attended the December parliament, she observed bitterly that 'Bothwell might as well have been there as he,' suggesting that they were both equally guilty of Darnley's death.[4] Huntly was courted by the prospect of a future marriage between his five-year-old son and Moray's two-year-old daughter, Elizabeth. He had earlier come to an agreement with Moray. In return for Huntly finally renouncing all claims to the earldom of Moray, the future Regent backed his restoration from forfeiture.[5]

The Queen deposed and disgraced, her son and successor a babe in arms, and with no rivals for the regency, Moray was king in all but name, as was his destiny. And more: he fulfilled the archetypal role of the godly magistrate in Protestant hagiography.[6] Throckmorton, the English ambassador, observed how the new Regent 'went stoutly to work, resolved rather to imitate those who had led the people of Israel than any captains of that age.'[7] The General Assembly of the Kirk exalted in his elevation: 'God of his heavenly Providence hath reserved [him] to this age, to put in execution whatsoever by his law he commandeth.'

Soon enough God would show where his favour lay when Moray had to contest his sister's attempt to retake her kingdom after she escaped from Lochleven Castle on 2 May 1568 and headed for the west to raise support. Moray's position was precarious. Her escape from confinement and the revocation of her abdication divided the country. Families were split in their adherence to Queen or Regent. Although Regent for the whole kingdom, Moray's sympathies lay strongly with the Protestant faction. This could not but alienate the Catholics who had been part of the loose coalition which had leagued against the adulterous and murderous Queen but now wavered towards her once more. Athol, Caithness, and the Bishop of Moray condemned the Regent's religious legislation. Religious affiliations, however, did not always define allegiance. Not all the nobility were enamoured of the prospect of a protracted regency by the royal bastard. It was the removal of Bothwell and his baleful influence on the Queen that had galvanised them, not the prospective elevation of her brother. The Hamiltons in particular, to whose territories she fled, and whose claim to the throne was legitimate, had little love for Moray who had usurped their ancestral rights to the regency. With Bothwell departed the scene, Eglington and Huntly, who both had reversionary rights to the crown,[8] and others of the Catholic nobility – Athol, Caithness, Cassilis, Crawford, Sutherland and Montrose – were again firmly in the Marian camp. Yet it was the Protestant Earl of Argyll, animated by animosity to Moray and loyalty to the Queen, who supplied her greatest support. Within a week of Carberry he had deserted the confederacy and aligned himself with the Hamiltons. Nor was he the only Protestant to adhere to her cause: the lords Livingston, Fleming, Boyd, Crichton, Hay, Ogilvie, Maxwell and his son, Herries, all signed the bond that Hamilton drew up affirming their loyalty. So too did James Stewart, the lay abbot of St Colme.[9] The majority of the bishops were also with the Queen, but their support was essentially moral rather than military. To the Queen's cause rallied in total some 5,000-6,000 men largely from the Hamilton areas. Argyll was her lieutenant general.

Moray was in hostile territory and heavily outnumbered. Some of his followers may have wavered but not the Regent. He knew that withdrawal in the face of the Queen would be construed as flight, and that his only chance was to strike before the northern levies of Huntly and Ogilvie could join the royal forces. In his favour he had some staunch supporters in Morton, Glencairn, and Mar, as well as many of the lesser nobility such as Ochiltree, Ruthven and Innermeath. Even Home, a Catholic and a bloody Borderer, foiled an attempt to seize Dunbar for the Queen, and arrived with 600 men for the Regent. Within ten days Moray had mustered 4,000 men, including a large detachment from Glasgow, cannon from Stirling, and the royal archers and hagbutters from Edinburgh.[10] It soon proved that Moray had more resolute troops than his adversary and two commanders of real calibre in Kirkaldy of Grange and the Earl of Morton who took the vanguard.

Nor did he have to face Huntly, since once again the latter took no part in the proceedings. He was in the north, perhaps bought off by the prospect of marrying into the Regent's family, or perhaps relishing a mortal struggle between the siblings who had wreaked such havoc on his house. Mary, abetted by her brother, had brought about his father's destruction; by his inaction Huntly would ensure her own. On the other hand, perhaps he had merely been caught off guard by the speed of events, as it was reported that he was on his way to the Queen at great speed.[11] In any event he was to be the backbone of her support in defeat.

Meanwhile Mary began to march from Hamilton to the rock-fortress of Dumbarton held by the ever-loyal Lord Fleming. Had she reached it she could have remained there secure until reinforcements reached her from the north. Moray might then be eradicated and Mary restored. Moray stalked her, and finally forced her into an unnecessary fight. When the two armies met at Langside on 13 May 1568 Moray's more seasoned troops triumphed. Caught in a lane by enfilading fire the royal van was momentarily driven back. They regrouped and pressed forward uphill. There they encountered the fresh Border troops of Morton and Home who pushed them down again at the tips of their pikes. Moray in the centre ordered a charge and the Queen's troops broke and fled. The fighting had lasted barely forty-five minutes and casualties were light – no more than 300 and possibly half as many – owing to Moray's command that 'prisoners should be brought in rather than corpses.'[12] Mary's forces scattered. Three days later the friendless Queen impulsively deserted her own supporters, thereby undermining their ability to resist, and fled to England to her wretched but well-deserved fate. She threw herself on the mercy of her 'loving cousin' and found that she had fallen into the clutches of a jealous rival.

Mary was an abject failure as a monarch and as a person. Fatherless from birth, she had craved the support and sustenance of a male figure. Her second and third marriages were both manifestly foolish. Both husbands were perilously inadequate figures, both ambitious, both arrogant, both contributing in their own way to her downfall and their own. The only man of calibre was her brother who, though envious of the throne, was content to serve her well while he remained the power behind it. When Darnley usurped Moray's place, the latter became an enemy and not a friend, finally finding another monarch to dominate, Mary's infant son. He was ultimately going to desert, betray, or replace her whoever she married. There are in this little tragedy some tantalising hypotheticals. Had Moray not been her brother and a bastard, would they have married, and together been a force in the land? Had Elizabeth been a man and of the marrying kind, would the union of the crowns come fifty years earlier? Scotland had never before had a Queen regnant; England had known only three – Matilda, Mary and Elizabeth. It is a strange and unique irony that both countries should be ruled by queens simultaneously.

Mary's subsequent exile and imprisonment, while demoralising the Marian Party, did not leave Moray unchallenged or all-powerful. The Queen's fate and future were not yet obvious and many longed for her return. For five years the Jacobite and Marian parties vied for dominance and Scotland teetered on the verge of all out civil war. Three of the four regents were to die in the office to which they succeeded relentlessly from 1568 to 1573.

The Duke of Chatelherault, the Earl of Argyll, and the fifth Earl of Huntly formed the opposition triumvirate. In July 1568 they conferred together in Largs, their aim being to restore legitimate government and their Queen. Having taken counsel together, they dispersed to their own respective arenas. Chatelherault commanded the considerable strength of the Hamiltons in the south-west; Argyll was supreme in the north-west; but it was Huntly, acting as usual as a Vice-Regent, who virtually established a provisional Marian administration in the north-east, commanding an area extending as far south as Angus and as far north and west as Inverness-shire. A large group of northern lairds rallied to him and subscribed to a bond, amongst them the three Gordon lairds who had failed to follow the fourth Earl in 1562. The prospect of serving for the Queen rather than against her dramatically altered their position. Amongst the signatories of the bond were John Grant of Freuchy whose father had signed a bond of manrent with the fourth Earl in 1546, Duncan Forbes of Monymusk, a leading Protestant burgess of Aberdeen, and most prominently, Lachlan Mackintosh, chief of Clan Chattan. This resurgence of the Queen's party presented the Earl of Moray with a strong challenge to his authority as Regent and threatened a number of Scottish burghs which had been seen to take the Regent's side against the Queen. Dundee and Perth feared assault by Huntly, Fife was under threat, whilst independent Aberdeen was blackmailed into siding with the Earl.[13]

The Granite City was effectively capital of the north-east. It was a handsome and proud town, with a population of about 7,000 living in sturdy houses built out of the local hard stone.[14] Control of the burgh with its busy port and network of trading contacts with northern Europe was absolutely vital to the survival of the Queen's cause. Theoretically there should have been a substantial identification of interest between her supporters and the burgesses who dominated the town. Many of Aberdeen's chief citizens were Catholics or Catholic sympathisers, open or covert. The Reformation was slacker and more stretched in this northern outpost. It was isolated from the centre of government in Edinburgh and used its isolation to good effect. Most of the time it could ignore the commotions convulsing the Lowlands of the kingdom. Similarly it was in the interests of the city not to take sides if it could avoid it. No one knew who would win. The burgesses certainly wanted strong central government. When it was weak they were deprived of the protection necessary to maintain their prosperity and independence. It mattered not if this strong government was Mary's or her brother's. The crown would protect and keep distant. Huntly, however, would not. He was the power in the north and wanted, as had his father, to dominate the city as much as he did the countryside. The Aberdonians, by aligning themselves with the Queen at this juncture, might be backing the losing side, and would be losing their hard won independence. They would put themselves in thrall to Huntly. Thus the fifth Earl, like the fourth, found it impossible to create any strong party within the city. What he could not win he would have to take.

At the end of July 1568 Huntly came to Aberdeen with 1,500 men and 'threatened extermination against the provost' (Thomas Menzies). This was no idle threat. The following month one of Huntly's lieu-tenants, John Leslie, besieged the provost's house and forced the town to yield to the Earl. Huntly even had the temerity to make off with one of the King's cannons to intimidate any resisters. Like a scarlet pimpernel he moved fast, struck hard and seemed to get everywhere. With a large force of cavalry he almost managed to capture Morton, the Chancellor, and other members of the King's council. Like a highway robber he seized goods from an itinerant Edinburgh merchant. He managed to take the royal castle at Dingwall from Moray's supporters. 'Moray-land' was at his disposal, and he appointed one John Innes (alias the 'sweet man') as chamberlain 'to spoil that patrimony.' In this way did Huntly lead the Marian party north of the Tay with a reluctant and nervous Aberdeen as its capital. 'Huntly reigns in the north' bemoaned Kirkaldy of Grange to the Regent, and none 'of us can see the end of it.'[15]

In the spring of the following year, however, Moray was growing in confidence and power, while the Marians were vacillating. He galvanised his supporters and ordered a general muster of the kingdom. His aim was to divide and conquer. In March he overawed his southern opponents into concluding a treaty of peace at Glasgow. It was agreed that there would be an immediate cessation of hostilities pending a convention of the nobility in April, which would settle the affairs of the state and deliberate on the measures to be adopted towards their captive sovereign. The convention would comprise the Regent, the Duke, and the Earls of Huntly, Argyll, Morton, Mar, Athol, Glencairn and Lord Herries. Chatelherault and his adherents agreed to acknowledge the authority of the King, on condition that all those who had been forfeited for their allegiance to the Queen would be restored. When the convention met at Edinburgh, Huntly and Argyll were notably absent. Chatelherault attended, but refused to sign the requisite declaration. It was enough. Moray ordered his arrest and that of Lord Herries and they were both made close prisoners in the security of Edinburgh Castle.[16]

Argyll and Huntly had refused to sign the pacification at Glasgow, but were now isolated in the north. Moray had out flanked them, controlled the southern half of the kingdom and was backed by the power of England. Argyll broke ranks first, and, acknowledging the King's authority was immediately restored into favour. Huntly, the last of the Queen's lieutenants, finally yielded to the present realities and submitted to the triumphant Regent at St Andrews on 10 May 1569. Huntly acknowledged the legitimacy of Moray's governance, surrendered his artillery, interceded for his followers and gave hostages for his good conduct. Moray was unchallenged in the realm, and would subdue it to his will. He immediately demonstrated his power in Huntly's heartlands themselves, arriving in force in 'these broken north parts.' He drove a wedge between Huntly and the burgh of Aberdeen, discharging the latter on the ground that its affiliation to Huntly had been coerced, but massively fining the former. For the rest of the civil war Huntly had to tie up much money and many men in securing the burgh for the Queen. The Regent proceeded to Elgin and Inverness dispensing heavy fines on all those who had willingly assisted their Earl.[17] By July Moray reported to the English that 'none of the great mass of the north, or very few, are disobedient.'[18] Their agent concurred: 'All is quiet' on the northern front.

Moray next purged the court. Mary's loyal secretary, Maitland, and Sir James Balfour were placed under house arrest on the charge of the murder of Darnley. Not for long. The former's old associate Kirkaldy of Grange, a recent convert to the Queen's camp and the keeper of Edinburgh Castle, fearing for his friend's safety at the mercy of the duplicitous Regent, attacked the house in which Lethington was confined and carried him off to the safety of the fortress. There, in the very centre of the heart of the kingdom, the most loyal Marians maintained their isolated defiance, a constant irritant and embarrassment to the Regent, whose hegemony was otherwise unchallenged. They too would be subdued in good time no doubt, but good time was not granted to the first Earl of Moray.

On 23 January 1569/70 Moray was murdered as he rode through Linlithgow on his way from Stirling to Edinburgh. The assassin was one James Hamilton of Bothwellhaugh, a condemned prisoner after Langside who lost his estates but kept his life due to the mercy of the Regent. He cancelled his debt by killing the creditor. In this he acted with the connivance and encouragement of his uncle, John Hamilton, Archbishop of St Andrews, from whose house the shot was fired and to whom the assassin fled for succour. Knowing that the cavalcade would ride through the congested High Street, Bothwellhaugh took up position in the gallery, which commanded a full and unobstructed view of the street below. He placed a feather bed on the floor to muffle his booted footsteps and a black sheet on the wall opposite to lesson the danger of his shadow being projected by a sudden burst of sun. A horse was saddled and waiting for him in the stable at the back of the premises. While he waited for the arrival of his prey, he made a hole big enough for the barrel of his gun just below the lintel of the widow. He loaded four bullets and took up position.

Moray and his retainers made slow progress along the street, impeded as they were by the crowds come to watch. As he rode past the archbishop's house, the Regent presented an easy target. Even so the bullet that hit him penetrated the pelvis but did not kill him outright. Bleeding freely, the Regent nonetheless managed to walk to the nearby palace, but it soon became clear that the wound was mortal. In this regal setting, he died just before midnight, according to a hagiographer calmly and without reproach, beseeching clemency for his assassin and praying for his King.[19]

The Hamiltons rejoiced in their handiwork, assembled in Glasgow with a 140 horse and eighty harquebusiers, and confidently prepared to march on Edinburgh to free their Duke. Defections from the King's party there were aplenty, but the general uprising that the Hamiltons had hoped the assassination would provoke failed to materialise. Controversial though Moray's rule was, his popularity eroded by his deference to England and his duplicity towards his rivals, the manner of his murder and the dignity of his dying, brought about an immediate and dramatic rehabilitation. It almost united the nation in grief and anger. Black-letter ballads were composed to express the popular lamentation. 'The death of my Lord Regent,' the *Diurnal* records, 'was the caus of great dolour.'[20] The dolour was not confined to Scotland. 'His death was lamented by all good men,' commented Buchanan, 'and especially by the English to whom in all the vicissitudes of providence throughout his life, his virtues were more known than to any other nation.' A strangely tearful Elizabeth belatedly realised that she had lost her 'best and most useful friend in all the world.'[21]

The state funeral did not take place until 14 February. The dead Regent's body had first to be brought from Linlithgow to Stirling, where crowds lined the streets, mourning. From there it was taken by water to Leith. In solemn procession it was carried to Holyrood where it lay in state. In its final journey from the palace to the High Kirk of St Giles, Kirkaldy of Grange led the way carrying a banner before the bier. The pallbearers were the principal Protestant peers: the Earls of Morton, Mar, Glencairn, and Cassilis and the Lords Glamis, Lindsay, Ochiltree and Ruthven. Behind them thronged the magistrates and citizens of Edinburgh. Alms were distributed to the poor as the cortege wound its way up the Canongate and passed the Cowgate. Through the great west doors of the High Kirk, and up the main aisle the mourners moved in silence. Before its internment in the crypt beneath St Anthony's aisle, the coffin was lowered into place in front of the pulpit for the Ezra of the nation to consecrate the passing of its Nehemiah. In his sermon on the text 'Blessed are these that die in the Lord,' John Knox, 'with his one foot in the grave'[22] could still move the 3,000 strong congregation to tears for the greatest Captain in the Scottish Israel. The 'Good Regent' was becoming the first Moray martyr.[23]

THE REGENT LENNOX 1570–1571

Not all bemoaned the Regent Moray and his passing. France and Spain were loud in their delight, and Spanish aid to the Queen's party became more open and more generous. During the five month vacuum created by the Regent's death the Marians waxed in strength while the 'son's party daily decay[ed].'[24] Her champions were everywhere active and unchallenged. Chatelherault, Argyll and Huntly all claimed to act as Mary's lieutenants in their respective spheres. Moray's boast that he would Protestantise the north had proved vain and no consistent attempt had been made to dismantle the infrastructure of Gordon power. Moray's allotted time was too short, his primary interests were elsewhere, and the hold of the Gordons was too secure, built up over generations by family alliances, loyalties of kinship and manrent, mutual prosperity and common culture.

Huntly, impregnable in the north, held a 'secret' or Privy Council in Aberdeen and by mid-June the 'haill earls, lords and barons of the north parts' had gathered in his support. Athol, Crawford, Ogilvy and Lord John Hamilton, the commendator of Arbroath, formed the nucleus. Huntly promised no reprisals and at the same time recruited as many experienced soldiers as he could get – especially those recently discharged Moray's service. He was so diligent in the north that the English remarked that he had caused the 'Queen's majesty to have universal obedience there.'[25] He even tried – despite the document he had signed – to get a couple of his own 'falcons' and the royal jewels back from the dowager Countess of Moray, another point of discord between the two neighbours.[26]

Matthew Stewart, the Earl of Lennox became Regent on 15 July 1570. The Hamiltons, having rid themselves of Moray, were presented with an even more inimical replacement. He was, as the King's grandfather and nearest adult male relative, the natural choice, but southern support and the gold that accompanied it clinched the matter. England, the gaoler of Mary, was determined to see her cause thwarted at home. Lennox, however, was seen as Elizabeth's creature, and this patronage alienated further those who feared English hegemony and favoured Mary's restoration as a bulwark against it. Huntly rather accurately branded the Regent as an alien, a lackey of England, a traitor bought by English gold. Lennox felt forced to counter Huntly's 'scandalous misreports' with a ridiculous public proclamation that he was a 'Scotsman of the royal blood and surname.' Only Morton was staunch in support.[27]

Military counters to the new Regent were soon afoot. Chatelherault mustered in the south-west; Argyll and his men made ready to ravage the Lowlands; and Huntly moved towards Brechin with his forces. Huntly complained Lennox to the Earl of Sussex, not merely resisted the King's authority but under pretext of administering justice, oppressed all of the King's supporters within his sphere of influence. He 'sets out letters' and held courts in the Queen's name, issued proclamations calling out all the men in the areas of his influence to meet him in 'warlike manner' at Brechin, and his men forced reluctant officials at sword point to make the proclamation.[28] Along with Argyll and Chatelherault Huntly even intended to call a parliament at Linlithgow. The Regent seemed powerless to impose his will on these mighty lords of the realm. Lennox had the money but lacked the men and the authority. In contrast to Huntly, he had only managed to buy up 'a band of young soldiers of little experience,' not the sort who could trounce the rebels in their own homelands.[29] England alone could

provide the resources and England as usual was reluctant to involve
herself too deeply in the quagmire of Scottish politics. A little bribery
here, a few guns there, but nothing approaching a decisive commitment
could be got out of Elizabeth. Nonetheless, Lennox and Morton
assembled such forces as they could, and in August 1570 marched
against Huntly, stormed Brechin Castle, and strung up thirty-four of
the garrison before Huntly's own house. In a further pre-emptive
attempt to eliminate potential opposition in the heart of the kingdom,
the Regent took Castle Doune from its suspect captain, Lord Saint
Colme.[30] Meanwhile the English, under Sussex, raided the Borders to
assist their ally's manoeuvres inland. Such successes were enough to
restrain but not subdue the Marians.

Sussex first of all proposed a truce in October 1570, stipulating that
Chatelherault, Huntly and Argyll should cease hearing all civil actions
and criminal justice should be administered in the King's name and not
their own or that of the Queen. When peaceful overtures failed, as they
soon did, civil war resumed. The decisive victory, somewhat surprisingly, went to Lennox. This was the dramatic capture of the formidable
Dumbarton Castle by Captain Crawford of Jordanhill in April 1571.
Within its walls was a rare prize, John Hamilton, the infamous
Archbishop of St Andrews. He was taken in triumph to Stirling and
ignominiously hanged in his full episcopal vestments for his part in the
assassination of Moray. The Queen's men, starved of funds and
resources and exhausted by continuous struggle were severely
weakened. The fall of Dumbarton was the death not just of an errant
archbishop but of any further hope of foreign aid. In August Huntly
and Chatelherault were forfeited.[31]

Yet Edinburgh Castle still held out under the redoubtable Kirkaldy
of Grange. Who held the citadel commanded the city. In May, while
the Marians gathered in the traditional assembly point of the tolbooth,
the Regent had been forced to hold his parliament in the Canongate,
a point less vulnerable to cannon fire. Even so, the assembly was
dubbed the 'creeping parliament' from the number of times that its
members had to take to their hands and knees to avoid salvos from the
castle. In September Grange cheekily determined to summon a parliament in the capital while the Regent convened his own in the greater
safety of Stirling. Both bodies denounced the other as traitor and passed
acts of attainder against the nobility attending their rival. While their
legislative authority might not pass beyond the city gates the Marian
forces could. Grange purposed on a surprise attack on their rivals.
Huntly was loud in support. In command of a striking force of sixty
mounted hagbutters and 340 Border horse they sallied forth on the
night of 4 September 1571 to raid Stirling. Their guerilla action
achieved little but the death of Lennox, who was stabbed in the back

by Captain James Calder in the course of the skirmish. The Regent's death, confessed Calder on the rack, had been ordered by Lord Claud Hamilton and Huntly – in revenge for the killing of the Archbishop of St Andrews. Some, at least, considered that this assassination made the raid worthwhile!

THE REGENT MAR 1571–1572

John Erskine, Earl of Mar, governor to the young King, succeeded Lennox in the unlucky position of Regent. Argyll and Morton both contested the election but the majority of the nobility declared for Mar, who was considered more honest and less ambitious than his rivals. It was a good choice. Although he ruled for only thirteen months before his own death in October 1572, in that short time he accomplished a considerable reconciliation, winning over several magnates to the King's side. He may have thereby weakened the Marian party but Huntly still eluded him and, through the agency of his ruthless brother, could engage in guerilla warfare in the north.

Huntly would not come to heel, especially when the rival 'King's lieutenant' was William, seventh Baron Forbes. The Gordons and Forbes, as we have seen, had been 'harbouring deadly feud, of long rooted between them,'[32] a division intensified by the breakdown of the marriage between John, the master of Forbes, and Huntly's sister, Margaret. In 1571, some sources preferring 10 October but the majority favouring 17 October, the first engagement between the two families took place at Tulliangus, on the northern skirts of the Correen Hills. Huntly's brother Adam Gordon of Auchindoun, popularly known as 'Edom o'Gordon,' got wind of a major clan gathering there under 'Black Arthur,' Lord Forbes' younger brother, and a mortal enemy of the Gordons. With Huntly absent in Edinburgh, Adam took the initiative, hastily mustering his friends and followers, and making straight for the convention. There, in the enemy heartland, almost within sight of Lord Forbes' seat of Drumminor, he routed the superior Forbes forces, inflicting heavy casualties in the battle, and heavier in the pursuit. Some 120 lost their lives and others their liberty, including Lord Forbes second son, William of Fodderbirse, a valuable prisoner. His uncle, Arthur, fought his way out of the carnage but was fatally stabbed through a joint in his armour when he stopped to drink from a burn.[33]

The master of Forbes fled south to safety and succour. There he was granted a commission of lieutenancy from the Regent Mar, and levied troops sufficient, he hoped, to 'daunt and suppress' Adam and avenge his uncle. Accompanied by the son of the Earl Marischal, he marched north with an army of 600 horse and two companies of hagbutters under Captain Chisholm. Adam, his force augmented by sea-borne troops sent by his brother, had been warned of their approach, and was more than ready for them. Forbes and his men, assembling at Brechin, crossed the Cairnamounth Pass and descended the River Dee as far as the Justice Mills on the outskirts of Aberdeen. They found that the lands round the Dee had already been despoiled to deny them provision. Fatally the invaders decided to split their force, one company under the master of Marischal continuing north, the other under the master of Forbes veering east to take Aberdeen.

On 20 November 1571 with an army of 900 men, Adam came upon the latter detachment at Crabstone near Aberdeen. The ensuing massacre lasted an hour and left 300 of Forbes' men dead and 200 – including the master of Forbes – taken prisoner.[34] Forbes was lodged in Spynie Castle where under the roof of the Bishop of Moray he suffered the further indignity of seeing his estranged wife cavorting with the bishop's natural son, the parson of Kinoir. Forbes subsequently divorced her.

Effectively unopposed after Crabstone, Adam Gordon 'passit to all places of the Forbes and tuik them perforce and causit them to be keipit in his name.' They were despoiled of their valuables, and cattle and other livestock were driven off. Aberdeen was occupied and Adam's word was law 'fra the water of Dee north.'[35] The Forbes had been defeated in the field but they remained in control of a number of strong points, most notably Drumminor and Corgarff. To hamstring any attempt at revival or retaliation, Adam acted against both. He sacked Drumminor in person, and despatched a detachment under the command of Captain Kerr to the recently built Castle of Corgarff in the valley of the River Don. In style and plan the castle was typical of contemporary small houses of the gentry being built throughout the country. Its nucleus was the tower house, which consisted of a storage basement surmounted by a hall, and upper floors containing private chambers. Surrounding the tower and its adjacent buildings was a relatively small perimeter wall. Margaret Campbell, the wife of Forbes of Towie, whose seat it was, refused them entry and fired on their leader. Thus provoked, the assailants set the tower on fire, the lady and twenty-seven others in the house perishing in the blaze.'[36] Corgarff's destruction effectively ended local opposition to Huntly but built up enormous bitterness against the Gordons. The savagery was commemorated in the Ballad of Edom o'Gordon, and Adam was awarded the contemporary sobriquet 'the Herod of the North.'[37] His depredations continued into 1572 when with a force of 1,600 men he took 200 prisoners at 'Brighen,' killed some notables and wounded several others. He than extorted a ransom from the young third Earl of Montrose, took Arbroath and captured the laird of Dunne's house with three or four field pieces within.

Suddenly, on 28 October 1572, the Regent died. His death was a result of natural causes, but precipitated, some said, by disappointment 'because he loved peace and could not have it.'[38] Mar, in the short time allotted him, had failed to end the civil war and the ensuing chaos. This fell to his able but far more ruthless successor, James Douglas, Earl of Morton, who was elected unopposed as Regent on 24 November 1572.

THE REGENT MORTON 1572–1580

The new Regent had strong support and was a strong man, a typical Douglas, accustomed to command and without scruple. He would prove a longer-lived and more determined Regent than his predecessors. He started with an advantage. In the months immediately prior to his accession, the position of the Catholics had been steadily weakened by the news of the St Bartholomew's Day massacre of French Huguenots in August 1572. England, whose paranoia was not without reason, became even more determined to prevent a Catholic resurgence on her northern border. Consequently, Morton and the Protestants had the unusually active backing of a near and powerful neighbour. Huntly and the Queen's party were tired, isolated and demoralised, their defiance on the wane. Morton decided to harry his foe. Huntly's lands had already been forfeited for treason but Morton became vigorous in his pursuit of them. Lachlan Mackintosh, for instance, was allowed to keep the lands granted him by the rebel Earl but had to swear allegiance for them to the crown.[39]

These factors had a salutary effect. On 23 February 1572/3 Huntly and other Marian magnates were induced to sign the Pacification of Perth in which they recognised the King and the regency government. All sides now accepted the settlement. Mary would not return. James would soon rule in his own right. Better to accept the inevitable, welcome the prosperity that would come with peace, and maintain the traditional authority each magnate had long enjoyed in his domains. The Pacification of Perth was not so much a defeat or surrender on the part of the Marians as an acquiescence in the inevitable, and an accommodation with the government which they could not overthrow and with whom they had to live. Huntly and his friends had not been defeated and his power in the north remained largely untouched. This was demonstrated during the very sitting of the conference at Perth when Adam Gordon attacked and defeated Lord Forbes in Aberdeen, finally quashing any aspirations he might have had of exploiting the victory of the King's party.[40] It was to be Adam's last triumph. Shortly afterwards he sought the intercession of Elizabeth to reconcile him to the Regent but in the meantime, along with Thomas Kerr of Fernihurst, prudently absented himself from the kingdom. [41] He left many enemies behind. One such, Arthur Forbes, a son of Lord Forbes, and nephew of his slain namesake, pursued him to France and attempted his assassination but was himself apprehended and his body broken on the wheel.[42] On his return to Scotland Adam was warded in Blackness by Morton, not being released until January 1575/6, four years before his death.

Morton was determined that there were to be no feuds arising from the war and no excuses for further violence and disorder. The master of Forbes was to be released from Spynie Castle, but only after paying £705 expenses incurred during his detention.[43] With the north settled, Morton could excise the cancer at the heart of the kingdom, the defiance of the garrison in Edinburgh Castle. In May it fell. Kirkaldy of Grange was executed along with his brother, James. Maitland of Lethington, to the last living up to his contemporary sobriquet as the Scots Machiavelli or 'Mitchel Wylie,' escaped the same fate by his premature death. Most of the others, including Lord Home and John Maitland, Lethington's brother, were allowed to live, and, after a short confinement, leave. Punitive measures were unnecessary. Resistance to the Jacobite cause was over.

Whatever residual menace there was, however dormant, it lay in the north-east. Although after the Pacification Huntly lived chiefly in his own dominions scarcely taking further part in public affairs, Morton was determined, as Mary had been before him, to challenge the Gordons' potentially dangerous, and always over-weening, regional hegemony. Where better for a showdown than Aberdeen, again to suffer for its exploitation by Huntly during the civil war? In the late summer of 1574 Morton came north in an expedition that would stamp his authority on the kingdom and curb the power of Huntly. Just as with Mary the English ambassador was brought along to report this show of Reformation zeal to the Queen in the south.[44] So too were a number of the nobility and, most importantly, Lowland levees.

Protestantism was an alien innovation in Aberdeen, dividing communities and endangering long-standing notions of order and hierarchy in local society. St Andrews and Edinburgh might be centres of committed and triumphant Protestantism, but in Aberdeen outward conformity was a veneer covering older loyalties and affections. When need be, the city, like its Earl, could gird itself in reformed righteousness which would at least show obedient conformity if not enthusiasm. The agile inhabitants were two-faced, always presenting the correct appearance when in public, bowing the knee to the prevailing orthodoxy but keeping their fingers crossed behind their backs. When Mary had embarked on her visitation in 1562 Aberdeen had belatedly instituted a Kirk session. This outwardly conformed to the decrees of government and the Queen's express intent to maintain the religious settlement but its obvious superficiality cannot have displeased her as a Catholic monarch. With Morton it was different. Zeal for the reformed faith was part of his temperament.

Much of the conservation of old customs and beliefs would be offensive to him. Morton demanded greater conformity and a rooting out of the vestiges of Catholicism. Only the Sabbath was to be celebrated, other festivals were prohibited. The parish church of St Nicholas was to have its organ and pews removed. Images and crucifixes were to be burnt. When he turned his back his orders were tardily implemented and some were openly defied. It took an age – and further rebuke – for St Nicholas to be reordered. Some statues and crosses were destroyed but many were not. Some holidays were still observed as days of rest, if not of devotion. Craftsmen refrained from working on Christmas day, grammar school boys played truant from school. The mass could still be celebrated in Old Aberdeen and in some large houses in the vicinity. In 1575 Lady Jean Gordon of Fyvie was put on trial for hearing mass. Catholic devotion and traditional practices were able to continue, at least privately, as long as the Earl of Huntly's hegemony in the region provided a safe haven for his co-religionists.[45]

It came as a considerable blow when on Saturday 19 October 1576 Huntly, seemingly in the prime of life, was suddenly struck down on the field, as his father had been before him. The field, however, was not one of battle but of football. Saturday was a day for recreation and sport. In the morning he had been out hunting and had killed three hares and a fox. After lunch at Strathbogie there was football, at that time – as now – 'more a friendly kind of fight, than a play or recreation.'[46] Huntly, an avid if elderly player, collapsed in agony after his second kick. He was wrapped in a cloak and led off the field, supported by his brother and friends. They laid him within the great chamber of Strathbogie. He lingered on for twenty-three hours, unable to speak, vomiting blood 'black like soot.' He died at six or seven o'clock the same evening. Richard Bannatyne gives us this memorable, if partisan eyewitness account. He was certainly of the view that the Earl's undignified demise was a judgement for his involvement in the murder of Darnley.[47] As one would expect, the author of the House of Gordon attributed the Earl's demise to apoplexy. Given that other members of the household exhibited similar symptoms, though without vomiting, and finally recovering, it looks more like that common scourge, food poisoning. Whatever the cause Morton would have considered it divine retribution. The following Tuesday William Urquhart, 'a furrigioner of Aberdeen,' came none too soon to Strathbogie and embalmed the decomposing body. It was then borne to the chapel to await burial in the family vault in Elgin Cathedral.

Although sandwiched between the more considerable figures of the fourth and sixth Earls, the fifth Earl of Huntly was a man of some stature in his own right. His features are not so clearly delineated as those of his father or his son, he is less colourful than either, and he lived less long. Although a champion of the lost Marian cause, depicting him as a 'valiant, liberal and constant man [and] a true and faithful servant to Mary,' may be stretching the point.[48] Religion did not seem to mean much to him. He was prepared to sacrifice principle and party for personal gain. He was damned as being 'not very wise, inconstant, factious and insolent,' but this assessment was that of the English who had reason to fear his resurgence. He was described by one observer as being a man 'full of malice against his enemies,' but such a criticism could be made of many of his contemporaries.[49] Huntly not only survived in interesting times – no mean feat – but in addition, after the near terminal catastrophe of Corrichie, he re-established his family as the holders of one the great earldoms of Scotland. His sudden death, however, so soon after their defeat in the civil war, further shook the power of the Gordons.

The 'Cock' had ceased to crow. It was undoubtedly the 'belief that the Gordons could be successfully challenged, and the determination of the sixth Earl of Huntly to restore the power of his family, which lay at the root of his future feuds with his neighbours, and especially the fatal one with the Earl of Moray.[50]

PART III

THE 6TH EARL OF HUNTLY

AND

THE 2ND EARL OF MORAY

1567–1591/2

7

ST COLME'S SON
1567–1582

Oh! lang will his Lady
Look owre the Castle Doune,
E'er she see the Earl o' Moray
Come sounding through the toune!

Ballad of the Bonnie Earl o' Moray

Moray lies betwixt the Spey and Ness.... and is the first country of all Scotland for pleasure and commodity of fruitful trees. There are two towns in it, Elgin and Inverness.

Certayne matters concerning the realm of Scotland[1]

In 1581 James Stewart, the eldest son of Lord Doune, became, by marriage, the second Earl of Moray. The predecessor had been none other than the 'Good Regent' himself, the son of a king and brother of a queen. This was an extraordinary translation for a young man whose father had only recently been ennobled and whose immediate family were but the poor relations of the great. Fortunate marriages and canny diplomacy were the making of them.

Ironically, but unsurprisingly in the small world of the Scots nobility, James was a distant cousin of his future archrival, the sixth Earl of Huntly. His great-grandfather, Andrew, the second Baron Avandale, had married Margaret Kennedy, a granddaughter of the first Earl of Huntly. They had had three sons: Andrew, the first Lord Ochiltree; Henry, the captain of the royal guard; and James,[2] the grandfather of the second Earl of Moray. Third son he might be, but James knew how to prosper on the good fortune of his siblings. When Margaret Tudor, the widow of James IV, married for the third time in 1526, she did so to the captain of her guard, and in this way Sir James became brother-in-law to a dowager queen. A year later King James V, at his mother's behest, created Henry Baron Methven and granted James the stewardship of Monteith and the captaincy of Doune, the royal citadel in Perthshire.[3]

Possession of Doune was a mixed blessing. Its transfer to Sir James from its custodian for the past seven years, William Edmonstone of Duntreath, had been with much rancour and resentment. Its new keeper was kept waiting for a year until he could enter into his office. Edmonstoun, despite several orders and threats from the king, had refused to hand over the castle and was put to the horn. Despite an enforced reconciliation between the former keeper and his supplanter,[4] the grievance smouldered away for the next two decades and finally flared into murder when in 1547 Sir James was killed by his dispossessed predecessor in a brawl in the High Street at Dunblane.[5] He was succeeded by his nineteen-year-old son, James, the future father of the second Earl of Moray and the then commendator of St Colme.

During the Reformation the riches of the Church had been made available to men of note in England; Scotland followed suit. By the sixteenth century the monastic communities had largely ceased being vehicles of spirituality and had become little more than property owning corporations. By the late fifteenth century laymen could be, and were, placed in control over such institutions as commendators – 'protectors,' or administrators, and titular heads. Such an office could be a rich source of revenue.[6] One particularly desirable house was the wealthy Augustinian Abbey of St Colme situated off the north shore of the Firth of Forth on the island of Inchcolm. Hermits had already lived there for generations when the monastic community of 'black canons', as the Augustinians were known, was founded by King David I around 1124. Its patron, St Colme, is a shadowy figure about whom we know next to nothing. In the later Middle Ages he was identified with St Columba, the sixth century Abbot of Iona. Royal patronage and the foundation's association with St Columba destined it for easy distinction. Inchcolm was dubbed 'the Iona of the east.' In 1235 the priory was elevated into an abbey. The abbey church was doubled in size as the community centred on it grew and thrived. The buildings by Scots standards were lavish and well proportioned and nestled securely in a sheltered hollow. The island by any standards was picturesque. Boasting several of the beautiful horseshoe bays for which the area is well known, and with a natural harbour affording boats a safe anchorage, it was divided from the mainland by a narrow stretch of water known as Mortimer's Deep – so named after the Mortimer lords of Aberdour. But the community, in its relatively isolated tranquillity, was vulnerable to attack, especially in the balmiest months of summer and early autumn. It was repeatedly plundered by English marauders, the regularity of their assaults providing a dubious tribute to its prosperity.[7] So persistent was the threat that each year throughout the dangerously tranquil summer months the community took residence and refuge on their lands of Donnibristle on the neighbouring mainland a mile or so from the island. There they stayed, returning to Inchcolm only in late October when the danger of attack had receded. During their daily offices the monks implored their saint, in the words of their

Antiphoner, to 'preserve this choir, which praises you, from the incursions of the English.'[8] Their prayers were, for a time, answered since, despite these depredations, the abbey reached its apogee in the fifteenth century. For over thirty years from 1418 to 1449 it boasted as its abbot none other than Walter Bower, the Venerable Bede of his day and place, and author of the *Scotichronicon*, a history of Scotland from Malcolm Canmore to James II.

Yet less than a century later things had come to such a pass that after a particularly devastating English attack in October 1542 the then Abbot, Richard Abercromby, was induced to resign in favour of the teenage James Stewart, 'nephew of the mighty Lord Andrew Stewart of Ochiltree of the royal race of Scots,' who had 'been ready to defend and repair the monastery' after that attack.[9] He became titular abbot in 1543 and, three years later, at the age of eighteen, commendator of the abbey and its properties. These properties included the lands of Donnibristle, and the abbot's house situated there. Since James had effective control over its considerable assets, the secularisation of the abbey's wealth began. This was very much to the commendator's advantage but not to that of the abbey's erstwhile tenants. By 1545 the tenants of Donnibristle, Barnhill and Grange were complaining about 'rack-renting.'[10] Their complaints fell on deaf ears since their former landlords were awaiting their natural extinction in retirement on Inchcolm. The tenants may have breathed a sigh of relief when, after the fateful battle of Pinkie, James Stewart was displaced from his position by Sir John Luttrel who was appointed abbot by the Duke of Somerset.[11] There is no evidence, however, that an English appointee would be a more understanding landlord than his Scots predecessor. In any case, the remission, if that is what it was, lasted only a short while before James was reinstated. Apart from this brief interruption, the estates of St Colme were to remain in the Stewart family for good.

Despite the revenues he could extort, as a mere commendator James Stewart was still a young man of little political or social note. He was, however, intelligent, subtle and unscrupulous, an ideal combination for a man on the make in sixteenth-century Scotland. He sailed with whichever wind would best propel his own boat, in religion as much as in politics. St Colme needed powerful friends since he was in litigation with the Earl of Montrose over their respective claims to the captaincy of Doune and the stewardry of Monteith, the latter asserting that the Queen-dowager had given both of them to him in 1542.[12] The commendator made his moves well. In 1560 he threw in his lot with the Lords of the Congregation, now plainly in the ascendant. In April he was one of the delegates to the English Army at Preston, a delegation that included Chatelherault, Argyll and Lord James. In May he was the last of the signatories of the Treaty of Berwick, the treaty the Lords of the Congregation ratified with England while the English Army was besieging Leith.[13] In August he – along with many other lairds – attended the 'Reformation Parliament,' the parliament which effectively closed down the public manifestation of Catholic worship in Scotland.[14] Robert Keith gives a contemporary list of the earls, lords, clergy and others of the Estates that attended this packed assembly, beginning with James, Duke of Chatelherault and continuing in descending order of importance. In the list of commendators attending the parliament, St Colme was placed two thirds of the way down.[15] He had put himself as far to the fore of the Protestant party as a man of his station could aspire. If he were not in the first rank his patrons were. Yet, with the return of Mary, Queen of Scots, his position as a creature of Lord James was in no way diminished. No doubt on the latter's recommendation Mary entrusted him with a position of royal emissary to France and England in 1561-2. The English remained wary of him. The ever-perceptive Randolph warned his masters that though he seemed 'gentle and honest enough' St Colme was 'suspected of ambition, which may move him by all ways to serve [Mary's] appetite.'[16]

St Colme had begun his rise with the spoils of the Church, and the Reformation with its social realignments and redistribution of land would serve to promote him further. So too would marriage. On the promise of custody of his old home Castle Doune, at the relatively old age of thirty-six, he enhanced his position still further by marrying Margaret Campbell, eldest daughter of Archibald, fourth Earl of Argyll. Contracting matches with women who could bring greater prestige than their husband to the settlement was to be the way that this minor Stewart family would rise to position and power. The wedding took place on 11 January 1563/4 in the Lowland seat of the Campbells, the awesome and intimidating Castle Gloom, set sternly on an outcrop between the burns of Care and Sorrow. (James IV by act of parliament in 1489-90 approved the change of name from, the ominous and enigmatic 'Castle Gloom' to the prosaic and pretentious, 'Castle Campbell'. For a long time the old name persisted in popular use. I still use it). The Queen herself attended. The festivities included the ever popular banquets and the increasingly fashionable masques, one of which, for instance, depicted a sylvan scene with the cast disporting themselves as shepherds playing lutes.[17] Two months later James got the hereditary custody of Castle Doune and its lands.[18] He was not yet allowed the title 'Lord' – that would not come until 1581 – having instead to satisfy himself for the moment with a knighthood, bestowed by Darnley before the Queen on 15 May 1565.[19] He was in fact a fairly minor royal official, a gentleman gaoler, not yet a peer of the realm. On the positive side, his posting was near to the capital, and his castle, though badly in need of repair, was still majestic.

Doune is a magnificent example of a late medieval keep built for its strength, security and splendour. Its origins were suitably illustrious. Robert Stewart, the Earl of Menteith and first Duke of Albany, and virtual ruler of Scotland in the late fourteenth century, commissioned it, but it may not have been completed until sometime between 1419 and 1424 during the regency of his son, Murdoch. On his forfeiture in 1425 the earldom of Menteith and the Castle of Doune passed to the crown. With the crown it was to remain until it was bestowed on the Earls of Moray. Its location was a commanding one on the intersection of Highland and Lowland, close to the town of Doune in Menteith, Perthshire, and only eight miles from Stirling. Strategically situated on a tongue of land lying between, and at the junction of, the Rivers Teith and Ardoch, the castle is further defended by the steep slope of the ground all round and by several manmade ditches.

The approach is from the north, from which direction all the eye can see are the two formidable round towers linked by the great hall of the keep and the adjacent banqueting hall. Massive as it is along its northern front, the rest of castle tapers back with a forty-foot tall curtain wall surrounding a large open square where secondary buildings stood. This 'service area' is less well protected but it was also less essential. The castle was self-sufficient without it. The conception of the castle was a radical departure from that which had gone before. It was careless of its curtain wall, instead ensuring that the baronial residence was capable of independent defence.[20] Its entrance consists of a long vaulted passage passing under the great hall. The passage is flanked with a guardroom and well defended with wooden doors, strong iron-grated gates and a portcullis as well as apertures in the vault. The keep at the north-east angle of the frontage constitutes a large castle on its own. It has a separate entrance and no internal communication with the other buildings. Every turret, embrasure and latrine has a defensive function. If all else fell, it could still hold out. Attached towers increase its security.

Here would be the fittingly distinguished birthplace of the keeper's first son, most likely in the early summer of 1567,[21] yet another James Stewart. This child was soon followed by seven others, four boys and three girls: Henry, Archibald, John and Alexander; Mary, Margaret and Jean. Of this fair brood only Margaret was to die young. The young James would never have been bored for want of company. Indeed boredom was not to bedevil his short life. He lived in interesting times. It was insecurity that dogged his infancy. His birth coincided with the beginning of the civil war that was to rake Scotland for six years. In such shifting sands Sir James' tenure of Doune was never certain. He was merely a tenant even if his landlord were the monarch. His possession depended on the political balance of the moment. He was unprincipled enough to survive the intrigues of the mid century and hold onto his post come what may, but his constant vacillations and reputation for duplicity gave rise to persistent distrust at court. In 1566 he was accused of having a hand in the murder of Ricchio; later of being a sympathiser of the deposed Queen.[22] He was ordered to surrender Doune as a result. Although he soon regained it, dereliction of duty as royal gaoler almost reversed his rise. In the summer of 1569 the Regent Moray summoned him to appear before the council in Stirling to answer for the break from ward of Robert and Archibald Elliot, two notorious Border reivers. St Colme dutifully 'compeared' – surrendered himself – in early September and made his explanations. Moray gave him nine days to bring the two escapees before him or forfeit the surety of £500 each, which he had stood for them.[23] His success or failure is not recorded. When James Stewart was three or thereabouts, on 21 August 1570, his paternal home was put under siege by the new Regent, Lennox, who considered 'the Lord of Saint Colme a false and feeble tratour to the good Regent, a shame to the Stewarts.'[24] The castle yielded to him four days later. From the King it came, to the Regent it went. This, however, proved to be a mere token surrender since the chastised St Colme remained in post, and was soon imprisoning other dissidents on behalf of the Regent. By the time the civil war ended and the King's men had triumphed Doune had set himself firmly among their number. He had played the game well. He was to continue to do so for the rest of his life. There was greater security and prestige for the young boy in his father's impressive keep in Menteith than in the lovely surroundings of the more modest house at Donnibristle on the southern coast of Fife where his mother used to resort. It is likely that the young James would have spent the bulk of his time at the former residence, probably wintering in the latter. As he grew up he would thus have encountered many of the most prominent men in the land, for it was distinguished prisoners who were warded in such a place, and warded in style.[25]

If the future Earl of Moray was safe here, he was also cold. The family apartments were in the great keep. This fortification houses on its first floor the grand hall, entrance to which was gained by a steep and easily defended external stairway enclosed with a wall and guarded with a grated gate at the bottom. Northward facing, with large windows and vaulted walls it required some heating. A fine double fireplace placed at its east end is token of this need, albeit dwarfed by its surroundings and no doubt fighting a losing battle against the elements. Some would roast while others froze. From the hall a staircase leads to four private rooms in the tower, and to the floor above the hall. On this second floor is the drawing room which has another – and perhaps more effective – fireplace and a small oratory in the south window recess. Maybe a larger chapel was intended to be built in the southern wall where fine windows were inserted. If it were it was never carried out.[26] The upper storey contained similar accommodation, topped by a wooden roof. These were the private apartments for the keeper of the castle and his family. It is here that the young James would live, sleep and pray. For special occasions the staterooms of the castle would be used. Adjoining the keep to its west was the banqueting hall, a first floor building of expansive dimensions, large windows and cellars underneath. It too had a separate external staircase enclosed with a wall. When feasting took place there would be a wide display of fish, game and cured meats, and wine with comfits added.[27] At other times, especially in winter, the diet would be unimaginative and unvaried: oat cakes, porridge and broth, leavened with tough mutton and salted beef. The semi-circular tower to the north-west of the banqueting hall housed the kitchen and principal guest chamber as well as having a considerable defensive capability. Here visiting nobility or officers of state would be lodged. When the King came he would take the family apartments.

Being resident at Doune had the further added advantage of proximity to the King. It was near Stirling and not far from Edinburgh. The family basked in royal favour. The castle and its surroundings much appealed to the young monarch who frequented them as a 'commodious' summer retreat. There he could enjoy the salmon fishing in the Teith and Ardoch, and hunting the tall deer in the Braes of Menteith and the royal Forest of Glenfinlas, 'maist pleasant for our pastyme'.[28] The two adolescents, Lord James and King James, with only a year separating them, must have been regular playmates and friendships or enmities sown in those summer months may later have borne bitter fruit. Did James Stewart best the King at sport, outshine him in looks or reject him in love? Mere speculation. There is no hint of any dissension. And the King's treatment of both the fabric of his castle and of the family in custodianship of it seem to belie any animosity.

It is unlikely that the son of still so minor a man would be educated anywhere other than in Scotland, and he could have done much worse. The likes of Huntly, a scion of one of the most distinguished families in the realm, were polished by an education in France. Those aristocrats remaining at home were encouraged, even compelled, to get a fairly demanding education. An act of 1496 required all substantial barons and freeholders to send their eldest sons to grammar school from the age of eight until they were proficient in Latin, and then to university for three years 'so that they may have knowledge and understanding of the laws.'[29] Not all complied with this edict by any means, but a father who was at least as ambitious for his son as he was for himself, and who saw his own rise as the prelude and propellant to the rise of his offspring, would ensure that the young James fulfilled these requirements. The spirit of the age was changing and an unlettered aristocrat had begun to feel embarrassingly deficient.[30] The King himself, young James' contemporary, was the very model of the Renaissance man. To prosper at his court would require more than title and physical prowess. While partial to lusty good looks among his courtiers, James ultimately valued intelligence honed by education. Huntly possessed both attributes in abundance, as well as physical prowess. Moray was to demonstrate that, despite his father's best efforts, he could not compare.

But some form of education he did acquire. If Master James went to school its name is not known to us, but as a member of a family with aspirations he may have had a private tutor, a man 'learned in history, [and] upright in character,' and another symbol of distinction. Contemporary educationalists warned of the dangers inherent in 'cloistering from the common.' It encouraged 'the overweening of one's self, not compared with others.'[31] This was a danger that the young James was to fall prey to. Whatever the venue, the curriculum would include reading and writing in secretary hand, a cursive script full of strokes and abbreviations almost impenetrable to the modern eye, and a thorough grounding in Latin. In addition, the young James would learn to sing and play music, to dance and to draw. Sport and knightly exercises would take up much of his time. He would be a proficient horseman and archer. He would be trained in jousting and swordsmanship. He would play football with the retainers and the children of his servants. He would hunt on his estates with dogs or hawk. He would fish in the rich rivers embracing his home for salmon, trout, turbot and pike.[32] So in the environs of Doune the young James would grow into the tall and strong youth his contemporaries commented on, with a veneer of basic education clothing the wild barbarism of his physical and social development.

For university education the choice was between home and abroad. Catholic noblemen of the rank of Huntly would naturally look to Europe for their finishing school, but it was an expensive option and few could afford it.[33] For Protestants the obvious alternative was Oxford or Cambridge. The English were only too eager to encourage the shaping of the Scots gentry in their own universities and Elizabeth was ever ready to grant her licence to study in the south for two to three years.[34] There is no record of our subject at Oxford.[35] A James Steward [sic] is recorded as being a fellow commoner at Queen's College, Cambridge in the Easter term of 1584.[36] A fellow commoner was a socially superior sort of undergraduate, privileged to dine with the Fellows of the College. Such undergraduates were 'not in general considered as over full of learning,'[37] but were much sought after for their wealth and standing. Steward's registration appears only in the register of the college not that of the university and so we may conclude that this individual matriculated but did not graduate, the classic progress of a fellow commoner. Moray is absent from every account of transactions in

Scotland for the period 1584 and 1585. Thus this 'James Steward' may be the incognito Earl of Moray using Cambridge as a finishing school rather than as a repository of learning. On the other hand James Stewart is a common name, and by 1584 our James would surely have been styled in the matriculation register as Earl of Moray, a title he had held for three years by then.

It is more likely that the young man we are considering would have gone to university at a considerably younger age and would have done so in Scotland. It was not necessary to go abroad to acquire a decent higher education. The universities were very considerable both in number and quality for so small and poor a kingdom: St Andrews founded in 1412, Glasgow in 1451, and Aberdeen in 1495. Edinburgh was founded in 1583 when James was about eighteen years old and so would not have been his *alma mater*. Nor do its records indicate that he was a graduate of that institution.[38] Aberdeen had the single but 'noble' foundation of King's College, endowed by Bishop Elphinstone. Its disadvantages, however, were considerable. Isolated far away in the north, only recently 'liberated' from its adherence to the Old Faith, and being under the protection and influence of Huntly, it would have been most unsuitable for a thrusting young lord in a country increasingly Protestant.[39] Nor was his name included in the matriculation lists.[40] Glasgow was, in many ways, the best choice for an intelligent young man. Although poorly endowed and not at first rich in scholars, in 1574 it appointed a new principal, Andrew Melville, whose dynamism would revolutionise the course of studies not only in Glasgow but in the other universities as well. His achievement was to elevate Glasgow to parity with its more prosperous neighbours and ultimately to put Scottish higher education on a par with the best in Europe.[41] Glasgow, however, has no record of a James Stewart matriculating at this time.[42]

It was, however, St Andrews that was likely to win out. It was the most prestigious of the three southern foundations and it alone attracted well-bred students from all over Scotland. Situated on the east coast of Fife, not very far from Doune and even nearer to Donnibristle, the city was ideally placed for the young Earl of Moray and was closely associated with his predecessor to that title. The university consisted of two colleges, St Salvator's and St Leonard's. The former, founded by James Kennedy, was 'fair to look at and of good endowment,' but no other 'magnificent gift' had yet been made to the university.[43] Although the teaching had been uninspiring, dry and scholastic, in 1579 St Andrews too began the process of transformation. Within a year it had lured Melville away from Glasgow to become the first principal of the new college of St Mary's. It was probably to the revitalised St Andrews that Master James would go at about the age of thirteen, his time there coinciding with the transformation of the university and the arrival of Melville. The only contemporary James

Stewart mentioned in the records of St Andrews matriculated in 1575 and graduated in 1577. If this is our subject he must have been only eight when he began university and ten when he finished, an unlikely prodigy. The matriculation roll, however, stops in 1579.[44] Aristocrats often ended their university studies at about fifteen years of age. Thus 1580 or thereafter could have been the year of James' matriculation. His future career, however, does not suggest he benefited as much from the rigours of academe or the precepts of the principal of St Mary's as from the sporting opportunities the university's environs provided. It was the home of golf. The acquisition of learning was thought by many nobles to befit only 'mean men who intend to live by them ... but are no ways either suitable or requisite in Noblemen and such as are of any eminent rank of degree.'[45] Such views are likely to mirror those of the Earl of Moray. If he were an undergraduate at St Andrews, he may have topped off his time in Fife with an incognito year at Cambridge, to little more effect. Although there is no evidence that he went on a foreign tour, his father's horizons had been widened by his mission to France in 1560, and so may have encouraged his son to follow suit. However far he wandered, home was always Doune.

As with so many things royal during the minority of the King, Doune Castle was falling into disrepair. In August 1580 the captain had informed his master that the battling was becoming so ruinous as to render the castle uninhabitable in winter. James authorised the expenditure of the princely sum of £200 Scots for repairs. The work was put in hand almost at once under the King's master of works, Robert Drummond of Carnock, but in the event £320 Scots were spent repairing the tower head alone.[46] The patching up, if not a full scale renovation, would at least be finished in time to ensure a suitable home for their prospective daughter-in-law, Elizabeth Stewart, the eldest daughter of the 'Good Regent' and first cousin of the King, who was betrothed to their son and heir.

This extraordinary match, by which the son of a man not yet ennobled married the daughter of a man who had been all but king in his lifetime and a revered martyr after his death, was to 'the great misliking of the best part of the Earl of Moray's friends', who recoiled to see his daughter 'so meanly married as to the abbot of St Colme's son.'[47] That such an advantageous matrimonial alliance had come about was in no small measure due to the skill with which St Colme played his rather limited hand. His tactics were two pronged. He had ensured that he won the support of the King's first favourite, Esmé Stewart, Lord d'Aubigny, and he had consistently demonstrated his loyalty and usefulness to the young King.

Esmé Stewart had arrived back in Scotland from France in September 1579. He had all the right credentials of birth, breeding and looks to captivate the young King. He was James' second cousin, the first cousin of his father Darnley, and the nephew of the Regent Lennox. He became a father figure and more. Still strikingly handsome at thirty-seven, this dashing and exotic ex-patriot had quickly infatuated the thirteen year old monarch who showered titles and gifts upon him. In March 1579/80 he had been created Earl of Lennox and given command of the royal bodyguard. His star was in the ascendant, his influence was tangible and so with those had allied themselves to him, from the great – James Stewart, the recently elevated Earl of Arran – to the small – James Stewart, abbot of St Colme. It was a canny move, any friend of Lennox was a friend of the King and any friend of the King went well rewarded.[48]

Hanging on the tail of the royal favourite, keeping in with the increasingly powerful Arran, and making himself generally useful, St Colme had succeeded in advancing his own interests and ultimately those of his son. Most significantly he was to be part of the cabal that deposed Morton in December 1580. Among a whole series of royal grants that were made to St Colme in repayment for his loyalty – past and future – the most valuable was one of the earliest: the gift on 5 January 1580/1 to his son of the ward of the heritage of the late Earl of Moray, a gift which included the right to control all the lands and to determine the marriages of the two daughters of the murdered Regent, Elizabeth and Margaret.[49] Elizabeth, the elder, had succeeded to the dignity of the Countess of Moray, unprejudiced by the settlement of 1566 under which her mother had the earldom for life. Although the mechanism is not entirely clear, the earldom of Moray would pass to her husband on marriage.[50] The union was further facilitated by the fact that the two families were already linked by marriage. In 1571 the Regent's widow, Agnes, had married Colin Campbell, the future sixth Earl of Argyll. He was also the young James' uncle. Argyll naturally encouraged his wife to approve the marriage of his stepdaughter, the fifteen-year-old Elizabeth, to his thirteen-year-old nephew, St Colme's son. Neither child would have a say in the matter. They were to do their parents' bidding.

St Colme wasted no time. They were married within three weeks of the grant being made. The wedding itself took place 'on the other side of the water,' either at Doune or perhaps more likely at Donnibristle House. In contrast to old Castle Doune this was an altogether more urbane setting. The house itself was built not for defence but for comfort, not surprisingly since it was originally the residence of an abbot. The Stewart kings had attempted to build a Renaissance court centred on the capital, Edinburgh. For those on the make a country house within easy access of the capital was particularly desirable, and feasting and drinking for days and nights in a house with spectacular views of the river, a balmy haven in cold winter months, must have impressed – or irritated – rivals. The wedding day itself was on a Monday 23 January 1580/1, but the festivities lasted over a week, culminating in extravagant celebrations spanning the afternoon and evening of Tuesday 31 January 'the greatest day of solemnity.' A grand wedding celebration would put the seal of approval on the social arrival of an up and coming family and this must have ranked as the society wedding of the year. It was dominated by teenagers. The groom was thirteen, his bride fifteen, and the principal guest – now a cousin by marriage – the fourteen-year-old King. Another such 'cousin', the fourteen-year-old Francis Stewart, fifth Earl of Bothwell, would certainly have been there as well. The relatively ancient Lennox, of course, was also an honoured guest. The King took full part in the chivalrous pursuits laid on, riding at the ring, and – for a child – doing very well.[51] It was a triumph for St Colme and his son, since the latter's recognition as Earl of Moray seems to have taken place immediately after his marriage and he was styled as such as early as March or April 1581.[52] Their children – soon to come – would be born to the ermine.

The fifteen-year-old bride's beauty is nowhere alluded to, in contrast to her thirteen-year-old husband's. Contemporary descriptions of him as an adolescent and young man seem unanimous on this, though nowhere is he actually called 'bonny,' an epithet bestowed on him only much later.[53] He was the 'tallest and lustiest young nobleman within the kingdom.'[54] He was distinctive, if not distinguished, 'of very tall stature but little proof' as one perceptive observer commented.[55] 'Moray was the maist weirlyk man bayth in courage and person, for he was a comely personage, of great stature and strang body like a kemp (fighter).'[56] The memorial of him painted after his death hardly flatters, portraying him as rather well nourished, with heavy thighs and bloated torso. His look is haughty, his expression sullen, and his nose too prominent. Yet it is a death portrait, and in death the bloom soon fades.[57] At the time of his wedding, however, his looks and physique were just coming into full bloom, and his prospects were excellent.

For a son to marry a countess and for a king to attend their wedding boded well for the future prosperity of the Stewarts of Doune.[58] The father of the groom was soon to receive his own reward, ennoblement. He had served his King well and secured the King's enemies safely. Despite an escape attempt engineered by Angus, he held Morton captive in Dumbarton Castle until his execution the following summer. His death profited his gaoler enormously. Four days later St Colme was reimbursed for the sums of money he had expended, at the government's command, on the dead Earl's 'sustenation.' Morton's lands in Aberdour, forfeited to the crown, were bestowed on him. He was granted his abbacy in fee simple for himself and his children. It was now his personal fiefdom to do with as he would. Nothing was sacred to this rapacious arriviste. He immediately dismantled part of the church and sold the salvaged material to the town council of Edinburgh for the rebuilding of the tolbooth. It was almost his last act as 'protector' of the abbey, for the King, 'having respect that Sir James is descendit of his own blude,' created him Lord Doune by charter under the Great Seal on 24 November 1581.[59] His second son Henry was appointed commendator of the Abbey of St Colme's Inch in his stead.

As well as tending to his own advancement the new lord continued to supervise the affairs of his son and daughter-in-law, who were both still minors. He had already ensured his valuable offspring's future security. Acting as his son's administrator or 'tutor,' Lord Doune asserted his right to specific teind sheaves (tithes) or the fruits of certain vicarages, warning tenants and townspeople from meddling with them, taking possession of lands in his son's name, instructing the sheriff in regard to 'forthputtings and removals.' The father, all too aware of the fragility of his own rise, would let nothing escape that could give greater security to his son. As a result, by the time of his marriage Master James Stewart had land and income from Menteith, Glenfinlas, Donnibristle, Aberdour, Dalgety and several other places.[60] For the next five or six years all of their legal documents were either executed 'with the consent of Lord Doune' or by the young Earl as 'son and apparent heir to Sir James Stewart of Doune.'[61] Creditors wrote to Lord Doune when their patience finally ran out with the persistent non-payment of the Earl of Moray and his wife. In this he was walking in the shadow of his predecessor. John Wishart of Pittarro who complained to Lord Doune about his son's large unpaid bill in October 1586, was still writing repeatedly in 1588 about £333 6s 8d owed by the first Earl of Moray.[62]

The young Moray was exasperatingly different from his canny father. Letters and other documents kept in the family muniments reveal a headstrong and irresponsible young man, resistant to parental control, yet unable to fend for himself, a very modern depiction of the perennial clash between an adolescent, rebellious but dependent, and an adult, invariably right and infinitely irritating. Moray would not take advice, yet could barely survive without his father's resourcefulness. Money was at the root of it. Gambling and other debts were a constant source of friction with his parents. More serious was the poor way in which he husbanded his inheritance and the fact that he did so at a distance.[63] Rather than tending his estates, enlarging his interests and building up alliances in the north as Huntly had done, the new Earl was almost always in the south. As opposed to his northern inheritance, which was both strange and far distant, he naturally gravitated towards Doune, the place of his birth and upbringing, and Edinburgh, the seat of his ambitions. Like many members of the nobility he was eager to be within easy reach of the court, the centre of patronage, office, sinecure and influence. It was also much more fun for a young blade than northern provincial life.

In addition to these lures of the south, there had been no meeting of minds in marriage, and certainly no restraint on his behaviour. The teenage Earl of Moray seemed all too prone to put distance between himself and Elizabeth whenever he could. By putting personal preference above family duty, he was indicating a singular lack of understanding of the importance – politically as well as personally – of family gatherings. He had been married at so young an age, not for love but for advancement. Further advancement both for himself and for his father depended on acknowledging this reality and playing the role expected of him. The advancement he revelled in, the restraints of marriage he ignored. He was still a child. Lord Doune worried over, and at times reproved, a boy who was his own son before he was Moray's Earl. On one occasion, just a year after the wedding, having successfully made the boy's excuses for his failure to keep a rendezvous with his wife, the father wrote to his son at Doune, insisting that he cancel any plans to ride to Kinneil House – the recently built 'palace' of the Duke of Chatelherault – in Bo'ness, West Lothian – a more seductive lure than visiting his in-laws at Castle Gloom. Although enjoining his son to be 'merry and blithe', failure again to attend on his wife, Doune warned, would 'crab her at the heart,' and jeopardise some preferment that his father hoped to get from her mother, Dame Agnes, with whom he had 'grown very great again'. In the same letter, the ever-practical patriarch could not resist instructing his son in more mundane matters: 'command Andrew Stewart to get men to the park dyke before the sowing comes on. And ... look that ye see them at work and that they be busy until my homecoming.'

By the time the letter reached him, however, Moray was already at Kinneil. Not only was he where he was not meant to be but he was again short of money and even shorter of excuses. His angry father, while reluctantly sending him such a sum as he could 'not to play at cards and dice but to do necessary small business with,' ordered him to Doune the following Monday 'lest matters with your mother-in-law be seriously upset.'[64] Yet still Moray declined to put in the necessary appearance, instead planning to return to Kinneil. His father wrote to him once more, mixing moral blackmail with an attempt to get compliance with a concession.

> You know that the last time that you were there your good mother and wife were both angry because ye came not forward to visit them. Wherefore ye shall come hither to [Edinburgh] to visit your wife – and be in Kinneil one night on the way and another night going home again.

His mother likewise vented her displeasure at his behaviour in correspondence of her own to her wayward son.[65] Family duties were not his only failing. Lord Doune, who must have seemed like a meddlesome old man to a son revelling in his new-found opportunities, rebuked him for being as remiss at husbandry as at being a husband: 'I marvel that you did not set the men to work on the park dyke before sowing time, seeing I wrote to you for that same ...Your wife is very angry ... as you will know at meeting'.[66]

In another letter his father suggests that self-interest if nothing else should make James more attentive to his wife. Since she could not come south from Darnaway until eight days after Whitsun he should wait and escort her, 'for in doing that you shall do yourself both honour and profit and close the mouths of your enemies that speak largely on that behalf.' If he still needed money he should ask her 'to speak to her mother and get you the silver to get you your clothes and other necessaries that you have difficulty with.'[67] Doune, like all fathers, cannot resist chiding and chivvying his adolescent son. Among all the correspondence in the Moray archives, there is not a single letter by the second Earl. It may be that his letters to his family were destroyed in one of the fires that swept Donnibristle or it may be that he disregarded this irksome correspondence without deigning a reply.

In one respect Moray did his duty. He was fertile. In July 1582 his first son was born most likely the future third Earl.[68] In all Moray sired five children who were to attain adulthood. Fatherhood, his parents hoped, would act as a restraint on his waywardness and bring the couple closer together. It certainly provided another lever. Before the birth of their second grandchild, they offered to provide a retinue of servants to look after James, and his family, for up to a year, in return for which he was to sign over his pension of £500 Scots for that year, and 'to follow the counsels and admonitions of my said father in all things appertaining to his honour and mine'.[69] Some hope! Moray was proving himself to be a spoilt and selfish adolescent whom the responsibilities of fatherhood did as little to mature as the duties of station.

Lord Doune throughout his life had made a great success of self-promotion. He had carefully groomed his first son and heir to inherit and carry on the family fortunes. He had made him a staggering match, securing him an undreamt of earldom. But he could not make his son into something he was not, nor could he control what he had made. It was St Colme's tragedy that precisely that ambition and self-assertion, which was to secure the ultimate prosperity of his family, was also to lead to the murder of his child. James had been first cosseted and then transformed from being heir of a minor baron to being an eminent earl in his own right. That this extraordinary change happened to him at so young an age led him to believe that this was but the beginning of a meteoric career. Favoured in looks, by marriage, and initially by the King, he aspired to rise to ever-greater eminence, rivalling or equalling the achievement of his late father-in-law, the 'Good Regent'. The Regent's ascendancy had been made possible by his successful destruction of his northern rival, the fourth Earl of Huntly. A son (by marriage) of Moray was again in the north, so too was the grandson of Huntly. Elizabeth, Countess of Moray, had been promised as an infant to George Gordon, an alliance which would have united the two great earldoms of the north in the person of Huntly, ensuring his absolute and unchallenged hegemony. Instead she had ended up marrying James Stewart, propelling him as Earl of Moray into neighbouring rivalry with Huntly, and threatening his security. It was inevitable that they would clash. Here lay the seeds of the conflict that would destroy not the sixth Earl of Huntly but the second Earl of Moray himself.

8

TUA HOUSIS IN THE NORTH
1576–1584

There be tua famous houses in the north of Scotland, to wit, Huntly
and Moray. The house of Huntly is very mighty in men and guddis,
and so is Moray, but not comparable to the other, as all man knawis.

Historie of James Sext[1]

If two nobles of equal rank happen to be very near neighbours,
quarrels and even shedding of blood are a common thing between
them: and their very retainers cannot meet without strife.

John Major[2]

In religion doubted, and in affection French.
  The appraisal of Huntly in The Estimate of the Scottish Nobility, 1583[3]

The young heir to the Huntly title was only fourteen years old when his
father died so ingloriously on the football pitch. At the time he may
have been paying an extended visit to court since the young King was
said to be 'like to break his heart with gretting' because he would now
be deprived of the young Huntly as his playfellow and servant.[4] The
King, a virtual orphan, was easily disposed to adore those who could fill
the role of older brother or father figure. Esmé Stewart was to be the
prime example of the latter, the young Earl of Huntly of the former.

  Another who is said to have shed tears at the news, though they may
well have been crocodile ones, was the former Regent, the Earl of
Morton. He had made many enemies among the aristocracy. In March
1577/8 they inveigled him into offering his resignation from the
regency and secured his deprivation. The King from then on was to rule
in person though, as a twelve-year-old, through the advice of his
council. The wily Morton soon outwitted his opponents, however,
reasserting his authority the following month by seizing the King. Once
more he was the effective ruler of the kingdom, even if he had to forego
forever the title of Regent. He told the young Huntly's uncle, Adam
Gordon of Auchindoun, whom he had recently released from prison,
that 'for the great kindness that was lately contracted betwixt them, he
would be ane father to his fatherless, and protector to his friends and

servants.'[5] As father to the fatherless he would of course exercise complete control over the nephew of his erstwhile enemy. So it was to be. During the young Earl of Huntly's minority he was personally under the tutelage of Morton.

During this period Huntly's ample estates were administered by his Uncle Adam and from his death in 1580, by Patrick Gordon of Auchindoun. The young Huntly's was a rich inheritance in a poor country. By Scots standards but by no other he was an exceptionally wealthy man. The Scots nobility were not well off, either relatively, compared to their peers in England or France, or in absolute terms. Land and riches did not necessarily coincide. There were commoners with as much or more than the nobility. In 1577 John Kennedy of Ardmillan left £3,333 6s 8d in his will, in the following year Nicol Elphinstone of Shank left £2,666 10s 0d and in 1585 John Grant of Freuchie, who must have been one of the richest men in the country, left £6,666 13s 4d. English intelligence reports for the period 1577 to 1583 show that many of the aristocracy were facing ruin as a result of the civil war and the ensuing instability. The period of tranquillity brought by the personal rule of King James, however, was mirrored in the rising prosperity of his nobility. In 1575 James Hamilton, Duke of Chatelherault, once Regent of Scotland and the young Huntly's grand-father, left a meagre £1,604. By 1589 the great Hamilton estates brought in an income of nearly £5,000. Huntly too would prosper and by 1600 his vast lordship of Strathbogie and Lochaber would bring him an income of £4,445.[6] He would need it for he had a reputation as a prodigal spender and in particular liked to build in style.

But these estates and revenues were at present for his guardians to worry about, and only in the future for Huntly. In his mid to late teenage years he was educated as befitted his station at the University of Paris and at the court of Henry III in the cosmopolitan culture of Catholic and Renaissance Europe. Huntly's self-imposed educational exile had both freed him from Morton's immediate influence and kept him out of any danger that the turbulent times of the quasi-regency might have posed to the scion of the leading Catholic family in Scotland. The Catholic Church had high hopes of 'Rome's rising star' whose destiny – it was devoutly hoped – would be to restore 'the worship of God in Scotland one day.' And Scotland was the Catholics' 'chief hope.' Her King was heir to the throne of England and was initially thought well disposed to the faith of his mother. The following few years would be crucial. On a Catholic king in Scotland, supported by a loyal and orthodox nobility, depended 'the conversion not of England only, but of all the north of Europe.'[7] A young man in whom such flattering but fanciful hopes were placed by the losing side in the sectarian struggle was safer abroad during his formative years than at home.

While Huntly was 'furth of the realm' matters of some importance to his future northern territories came to a conclusion in April 1580 when the great feud between the Gordons and the Forbes was settled in the Privy Council. As we have seen, trouble between those bad neighbours had been simmering for years and every so often came to the boil. In July 1578, when Parliament met, Lord Forbes had complained that a number of his kinsmen were being evicted from kindly tenancies which they held in lands owned by Huntly and that they were being victimised for their opposition to the Gordons during the civil war. The local feud fast became a trial of strength between the two major factions in government: Morton's and the newly elevated Earl of Lennox's. Parliament appointed a commission to investigate the dispute, and in November 1578 the Gordons were found to have brought dishonour on the King by breaking the Pacification of Perth.

Events, however, were to move quickly against the Forbes' interest, as the rise of Lennox and the irrevocable eclipse of Morton at the centre of government altered the balance of power in Edinburgh and in the North. In March 1580 there was a skirmish on the shore at Dundee in which Sir George Gordon of Gight and Forbes of Tollie were among the slain. The Privy Council, fearful of spiralling violence, decided to impose peace, appointing another commission to investigate. The Chancellor, Argyll, represented the Gordons, and Morton himself the Forbes. In April the principals of both clans assembled in Edinburgh to negotiate terms. Parliament made a *volte face*; reversing its earlier decision and holding that the claims Forbes had made in 1578 were against the Pacification of 1573. He was forbidden to raise the matter again. Peace was imposed between the parties although feuding was to break out again in 1589 and continue until 1597.[8] The outcome of this issue was proof positive that Morton, whose will had been decisive in 1578, was by now almost a spent force. His enemies moved in for the kill. On the last day of December 1580 he was accused of involvement in the murder of Darnley and imprisoned. Despite the protestations of England and the Kirk, six months later he was dead, beheaded in Edinburgh, a victim of 'the Maiden.' He had finally fallen foul of the machinations which Lennox and his supporters easily worked on the ill-disposed King, and of a mechanical decapitating device which he had himself introduced into Scotland.

Shortly thereafter in July 1581 Huntly returned home to his northern territories. There he found a new neighbour and rival, some years his junior and his equal only in title, the recently elevated James Stewart, second Earl of Moray. For a while these two young men lived in relative harmony or at least mutual tolerance, but it was only a matter of time before it became obvious that there was not room enough for 'tua famous housis in the north.' For the present, though, Huntly bided his time. Despite being young, 'hot and hardy,' employing brute force and even savagery when expedient, Huntly was equally able to prove 'a provident and politic man, slow to engage himself in any faction or quarrel of state' until the advantage was his.[9] Before he could physically take on a fellow peer, and one whose family was so firmly in royal favour, he first had to consolidate his power base both in the north and at court.

In the former, with the resolution of his feud with the Forbes, he could avoid local conflicts until he had restored the estate to what it was before the forfeiture of his grandfather. The restoration of his power, influence, and wealth took personal form in the dozens of bonds of manrent he entered into with his neighbours over the years, and concrete form in the 'the glorious and magnifick structures and monuments [which] remain unto posterity at Strathbogie, Bois of Gight, Pleughlands, and several other places.'[10] He was 'adjudged by all who dwelt before him' and even by his enemies to be 'successful in all his enterprises and a good and just neighbour.'

But it was the King he played best. He astutely concentrated on his close relationship with the young James 'to whose humour he doth wholly bend and apply himself,' and avoided being drowned in the factionalism so prevalent in a court during a minority. At all he was adept. Although during his long career he was to prove to be one of the most arrogant and devious magnates in the kingdom, throughout the years he never jeopardised the valuable intimacy he had fostered with the playmate of his youth. From their earliest acquaintance he used an easy and engaging familiarity with his younger cousin. Once, on his arrival at court, he forgot to bow. Realising his *faux pas* he begged pardon and excused his want of respect by saying he was just come from a place where everybody bowed to him. He always remained 'a great favourite of King James who loved him entirely,' and who could trust him implicitly. By the time of his return from France, Huntly had become a young sophisticate, fluent in both French and Latin, adding to his attractiveness to an erudite but lonely King. Suggestions that Huntly was 'shallow witted' and 'a most semple man' who was only saved from himself by 'shrewd counsellors' whose advice he followed are preposterous smears. He could have been the model James had in mind when he later commended to his son those who 'garnished' the court.[11]

He acted with a deftness beyond his years in the crisis of loyalties produced by the 'Ruthven Raid'. This was the counter-blast to the demise of Morton. The Protestant party was increasingly hostile to the French bias of the government and the dominance of Esmé Stewart and his unsavoury associate, James Stewart, recently created Duke of Lennox and Earl of Arran respectively. Fearful that James would be induced to renounce the throne in favour of his mother, the ministers drew up a list of grievances and boldly presented them to an astonished King. For once he, and his favourites, underestimated the determination of the forces ranged against them. On 22 August 1582, having been warned by the English ambassador that Lennox intended to move against them, the Protestant faction led by Lord Gowrie struck first, seizing the teenage King while he was visiting Ruthven Castle in Perthshire. He was made fast prisoner. A rescue attempt by Arran was easily frustrated and Arran found himself a captive along with the King he had come to save. This seditious seizure of the King's person met with the full approval of the General Assembly of the Kirk as an act of Reformation that had preserved the True Faith from evident and certain dangers, and the King from no less evils. The English too were exultant.[12]

Huntly was quick to show his allegiance. In September he was recorded by the English ambassador as being one of the earls who 'sided wholly with Lennox.' In so doing he allied himself to a strong band of nobles including Arran, Sutherland, Athol, Bothwell, and Crawford whose ultimate aim was to secure the deliverance of the young King. Moray was described as too young to take sides.[13] An abortive attempt to seize James in Holyrood was called off.[14] The position of the Duke of Lennox was now unsustainable. James was compelled to order his beloved Esmé into exile for 'disturbing the government.' This was intended to remove him from the realm temporarily until James could reinstate him in triumph. He was never to see him again. Lennox died in France the following May. The King was desolate in his bereavement and ever more resentful of his captors who had humiliated him and effectively killed his mentor. They would pay for their disloyalty just as Huntly's loyalty towards James' first favourite, father figure, and familiar friend, would be well rewarded. He would receive Paisley and Buquhan's lands to add to his vast estates. And he would bask in the King's good favour.

Meanwhile Lord Doune was also to be a beneficiary of the Ruthven affair. He was already ensconced in the same camp as Huntly, and made himself invaluable by arranging for Huntly, Athol, Argyll and Marischal to rendezvous with the King at Falkland, no doubt to make preparations for his escape. This was not long coming. On 25 June 1583 the King rode out from Falkland Palace, eluded his captors, and took refuge in St Andrews Castle. Huntly and the others were already there by prior arrangement. Arran was immediately restored, and Mar and his associates fled to England. Gowrie, who had cannily procured a pardon, stayed put. This dealing on the part of Doune got caustic criticism from Francis Walsingham, the new English ambassador, who predicted his downfall. He could not have been wider of the mark since, inexorably, Doune continued the advance of his family. On 17 June, before James' escape, Argyll had leant his ambitious nephew another helping hand, entreating the King to baptise the young son of the 'daughter of the Earl of Moray who had been married to the eldest son of the laird of Doune,' an indication both of the importance of the Moray family and of the reluctance of the English to award the title of earl to the mere husband of the Regent's daughter.[15]

The strength of James' feelings for Huntly, now that Lennox was dead increased, as the King's intervention in his love life reveals. Huntly had become enamoured of the daughter of Sir Thomas Kerr of Fernihurst. This came about when Huntly helped to secure the safe recall of the Catholic laird who had been banished for his part in the murder of Darnley. He entered Scotland in September 1583 and for a while stayed with Huntly at Strathbogie waiting for his complete reha-bilitation. Kerr's wife Janet impressed upon him how he was 'mekill bund to that gentil man for his gud offyces and contenuall payne and travel.' So indebted that he ought to give the good Earl his daughter in marriage. James was vehemently opposed and declared his views in such terms that the ardent lover fell ill of grief.[16] James kept Huntly all the more with him, until his ardour wore off. He was only reconciled to Huntly marrying when the object of his affection was Esmé's daughter. This may well explain James' extraordinary loyalty to and affection for Huntly throughout his life. He was a reincarnation of his first love.

Huntly had successfully wooed the King. Keen to be secure against any eventuality, he then turned his attentions on the King's mother. Again aided by Lady Fernihurst, who commended the young Earl to the exiled Queen, he began a correspondence with Mary. She welcomed contact with one so close to her son. Huntly on his part declared that for her sake he would anxiously watch over James. He was as good as his word. Prompted by Elizabeth, the Hamiltons and Ruthvens rose in the spring of 1584 in another attempt to seize the King. Their plot came to nothing. The chief contriver, Gowrie, was taken prisoner and executed for this treason if not his last. His co-conspirators fled to Berwick. Huntly took a prominent part in the suppression of the confederates. His services on the part of James were acknowledged by Mary.[17]

While Huntly learnt the subtle crafts of diplomacy and honed his skills of charm and flattery, Lord Doune was for the first time over-playing his hand. He obviously enjoyed centre stage and as one newly ennobled wanted to make his mark. He began to see himself as equal to any in the realm. For the first time he turned coat on the King and aligned himself with the Protestant faction. Styling himself the 'father of the religious and well-affected in Scotland', with astonishing temerity, he had written to the King in December 1583, demanding a stay to a feared persecution of the Kirk, and concluding that otherwise he would be the last of his name that should reign in that realm. This was no way to address a King now shaking off the thralldom of childhood and coming into his own. A few months later Doune again admonished the King when James excepted the son of Sir James Balfour from the prescriptions imposed for his involvement in the murder of Darnley. 'Downe denied and withstood the matter, saying, "God forbid that the King should so little regard his father's murder." James retorted tartly, "You forgave your father's murther, why shall I not forgive mine?"'[18]

His son was also getting beyond himself. The death of Colin Campbell, the sixth Earl of Argyll, in September 1584 while staying with Moray at Darnaway left a minor as heir. The great strength of Clan Campbell was fragmented as rival factions sought to control it. An opportunity seemed to present itself for someone to fill the vacuum. The obvious contender was the Earl of Huntly, but the Earl of Moray saw himself as equally in the running: Argyll was his step-father-in-law, had died at his house, and had made his will there. Huntly had the land, the retainers, and the personality to rank as one of the greatest aristocrats in the land. Moray had none of these. Only an immature novice could have put himself on a par with Huntly. The Gordons had been unchallenged in the north for so long and Huntly had entrenched his position so well that any attempt by the Morays to improve their lot at his expense would come as an affront and would not go unchallenged. Huntly would deeply resent any incursions into territory where for so long his family had reigned supreme. If there were now two houses in the north, one alone was built on rock, the other on sand.

9
BANGING IT OUT BRAVELY
1584-1588

Every great personage in that realm pretendeth to be a king, and thereby take liberty to commit strange and great insolences and oppressions on the weaker sort.

Francis Walsingham[1]

The natural sickness that I have perceived [the nobility] subject to in my time hath been a feckless arrogant conceit of their greatness and power... For any displeasure, that they apprehend to be done unto them by their neighbours, [they] take up a plain feud against him, and (without respect to God, King or commonweal) ... bang it out bravely, he and all his kin, against him and all his.

James VI[2]

The first violent incident in 'the deadly feud notoriously knawin' between the two Earls was in June 1584 when Alexander Leslie, a tenant of Huntly, killed one Sym, a Spey fisherman in the employ of Moray.[3]

Disputes over fishing rights were no mere childish spats over demarcation lines between bad neighbours. Hard-pressed landowners viewed the rich revenue from the rivers as vital to their survival. Fishing the salmon on a commercial basis was a source of considerable profit in the north, and a right jealously guarded. It was estimated that salmon accounted for a third of the value of fish exported from Scotland at the beginning of the seventeenth century.[4] The income from fishing could finance the sort of lifestyle to which the great earls of the north aspired. Aberdeen was the most important centre in Scotland for the trade in cured and salted salmon. Of all the rivers in Scotland the Spey was the richest in fish. George Douglas, late Bishop of Moray, had granted the fertile lands surrounding his palace at Spynie and the Spey fishing rights to the Regent Moray, rights, which descended to the second Earl. However, after the bishop's death, Huntly had instigated litigation in an attempt to have the dowager Countess's titles to Spynie reduced. As a result he had taken possession of the Spey fisheries, the Castle of Spynie, and all the bishop's goods. Dame Agnes had been in legal dispute with Huntly ever since.[5] This dispute the new Earl of Moray fell heir to.

The sixteenth-century Scots historian, John Major, bemoaned the truism that 'from the beginning of time families at strife with one another make bequest of hatred to their children; and thus do they cultivate hatred in the place of God. So had it been in the days of Abraham and Lot when even the shepherds would not keep the peace.'[6] Whatever may have been the case among the Patriarchs it was certainly true that Scotland had long had an unruly nobility. Hereditary blood-feuds arising out of perceived slights or rival claims were the pastime of the gentry and aristocracy of Scotland, and Scottish history has been described − not unfairly − as one 'long brawl.'[7] Foreigners considered Scotland to be a: 'kingdom under arms, for all the friends of one faction mistrust all those of the other faction; insomuch that not only the nobles are in arms, but churchmen, friars and peasants travel through the country only in large companies, and all armed with jacks, swords, bucklers, and a half-pike in hand.'[8] Violent and eager clashes between rivals and their retainers such as the one that engulfed Sym should come as no surprise.

Youth, of course, was the unavoidable and inevitable spearhead of feudal aggression. War, disease and murder kept the peerage young and aggressive. The average age of the higher nobility in 1587 − the Duke of Lennox, Lord Hamilton, and twenty-two earls − was around twenty-seven. Seven of these were children, two were in their late fifties, three were middle-aged, and the remaining twelve were in their twenties and early thirties. These young men − Glencairn, Athol, Bothwell, Caithness, Errol, Huntly, Mar and Moray − were to be responsible for a great deal of violence over the next few years.[9]

The worst example by far was Francis Stewart, Earl of Bothwell. The son of one of James V's bastards and the nephew of Mary's third husband, he was the cousin of the King as well as being of an age with him. Like many another Border reiver, he 'lived for violent action, riding from Protestant or Catholic plot to Border brawl.'[10] Neither of his religions restrained his propensity to sudden and savage violence. A football foul had led him at the age of seventeen to challenge the master of Marischal to a duel, an encounter thwarted by the Earl of Angus who had brought it to the attention of the King. The latter had used his offices to reconcile the two young hotheads.[11] Five years later Bothwell had stabbed Sir William Stewart to death in Blackfriars Wynde in Edinburgh. During a drunken argument between the two young men Sir William had bade him kiss his arse. Bothwell drew his sword and thrust it into Sir William's back forcing it out of his belly.[12] On another occasion Bothwell and a retainer had taken on Robert Kerr, the laird of Cessford and his servant outside Edinburgh and had fought until Cessford withdrew.[13] His own brother-in-law complained of the trouble he had to keep him in order. Duels, drunken stabbings and the like were commonplace among the aristocracy. Bothwell's actions, however, took him beyond the usual wild spirits. His attack on the Edinburgh tolbooth to free one of his retainers, his association with witchcraft and sorcery, and his madcap attempts to unseat King James, throw serious doubt on his mental stability. He was, in short and certainly in the King's eyes, an impetuous, arrogant thug 'walking along the dark edge of insanity.'[14] In our day would be labelled a psychopath. He was not alone among the nobility.

Education – or the lack of it – was held to blame for irascibility of the nobility. In 1521 the ever perceptive John Major lamented the fact that 'the gentry educate their children neither in letters nor in morals – no small calamity to the state.'[15] Over sixty years later the diarist, James Melville, indicated that there had been little improvement: 'The nobility and gentlemen are unlearned themselves, and take no delight to have their children and friends brought up in lettres, to the great reproach and shame of the country and their own great hurt and dishonour.'[16] The critics of this philistine attitude on the part of the nobility believed that aristocrats 'endowed with reason' would not only find it much easier 'to live together in peace' but would no longer 'stir up sedition.'[17]

Despite the veneer of culture some of the senior aristocracy aspired to, formal schooling seemed to do little to undermine the lessons taught at home or diminish the habits of violence inculcated in childhood and youth. As soon as they could walk they would ride, and hunt and fight. Disciplining such hot-headed and headstrong youths could be a perilous task. In one notorious incident, grammar school pupils – led by 'gentlemen's bairns' – seized their own school and shot and killed a town official in defending it. They had been denied a privilege they were accustomed to, and 'a number of scholars ... made ane mutiny and came in the night and took the school and provided themselves with meat, drink, hagbuts, pistols and sword.' They reinforced the doors of the school and refused to let in their master, or any other, unless they were granted their accustomed privilege. The provost sent a baillie called MacMorrane to put the school in order. He went to the school with some officers and demanded entrance, which was refused. MacMorrane and the officer tried to knock the door down using a large timber beam as a battering ram. One scholar 'bade him desist from dinging up the door with the gest or else he swore he would shoot a pair of bullets through his head.' The baillie carried on and from a window William Sinclair shot him through the head. 'The bairns' were excluded from the school, and given detention in the tolbooth for this insubordination, but were soon released without further punishment.[18]

Noble-born adolescents even had 'youth clubs' to foster their aggressive self-reliance. In the north-east the 'Society and Company of Boys' otherwise known as 'The Knights of the Mortar' was established to instil manly virtues and camaraderie, but soon degenerated into a violent and criminal fraternity whose members prowled the land armed with hagbuts and pistols committing 'robberies, slaughters and oppressions.' They bound themselves with solemn oaths of loyalty to the gang and to each other, and would unite in support of any member in his quarrel with any outsider. To slight or cross one was to slight or cross all. They were no respecters of persons and none but the mightiest was immune from their threat. The Edinburgh authorities could fume and vent their spleen in issuing edicts about such 'seditious assemblies.' They could demand the summary suppression of such 'detestable fellowships,' but were impotent in the face of the indifference of local authorities who did not necessarily share their monochrome view. The delinquency of such young men was often ignored by their elders since their ruthless and reckless comportment marked them out as the ideal agents for a little intimidation here and the odd act of elimination there. The 'Society of Boys' provided a fertile recruiting ground for the likes of John Gordon of Gight and his associates. The sixth Earl of Huntly, not usually noted for his patience and restraint, was indulgent to a fault, and was strongly reprimanded by the Privy Council for his 'lang patience and connivance' in not suppressing these 'debauched and lawless lymmers [rogues].'[19]

Violent temperaments were easily armed. Weapons came readily to hand, and the prevalence of rapiers worn at the waist, and pistols light enough to be carried in a belt, meant that street fighting became increasingly lethal. There had been a proclamation as far back as 1567 prohibiting the wearing of guns or pistols or 'any sicklyke fyerwork ingyne' under pain of death, the King's guard and soldiers excepted.[20] The refined English agent, Thomas Randolph, found the coarseness of Scottish culture hard to take. He wrote to the Earl of Sussex: 'It is but a late practice to shoot men with arquebuses, which begins pretilly to increase. God make me quit of the country.'[21] Scotland could be typified in 1585 as a land where 'every man carries a pistol at his girdle,'[22] in lands where every man did, any confrontation could easily end up as a homicide.

Major spoke of the senior tenantry of the great earls, those who had servants to cultivate their plot and whose sons went into service as the lord's retainers – holding their lord in devotion, looking forward to his feuds, and keeping horse and weapons so that they could make his quarrel their own, 'be it just or unjust ... if only they have a liking for him, and with him if need be [they will] fight to the death.' They welcomed any provocation, were ready to see slights and returned 'any blow upon the spot.' Those tenants who were not so enthusiastic about getting involved in their landlord's quarrels were drawn in by their utter dependency on him. The power of eviction was a serious incentive. Under the feudal system it was also the case that any injury, be it ever so slight, to either man, beast, or property was perceived to be injury done to that man's lord. To fail to avenge that injury was a disgrace and a dereliction of duty. The defence of their vassals and dependants was a constant cause of the outbreak, and of the continuation, of a quarrel between one great noble and another. 'If he could not defend those who looked to him for protection, the very reason for his existence was at an end.'[23]

There was always the very real danger that violence begun between two individuals could conflagrate a large area and feuds begun in the provinces would spill over into the court or on to the streets of the capital. In Edinburgh there were 'frequent slaughters, bloodshed, arson and open robberies, thefts and oppression.' Street violence was no novelty in the 1580s. In 1585 the Privy Council warned those attending court to 'contain themselves in honest behaviour and quietness,' nor to attack one another 'for auld feud or new' under pain of death.[24]

The only law in country parts was that imposed by the aristocracy. It has been well said that while it is 'correct to see Scotland as a feuding society, it is wrong to see it as a lawless one.'[25] Feuds were resolved locally, on the principle of compensation rather than retribution. Feuding parties could be bought off, and frequently were. The acquisition of money or land was ultimately more satisfying to a family at feud than the sight of the dismembered corpse of their enemy. Ultimately that may be so, but the emotions stirred by the shedding of blood engendered years of violence and depredation before any armistice could be agreed. And violence had tentacles. When aristocrats were at feud, or even just at loggerheads, their retainers often settled their own scores, confident that they had a licence so to act and of protection once they did. The great nobles may not have incited all the violence, but their actions or example promoted it, and their own feuds sanctioned it.

Two murders, both of them in the same month of May 1587, both of them of Grants, and both of them by henchman of Huntly, were cited as being elements in the feud between Huntly and Moray,[26] despite the fact that a truce was in operation at the time. Alan Grant, kinsman of John Grant of Freuchy, was killed in Drumbulge by Alexander Gordon of Lesmour. This was trumped by the savage despatch of the son of Alistair Grant. He was suspended by the 'bagestanes' (testicles) by Patrick Gordon and five or six accomplices. They bound his head and feet together 'in the crook', and beat him to death. Though perhaps unjustified, the assumption that Huntly had put his kinsmen up to these killings was a natural one.

The falling out between Huntly and Moray was uppermost in the King's mind when in May 1586 he called a meeting at Holyrood of all those among his nobility who were at feud. Huntly and Moray both attended: they shook hands; they drank to one another; and the King led them – like lovers or schoolchildren – hand in hand to Mercat Cross where the city put on a grand banquet. The King drank peace and happiness to all; 'the like thing was never before seen in Edinburgh.'[27] Huntly we are told was soon 'stricken with a frenzy,' perhaps a late response to this unnatural and uncharacteristic effeminacy.[28] James, on the other hand, placed great faith in such liturgies of reconciliation, and was always more willing to welcome the penitent than to punish the incorrigible. He wanted to bridle and tame the aristocracy, not extirpate it.

This was no sign of weakness, however. During the adult years of his reign James imposed his will on the fractious aristocracy who had made his childhood and adolescence so unstable. His mother had been deposed and exiled by them. He had suffered the indignities of a long minority when he seemed to be a mere pawn in the hands of his leading nobles. James had observed that the swollen power of the lords arose from the fact that for forty years or more, the kingdom had been governed by women, little children, and traitorous and avaricious regents.

> During the divisions and troubles happening in that time the nobility by an unbridled liberty had become so audacious in leaning on those who commanded them, that now it is not possible to subdue and reduce them all at once to their duty, but that little by little he would give them in good order...

And so he did. When he entered his majority on 19 June 1587, his first appointment as Chancellor was Sir John Maitland whose brother had served Mary in the same office. For the following eight years, until his death in 1595, this 'man of rare parts'[29] was the prime political influence on the King. He could command his master's intellectual assent and amuse him as well. But above all this was a man whom James could trust. He was the King's man first and foremost.

The two subtlest politicians in the realm, the King and his Chancellor, were to prove the most successful practitioners of the games aristocrats played, and were the prime beneficiaries. The one had to rule the kingdom, manoeuvring for space between the competing claims of his nobles; the other had to administer the affairs of state, without a powerful clan or clientele to support him. A hopelessly divided and easily affronted nobility they learned to play off brilliantly. The Chancellor ran risks, taking the brunt of their disquiet and deflecting it from his King. Archbishop Spottiswood observed, that 'no man ever carried himself in his place so wisely nor sustained it more courageously against his enemies than he did.'[30] Wisdom and courage were both required of the meritocratic Maitland when confronted by the ire of an ancient and arrogant aristocracy. The Earl of Huntly was a prominent figure among that group. Protestant and Catholic lords, so often at daggers drawn, would unite in their detestation of this shadow of the King, but not all their efforts could depose Maitland from his position near the throne. In contrast to the calm professionalism of his Chancellor, the King considered that the histrionic attitude of his nobility was a reversion to infantilism and squabbling. Privy councillors they might be, but the major offices of state were placed in the hands of the *noblesse de robe*, which he and Maitland created and it was from this group that James took his political advisers. He did had not wish 'ever to advance any earl or lord, but only simple soldiers and gentlemen ... whom he could always ... ruin ... as easily as he had made them, but if these earls were in their places it would not be in his power to have his will of them,' he confided in the French ambassador.[31] He consistently excluded them from the sphere of royal administration. Nonetheless, James remained friendly with many of his nobles. He enjoyed their company but not their pretensions. On the other hand he left them well alone in their own shires. Apart from the judicial legislation of 1587 James and Maitland made no effort to shake the aristocracy's local pre-eminence.[32] They were safe in their spheres so long as they did not impinge on his or threaten, by their puerile feuds, to plunge their localities into civil war. This remained a real danger throughout the remainder of the sixteenth century.

The north, far away and isolated from royal control, was always a prime flashpoint. As rivals regrouped, as old allegiances were broken, and as new alliances were forged, the hegemony of one earl or chieftain or another was threatened. Despite the royal reconciliation imposed on the two main protagonists, the winter months of 1586-7 were disturbed by another dispute involving Huntly, this time with John Stewart, fifth Earl of Athol. Athol sent men to plunder the lands of Drummond of Blair, who had switched from Athol's lordship to that of Huntly, and of Menzies of Wemyss, who was wavering. This was known as the 'Ronie Rode' because it happened when patches of ice (rones) covered the road. Huntly outlawed the raiders; Athol gave them succour. Both lords began levying forces, and when the King intervened telling them to settle by law, Huntly refused to yield, insisting on his rights to deal with the matter in his own courts. To forestall further trouble, the Privy Council hastily convened and found in Huntly's favour.[33] By sheer bravado, not to say arrogance, Huntly had triumphed. He was the King's officer, and in this case right was on his side. Such factors were not enough to quell the mutterings of those who thought the King over partial to his lord lieutenant.

This partiality was both political and personal. James, believing that the most significant opposition to his claim to the English throne would come from the Catholics, both in England and abroad, adopted a policy of leniency towards the leaders of Scottish Catholicism, notably Huntly. Huntly, he had reason to believe, was more loyal to him, and the benefits he could bestow, than to the old religion and a losing cause. Perhaps it is true that James' coddling of Huntly would not have gone as far as it did if he had felt more confident about the English succession,[34] but personal affection tended the King in the same direction. Huntly was described to Walsingham as 'a great courtier' knowing more of the King's secrets than any other. He even 'lay in his highness' chamber' in Holyrood, a privilege bestowed only on the closest of the King's intimates. Just how intimate George and James were, is open to conjecture. Sir Lewis Bellenden, the Justice Clerk, while deprecating the fact that the Earl of Huntly '[lay] in his majestie chambre and preaces papistrie' took comfort from his observation that although Huntly be 'ane papiste he was not so precise as he had not rather lyie in a faire gentlewoman's chambre than either in the Kinges or yet where he might have ane hundrethe messes.' This familiarity, however, made the more distant and less cynical English nervous. Even treasonable dealings with Spain could not dent James 'extraordinary affection to Huntly' and the Earl could 'persuade his majesty to any matters to serve his own particular or friends.'[35] This continued to place a question mark on James' adherence to the Protestant faith, a matter of crucial importance to the English and his own subjects.[36]

Possessive as he could be, James took a paternal delight in the marriage of his favourites if it was to someone of whom he approved. Huntly was no exception. Having frustrated the amorous inclinations of Huntly towards Kerr of Fernihurst's daughter, the King took the lead and in September 1586 arranged a contract of marriage between Huntly and Henrietta Stewart, eldest daughter of his beloved Esmé. The King instructed Huntly to send to France for her and granted him 5,000 merks towards the expenses. Thus would he entwine the two main strands of his affection. Huntly finally married Henrietta on 21 July 1588. This coupling proved beyond doubt to himself and the world that he was firmly ensconced in royal favour. The wedding itself was to take place in Holyrood. James took an extraordinarily paternal interest in its detail, writing in person to the laird of Abercairny to get him such scarce commodities as venison, wild fowl, fed capons, and such others as he could procure in time.[37] For the celebrations afterwards he even began to compose a masque in which he himself would take a part and which would have been a prelude to jousting. In it he saluted his 'brother dear/Who are prepared for glove or ring or any sport with spear.'[38] The masque was never finished but the marriage went ahead. The ceremony was presided over by Bishop Adamson of St Andrews in defiance of a resolution of the presbytery of Edinburgh who had required the Earl to give satisfactory proof of his steadiness to the reformed religion. Huntly's Christian confession was fairly fluid and his preparedness to 'turn Protestant for the occasion' satisfied the bishop.[39] James, acting in *loco parentis* as he loved to do, gave the fatherless bride away to Huntly. It was a wise match. Henrietta was fertile bearing nine healthy children.[40] In addition she proved 'a virtuous wife and a prudent lady,' a daughter in all but blood of the King and a great confidant of the Queen, well able years later to take control of the earldom when her husband was forced into exile and equally adept at representing his interests at court.[41]

Even after his marriage Huntly kept his personal ties with the King very strong. Over the winter of 1588-9 he more or less lived with James at Holyrood. James remained 'a most affectionate and loving prince' towards Huntly, swaying between the paternal and the amorous, signing himself 'your dad, James R,' as later he was notoriously to do to Buckingham, and admitting that his 'Good Son' was constantly on his mind: 'My good Son, I may on my saule swear unto you, that sen your parting fra here I was never ane hour unthinking upon you, but when I was sleipand and scarcely then.'[42] James had adopted the older Huntly, and like any good father he would forgive all and ultimately defend him against anything and anyone.

10

A PARTICULAR FRIEND
AND A GENERAL CHRISTIAN
KING
1587–1589

As ye have offended two persons in me, a particular friend and a general Christian king, so must ye make amends to both these ... repent you of all your faults, that in heart and mouth with the forlorn son ye may say 'Peccavi in caelum et contra te' [I have sinned against heaven and against you].

James VI[1]

Huntlaeus homo minime ambitiosus, minime turbidus, sed ad quietum proclivis.
[Huntly is man little given to ambition or to faction but one who inclines towards the quiet life.][2]

During the height of his dispute with Huntly, the young Moray contemplated a three-year continental tour to France, Flanders and Germany. He wanted a 'finish' befitting his station to compensate for his erstwhile rather parochial education. He asked for, and immediately received, a passport for this purpose.[3] The King would be relieved to see him go. His tenants reassured him that they 'would do very well' in his absence. His wife, who was at Darnaway a lot more often than her husband – as the one-way correspondence shows – agreed, with the caveat that he tied up all loose ends before he went, 'the neglect of which will cause many here to have an evil opinion of you.'[4] Even his father seemed anxious to get him away for a while, perhaps in the hope that foreign travel would exhaust his pleasure seeking and bring some maturity, and that he would return with a greater commitment to his responsibilities and not just a readiness to spend his father's money, neglect his tenants, and quarrel with his neighbours.[5] The tour never took place. It may have been partly because the feud with Huntly was growing more intemperate. Enmity would keep him at home where duty had singularly failed. The main reason, however, was financial: he simply had no money for such an expedition. Despite his father's careful husbanding, Moray's income did not match his life-style. At the time he was contemplating foreign travel his finances were in a parlous state, and he was getting increasingly into debt as the large number of unpaid bills ending up on his father's desk testified.[6]

Times were hard, even for the nobility, at the close of the century. In the two decades between 1585 and 1605 there was a dramatic fall in rural incomes brought about by a combination of high inflation and a succession of poor harvests. Debts mounted inexorably. All the nobility were affected but the feckless more than the rest. Lending had been made easier by a relaxation in the laws against usury; borrowing was an alluring way to pay for today by mortgaging the future. Even the more prudent had to borrow; the imprudent had to hazard their estates.[7]

In many cases, Moray's included, the costs of several residences compounded the problem. The refurbishment of Moray's country seat of Darnaway was a major expense since no expense was spared, and the Darnaway estate did not bring in the revenues it should have done because of the poor way it was managed and its susceptibility to hostile depredations, cattle rustling and over-fishing. 'There is nothing at Darnaway,' her agent quipped when despatching to Lady Moray a parcel of the finest hand plaid to be got in Elgin, 'but great expense and daily spending.'[8]

Large debts were regularly accrued – if not always paid – for the Earl's town house in Leith. In September 1588 Moray paid £342 for eight tons and a puncheon of wine. In March 1590 he owed £205 to an Edinburgh merchant, John Reid, for domestic supplies, a bill that was not paid until August – and then it had to be paid with interest and by Lady Moray. In August Moray also settled his tailor's bill: 1,000 merks. The following February £100 was owed to another merchant, James Lauder, for furnishings. It had still not been paid in July despite several reminders. He owed 600 merks to William Duncan of Dundee for goldsmith work including a gold belt and chain.[9] A silver basin and laver and gold goblets 'according to the new fashion' were sought from the best but most expensive source, George Heriott, the King's goldsmith. Creditors were getting canny. Michael Gilbert, the factor John Leslie informed his lord, would not give him the cup he wanted without ready money and even the goblet upon which the Earl had his arms engraved would not be released until he sent money. Those not so canny rued the fact. William Stalker, the jeweller, was not paid for over ten years. With his inheritance of the late Earl of Moray's title and lands the second Earl also inherited his predecessor's debts, and year by year there were demands for their repayment. The sums were considerable. John Wishart of Pitarrow, the son of the comptroller under Queen Mary, made repeated demands for the payment of £333 6s 8d owed to his father by the late Regent. James

Findlayson, a burgess of Dundee, was owed £2,017 6s 8d; money still not paid in full at the close of 1591.[10]

Lord Doune took matters into his own hands, arranging for the despatch to his son of 3,000 merks, and securing on his behalf a £1,000 loan from Andrew Abercrombie and Alan Cowtis, good friends of the family. Doune wrote to his wayward son, telling him that these vital injections of cash were conditional on his attending a meeting with the lenders at Donnibristle the following Sunday night, but that he should get there the day before at the latest, so that they could consult 'on your hard turns that fall in great heaps.' Young Moray, in such trying times, would need all the support he could get. His wife had been seriously ill and her father-in-law prayed that God 'give her strength to get on her feet for to meet the perilous turns that are practised against her and her bairns.'[11] An ominous note.

National necessity and royal command, however, at this time enforced an uneasy co-operation between the two houses. The threat of the Spanish Armada meant that in August 1588 Huntly and Moray were both appointed commissioners to guard the north, Huntly for the swathe of shires along the north-east – Cromartie, Inverness, Nairne, Forres, Elgin, Banff, and Aberdeen – Moray for the far less significant central area between the Rivers Ness and Spey, 'baith hieland and lawland.' Their enmities seemed to be quenched 'yet the sparks lay only under the ashes which small occasions might ... cause to break into great flames.'[12] Continuing incidents on Speyside, where tenants of their respective earls regularly came into contact and where such contact often led to bloodshed, constituted just such 'small occasions.'

Rumours in Edinburgh of a successful landing in Moray's territory and his Papist leanings, unfounded though they were, undid what standing the commission gave him with the King, and showed the distrust in which he was held. Huntly was a Catholic, strong willed but high minded and utterly loyal to his King; Moray was immature, petulant and fickle. Such characteristics led not to royal approbation but to distrust and distance. Over the next few years, as Huntly assiduously attended the sederunts [meetings] of the Privy Council, Moray and even Doune, both now out of favour, gave up on them. Between August 1587 and July 1592, Huntly is recorded as attending eighteen, Moray none, and his father, Lord Doune, only one.[13]

They were not alone in regarding the predominance of Huntly with disquiet. Bothwell was jealous, the recently appointed Chancellor, Maitland, uneasy. The latter trusted neither Huntly nor his faction. He was deceived neither by their show of piety or by their flattery.[14] His fears increased as he heard of a conspiracy on the part of the Catholic faction to ambush him in Fife early in October. He reported his concerns to the King. However strong his personal affection for Huntly, James would not let it blind him to the dangers. He ordered Huntly back to the north and advised him to look to his religion if he valued his favour.[15] Huntly, always sensitive to political realities, quickly realised he had overstepped himself and changed tack. He informed the King of the plot, told him he had nothing to do with it, and was formally reconciled to Maitland.

His reward for this return to favour was considerable. On 28 November 1588 he was appointed captain of the guard at Holyrood. With the office came the right to appoint followers to the guard. It would soon be reported that all the 'beloved' royal servants in 'chamber or stable' were clients of the Earl of Huntly.[16] Such powers of patronage were an important means of repaying past service and ensuring future dependence. But more: under a long line of regents, he who had secured the King's person had controlled the realm. It was not so under self-rule, but the office of captain and the influence it accorded, was still a very powerful perk. Huntly's accession was a bitter blow to Bothwell who had been vying with him for months over this prestigious position. The animosity between the two reached such a pitch − 'even to stabbing and shooting one another'− that it was feared that 'if the king take it not up in time it will cost one of their lives.'[17]

James was adept at this sort of thing. He stepped so dextrously between the rival earls 'that neither of them can tell who hath him surest, and he telleth some secretly he will be no maintainer of factions, therefore he will be no partaker with anyone, but will show himself when time serves.' Ultimately it was to be no contest. Despite his self-aggrandisement and the occasional disloyalty that accompanied it, Huntly was the King's friend and, in the last resort, he was trustworthy. Bothwell was neither. In addition to royal favour Huntly could call on his old allies and co-religionists, Errol and Athol, to support him in any emergency. Bothwell had no loyal friends or supporters, with the exception perhaps of the feckless Earl of Moray his cousin german, two losers who found solace in each other's arms. At times court factions would seek Bothwell's support as 'an undertaking man,' a grudging tribute to his personal dynamism and ability to muster men to a cause. But he was rightly considered fickle, and no party could be sure of him: 'feared of both sides, trusted by neither' was his disastrous political epitaph, one that ensured his ultimate failure. 'The king and all good men [were] weary of him.'[18]

Maitland was reconciled. Bothwell was outrun at court. Moray was isolated in the north. With his unrivalled influence at court and in closet, with his regional hegemony and local lieutenancy, Huntly was in power and strength second only to the King. Even Queen Elizabeth was uncharacteristically disposed to look favourably upon him.[19] Perhaps she recognised a fellow professional in the game of politics.

The more usual English position was distrust. They were never sure whom they could rely on to serve their interests in Scotland. Scottish politics were every bit as confusing as English observers thought them to be. 'It is hard to judge today,' lamented the English ambassador, William Ashby, 'what will be tomorrow, especially in this court suffering such alteration and "waltering" as is incredible.'[20] No alliance was for long. Fidelity was a shifting sand. Constancy was of a moment. Old enemies united against old friends, whoever was the common enemy, whoever was the current dominant force. In their desire to ascend to the summit of power they would join hands with their rivals on the ladder to pull down those above them on the steps. And so it would go on. Even religion was not sacred. A generation before everyone had been Catholic. Old loyalties were often superimposed on new, and all loyalties were fluid. Huntly was not unique in swinging easily between his long-term, innate and in-bred Catholicism and, from time to time, a pragmatic assumption of fidelity to the Kirk. As he could embrace the new religion so others could rediscover the old. The English had long suspected Moray's father of 'Papistical leanings,' and in one dispatch to Francis Walsingham Moray himself is called not only a Papist but also a friend of Huntly. Ashby was also under the impression that Moray was in the same faction as Huntly and the Chancellor.[21] If it were the case that Huntly and Moray were for once aligned it must have been for some short-term political advantage. It was another indication that Moray was capable of all the political ineptitude of his friend Bothwell.

English approbation of Huntly was not to last. In February 1588/9 rumours reached Elizabeth that three Englishmen who had escaped the Tower while awaiting their fate for assisting Mary had been received into Huntly's house. Worse was to come. In the same month a young man called Thomas Pringle was intercepted south of the border bearing letters in cipher to both the Duke of Parma and Philip II of Spain. The writers – or so it seemed – were Crawford, Maxwell, Errol, Lord Claud Hamilton and Huntly and they wrote in the name of the Roman Catholics of Scotland. Huntly professed his adherence to the Catholic faith. His apostasy he explained as a tactical ploy. He had had to choose between subscribing to the Protestant articles of religion and exile. By remaining at home and subscribing he had been able to secure many of his own men in the royal bodyguard and was strongly placed to become master of the King's person. He lamented that the Armada had not landed in Scotland where it would have found plenty of allies, and promised that even then if 6,000 men were sent an invasion of England would be launched within six weeks of their arrival. Mar, Glamis, and Bothwell were among others implicated in this damning correspondence. Elizabeth sent the letters to James with a letter of her own demanding the immediate imprisonment of these dissembling lords. She expressed her dismay that James seemed to hold such traitors 'near and dear.' 'Good Lord,' she exclaimed in her blunt exasperation, 'methinks I do dream. No king a week could bear this.'[22]

Yet bear it he did. James would not read the letters. Huntly denied their authenticity and alleged that his enemies had counterfeited them, always a distinct possibility in the sixteenth century. James believed him at first, until compelled by English insistence to accept the letters as genuine. The irate and impatient Elizabeth demanded action. James could do not less than imprison him for a time in Edinburgh Castle but without the rigours that England expected.[23] The King's belated disappointment with his friend seems to have been genuine but short-lived. After receiving an entreaty from Huntly that he might speak to him, James wrote in his own hand to the incarcerated Earl: 'What further trust can I have in your promise, confidence in your constancy, or estimation of your honest meaning.' Huntly had offended both his King and his friend. He must make amends to both. To the King he must conceal nothing, reveal his associates and the extent of his plotting. To the friend he must repent all his faults and entrust himself into his hands as a prodigal son to his father against whom – as against heaven – he had sinned.[24] It was a breach, not a rupture, in their long relationship.

The following day, 1 March, the King went to dinner in the castle, where he gave Huntly leave to send for his wife, friends and servants. The next day he went to visit him again. The King 'kissed him often, and protested he knew he was innocent.'[25] The English agent, Sir Thomas Fowler, could only wonder at the King's 'strange, extraordinary affection to Huntly,' which enabled the recipient to 'persuade his majesty to any matters to serve his own particular or friends.' When the king wanted to mollify Elizabeth – and he was loath to offend her – he would 'yield and promise much,' but when 'Huntly or his solicitors come in place he forgets all and many say they doubt him bewitched.' Fowler had no doubts that James was genuinely Protestant, 'a mortal enemy of Popery' and well disposed to England, but he was still very young and prey to flattery. His support for Huntly was not an indication of a secret hankering after Rome but was born out of strong personal affection – 'overgood' as the English termed it.[26] The King indeed sought to 'persuade him from papistry,' and thought he had prevailed. Huntly 'subscribed to the Church whereat the king rejoiced exceedingly.' A couple of days later, on the 7 March, Huntly was released. That night he spent in the King's bedchamber. Five days later he was restored as captain of the guard. Again the King dined at Huntly's house 'and so from day to day ceased not to show what favour he could devise.' Significantly Huntly avoided all matters of state but proved the King's boon companion in sport and pastimes and was adept at flattery.[27] He was being exactly what – in James eyes – a nobleman ought to be.

The King's next godly task was to try to bring about a reconciliation between his favourite and his Chancellor who was 'beloved in another sort,' both of whom in their respective ways were necessary to him and both of whom he wanted at court. With Huntly at the heart of government Catholics could take comfort that their position was protected from the worst excesses of Protestant zeal. Huntly represented an essentially if erratically loyal conservatism far preferable to the sort of treasonous dissent to which a totally disaffected Catholic population could succumb.

Maitland on the other hand was at the centre of the Anglophile Protestant grouping so vital for James' greatest aspirations. Maitland irked Huntly. He embodied both the displacement of the nobility at the heart of government and an engagement with a heretical England antithetical to the Francophile Catholic party. As Lord Burghley had perceptively observed, Huntly's dalliance with Parma was largely motivated by 'a particular dislike of the Chancellor than any common cause,' and Spanish money, regularly solicited and regularly received, was used to enhance his own position rather than directly advancing the Catholic interest. Consequently, although a reconciliation of sorts was patched up 'it never lasted forty days without some suspicion or jar.'[28]

The wary Chancellor remained concerned about Huntly's control of the guard and the threat to the Protestant cause and to his own safety that that control constituted. He refused to come to Holyrood without his own guards and persuaded the King to grant him a commission to raise 100 horse around him, ostensibly to apprehend 'offenders to religion, the realm and James himself,' but really to provide a safeguard for himself and, if necessary, the King. This impinged on Huntly's prerogative, as captain of the guard, to ensure the royal person. Maitland would not back down. He told James to his face that if Huntly remained in such a position of influence he would not have a Protestant left in Scotland to follow him. Rather, they would 'leave him to the papists and would provide securely for themselves.' The Chancellor was not finished. The King was blind to his favourite's dissimulation, he warned, and vowed no more to serve his majesty nor come to court so long as Huntly had charge of the guard. The Privy Council backed the Chancellor and argued long and hard that the King relieve Huntly of his captaincy and order him to leave Edinburgh and return north. James finally consented. To do otherwise would have brought the resignation of Maitland, an eventuality not to be countenanced. He was 'beloved of the king in another sort, for he manages the whole affairs of this country.'[29] Where political necessity and personal predilection clashed James was a 'general Christian king' first and foremost, before he was 'a particular friend.'

Huntly tried one last and unsubtle stratagem to maintain his hold on the King and sever that of the Chancellor. On 13 March, accompanied only by the English ambassador and Huntly and his friends, James went hunting. After this they were to dine together. During the morning despatches arrived which claimed that rioting had broken out in Edinburgh. Then Bothwell turned up, at that time thick with Huntly and ever ready to act as a desperado, soon followed by Errol with a dozen men. This was the former's first appearance since he had fled when Huntly was committed. Huntly met him and brought him to the King.[30] He related that a plot instigated by Maitland was afoot to assassinate Huntly on the return of the hunting party to the capital. Huntly protested that it would also be too dangerous for the King to return and urged him to go into safe keeping with him and his friends. It would not have taken a man as astute as James to see through this contrivance. They talked for an hour but the King was adamant and said he would rather die than go with them. He was no longer a child to be a plaything of overweening magnates. With that Huntly made off. He could easily have forced the King, but when persuasion and subterfuge failed, he would capitulate. It was a pattern to be repeated. James' trust proved ultimately well placed. Huntly made for Dunfermline, the King returned to an Edinburgh untroubled by violence.[31]

James was reluctant to make much of this but Maitland, as anxious for his own position as that of his master, immediately put measures in place to secure the King. The first was to discharge Huntly's guard. The next was to summon the city forces to arms. No attack came, but Bothwell did, a few days later, sent by Huntly to explain away the meeting and clear their names. The attempt was premature and disingenuous, the messenger inapt, 'using very hot speeches from Huntly in the name of the rest' until 'the king put him to silence.' Huntly then retired to Strathbogie, leaving a melancholy King who it was hoped would soon forget his favourite.[32]

Not if Huntly could help it. He may have made a tactical retreat to his own lands, but he left behind many of his friends, two of whom made a particular impact on the King. The more senior was the younger, the fourteen-year-old Ludovick Stewart, the second Duke of Lennox. He was 'so proper a youth, so wise, staid, active on horse and foot, courteous of such entertainment and carrying of himself, so pleasing to all men, being reasonable high and well made, as truly he is a paragon.' He was also the son of James's first paramour. Unsurprisingly, the King 'loved him as himself.' Lennox was as enchanted with Huntly as the King was with him. The elder but more junior was Alexander Lindsay, the younger brother of the eleventh Earl of Crawford. Not only was he 'the king's best loved minion, and a proper man,' but he was 'Huntly's wholly.' These two young men had the King's ear and worked such 'great effect for Huntly' that the Chancellor could not mend it.[33]

Despite his reverses, Huntly retained a dominance in the north and an influence in the south that Moray could not begin to match. Moray had constantly attended court in recent months but it availed him nothing.[34] He tried to put pressure on Huntly by having him put to the horn in March 1589 but his messenger who carried the message to Banff barely escaped with his life.[35] Horning – or outlawry – posed little threat to so powerful a peer as Huntly. It was in any case a blunt instrument as well as a short-term one since most of those outlawed continued to live undisturbed, knowing that the greatest threat came not from the crown but from enemies who tried to exploit their legal vulnerability. Huntly was not vulnerable, unless by his own actions he made himself so.

Within a month of his outlawry Huntly was acting the part, conspiring with Bothwell and Errol, Crawford and Montrose to challenge the pro-

English hegemony at court by ridding the King of his Chancellor and seizing the royal person. One night in early April the King was staying at Hawghton near Edinburgh when he received word that Bothwell had gathered forces in Kelso 'to free [him] from those who had prostituted him to England' and was bent on capturing him. The King took horse at midnight and eluded him. Bothwell rode with a mere 300 horse in pursuit. But James had been too quick for him and by three in the morning was safe in Maitland's house in Edinburgh. Bothwell had no choice but to withdraw to Dalkeith where he was joined by a further 300 horse and other followers and supporters including Crawford and Montrose. Simultaneously Huntly and Errol had successfully raised men in their domains. A crown official commented that the barons of the north-east were so dependent on Huntly that they have 'forgot their duty to their natural Prince.'[36] Thus began the Brig O'Dee rebellion, more a tantrum than a serious threat, motivated more by politics and position than by religious idealism, and aimed at the Chancellor rather than at the King himself.

Love Huntly as he might, James was not so partial as to neglect his duties as a king or fail to defend the security of the throne and the Chancellor who had done so much to sustain it. His head, when it came to matters of high state, as we have seen, ruled his heart. In any case his attitude to the psychotic Bothwell was very different from his attitude to Huntly, and the King vented most of his spleen on the former. James rallied the loyal lords, brought all boats this side of the Forth, and warned all towns to arm and resist. He issued a proclamation ordering all men to forsake the service of Bothwell and Huntly on pain of treason. The element of surprise gone and James' opposition apparent, the rebel Earls began to make their excuses: Huntly was come south to visit his wife; Bothwell had brought retainers as self-protection after a dispute with a neighbour. The King would have none of it. Furious with Bothwell's lèse-majesté, he was further enraged by the maltreatment accorded his herald and the contemptuous manner in which the proclamation had been ripped in pieces. He lacked both money and men, but James did not lack resolution. He was determined to stamp royal authority on his unruly nobles.[37] He marched from Edinburgh to Linlithgow to await the muster of the forces his name could command. Errol's keepers of his castles at Slains and Logiealmond were ordered to deliver them within six hours under pain of treason. The following day the King proceeded to Stirling and so into Fife in order to join with the loyal earls to put down the rebellion. Moray, unwisely, was not with him.

The rebels also lacked resources. They had not anticipated a protracted campaign. Huntly's forces were fewer than he had hoped for. Bothwell had overestimated the numbers he could raise especially in the Borders. He was soon reduced to thirty horse. Home, an erstwhile conspirator, deserted to the King. Bothwell, Huntly, Crawford and Errol withdrew north. Passing through Perth they captured Sir Thomas Lyon, the master of Glamis, having been forewarned that he had gathered forces to entrap them there. Crawford wanted him killed but Huntly and Errol forbade it. Crawford 'retired in discontent.'[38] The King followed apace even more irritated by the indignity inflicted on Lyon.

When on 18 April the King arrived at Cowie near Aberdeen, the rebel lords prepared for battle. Fearing a night attack, wrote one of his men, James 'would not so much as lie down on his bed but went about like a good captain encouraging us.'[39] When the rebels marched out of the city to the Bridge of Dee with 3,000 men, the King, although fielding a force of only 1,000, would not be intimidated. The rebel Lords had given out that their aim was to free the King who was 'held captive and forced against his mind' but the presence of the King against them gave the lie to this statement. Buoyed up by the rebels' superiority in men, Errol 'would have foughten,' but Huntly shied away from a battle when faced by James in person. Huntly freed the master of Glamis, and dissolved his army. James entered Aberdeen without loss. The laird of Grant, the Forbes and the Drummonds and others who lived around Huntly's lands came before the King to pledge their belated loyalty. Huntly in turn was made prisoner by Sir Thomas Lyon, and strongly guarded in the Tower of Torriesoul. James would neither see him nor speak to him, mortified that he had not surrendered to him in person. He sent the captive on to Edinburgh where he was kept under arrest in a strong house in the town.[40] Sir Thomas Fowler, Elizabeth's representative, urged drastic reprisals including his speedy execution. James would not go that far, excusing the wayward Earl as 'but young, merry, disinterested in matters of state, and easily led to evil or good,' but assured the ambassador that he would proceed against Huntly's supporters 'as well as ever his hounds hunted a hare.'[41] The ambassador knew that this hound had little taste for the kill. He went away marvelling at the contrast between the two neighbouring monarchs in their attitudes to treason.

Huntly was soon to be restored to favour. He wrote to James begging a private audience. The King initially refused this request, perhaps recalling how his resolve dissolved when they were together, but more likely to mollify the English. However, if an undated letter from James is attributable to this time, as its contents and reference to a trial suggest, he secretly advised Huntly how best to comport himself in his coming adversity and reassured him that he retained royal favour even if it could not be openly shown for a time.

> I troue ye are not sa unwise, milord, as to misinterpret my exterior behaviour the last day, seeing what ye did ye did it not without my allowance, and that by your humility in the action itself, your honouring of me served to countervail the

dishonouring of me by others before, but perceiving by my expectation that baith noblemen and councilors, to wash their hands of that turn, and lay the haill burding upon me, I thocht the hurting of myself and their looping free could be na pleasure nor wiell unto you, for gif that impediment had not been, assure yourself I would fainer have spoken with you than ye would with me for many causes that were langsum [lengthy] to write. Always assure yourself, and the rest of your marrowis [comrades], that I am earnester to have the day of your trial to hold forduart [forward] than your-selves, that be our services thereafter the tyranny of their mutins [legal action] may be repressit [repulsed] for I protest before God in extremity, I love the religion they outwardly profess, and hate their presumptuous and seditious behaviour, and for your part in particular I trowe ye have had proof of my mind towards you at all times, and gif of my favour to you ye doubt, ye are the only man in Scotland that doubts thereof, sen all your enemies will needs bind it on my back.[42]

Acting on this advice, Huntly petitioned for a speedy trial or voluntary banishment. Bothwell who had been gathering troops in the south, now dissolved them when he heard of Huntly's capitulation and made abject surrender on 11 May in a formal ceremony in Maitland's back garden.[43] The English did all they could – including bribery – to secure Huntly's conviction and execution. The nobility however were afraid 'to toche him in blud' and meant to arraign him, convict him but stay judgement, proceedings past the comprehension of the English ambassador.[44] Even more than the nobility, the King would have him pardoned.

On Saturday 24 May Huntly, Bothwell and Crawford were arraigned and tried, the trial lasting until two o'clock on the Sunday. Huntly pleaded guilty, as did Crawford. Bothwell was found guilty by his peers – Hamilton, Angus, Marischal, Marr, Athol, Morton, Seton, Fleminge, Yester, Dingwell, Awtrye, and Home. The leaders of the Kirk clamoured for their execution but without any realistic prospects of securing it. That evening the King went to dinner with Sir Thomas Fowler and inveighed against Bothwell and Crawford, 'showing great misliking for them.' In contrast he spoke warmly of Huntly's confession as showing him a plain man corrupted by others, especially Montrose, Errol and Bothwell. Bothwell was by far the greatest enemy, 'a bloody man infected with all notorious vices.'[45] To James he had become the bogeyman and all errors into which others fell could be attributed to his malign – even Satanic – influence. The following Monday brought judgement. Huntly was absolved from treason since his actions were solely against the Chancellor, not the King. A brief warding a few miles from Edinburgh in Burtyke

Castle with daily rides out of his prison 'to take the air' was the extent of his punishment.[46] Where Huntly was concerned James would scold but never too severely and never for very long. The rehabilitation of his friend he rather rushed on this occasion. He restored him to the captaincy of the guard, returning things to the status quo before the rebellion had begun. Maitland was livid and again threatened to resign. Again it was clear that he was serious. Huntly was removed from this sensitive office and once more sent back to the north.

Having survived royal displeasure but being deprived of office in administration, Huntly wisely resolved to his reinforce his hegemony at home. Assiduously he built up his strength with bricks and mortar and with flesh and blood. He built for substance and show. He erected a new stronghold in Riffen in Badenoch near to his hunting forests, and he enlarged his house at Bog of Gight.[47] There his first-born was baptised into the Catholic faith by Robert Grant. Huntly might play religion as he played politics, but when it came to the matter of his son's ultimate salvation there was no prevarication.[48] Huntly cultivated fields and friend-ships and created alliances. He made a bond with Errol to keep 'sure and infallible affection, goodwill and friendship to each other, and defend one another against all other persons, the king only excepted.'[49] He was frequently present on his estates, and, when he was absent, loyal Gordons were everywhere looking after his interests and impressing his will. They were also constantly taking advantage of the disorganisation and demoral-isation on the Moray estates nearby.

Those estates received one fillip: a royal visit. The King decided to tour Grampian to supervise the process of collecting fines and pledges from those lately involved in rebellion. He was accompanied by – among others – both Glamis and Moray. On 14 July they stayed together at Darnaway, the first royal visit there since Mary's stay in 1562 and a sign to Huntly that the King had other friends in the north. It was almost as unusual for Darnaway to hold its Earl as its sovereign. Moray may not have gone on a continental tour but his presence in Scotland did not equate with his presence in the north. His usual absence did not make the task of those who had to administer the earldom any easier. With the exception of the loyal and trustworthy George Dunbar, his sheriff, the quality of those he appointed to run his estates was in question.[50] This was a serious omission when he was so often far from home and communications being as poor as they were. Industry and trustworthiness were the indispensable qualities of such agents.

William Douglas of Earlshill, his bailiff, represented the visible and public face of his authority, presiding over the barony court, administering justice, and punishing felons, assisted in this by sergeants and other officers. He wrote to Moray about the disposal of three thieves they had caught. Some 'broken men' [outlaws] were to be released soon and

Douglas would know the Earl's will should they enter his lands. On the same day Douglas wrote to the Countess, at greater length, informing her of threats from 'a band of loose men who belong to the late John Fressell of Knok, especially tua of his bygotine [bastard] sons who are common thieves' to kill him if he entered the lands of Auchindowir that the Earl had given him 'in tack.'[51] This correspondence suggests that the Countess was as much, or more, involved with life in the north than her husband. It also betrays a pestering anxiety or lack of decisiveness on the part of the bailiff. His incapacity when on duty was matched by his frequent unauthorised absences from that duty. But who was to check and keep account? Similarly the large number of complaints from tenants to the sheriff evidence their distrust of, and discontent with, his chamberlain, the chief financial officer of the estate, who should have dealt personally with all matters relating to the administration of his lands and livestock, and the gathering of rents. The chamberlain construed his remit so narrowly as merely to ensure that 'his wife's bairns' had some rent, neglecting some duties and carrying out others without concern for either the human cost or the effect on the reputation of his master, the absentee landlord.

Dunbar was the one officer who bore the brunt of the local discontent with how affairs on the Moray estates were being conducted, being 'daily cumbered with the complaints of your Lordship's poor folks how they are molested by great and small who are neighbours to your Lordships lands, and no man to find fault with the same.' James Torrie of Logie, for instance, reported that rustlers had driven off his cattle while he was away with the Earl in February. They had been thwarted by the intervention of 'good friends and neighbours within the forest of Darnaway' who had chased them so vigorously that they had been forced to abandon the cattle to escape with their lives. Every day Torrie went 'in fear of [his] life of lymmers but if your Lordship was in the country they would stand in more awe and I would fear them less.'[52] In Moray's absence brigandage became ever more bold, rents were resisted and encroachments were made on his tenants' rights and his own lands. One such neighbour had caused ditches to be made on Moray's lands and appropriated the same to the tenant's injury. One young man called Garnside troubled tenants in their pasturage and the men of Rothes sought to appropriate Glen Corremel. All Dunbar could do is to tell the tenants 'to defend their marches,' but they were overwhelmed. 'This is one part of the news of this country,' he ended, 'but I am more angry that your lordship's land is lawless than anything that ever I saw.'[53] Dunbar's frustration with his Lord is impressed on every letter. Moray was too seldom in the north and he had 'too few Stewarts living upon his lands.'[54]

The dangers of this neglect were made all the worse by the King's departure from his kingdom. James had come of age, quieted his nobles, and imposed his will. He must now ensure the succession. On 20 August 1589 he married Anne of Denmark, by proxy. Accompanied by his Chancellor, he sailed for Denmark to marry her in person. She was fourteen, her husband twenty-four. Her portraits show a rather plain, masculine looking woman. She would be good breeding stock; he would do his dynastic duty, but for more sustained relationships the King would always look elsewhere.

The King was out of Scotland for many months, a long and vital period when the enmity of Huntly and Moray grew unchecked, fostered if anything by the intervention of Bothwell who had been left in charge. Given Bothwell's recent history this was an odd appointment, but James was always inclined to give a second chance to the most wayward of sinners in the hope that by giving them responsibility they might live up to it. The alternative was Huntly, and Maitland feared him far more than he did the erratic Bothwell. The Chancellor thus supported Bothwell as Regent in the King's absence. To secure his position against Huntly, Bothwell in turn allied with Moray, Athol and other the Stewarts. He then ostensibly tried to use his good offices to end the feud between Moray and Huntly.[55]

Fishing and property rights on Speyside were still the main matters in contention. Huntly in a sly letter to the Clerk Register had got his case in first, pledging his good behaviour in the King's absence in Denmark, but hinting that this would be all the more assured were the King to find in his favour over the Bishop of Moray's estates.[56] The King left the country without deciding the issue. This apart, Huntly, as ever, was getting the better of his neighbour. He could take what advantage he pleased and many of the incursions complained of by Moray's stewards were of his men poaching and encroaching on his neighbour's properties. Impotent in the face of these depredations, in frustration Moray resorted once more to the law. He and his wife had Huntly put to the horn for not desisting from 'all entering and putting of cobles [short flat-bottomed rowing boats], coracles and nets upon the water of Inverspey and fishings thereof' and for 'molesting them in their twa part cobles fishing, coracles and nets fishing of the said water.' In addition Moray filed a claim for £800,000 for damage to his property during five raids by Huntly on his lands.[57] The year ended on an ominous note:

> Disdain and Envy, that still invade the mind of man to corrupt all friendly tranquillity, did so assault the mind of the Earl of Moray that he fell out with Huntly, which turned at last to his own ruin.[58]

11

DISDAIN AND ENVY
1589-1591/2

His Majesties peaceable good subjects over all his realm have been troubled heavily with bloodshed, stowth, reiff [plundering], masterful oppressions, convocations and other enormities, to their great hurt and skaith [injury] without redress or punishment of the offenders.

Acts of the Privy Council, 1582[1]

It is notourlie knawin to the lords of counsel quhat deidlie feiddis, querrellis and contraverseis hes fallin out amangis noblemen, barons and utheris, universallie ouer all the parts of this realm, be granting of private commissiounes of iusticiare and lieutennendre to certain particular persons, quhilkis for the mast ware purchest, nocht samekill upone ane desire they had to the executioune of iustice and puneschement of offenders, as to be revengit upon persons aganis quhome they professit evil and iniquity... George Earl of Huntly ... under cullour thairof hes soucht the liffis and blude of [John Earl of Athol, James Earl of Moray, Simon Lord Fraser of Lovett, Lachlin Mcintosh of Dunnachtan, John Grant of Freuchy, John Cambell of Caddell [Cawdor], Patrick Dunbar of Boigholl and others] thair servandis, proper men, tennentis, dependeris and partaikeris.

Decreet of the Privy Council, 1590[2]

Things rapidly worsened with the new year. Huntly had scornfully ignored the legal proceedings instigated by the Morays against him. In April 1590 they took out letters of treason for his disregard of the horning. He was charged to deliver his castles and to enter into ward in the royal prison fortress of Blackness on pain of treason.[3] The messenger tried to deliver the letters to Huntly at Bog of Gight or Strathbogie but, as he plaintively put it, he had 'no power to apprehend such a man.'[4] Another of Moray's servants, James Stewart, 'barely escaped with his life' when registering the Earl of Huntly at the horn in Banff. Huntly, understandably 'very commovit' [enraged] at being put to the horn, as Moray's bailiff, William Douglas, warned, took the initiative and summoned his noble neighbours and Dame Elizabeth to appear before the Privy Council to justify their actions against him.[5] The sort of overblown posturing and impotent escalation Moray had engaged in could not be sustained in the light of public scrutiny. Moray failed to appear. Huntly in person protested to his fellow councillors that since he 'had passed personally to the shore or waterside of the said fishing and his cobbles drawn from the said water and discharged his fishers of any further fishing with the said cobbles, nets or coracles' the letters of treason should be suspended.[6] They were. The King, recently arrived back with his fifteen-year-old bride, made it plain to Moray that he would not tolerate this easy recourse to dreadful remedies for petty injury: he 'mislikes no order in the realm worse than that of passing to the horn.'[7]

James was clearly not happy with the comportment of the nobility he had left in charge on trust for several months. His natural anxieties primarily focussed on Bothwell. His mistrust of that Earl had been resurrected when, returning from Denmark, the royal ship had almost foundered in a storm. James was suspicious, and his suspicions increased when several supposed witches whom he had had arrested implicated Bothwell in the storm. Maitland in all probability framed him, playing on the King's credulity. James, so level headed in most things, was credulous in the extreme when it came to witchcraft and he prided himself on his detailed knowledge of the phenomenon. Since the days of Macbeth it had been viewed as a seditious compact with the Satanic powers, designed to usurp the divine institution of kingship. Spurred to action by fear and anger the King personally led troops to North Berwick in an attempt to discover a 'Black Mass' in which Bothwell was thought to be involved. He was increasingly concerned at the prospect of a powerful Stewart faction grouping itself around the wayward Earl, co-conspirators in vice. On the departure of his wedding guests, James had contemplated placing Huntly, Errol, Bothwell, and Montrose in ward to prevent future mischief. But he changed his mind. He will 'rather seek to keep two factions,' wrote Sir Robert Bowes, the English ambassador, 'or else by fair means to unite all together.'[8] This policy the King consistently pursued.

He did so in the face of strong opposition from his Chancellor and the stern advice of Elizabeth that he should suppress rather than conciliate the northern earls. 'It will make him to be the better obeyed whilst he reigned,' wrote Burghley, 'and therein facies hominis is facies leonis' (the appearance of the man is as the appearance of a lion).[9] The Earl of Worcester, as English envoy with the Garter, appears to have extracted a promise from James that he would take stern measures. The King told Bowes that he remembered his Queen's advice and would keep his promise in good time. Bowes ruefully noted that there was 'no surety of the accomplishment of his promises.'[10] They were more easily made than enacted. James was concerned enough about Elizabeth's reaction to his procrastination to instruct his ambassador, Sir John Carmichael, that in the event of his lenity being misconstrued his answer should be that whereas it was true that James was 'naturally inclined to clemency, abhorring rigorous extremity unless by justice and mere necessity enforced thereto' it was the experience of Scottish kings when dealing with their people that 'a rigorous procedure has often rather moved not repressed rebellions.' This fact inclined the King all the more 'to abstain from hard procedure.'[11]

The Scots Kirk was as opposed as the English Queen to any manifestation of Christian charity on the part of their King. The godly ministers misliked James' propensity to lenity and only grudgingly were brought to approve the royal dispensation of mercy towards his enemies. At a meeting of the council, that ministers of the presbytery of Edinburgh attended, it was generally agreed that the confederates of the Brig O'Dee rebellion should be received, under certain conditions, back into the King's grace. As a result, Errol was detached from his associates and reconciled to the King and the Chancellor. From another confederate, Adam Gordon, the laird of Auchindoun, James received the original roll call of conspirators, the 'bond of the rode of the Brig O'Dee,' and thus secured a hold over the others. Another six months passed, and Huntly, despite Maitland's protests, received a full remission for all his offences.

Circumstances had proved too strong for the Chancellor. Incessant intrigues at court threatened to undermine his position and to jeopardise his policies. He had tried to remain neutral or at least noncommittal. He had resisted the offers of the Catholic party, and the plots of the notorious master of Gray. Moray had incautiously tried to inveigle him into the Stewart faction at court. The canny Chancellor would have none of it, predicting that the association 'shall one day stir some trouble in this realm.'[12] But his position had been weakened by the discords among his Protestant fellow-councillors, the main cause being the jealousy and ambition of the master of Glamis. Glamis had been the mediator for Errol, and had been supported by Morton and Mar. The Chancellor confessed to Bowes that he had been compelled to agree with Huntly by the King's express commands 'and he acknowledgeth that by the sight of Glamis' secret courting of these noblemen, for his own strength he was driven to show the more favour to [the Spanish faction].' He could not bear alone the burden and wrath of all malcontents.[13]

Huntly's fortunes were once more in the ascendant. As they rose the House of Moray took a dreadful blow. On 20 July 1590, its only begettor, Lord Doune, died. The Earl of Moray, so long reliant on his father for advice, admonition and support, was on his own. The wealth of experience of the one in matters of courtly intrigue and politics was replaced by the immaturity, impetuosity and inexperience of the other. The extent of his day to day responsibilities – the drudgery of estate administration – had doubled as he added his father's lands in the south to those he already mismanaged in the north. It was another reason for him to further neglect the latter. Only a month after his accession to the lordship of Doune, his cousin William Stewart of Seton, displaying the bluntness of a man frustrated beyond endurance, wrote warning Moray that his enemies were taking steps to encroach on his lands in the north:

> They talk a great deal about how their possession shall serve them for a good claim and that they shall cut your tent ropes if you come there. I cannot abide the proud speaking in these snafflers ... My Lord, you had never the like to do since you came to manhood, so that by the handling of this turn you shall get esteem or simple contempt of all men and [if you do not act resolutely] it shall give occasion to every man bordering your lands to oppress your tenants and shame your self ... For as God lives, rather than have you not do this turn as you should, I had rather for my own part be banished from the country all my days.'

Seton saw daily the depredations committed. He had fulfilled his duty – and exonerated himself of any responsibility – in appraising Moray of them, and 'if after advisement you neglect the same yourself, the burden will lie on your own shoulders.'[14]

The taking of liberties by lesser men when their lord was away, and continual encroaching on Moray's rights and privileges, both fomented by Huntly, provided constant friction. 'The dismal contention' between the two northern Earls now broke out in open rupture.[15] Moray had letters of inhibition issued against his rival, but Huntly ignored them.[16] In brazen response he persuaded the King to turn over Spynie Palace, the erstwhile residence of the Bishops of Moray – and another property in dispute between them – to Alexander Lindsay, Huntly's young protege. In the face of this provocation Moray could do nothing. The forces ranged against him were too great. Were the balance to change, however, Moray would seek to be the centre of opposition and its main beneficiary.

An opportunity soon arose in autumn 1590, when a number of grievances coalesced. Huntly's aggrandising plans had been frightening his neighbours for some time. He had recently built Riffen Castle in Badenoch, stamping his presence on the geographical heart of the Highlands, which comprised the upper strath of the River Spey. Badenoch, as we have seen, was home to members of the ancient Clan Chattan, which included the Mackintoshes of Dunnachten. Their chief, Lachlan, fearing that this was a prelude to his family's final subjugation, renounced his traditional, if reluctant dependence on Huntly, and threw in his lot with the neighbouring Grants, another clan, erstwhile retainers of the old earldom of Moray, that had long vacillated between friendship and rivalry with the more dominant House of Huntly. Their laird, John Grant of Freuchy promised to assist, maintain and defend Lachlan 'in case any earl within this realm wrangeously [illegally] or by ardour of law, by themselves and their assisters, by force or violence, invades, troubles, molests, or pursues the said Lachlan.' The Grants also managed to draw in many of the Dunbars who lived between Inverness and Forres, all of whom had the Earl of Moray as their patron. On 1 November 1590 a general bond of mutual assistance was made in which Moray, Grant, and John Campbell of Cawdor were joined by Athol, Lovat, Stewart of Grantully, Sutherland of Duffus, Grant of Rothiemurchus and Grant of Bellintone.[17] Huntly's traditional satellites were being subverted by the usurper, Moray. His position in the north was being jeopardised by this coalition of malcontents. Behind this turn of events, Huntly feared, lay the hand of Chancellor Maitland. He was probably right to so suspect. At court the Chancellor had been overruled by James when the royal favourite had been reinstated. If an opportunity arose in the north to rein Huntly in Maitland would welcome it. According to the *Historie of James Sext*, Maitland was perfectly prepared to play the politics of divide and rule, and actively incited Campbell of Cawdor and the laird of Grant to 'engender jars' between Huntly and Moray.[18] Fomented or not by the machinations of Maitland, jars there were aplenty.

The 'jar' finally sparking the whole feud into fire arose out of a November marriage in Ballindalloch, the very heart of Grant country. When the laird of Grant died, leaving a rich widow, his kinsman, the tutor of Ballindalloch, John Grant, tried to stake his claim to some of her inheritance. She just happened to be the sister of Alexander Gordon of Lesmour and appealed to him for help. His eldest son, James Gordon, was despatched to her rescue and rode to Ballindalloch with his friends to have it out with the tutor. Tempers quickly flared, and the two parties came to blows, an encounter which left servants on both sides injured but the Gordons the victors. To secure their hard won gains and strengthen the position of their kinswoman, the family of Lesmour persuaded John Gordon, brother of the laird of Cluny, and one of Huntly's most beloved friends, to marry her. At the celebrations home-distilled whisky flowed and tempers flared. John Grant quarrelled with the groom and, 'after some jars,' killed one of his servants on the high road. John Gordon reported the murder to the justices, Grant was denounced rebel, and commission was given to Huntly as sheriff of the country to apprehend him.[19] Branding one northern magnate an outlaw and making another his pursuer was bound to cause increased bitterness and resentment. So events were to prove.

Huntly went to Ballindalloch Castle to apprehend Grant and his accomplices. On 2 November he took the house by force but those he sought were not within. The whole clan was affronted. The new laird of Grant promised to answer a summons to hand the felons over, but broke his word and failed to appear. He was denounced as rebel. The Grants, Chattans and Dunbars all looked for support to their new champion, Moray, who in turn called on Athol to assist in curbing

Huntly's pretensions. Cawdor, Mackintosh and Grant advised the earls to seize the opportunity 'and now or never afterwards to resist the House of Huntly and to make themselves strong in the north having at this time so great a party and being so well friended at court.'[20] Such an alliance against Huntly was much more serious than a man's murder. Huntly's policing operation to catch a killer had provoked a war.

He discovered that Moray, Grant and the others were to meet on 22 November with their confederates in Athol's house in Baweny in Forres. Taking 200 armed men with him Huntly decided to make this first meeting their last and dissolve it by force. He and his men arrived too late since Athol and Moray had already returned to Darnaway. Huntly dispatched an officer at arms with a dozen men to arrest the participants in what he considered to be an illegal conspiracy. Before they could get near to the house a large group of Moray's, Grant's and Mackintosh's retainers rushed out, and saw them off, firing pistols as Huntly's men retreated.[21]

This was a serious affront to Huntly's delegated authority as law officer of the crown and not one that could be ignored even by a less belligerent lieutenant than Huntly. He increased his force to 300 men and went himself to Darnaway to apprehend Grant who was holed up there with Moray and Mackintosh. Anticipating this move, however, Athol, Grant, Cawdor, and Mackintosh had taken to the hills. Moray remained in his well fortified, manned and provisioned castle, convinced that the raid, ostensibly directed at the apprehension of John Grant, would not stop at his own murder. For once he may not have exaggerated the danger, nor underestimated his opponent. In a petition of exemption from the Earl of Huntly's commission, made to the King's council the following January by Athol, Grant of Freuchie and others, the petitioners cited this attack on Darnaway as 'a maist queer and cruel enterprise ... they would have entered by force and craft and would have killed Moray and his family and servants if God had not defended them and provided remedy thereto.'[22] Moray refused Huntly entry. Huntly's men could only circle the castle on horseback. Those holed up behind such thick walls could taunt and irritate their powerless pursuers. There was a discharge of muskets from the fortifications and John Gordon, the hapless master of the murdered servant, was struck by a lucky shot which entered in at his mouth and came out of his neck, killing him instantly.[23] Enraged but impotent before such strong walls and so many armed defenders, Huntly was forced to withdraw. The resentment he felt for his rival was made even more personal by the death of his friend, and even more bitter by his inability to chastise his ingrate, erstwhile retainers. A recently ennobled upstart had publicly worsted him. To deal with Moray he would need to catch him off guard, away from his friends, and out of his territory.

1. Lord James Stewart, first Earl of Moray by Hans Eworth.
2. Mary Queen of Scots (The Deuil Blanc Portrait).

3. [Top right] Approach to Linlithgow Palace, where the mortally wounded
Moray went to die.
4. [Top left] Commemorative Plaque near the scene of Moray's assassination.
5. [Below] St Giles Edinburgh, tomb of the Regent Moray

6. Double portrait of Mary Queen of Scots and James VI, sixteenth century.

7. [Top] James VI aged 29 attributed to Adrian Vansen.
8. [Bottom] Queen Anne aged 19 attributed to Adrian Vansen.

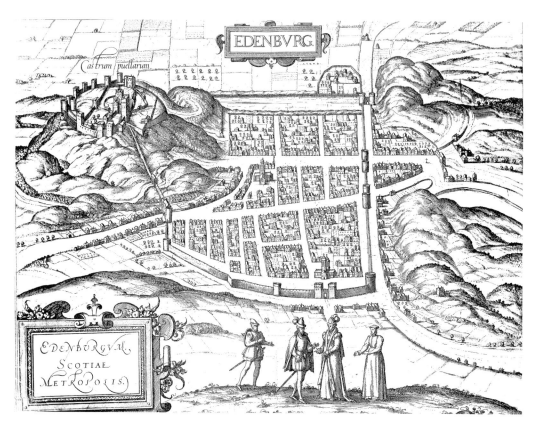

9. Edinburgh *c.* 1582 from Braun and Hogenburg's *Civates, Orbis Terrarum,* vol. iii.
10. Moravia- Morayland- by Timothy Pont.

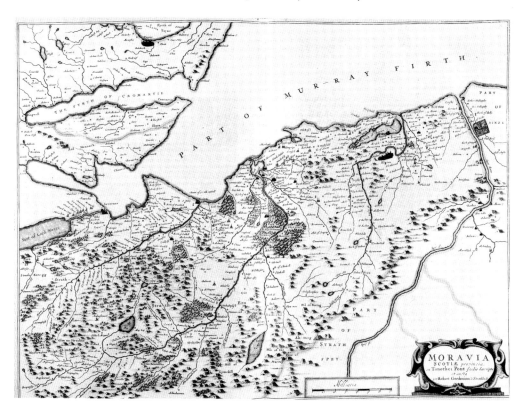

11. [Top] Doune Castle
12. [Bottom] Kilmadock cemetry, burial place of the second Earl of Moray

13. [Top] Donnibristle Bay, near Aberdour and Inverkeithing, showing Inchcolm in the background and the horseshoe curve of the beach where the second Earl of Moray was killed.

14. [Bottom] Aberdour Castle, showing the east-end, very probably similar to Donnibristle House at the same time of the murder of the second Earl of Moray

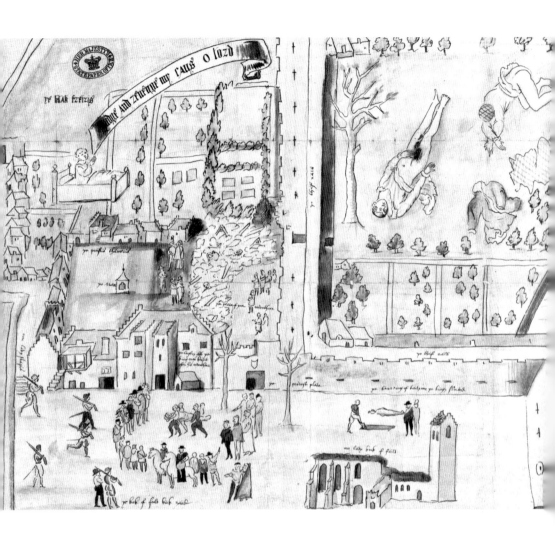

15. The Darnley Murder sheet, sixteenth century.

16. The Carberry Banner, sixteenth century.

17. The Darnley Memorial by Livinus de Vogelaare.

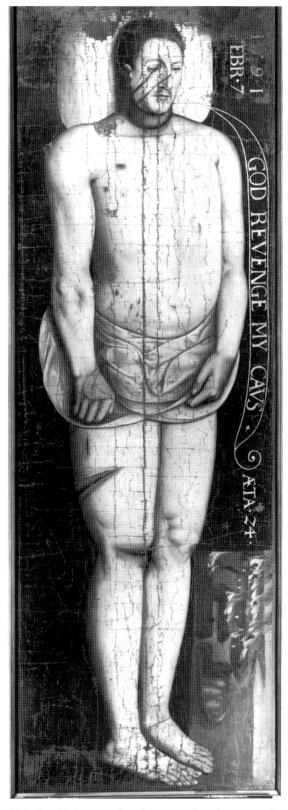

18. The second Earl of Moray after his murder, by an unknown artist
('The Moray Memorial').

19. [Top] The doubtful portrait of the 2nd Earl of Moray.
20. [Bottom] The Marquis and Marchioness of Huntly.

21. [Top] Huntly Castle from the south, showing great oriel windows, the inscriptions above 'George Gordon, First Marquis of Huntly,' and below 'Henriette Stewart, Marquisse of Huntly, and the great tower.
22. [Bottom] Huntly Castle from north-west.

33. [Top] Blackness Castle, the royal prison where Huntly was confined
34. [Bottom] Archibald Campbell, 7th Earl of Argyll by an unknown artist.

Huntly regrouped. His men even fortified the kirk and steeple of the church in Elgin, damaging it in the process. A summons was issued that Moray and his men appear at the next justice ayre in Elgin to answer for the slaughter of John Gordon.[24] Moray, assisted by Athol, prepared to resist further retaliation. This was no mere forest fire, easily extinguished: the north was on the verge of conflagration. 'A broil [had] fallen out' wrote an anxious Maitland to Lord Burghley, 'which has set the whole north in two parts, having taken arms on both sides.'[25]

At this point King James intervened to stop things getting even more out of hand. He would knock these arrant heads together. He sent letters to all the parties discharging their forces, and revoked the commission granted to Huntly for the apprehension of Grant. He commanded both Huntly and Moray to cease hostilities and remit the matter to law. Huntly tried his usual ploy of appealing directly to the King. He hurried south, but when he was still ten miles off Edinburgh he was commanded to ward in St Andrews. Similarly Moray was commanded to Stirling, and Athol, Grant and the rest to Perth.[26] When both sides had been successfully isolated, in mid December the King ordered the protagonists to Edinburgh with a limited number of retainers. Stretching royal forbearance, both arrived with far greater numbers than the proclamation allowed. Bothwell was also there with his men, and the streets seethed with angry factions spoiling for fights.

The King and council tried to adjudicate between the parties and bring some reconciliation. The deft Huntly managed to get his oar in first. Before the Privy Council he presented a supplication against Moray having taken part with the 'discontents in the north.' In riposte, Moray, Athol, Grant and the others maintained that Huntly was the aggressor, not they, citing many murders and other depredations committed by the Earl and his Gordons. Moray and his friends petitioned for exemption from the commission of justiciary and lieutenancy granted to Huntly, asserting, not unreasonably, that he would use the commission to settle old personal scores against them. Moray further asserted that Huntly's commission had been suspended by letters raised by the laird of Grant and his tutor. Not only had the suspension been published at the market cross in Elgin but also Huntly had been personally served with a copy on his six-mile journey from Elgin to Darnaway. Huntly angrily denied that he had received the letters before the death of Gordon at Darnaway and denounced the evidence of service as 'fals and feinit.'[27]

The Privy Council tried in the interests of peace and reconciliation to be as even handed as possible, examining all the relevant witnesses. After lengthy deliberations they found that 'the execution and endorsement of the said letters of suspension' had been forged and that Huntly had acted 'in the king's good service.'[28] Nevertheless a proviso stated somewhat optimistically that 'this declarator is not to be prejudicial to the Earl of Moray or any of his accomplices in their lawful defences in the criminal judgement when they shall happen to be called for the slaughter [of John Gordon] before his Highness' justice.'[29] Continuing in this spirit of even-handedness both Huntly and Moray were required to give caution of £20,000 Scots to keep good order in the country, and Grant of Freuchy and Campbell of Cawdor £5,000 apiece 'to underlie the law for the slaughter of Gordon, and not to disquiet the country.' Athol alone escaped censure, and as he was not present at the murder, no bond was taken from him.[30]

Despite this attempt to impose even-handed sanctions, Moray was aggrieved. This feeling of grievance was compounded when at the request of the Countess of Huntly her husband's bond was suspended for fifteen days. Moray gave voice to his anger, publicly noting the King's partiality towards Huntly against his own kith and kin, the Stewarts. Bowes concurred in this judgement although he conceded that the King's desire to conciliate the two sides was genuine enough. Rumours abounded of further machinations afoot, rumours that reached England: 'it was said that he has given commission to Huntly to apprehend all under Athol, Moray, and their friends who are at horn, but that Huntly will not hastily execute this and so hinder the agreements sought by the king.'[31]

James resolved that the bitter rivals had at present to be kept apart. Huntly was ordered to withdraw from Edinburgh, Moray was commanded to remain. There he was far from friendless. The Stewarts were his kin, and Bothwell in particular, always eager to stir up trouble for his own advantage, took Moray's part before the King and council and in the streets. His assistance was likely to be more effectual in the latter than the former arena. The Chancellor, whose distrust for Huntly was never far from the surface, made up with Athol, Moray and the Stewarts. The Duke of Lennox, another Stewart, whose support for the Moray faction had been hoped for, was the exception, neutralised by the fact that Huntly was his brother-in-law. The King thought him the ideal intermediary, 'loving both parties to work the reconciliation,' a task in which his willingness far outstripped his power.[32] Impotent in Edinburgh and anxious about what was transpiring in the north, Moray and Athol sought leave to return home. Permission was not granted. Thus confined, Moray's youthful frustrations were taken out in street brawling. Unable to come to grips with Huntly himself Moray picked a quarrel with one of his rival's most valued servants, John Drummond, and 'kuffed him openlie in the Tolbooth.'[33] It was small recompense for his frustration.

Confident of his power in the north, Huntly wanted to demonstrate it in Edinburgh as well, and so returned to court along with a good many retainers. James was pleased as ever to see Huntly but not so his armed men. Moray and Athol were pleased to see neither. Anticipating some plot for revenge on Huntly's part, they rallied support among the Stewarts. Moray, seeking friends where he could, rode to one of them at Kelso, none other than the errant Earl of Bothwell. There could be only one reason for this assignation: to get Bothwell active participation in any bloody encounter in the capital. This rash action on Moray's part seemed designed to displease the King.

> Bothwell and other Stewarts have warned their friends to attend here, but the king has given order to restrain them, and sent to Bothwell to remain at home. He likewise sent John Drummond – Huntly's servant in great credit – to Huntly, to will him to retire to his house. Moray and Athol, seeking this day to have spoken with the king, could not have access, wherewith they are deeply wounded.[34]

Finally in bleak mid February, when the king assumed that their tempers had been cooled along with the temperature, the respective parties were allowed to leave Edinburgh.

Back in the north the indefatigable Huntly went to work dividing his enemies and forging and re-forging alliances of his own. The furious eddies of clan life and loyalty, and the ever-present opportunism, meant that this task, for as subtle and powerful a tempter as Huntly, was never difficult. He successfully split Clan Chattan. The Macphersons of Cluny who were his tenants in Badenoch were the first object of his persuasion. By thus detaching the Macphersons from Clan Chattan he opened up a way to the rest. His kin were everywhere, and everywhere they were men of substance. The Earl of Sutherland was a Gordon, and Gordon lairds littered the north-east. In March, Alan Cameron of Lochiel made a bond of service to Huntly in which he particularly promised to assist him against Mackintosh of Dunnachten and Grant of Freuchie, in return for Huntly's promise never to receive them into his favour until Alan had been given satisfaction for any hurt incurred in the course of his service to Huntly against them.[35]

Later some observers saw in this the nucleus of a nation-wide conspiracy to destroy Moray, Argyll, and Campbell of Cawdor. Moray was to be shot while hunting in the woods of Doune.[36] Argyll and Cawdor would meet a similar fate. The Highlanders were to do the killing in return for protection and preferment. Morton, McLean of Duart, Stewart of Appin, and MacDougall of Dunolly were thought to have been drawn into the plot. So too was Maitland, on the promise of being rewarded with lands in Stirlingshire by Archibald Campbell of Lochnell, who was to succeed Argyll. Whether so extensive and well planned a conspiracy existed or not, Huntly's manoeuvring was undoubtedly engineering a major confrontation.[37]

In preparation for this Huntly planned to come to Spynie Palace and plant his forces in Elgin to which 'he drew many of his Highlanders who daily spoil all passengers and many inhabitants thereabouts.'[38] Despite strong protests from the burgesses, he ordered that the cathedral be fortified and manned. To counter this threat, Moray and Athol gathered their forces at Forres within eight miles of Elgin, thinking 'themselves strong enough for Huntly and all his forces, in case the king shall stand indifferent between them.'[39]

The King of course, was far from indifferent. He would again try to separate the warring parties. The Privy Council on 16 March ordered Huntly under pain of rebellion not to cross west of the Spey. Moray was not to go east of the Findhorn, nor Athol north of Skarkeith. Like naughty boys 'grounded' by their parents, they were told to leave each other alone and keep out of each other's way. Once again both Huntly and Moray were ordered to Edinburgh and told to sign bands to keep the peace. With Moray away, Grant and Macintosh kept armed guard at Darnaway against any ploys by Huntly. He bided his time, remaining at ease in Strathbogie.[40] A kind of snarling peace was restored.

The King's patience with tiresome aristocrats was exceptional and much commented upon. But James was a specialist in reconciliation long before the time when it was fashionable. Most unfair murmurs against the King for his 'careless guiding and government' were regularly heard not only from some of the nobility, as would be expected, but also from the lower orders. Street-fighting and murderous duels between rival gangs in Edinburgh and Aberdeen were causing concern among merchants and burgers increasingly anxious that disorder would harm their enterprises, a concern that was incomprehensible to clan folk, accustomed to bloody encounters in the glens. Among the urban leaders the King's policy of trying to conciliate the factions rather than punish them was misconstrued as weakness. He would hold in preventive custody one day and set free the next. It was the royal equivalent of detaining the drunk and disorderly overnight in the cells and releasing them without charge when they had sobered up. Likewise, Moray, Huntly and their men were a constant nuisance, but no more. The throne was exasperated but not under threat.

That was not the case where all aristocratic behaviour was concerned. In 1591 the Earl of Bothwell stepped forth as the ringleader of a new disorder which was to haunt James for the next four years. Bothwell, old-fashioned baron that he in many ways was, craved power and influence in the state befitting his station if not his deserts. His arrogance and impetuosity, his unstable character and the unsavoury rumours surrounding him, all made him suspect to the King. Having entrusted him with the regency during his absence abroad, since his return from Denmark James had persistently denied Bothwell the status and recognition he thought he deserved. Instead he was warded in Edinburgh Castle to await trial for treason. Protesting his innocence, he claimed that the whole witchcraft allegation was a plot by Maitland to ruin him. It may well have been so, since Maitland had the motive, and knew well the anxiety that James had for his own safety, and the credulity of the King in matters supernatural.

Bothwell's burning resentment towards this 'puddock stool of the night,' for overshadowing 'an ancient cedar' such as himself, and for being behind all his misfortunes, knew no bounds.[41] From being a delinquent on the streets, the psychotic Earl had become a danger to the state. Bothwell's obsession with the Chancellor was mirrored by the King's obsession with Bothwell, and the threat he posed, an obsession that grew with every action of his unruly kinsman and subject. It was even rumoured that the Earl had an illicit relationship with the Queen, as was later to be said of Moray.[42]

Moray and Bothwell were cousins german. The first overtures in the last act between them were initiated by the latter when he sought Moray's assistance in his forthcoming trial. Moray was nearby at Doune. Bothwell wrote to his 'very good Lord and brother' complaining that 'matters here go otherwise than I looked for' and that he was to be put on trial:

> I understand your Lordship has a promise of his Highness that he shall be present at that trial which will in no way be closed to you, and therefore I must request your Lordship for my cause to be present here, to the end that you may see my innocence made known to all the world. Not that you should request any benefit for me at His Highness's hands but that I may receive the most extreme trial that can be tending to equity, law and good conscience ... And if from this trial your Lordship and other friends shall absent your-selves I doubt not God shall try the same to his glory and my perpetual honour and comfort.[43]

Moray's response was tardy and less than full-hearted:

> My servant Andrew Stewart has shown me that your Lordship is desirous that I should come to Edinburgh with diligence for your cause. I have such earnest causes of my own to do that it is not possible to me to come so shortly, as this bearer Andrew Stewart will show your Lordship. I understand that there will be sufficient number of your friends in Edinburgh to be cautioners for you. And if this matter stands on my presence and cannot otherwise be settled I shall be ready to come on your notice.[44]

Moray wrote to Maitland in similar vein, asking that in his absence others be allowed to stand caution.[45] With his kin showing such lacklustre support, Bothwell was not prepared to chance a trial. He made his escape. James ordered his pursuit and forbade any intercourse with the renegade.

Moray's continuing support for Bothwell, half-hearted though it was, would not have gone unnoticed.

During the summer Moray remained inactive at Doune while his position in the north was constantly weakened. One of his tenants, David Ross, switched his allegiance to Alexander Lindsay, the newly elevated Lord Spynie and the appointee of Huntly. A few days later another tenant brought to Moray's factor, John Leslie, six arrows that Ross's son, John, had shot at him. Leslie informed Moray that after her Ladyship's departure he and George Dunbar had captured 'the lymmers' – both David and John Ross – and had publicly humiliated them by a thrashing so savage 'that I trow they shall not be well before Whitsunday.' Lord Spynie was enraged when he heard 'that the first man that ever he gave maintenance to in Moray had gotten the greatest shame that ever was done a gentleman.' Nothing but Leslie's life would content him. Unconcerned at this threat, Leslie wrote to Moray for a commission for the execution of the troublesome elder Ross, a commission that Moray had failed to leave with Leslie.[46]

> Therefore my Lord, send me word what thinks your Lordship
> best to be done with David Ross, for if your Lordship suffer
> this opposition it will cause greater men than he to mistake
> your Lordship. If your Lordship would have his life, send me
> word and I shall either get it for you or get you one as good.[47]

At the same time Leslie had written to a Mr Andrew inviting him to carry out the execution. Frustrated by the lack of reply from his absent master, Leslie wrote again complaining that by the dilatoriness in his instructions he was 'ill-served.' He was particularly concerned by a rumour that his lord had been yielding to pressure to let both David and John Ross go with a caution: 'If you so do the country will cry out on it for they are guilty in six or seven points.' On the wider scene, acting as his lord's eyes and ears in the north, he gave information about Huntly who 'has all his people in readiness with nine days' provisions, but where he goes to God knows. The rumour here is that he is going to Inverness to hold a court, and in his homecoming again he'll take up a Mackintosh escheat' (forfeiture of property). Given the depredations of Spynie's men and the presence of the over-mighty Earl, the faithful Leslie was so bold as to 'marvel much why you send not the harquebuses you promised, knowing the place to be desolate.'[48] Moray was neglecting to take even elementary precautions.

His fears were soon justified. On the same day as he had written to Moray the first time

> James Gordon, accompanied with the number of sixteen
> Gordons – gentlemen all – came to your Lordship's boats and

cobbles of Spey and have broken them and cut your Lordship's nets and laid all your coracles on land and beaten your Lordship's servants that work at your fishing – and Jakie Maweir escaped very narrowly with his life.

While Huntly himself led his people, in Moray's absence his men were incapable of uniting against the threat. Leslie implored him to visit soon, as otherwise his absence would be misconstrued by Huntly who would think he had carte blanche in the north.[49] Leslie was now gravely concerned that Huntly would attack Darnaway either on his way to or from Inverness:

> My Lord, this is a masterless country at this present, for there is no man in Moray that may put twenty men together. There is no man here but has received sure warning of Huntly's journey and has put all his gear aside. Therefore, My Lord, haste you home ... For if they get [Darnaway] house we shall all be hanged over the wall.[50]

The sense of being isolated in the north, far from succour and under ever-present threat, and the recognition that their Earl had abandoned them, magnified the fears of Moray's retainers and justified their reproaches. In the event Darnaway survived unscathed. No assault materialised. But Huntly's poachers continued to cause great loss to Moray's fishings.[51]

Huntly had played his part both in the countryside and at court with considerable deftness. At home, as he so often was, he could impress with his vigour, take advantage of the disorganisation of Moray's minions, and consolidate his power base. At court he could rely on his unique favour with the King to secure his interests. He was also the strong and loyal hand James needed against the outlaw Bothwell who was continually threatening to kill the Chancellor and always eluding capture.[52] By contrast Moray, his father dead and himself compromised by rumours of his association with his errant cousin Bothwell, could only seethe over his lack of influence in court and council, and, absent from his earldom, see his position in the north gradually erode.

To consolidate his hegemony Huntly wanted the royal imprimatur, the Lieutenancy of the North he had lost after the Brig O'Dee rebellion. The King was at his summer hunting lodge in Falkland and there Huntly and his wife attended him assiduously.[53] Initially rebuffed, he paid court with determined charm. He even tried to get Bowes to intercede on his behalf. The ever-circumspect agent sought advice from England before committing himself to assist this unlikely client.

> Huntly is become a very great courtier, and has made such liberal offers to serve the king and 'keep his quarterage against

the king's rebels' that the king much cherishes him for the same. The lieutenancy of the north is made ready for him.[54]

Huntly's enemies realised that they would have to take concerted action to oppose him. In Dunkeld Athol, Moray, Argyll's commissioners and possibly even Bothwell – a fugitive from justice – met to decide on united action.[55] The meeting led to no more than the expression of a common apprehension. Should Huntly be confirmed in his lieutenancy feud could progress to civil war. But what could be done? Bothwell was an outlaw on the run; Moray had lost the protection of his major ally. In September 1591 Huntly was again granted the office he desired. The worst fears of his enemies were realised, at least according to the tabloid reporting of 'an Englishman in Berwick.' 'Lyke young men bothe ther consenttes according,' Huntly got James' leave to go against his enemies with fire and sword and a whole series of violent clashes were occasioned as a result of his intervention in the affairs of his neighbours in accordance with his commission of justiciary 'under colour and pretense to punish trespassers and malefactors [but] meaning no other thing but to be cruelly revenged upon us [and] for uttering and execution of every hatred and injury conceived by [Huntly] against us.' Fact is not easy to pick out from rumour, and partisan exaggeration or invention was further distorted by transmission through many hands and over many miles. Propaganda tales of the treacherous desecration of Highland hospitality by one side and barbaric butchery of bairns by the other were disseminated in the streets of Edinburgh and taverns of Berwick. The Berwick intelligencer recorded them as truths for posterity, but was not even sure of the identity of his murder victim.

> Huntly treacherously sent to a principal great man to say that a certain earl known to be his friend was hunting near his house, and would come to his door and drink. This gentleman with his three sons and servants came out with bread, ale and wine to entertain him. But it was Huntly and his company who shot and slew the nobleman, his sons and servants. Some say it was Lord Boyd who was slain and with him a learned minister. In revenge the friends of the dead have sought out young children of Huntly's friends, learning abroad at schools, cruelly killing them.[56]

Savage encounters, doubtless exaggerated but with more of the ring of plausibility, were reported to the Privy Council. The laird of Lochaber and some septs of Clan Cameron, who adhered to Huntly, had killed forty-one of Mackintosh's men, and a force led by Alexander MacDonel Moidart, but acting under orders from Huntly, had killed twenty four of the laird of Grant's tenants, who had trespassed into Strathspey, presumably to rustle. In addition, Bowes reported, 'they have hurt the laird of Ballindalloch, seizing a great prey of cattle and sheep to Strathbogie, the House of Huntly.' Grant and Macintosh with the help of Athol, Moray and others were said to be preparing to invade Huntly's lands. Some action was expected about Strathbogie, notwithstanding Huntly's lieutenancy and his forces. Bowes warned his masters that 'more blood will be drawn unless the king prevent it.'[57]

In riposte Moray and his men broke down the dykes of Walter Kynnaird of Cubbin, one of Huntly's miscreants, and tried to break into his house to deliver summary justice. They were summoned by Huntly as lieutenant in the north 'for fomenting disorders there under cover of the letters of exemption obtained by them.'[58] The Privy Council despaired of 'the multitude of deadly feuds through which all parties having interest therein spares not to take their private revenge and advantage of others, disdaining to seek remedy by the ordinary form of law and justice, without fear of God or reverence of his authority.'[59] Once again James summoned the contenders – Huntly, Grant and Mackintosh – before him at Perth to try to reconcile their differences. He met with some success, and in October a contract was drawn up by which it was agreed that Grant and Macintosh would once again be received in the special favour of Huntly. The Earl of Moray, significantly, was left out of this concord 'otherwise than was promised.' This settlement further weighted the balance of power in Huntly's favour to such an extent that by the close of 1591 he was once more the unquestioned master of the north.[60]

Moray's position at court was simultaneously dealt another heavy, indeed fatal, blow by the death of his wife Elizabeth, probably in childbirth, on 18 November 1591. Though they had never been a close couple, her death was a disaster for her husband whose position derived almost all of its strength from the fact of his marriage to the daughter of the Good Regent, the uncle of the King. Thereby he had gained his title and lands. Bowes observed to Burghley that since his wife's decease Moray found little favour at court. The King was distant, and the Chancellor, always lukewarm, had become decidedly cool. 'Sparks of jealousy' were still seen in the Chancellor towards the Stewarts – Moray and Bothwell. But there was a larger reason. Maitland, despite his recent elevation to the peerage as Lord Thirlestane, had found his position weakened by the death in 1591 of his old ally, William Douglas, Earl of Angus and Morton, 'the ministers' king' as James had called this redoubtable Protestant. The successors to the two earldoms were for different reasons hostile to Maitland: the new Earl of Angus, Douglas' son, was a Catholic; the new Earl of Morton – Douglas of Lochleven, the half-brother of the Regent Moray, was an ancient enemy of the House of Lethington. Maitland needed to shore up his position as best he could. Moray had squandered whatever capital he had once had with the King and was a spent force. The Chancellor accordingly drew closer to Huntly and the Catholic party for support.[61]

Huntly was supreme in the north. Moray was impotent at court. Unable to get redress for the wrongs he felt were being done him, unable even to get a sympathetic hearing, Moray took the fatal step that would put him beyond the pale and in mortal danger. He was to pass from being an irritating and immature courtier and cousin of the King to becoming the tainted and treasonous confederate and cousin of the King's first enemy. This is the immediate and essential background to the Earl of Moray's bloody end. He retired sulking from court, and 'took plain part with Bothwell, who was still upon his enterprises.'[62]

Bothwell's enterprises included not only eluding arrest, but also taunting his pursuers by such provocations as riding under the walls of Edinburgh to dine in nearby Leith. They culminated on the evening of 27 December 1591 when he attempted to kill Maitland and seize the King. Getting into Holyrood Palace by a back passageway he was discovered when one his men smashed down a door behind which some friends of his were imprisoned. The noise alerted the guard. Bothwell was nearly taken but escaped under cover of night and fled north. Some of his less fortunate minions were hanged the following day. The King – and his Chancellor – had had a lucky escape.

The English feared that James might 'be surprised by the Earls of Moray and Athol, who are more to be doubted than any other upon whom Bothwell doth hope.'[63] But of James they almost despaired since he was 'of a disposition that will hardly believe such matters till they be too evident,' and even if proved beyond doubt he would still not be dissuaded from 'the field and his pastime for any respect.' However, this attempted palace coup had unsettled the King. He was furious, frightened and affronted. The Kirk offered him no solace, one of the clergy warning him that the noise of Bothwell's hammering had been a divine warning. Demonic threat, more like. Angus, Mar and Morton were all suspects. But it was the Stewarts as a whole who fell under the shadow of the Satan. Lennox was believed to have been implicated since one of his retainers, William Stewart, had taken part and fled with the rest. Despite the King's laudable reluctance to credit ill report, the whispering campaign against Moray had its effect. A rumour – conceived or fostered by Huntly – even suggested that he had been one of the Holyrood desperadoes. It was more reliably reported that he was hiding the fugitive.[64] His whereabouts were unknown. News that he was put to the horn for harbouring Bothwell did not reach him for some time since he had not condescended to inform his servants in Darnaway of his movements.[65]

The King wanted Bothwell caught and tried for treason. Almost certainly he would have been put to death. Huntly and Lennox – quickly rehabilitated and eager to show his loyalty – were commissioned to hunt him down and those who had supported him. Thus Huntly received what he later claimed was the blank royal commission under which he was authorised to act against Moray.[66] Until 5 February they were actively engaged in their pursuit, scouring the west coast for a Bothwell, clothed in beggar's attire, trying to get a ship for Spain or France. They did not find him but Huntly arrested a John Smallet who confessed to being privy to the conspiracy at Holyrood House and who 'discovered many matters not before revealed.' One of those matters may have been the extent of Moray's involvement in the plot.

James had good reason to think that Moray had abetted Bothwell, at least in his escape. Association with the nefarious actions of the detested necromancer was the most puerile and perilous position for the Earl to place himself in. Encouraged by Maitland the King ordered Lord Ochiltree to bring Moray to Edinburgh ostensibly for a reconciliation with Huntly and on promise of royal pardon.[67] Generous Jacobites may take this offer at face value, another instance of James' conciliatory nature and endless forbearance with an errant nobility. He had after all employed the good offices of Lennox in a similar mission a year before, but by this time he could no longer be described as neutral. The English agents at first took this view, reporting that James and Maitland were convinced that the chief danger lay in persistence of 'secret grudges' against the Chancellor and were 'earnestly to work good reconciliations amongst these parties to pull up the root of their hatred and prevent these dangers.'[68] Others see the order as a means of preventing Bothwell getting shelter in the north, or even as an instrument to bring Moray to his death. On the earlier occasions the disputes were between members of the nobility, but Bothwell and his associates had aimed at the throne itself. Moray, if thought to be aiding and abetting a traitor, was tainted with treason himself. Under this shadow of suspicion, the young Earl was lured from safety to within striking distance of Huntly. Why did he come?

The messenger as much as the message may be the answer. Andrew Stewart was thirty-one years old, and had only just become the third Lord Ochiltree.[69] He had succeeded, not his father who had died young but his grandfather, Moray's great-uncle. The grandfather was a well-respected peacemaker and Protestant, commended by his life-long friend and son-in-law John Knox himself as 'a man rather borne to maik peace, than to brag upon the calsay [street].'[70] The grandson was close to the King, being the nephew of the royal favourite, James, Earl of Arran. Protestant though he was, he had no love for Bothwell who had killed his uncle, William, in a street fight in Edinburgh. On the other hand, although he had been commissioned with Huntly and had ridden with him in the pursuit of Bothwell, he was not Huntly's man. His family's reputation and his lack of partisanship in the politics of the north would make him the ideal broker. The King both liked and trusted him. Convinced of the King's sincerity, he would be a persuasive influence on Moray, whose kinsman and friend he was. The last letter Moray was to receive was from Ochiltree telling him of his commission.[71]

And so in late January 1591/2 Moray, in the company of Ochiltree, took his fatal and final journey south from Darnaway Castle to Donnibristle House. His departure had been sudden and precipitate as a letter from a friend in Edinburgh, taking him to task, shows: 'I find great fault with much that your Lordship does and especially of keeping such things from me ... not advising me of Your Lordship's journey to Donnibristle.'[72] Moray in his last days was as reluctant to put pen to paper as ever he had been. Having seen Moray to Donnibristle, Ochiltree returned to court and reported that the Earl had submitted himself to the King's order. His attempt at reconciliation was 'near at a point.'[73] On 5 or 6 February Huntly returned to court from pursuing Bothwell, and learnt of Moray's whereabouts. According to Calderwood, Huntly, the king, and the Chancellor were alone privy to this information. Not for long. It was soon 'the bruit of the town.'[74]

12

FASHION AMONG THE BEST SORT

Monday 7 February 1591/2

Ye Highlands and ye Lawlands,
O whare hae ye been?
They hae slain the Earle o' Moray
And hae laid him on the green.

Ballad of the Bonny Earl of Moray

It is but a late practice to shoot men with arquebuses, which begins prettily to increase. God make me quit of the country.

Thomas Randolph[1]

It is the accustomable fashion of this country, specially among the best sort, to styk or shoot with a piece or pistol such one as ... gave them cause of offence, and not to raise an army to charge and molest the whole realm.

Thomas Fowler[2]

Moray foresaw no danger. He could have stayed at his own stronghold of Doune and still have been within ready access of Edinburgh. Instead he chose the greater comfort and convenience of Donnibristle, his widowed mother's manor house on Dalgety Bay near Aberdour in Fife.[3]

Donnibristle House stood commandingly upon a small headland on the water-worn shore of the Firth of Forth, midway between the old kirk of Dalgety and the ancient royal burgh of Inverkeithing. The island and Abbey of Inchcolm lay just offshore, as though moored in the bobbing sea. The prospect, unusually for Scotland, was south facing, and so the house and its occupants were spared the bitter winds of the north. The bay before it was horseshoe shaped and provided a tranquil spot where seals came to play. This temperate idyll was the place to be in the dreich season of the year. The court was another attraction since during the winter months the King would stay in Edinburgh and the centre of social life would be there. Donnibristle was but an easy ride to the capital. Often, of course, the Firth would be impassable and the Queen's Ferry would not sail the considerable distance from shore to shore, but at other times in the cold but clear days of winter the journey to Edinburgh could be accomplished in a matter of hours and in the light of day.

In this domestic and essentially female milieu, the Earl had few retainers in attendance. His sheriff, Patrick Dunbar of Boigholl, and a servant of his called 'Boeg' are the only ones we hear of. The Earl's mother was likely resident, coming from Doune Castle to winter in the greater comfort and warmth of her southern seat. By this time Lady Margaret was in her mid-forties and would rarely venture to the capital or the court. But at least she was near the centre of things, and could expect friends to visit and gossip to seep through. She doubtless welcomed the prospect of seeing her recently widowed son and her grandchildren whom he had brought with him. In addition, at least one of her daughters was with her.[4] So too would be a retinue of domestic servants, but not men-at-arms.

Originally the residence of the Abbot of Inchcolm, Donnibristle House had passed to Moray's father as commendator of the priory. In its origins it would have been built more for comfort than defence. In its development it would have been modified for even greater domesticity in keeping with the architectural developments of the times. In 1592 it was likely to correspond to the sort of fortified manor house being built or renovated all over Scotland in the late sixteenth century by lairds seeking status and ease, and able to pay for it from ecclesiastical pickings. Defensive features such as iron-grilled doorways and windows, gun-loops, open parapets and angle-turrets gradually disappeared, or were converted to ornamental purposes. Other forms of external embellishment, including heraldic panels and inscribed lintels and pediments, likewise became popular, as did wooden panelling and ornamented ceilings inside. Dining rooms replaced medieval halls, panoramic windows on all floors replaced upper story slits. Greater privacy was provided by according each room separate access from turret stairs, greater delicacy by banishing the kitchen to the furthest reaches of the house.[5]

Over the years Donnibristle House has been several times gutted by fire. Nothing now remains of the Jacobite structure. There is no description of it and the only depiction, an inset in the Moray Memorial, the death portrait of 'the Bonny Earl,' shows it in flames. From that crude sketch Donnibristle in 1592 seems to have been a large stone-built two or three -storey manor house with various outbuildings and a stack yard forming a corral surrounded by a low level wall with two undefended entrances. It was similar in appearance to Newton House, a fortalice built in the second half of the sixteenth century by the Edmonstone family and situated in the shadow of Castle Doune, but probably its closest extant likeness is to be found in a neighbouring property a few miles along the coast, the early seventeenth century east wing of Aberdour Castle, an elegant development of the Mortons.[6] While the stone walls and roof of Donnibristle would have been sufficiently high and sufficiently thick to withstand assault by a small skirmishing party and the windows and doors secure enough against casual intruders the house was not designed to repel any sustained or prolonged attack by a determined force. Its regular 'garrison' of cooks, stable boys, and maids could put up but paltry resistance. It was neither a defensible nor a strong house. It was 'not able to be kept' as the English agent, Roger Aston, described it.[7] One 'improvement' – a flue – was to prove fatal to the young Earl.

Moray must have been quite content. He had the trustworthy Ochiltree's assurance that the King meant him well. Two miles from the Queen's Ferry, and fourteen from Edinburgh, he was well positioned to attend court at his pleasure while dwelling secure in his own lands. But just as he was fourteen miles and a risky river crossing from danger from the south so he was distanced from the affairs of court. Moray would probably have no cognisance of how intimately he was being aligned with the wayward Bothwell. Similarly, Ochiltree, on his expedition to the north, would have had no knowledge that this association had reached such a dangerous level of proximity. However, a letter from Edinburgh on 25 January should have put the Earl on notice. His friend, Andrew Abercrombie, warned Moray of a summons that had been sent to Darnaway ordering him, under pain of horning, to attend a secret session of the Privy Council to answer for his 'receiving of my Lord Bothwell on a day of December.'[8] The court was to meet in Edinburgh on 31 January but the meeting never took place, perhaps because of Moray's absence. Did he fear to go or disdain to attend? Arrogantly refusing to submit to royal command would not have been out of character. Had he been notified of its timing? It is quite possible that Moray and the missives passed each other on the roads. But why was he not summoned from Donnibristle? The King and his Chancellor knew he was lodging there. He was doing so at their behest! Did the King secretly hope that he would fail to appear and so could be outlawed? Of this there is no evidence, but, whether or not he received notification, the effect of Moray's failure to answer the summons, was to put him beyond the pale. If this friend of Bothwell would not come voluntarily to the King he had something to hide, and the King would have him hunted down and brought in by force.

The trusting Ochiltree suspected nothing amiss, unless one small incident gave him cause for concern. Since 21 January, as part of the attempt to apprehend Bothwell, an embargo on all the ports was in force by order of the Privy Council, forbidding any boat to sail which had not divulged the names of those it was carrying. But ferry crossings had not been specified. Either the day before or the day of the murder (the 6 or 7 February) – the source is confused on this point – Ochiltree tried to cross over the Forth to meet with Moray. On reaching the Queen's Ferry he was turned back. The King had that very day ordered that no boat should pass. Assuming that this was to prevent Bothwell or his confederates getting over the river, Ochiltree returned to Edinburgh to seek a permit. The King denied any knowledge of the restraint at the ferry, and persuaded Ochiltree to remain in Edinburgh that night, and to accompany him hunting on the morrow.[9] The King's undiminished appetite for the chase may have served to calm any fears Ochiltree was harbouring, although one account had him place all his men in arms in readiness to cross over to Donnibristle. Hearing of these preparations, the King ordered the bailiffs to stay all Ochiltree's horses within their stables.[10]

If Huntly was to act against Moray, he must do so at once. Ochiltree could be fobbed off for only so long. On the morning of Monday 7 February the King went hunting, his favourite pursuit. Armed with his commission of fire and sword to 'execute justice on the accomplices in Francis Earl of Bothwell's raid on Holyrood House,' Huntly interrupted the royal hunt to tell the King that he had 'a purpose of Mr John Colven [Colville],'[11] one of the participants in the Holyrood raid, and others of the Bothwell faction, and that he would 'pass over the water' in pursuit of them. The King was well aware that over the Forth lay one of Bothwell's leading accomplices and Huntly's archenemy. If, despite later denials, the Queen's Ferry had been closed either Huntly was exempted as a royal commissioner or else he received express permission to cross. That permission would have come from the King. His royal master informed of his intention, and sanction for the pursuit given – tacitly at least – Huntly spurred on his way to rendezvous with his men. He had already primed a large group of his trusted friends and retainers to meet him at the ferry.

He had picked them well. Thirty individuals are named by the Privy Council in addition to Huntly. Most were Gordons. Some were close associates and retainers. Several were prominent 'Papists.'[12] Together they constituted a band of desperadoes. William Gordon, fifth laird of Gight, in particular, was a man of violent temperament and volatile temper who was reputed to have committed at least four murders in the past, two of them being of family members. Perhaps it is apposite that he is the ancestor of that amoral swashbuckler, Lord Byron. A William Leslie, the younger of Warthill, was his first victim. Next, on Christmas Eve 1576, after a quarrel with Thomas Fraser of Strichen, the step-father-in-law of his sister Margaret, Gight followed him onto the bridge of Deer and struck him one blow with his two handed sword, killing him on the spot. For this deed, as was common practice at the time, he had to pay 5,000 merks in compensation. No further killings are attributed to him for eleven years when he more than made up for this prolonged pacivity. On 28 November 1587, along with the laird of Lesmour and Captain John Gordon, he killed John Keith of Cryallie, and only four days later he murdered his sister Catherine's husband, John Keith of Clachriach, at the justice port in Aberdeen. On that occasion Huntly had given young Gight refuge in Linlithgow and would not hand him over to the King's justice.[13] This debt was now to be willingly repaid. James Gordon, the heir to Lesmour, had also been involved in the murderous assault on Alan Grant in 1587, and it is likely that in those violent times many if not all of the other participants would have had bloody histories, their experience and temperament qualifying them for the raid on Donnibristle. Some, of course, had old scores to settle with Moray, most especially Thomas Gordon of Cluny whose brother John had been shot and killed during the failed assault on Darnaway two years before.

Those worthy of being named numbered about thirty. That is the minimum force Huntly had at his disposal. But it is more than likely that in addition there would be numerous but anonymous foot soldiers with them. Their numbers grew as the year passed. In 1595 Henry St Colme asserted that there had been 'eighty or thereby of horse and foot.' David Moysie in his *Memoirs* increases this figure to 'six or seven score.' A reasonable estimate is in the region of sixty to eighty, the sort of number of retainers that Huntly could readily raise. Whatever the precise number it was a heavily armed military force that Huntly had assembled, equipped with 'jacks [body armour], steel bonnets, long culverins [handguns], harquebuses, pistolets, swords and other weapons invasive.'[14]

In the afternoon of Monday 7 February 1591/2 – thirty years almost to the day after Moray's father-in-law had displaced Huntly's grandfather from the earldom of Moray – Huntly and his men crossed the Forth and proceeded to Donnibristle House. Precisely what happened then we shall never know, since no first-hand account exists, just the reports of the English agents who gleaned their information from a mixture of partisan participants and wild rumour. On top of their assessment has been laid a deep layer of legend. Thus the following account is but a best approximation to the truth.

The actual time of the fatal encounter is unclear, one authority stating that it happened in 'fear [broad] daylight.'[15] Most probably the journey, the attack, and the murder spanned both light and darkness since in February the night comes early. It was not an easy ride, in the gathering gloom along a coast road shrouded in sea mist, but at least it muffled their approach. They arrived at twilight. The beacon light on the watchtower at Donnibristle had not yet been lit,[16] but horses hooves hitting hard ground would have prevented a complete surprise attack. Their approach was detected and the house secured against them as best it could be. Doors were locked and bolted, windows shuttered, and guns got ready. Moray had been under siege from Huntly before, but that was in Darnaway, where both his fortifications and manpower were much greater. His defiance, however, towards the royal lieutenant was the same on each occasion.

As Huntly's men surrounded the main building, Captain John Gordon, cousin to Huntly, brother of the laird of Gight, and a veteran of the Flemish wars, 'broke before all others into the court and called aloud to Moray that they were come thither to invite him to treat for composing matters; that Huntly had the king's order to conduct him to his presence; that therefore he should obey without a repugnancy, assuring him he should sustain no prejudice from them; that it would be vain for him to refuse obedience, since they were stronger than he, and had orders to use violence in case he refused to obey.' While he was thus talking, one of the defenders fired a hagbut from a window and mortally wounded him.[17] Further shots may have despatched a few more of the attacking party.

Others, including Norman Leslie, managed to lay brushwood and 'corn stooks' from the nearby barnyard all around the base of the tower and set it alight.[18] The proximity of its winter provender and the modernising of the house were its undoing. The main bedroom had an enclosed garderobe or wall-closet, a recent development in domestic luxury, a contemporary example of which can be seen in the central range of the neighbouring Aberdour Castle. The smoke from the burning wood and hay was convected through the garderobe flue in the wall to the upper – residential – floors of the house, making them uninhabitable. Some yielded, some tried to escape. According to Aston, Moray had no choice. Surrender was not an option since he had 'made great request for his life' and it was only 'when he saw it would not be,' that he kept the house till his servants had all left him, and then devoutly said his prayers. 'He committed his children and the revenge of his death to Ochiltree, praying his sister then with him ... to make the same known to Ochiltree.'[19] In this depiction we see the instant portrayal of Moray as a pious Protestant martyr, the second of that name.

He would not wait for the inevitable. A chance of escape was afforded by the coming of darkness and the bravery of his sheriff, Patrick Dunbar, who volunteered to act as a diversion: 'I will go out at the gate before your Lordship and I am sure the people will charge on me, thinking me to be your Lordship, sua, it being mirke under night, ye sall come out after me and look if that ye can fend for yourself.' He issued from the burning pile and ran desperately among Huntly's men who butchered him, the *coup de grâce* being delivered by Robert Innes of Innermarky. Between three and four other Moray retainers were hurt, one at least, a man called Boeg, being slain.[20] According to an Aberdonian chronicler six of Moray's companions were slain with him, but this is out of kilter with all other accounts.[21]

Moray had been so burnt that he could not hold a weapon in one hand, but in the darkness and in the confusion created by Dunbar's diversionary tactics he ran down a back passage into the garden and from thence out of the gate to the seashore – the green – which was only a few 100 yards distant. He found no boat to make good his escape but lurked among the rocks, thinking he was safe in the gathering darkness. And so he might have been had his own steel skullcap not betrayed him. The silk ribbon that secured its cloth cover had caught fire and sparks still rose from it. Unbeknown to him this acted as a beacon to his pursuers.[22] Aston makes the whole incident more heroic but also more prosaic, with the undaunted and unburnt Moray fighting his way through 'with his sword in his hand, and like a lion forc[ing] them all to give place.' He then ran straight into the arms and daggers of some of Huntly's men who had taken up a stand to prevent such an eventuality.[23] Whatever the mechanics of it, all accounts agree that he was caught on the shore and brutally despatched.

Who the actual assassins were is impossible to say, there being so many potential contenders. Aston, plausibly, attributes the killing to the passionate lairds of Cluny and of Gight, both of whom had lost a brother – one killed at Darnaway a year past and one mortally wounded at Donnibristle that very night.[24] Huntly names them along with Innermarky: all men with a grudge against Moray and all hotheads whom Huntly could not control.[25] They are the prime suspects. Other accounts make Gordon of Buckie the main assassin who slashed Moray on the face with his heavy sword and felled him.[26] These accounts, preserved in the tradition of the Moray family, also accord Huntly a more prominent and more culpable role, countering Huntly's claim that the murder was against his express instructions. Such obviously partisan traditions may seek to implicate Huntly more intimately in the crime than he deserves. On the other hand they may well have some basis in reality, suggesting that Huntly's followers wanted to compromise him as deeply as themselves in the crime, fearing he would disclaim them: 'you shall be as deep as I.'[27] An astute safeguard. According to varying accounts, Huntly, at Buckie's instigation, was forced variously to give some strokes to the corpse or even to deliver the *coup de grâce* – the final mutilating cuts to his face – whereupon Moray famously upbraided him:

> 'Huntly ... you Hieland stot (castrated ox or steer) ... you ha'e spoilt a far fairer face than yer ain!'[28]

He was 'cruelly demained,' as later reports have it.[29] That may have been the point: to disfigure his most distinguished feature – his face. His body as depicted in the contemporary memorial portrait shows several bullet holes in his chest, deep cuts to the right shoulder and thigh and left breast, and two neat parallel slashes running the length of the right hand side of his face from his eyebrow and nose to the jawline beneath his ear.[30] His bloody corpse was left where it had fallen on the sward. It was not, however, dismembered, as one early report maintained.[31] Moray was just twenty-four years old when he was murdered. According to a family document his last encounter with his old foe Huntly had lasted 'for the space of one hour or thereby.'[32]

His mother, his sisters Mary and Jean and his children were all saved,[33] although her family asserted that Dame Margaret was 'so suffocated by the fire' that she died a few months later.[34] The house was gutted by the inferno, with many of its documents being destroyed.[35] It was to remain a ruin for many years. Huntly and his men hurried from the scene, leaving the evidence stretched on the beach, the house burning like a torch in the night sky, and even one of their own on the ground. This was the mortally wounded Captain Gordon who was left behind since he was too badly injured to travel. His frugal companions relieved him of his purse, gold, and weapons and even 'his shanks were pulled off.' A servant, however, was left to tend to him. It was to be a costly service. They were taken in by the Baroness of Doune and 'cherished with meat and drink and clothing.'[36] There was, however, more to this than Christian charity. They were being succoured and kept alive so that they at least would face the full force of public justice and private revenge.

13

EXECUTION DONE ON CAWDOR:[1]
4 February 1591/2

It is commonly said that Huntly durst not have slain the Earl of Moray in the life of Calder, who was murdered eight days [*sic*] before Moray; so that all the murderers of Moray are now suspected with the murder of Calder.

Robert Bowes[2]

When every man carries a pistol at his girdle as they do in Scotland, it is an easy matter to kill a man through a window or door, and not be able to discover who did it.

Edward Wotton[3]

On the other side of the country another killing occurred whose coincidence in time and circumstance with the fate of Moray led many to think – then and now – that there was a link.

On the evening of 4 February 1591/2 the fifty-one-year-old Sir John Campbell, third thane of Cawdor (near Nairne in Morayshire), was sitting peacefully by the fire in his daughter's house of Knipoch, beside Loch Feochan, under the castle wall at Dunnone. He had arrived that day. Lying in wait for his arrival was Gillipatrick Oig McKellar. He planned to kill him from a safe distance. He had been supplied with a red stocked hagbut to accomplish this, but the plan was almost foiled when he discovered that the lead bullets were too large. McKellar was not one to be thwarted and chewed them to the right size. Finally he poked the hagbut through the window lattice and shot Cawdor three times in the heart.[4]

This news was not known in Edinburgh until after the death of Moray but when it was it was immediately attributed to 'Huntly's means.'[5] Two of his enemies were dead within days of each other, one by Huntly's hand, the other by his nod. Bowes considered that Huntly would not have dared killed Moray in the lifetime of Cawdor whose relation by marriage he was.[6]

At the time Maitland was not associated with Huntly in blame for the death of Cawdor, though he was accused of just about everything else. It was not for another two years that the fully fledged conspiracy theory emerged implicating a dazzling array of the Scottish aristocracy and revealing the Chancellor as the spider at the centre of the web. It did so in circumstances which cannot but undermine its credibility: a forced or frightened 'confession' by Sir John Campbell of Ardkinglas in June 1594 after he had been incarcerated and interrogated in Carnasserie Castle. He retracted these far-ranging allegations a month later and they were ignored and forgotten for 250 years until made public by the researches of the antiquary Donald Gregory. In 1837 Gregory had been ferreting around in the charter chest of the Campbells of Aird, a sept of the House of Cawdor, when he had come across papers relating to, and preserved since the time of, the murders. These detailed the history of the proceedings in the Cawdor matter.[7]

The origins of this alleged conspiracy were said to go back to September 1584 when Colin Campbell, sixth Earl of Argyll died, leaving a minor as an heir and a power vacuum in the west. The dowager Countess had custody of her son and was to be advised by a council of six leading Campbells: Archibald of Lochnell, Duncan of Glenorchy, Dougal of Auchinbreck, John of Cawdor, James of Ardkinglas, comptroller to the King, and Neil Campbell, Bishop of Argyll. Ardkinglas secured from the King the valuable feudal right of the ward and marriage of the young Earl. Cawdor, Ardkinglas and the bishop, as the signatories to all leases, soon eclipsed the other three counsellors in their influence on the affairs of the earldom. Lochnell, the nearest heir, was mightily offended at being sidelined. The sands soon shifted and as Cawdor rose ever towards dominance, relations between him and his erstwhile ally, Ardkinglas, ruptured to such an extent that they became murderous. When in 1590 at the age of fourteen the young Earl nominated his own guardians, rival factions, led by Ardkinglas and Cawdor on the one hand and Lochnell and Glenorchy on the other, ranged against each other. Cawdor and Lochnell were chosen. Ardkinglas was not. In June Cawdor's land agent in Edinburgh, James Wardlaw, warned his master that Ardkinglas had 'conceived a great anger towards you.'[8] Death, through natural causes, intervened when the latter died later that year before he could bring to fruition any plots of his own to eliminate his rival.

His antipathy to Cawdor did not die with him but was inherited by his son and successor, John. Cawdor's ever-growing supremacy – supported by many of the nobility connected to the family of Argyll, including the Earl of Moray – kept the new laird in the shadow, adding to his inherited sense of grievance. Glenorchy, equally anxious to curb the progress of Cawdor, worked upon this young man of 'weak and vacillating disposition,'[9] nursing his wrath.

What Ardkinglas claimed that he did not know at the time was that he was being worked upon in the interests of a far wider conspiracy, one involving Glenorchy, Huntly and Maitland himself, the great Machiavel of Scotland. Others allegedly party to the conspiracy were John, Lord Maxwell, Archibald and Duncan Campbell of Lochnell, John Stewart of Appin, Duncan Macdougall of Dunollie, and Lauchlin McLean of Duart who had his own grievances with Cawdor over his aspirations in Islay. They bound themselves together to achieve the murder of the Earls of Moray and Argyll, the latter's only brother, Colin Campbell of Lundy, and his guardian, Cawdor. Lochnell – as next in line to the young seventh Earl- was to get the earldom of Argyll, and in turn Maitland and the others would get a large part of its estates. The conspiracy had grown well beyond the narrow confines that Ardkinglas envisaged.[10]

While others were to act elsewhere Glenorchy undertook the assassination of Cawdor. He used all his guile on the young and susceptible Ardkinglas and taunted him into action, while keeping him in the dark as to the wider ramifications of the plot. Glenorchy proposed that they get 'some fit young man to shoot him on his travels or in a thatched house where he habitually lodged.' They in turn would kill the assassin and so no news of their involvement would leak out.[11] Ardkinglas agreed to implement this plan and a written 'contract' was drawn up and signed by him and Glenorchy at Inveraray.

Ardkinglas first approached his cousin, Duncan Campbell of Auchawillan, who refused to be party to the plot. However, he more easily secured the services of one of his own tenants and domestics, Gillipatrick Oig McKellar, in return for promising him a factorship. Gillipatrick's brother Gillimartin refused to take part but agreed to keep his mouth shut. One other man was in the know, Lochnell's brother, John Oig Campbell of Cabrachan. His estates were a few miles east of Knipoch, a place frequented by Cawdor whose daughter lived there, and a convenient spot for an ambush. Ardkinglas provided a hagbut, powder and shot, Campbell the location, McKellar the muscle.

As early as June 1592 Ardkinglas and Glenorchy were under suspicion,[12] but there was no proof, since McKellar had gone to ground. He evaded capture until 1594 when both he and Campbell of Cabrachan were arrested and thrown into prison. After brutal torture 'by the boots,' Cabrachan confessed his own share and implicated Ardkinglas and MacDougall of Dunollie. He suggested that there was a wider conspiracy involved but gave no details. The confession signed both his and McKellar's death warrants. They were executed forthwith. Ardkinglas and MacDougall were apprehended.

Ardkinglas, in turn under threat of torture, signed a 'confession' on 21 May 1594. In it he divulged the above account, implicating Huntly, Maitland and the others in a 'Great Contract' aimed at Cawdor, Moray, and Argyll. Cawdor's murder and that of Moray were connected in plan as well as in time, both separate strokes in one gigantic conspiracy.[13] The destruction of Moray was more than merely an episode in a private feud between two rival houses in the north. It was both the result and the cause of a vast network of conspiracy, which divided and distracted the whole country. So asserted the penitent Ardkinglas. There was, however, no evidence to substantiate these assertions. Documents were missing, and the explanations for this were weak. According to Ardkinglas, the first 'contract' drawn up between him and Glenorchy had been 'craftily taken away from him by the said Duncan Campbell of Glenorchy.' The second, which would have proved the wider conspiracy, had been shown to him by Glenorchy in an attempt to get him to sign it. There he had seen the signatures of a galaxy of Scottish notables appended: Maitland, Huntly, Maxwell, Lochnell, Glenorchy, Stewart of Appin and Macdougall of Dunollie. But Ardkinglas had refused to add his and so had never possessed a copy of the document himself. In other words, there was no documentary proof of any of that which he alleged.[14]

Glenorchy, of course, dismissed this account as a 'false, undutiful invention.' Argyll himself took no note of the allegations since he had Campbell of Lochnell and his brother James fighting at his side against Huntly at the Battle of Glenlivet a few months later, a battle in which both were killed by their supposed co-conspirators. Ensuing events seemed to justify their disdain. Freed from the torture, on 1 July 1594 Ardkinglas duly revoked his earlier confession, which he now claimed to have 'invented to eschew the trouble that might follow on me for Cawdor's slaughter.' He denied that Maitland, Huntly, Glenorchy or any others had been involved in any grand design. The feud was local and involved only the immediate and obvious conspirators: Ardkinglas himself, Gillipatrick, Gillimartin, and John Oig Campbell of Cabrachan. The following year, now he was at liberty, his conscience continued to prick him. As a result he made a longer retraction, confirming that he had made 'a worthless and slanderous invention.' He had done so as a result of being threatened with torture if he did not reveal details of a conspiracy corresponding with John Oig's testimony.[15] Despite or because of these retractions the Cawdors were convinced that evidence of the bond of conspiracy was being smothered and suppressed by intervention at the highest levels.

However, on 5 October 1595, Margaret Campbell of Cabrachan, widow of John Oig, decided to give her own testimony of what was told to her by Ardkinglas himself about the murder of Cawdor. According to her lengthy account he had asked her to consult witches on his behalf to mend things between himself and the Earl of Argyll. She pretended to know more than she did about Cawdor's killing and demanded of him a full account of the murder if she was to be able to do his bidding. He told her that his cousins, John and Patrick Campbell of Auchawillan, and his father's old friend George Balfour had cajoled him into picking up where his father had left off and compass the death of Cawdor. When he had tried to resile they called him coward and Patrick of Auchawillan said, 'Even if they had a bag full of fears in place of the laird of Ardkinglas, why might not they make a man of me?' Seeing himself so reproached he gave in.[16] Margaret pressed him further for details of a greater conspiracy. Gradually she found out the full extent of it and the great names involved. Her account is far too detailed to be other than a concoction; her story of witchcraft hardly lends weight to it, and she had an axe to grind against Ardkinglas who had survived his murderous activities while her husband had died as a result of his more marginal involvement in them.

As a result of these 'revelations,' in April 1596 the Cawdors brought letters of treason against Ardkinglas for 'murder under trust,' hoping to ferret out the wider story. His trial was set for September but on the appointed day when the King's prosecutors failed to appear the justice quashed the case for want of prosecution. The paranoia of the Cawdors grew wings, but there the matter rested apart from local reprisals. On 8 August 1596 Lady Jean Campbell of Ardkinglas had been ambushed near her home, stripped and put to the indignity of being whipped by her own accompanying servants.[17] Ardkinglas himself, however, escaped any retribution, and survived one assassination attempt.[18]

As with all conspiracy theories, far-reaching allegations based on partisan testimony are less likely to be true than the obvious explanation that Cawdor's death was yet another instance of a banal murder for local reasons. Such killings in Scotland were anything but uncommon. Ardinglas' declaration that there never was such a contract involving Maitland, Huntly and the others gains credence from the fact that he did not deny his own personal involvement in the murder.[19] Gillipatrick McKellar and John Oig Campbell had been executed in Dynone. The immediate culprits had been brought to justice, if their instigator, Ardkinglas was not. The Earl of Huntly would have rejoiced in the timely death of another old foe, but there is no evidence that he had his hand in it. The murder of the Earl of Moray was an act of opportunism rather than of premeditation; the killing of Cawdor the climax of a dispute within Clan Campbell. Nonetheless at the time, the coincidence of Cawdor's slaying and Moray's helped further to blacken Huntly's name and to ensure a broad coalition of those wanting to punish him personally and curb the invasive power of the Gordons. In particular, the young Earl of Argyll, angry for his friends and fearful for his own security, was eager for an opportunity to take revenge on the man he suspected had conspired against his life.

PART IV

THE 6TH EARL AND 1ST MARQUIS

OF HUNTLY

AND

THE 3RD EARL OF MORAY

1591/2-1638

14
'THE HORROR OF DINNIBIRSALL'
February–March 1591/2

The people cry out at the cruelty of the deed.

Roger Aston[1]

The murdour done of the erle of Murray, at Dinnibirsall, be the erle of Hountlie, on fear [broad] day-light, the king luiking on it with forthought, fellon hamsukin, and treason under tryst, maist crewalie with fyre and sworde, yit mightelie cryes and importunes the ear of the righteous inquyrar and revengar of bloode!

James Melville.[2]

[The Earl of Huntly] maist unworthelie and schamefullie murdreist and slew ... the Earl of Moray, being the lustiest youth, the first noble man of the kingis bloode, and one of the peiris of the countrey, to the great regrait and lamentacioun of the haill pepill.

David Moysie[3]

The King's actions in the immediate aftermath of the murder both facilitated Huntly's escape and kept a safe degree of distance between them. Huntly and his men returned to the town of Inverkeithing two miles west of Donnibristle. Situated on the Queen's Ferry road, it was a good place both to get news and if necessary to make a quick escape north. There, with one exception, they stayed the night. The exception was John Gordon of Buckie, then master of the King's household, whom Huntly despatched to Edinburgh as his emissary. He was to find James and inform him of what had happened before anyone else did. Thus Huntly's slant on events would be first in the King's mind before it could be poisoned by Protestant misrepresentation. Gordon went to Nicholl Edwards' house where James was staying, but was refused an audience. The King was to rise early the following morning to go hunting and on that account had retired to bed. Buckie took lodgings in the Canongate, hoping to deliver his message first thing in the morning. Again he was too late. The King had gone and Edinburgh was abuzz with report and rumour. Buckie could do no more now than save his own skin. As a prominent member of Huntly's entourage he was in mortal danger. At least the second part of his mission was accomplished: he had gauged the feeling in the capital and could warn his master to lie low.[4]

On the morning of 8 February James was innocently enjoying the hunt about Wardie and Inverleith, to all appearances ignorant of what had transpired over the Firth. Ochiltree noticed across the water smoke rising from Donnibristle. Perhaps a little disingenuously, since he was familiar with the house, James asked him to identify the spot. 'Ochiltree was amazed, partly blamed the King and craved leave to go to the rescue; nevertheless he was stayed.'[5] This staying prevented – by accident or design – Huntly's immediate apprehension. By the time Lennox, Mar and Ochiltree had returned to Edinburgh and heard of Buckie's presence he had taken horse, and although Ochiltree pursued him at once, he managed to get across the Forth unscathed. He found Huntly at Inverkeithing, 'who being at dinner, immediately on Buckie's arrival, rose therefrom, and slipt away in haste, not even paying his reckoning.'[6] He took refuge further along the Fife coast in Ravenscraig Castle, the impregnable fortress of Lord Sinclair. Sinclair was true to his duty of hospitality but mindful of the risk he was running, telling the fugitive that he was welcome to come in but would have been twice as welcome to have passed by.[7] Fortunately for his host, Huntly's stay was short, and he made for the greater safety of his own lands in the north.

However reluctant to acknowledge the obvious, the King could not evade it when he returned to the capital. There he found the streets 'swept with rumour and full of lamentation for Moray,' whose sudden demise created his popularity. There is no evidence that before his death he had been regarded with particular affection by anyone. Murder makes odd martyrs. The Protestant lords were furious. Had anyone other than Huntly been responsible they would have been less so, but here was a God-given opportunity to stir up popular clamour against the most powerful Catholic leader. Lennox and the Stewarts were further incensed by this outrage perpetrated on their House. Their retainers strode the streets, bringing the populace to the boil with lurid tales of foul murder until 'the people cr[ied] out of the cruelty of the deed.'[8]

The following day, the 9 February, Moray's grieving mother, Lady Margaret, brought her son's body and that of his sheriff by boat to Leith with a view to them both being paraded through the streets of Edinburgh and displayed at the Mercat Cross. The former, she intended, would then be buried with all pomp in the tomb of the first Earl of Moray, the Good Regent, in St Giles Church. James refused to countenance such a spectacle in the streets of the capital let alone such a burial in a royal tomb. He commanded the provost to prevent either Lady Doune or her son's corpse from entering the town 'until they knew more of His Majesty's mind.'[9]

Scapegoats had to be found to appease the popular indignation. The only ones directly to suffer for the murder were the mortally wounded Captain John Gordon and his servant, who had been nurtured and brought to Leith by Lady Margaret along with the remains of her son. The King first tried to circumvent the embarrassment of a public trial by granting Lord Spynie a warrant to take Captain Gordon from Lady Moray to Edinburgh castle 'to have eschewed the present trial of law.' Ochiltree again confronted the King on his hunt, warning him 'how far the murder touched His Highness.'[10] James, sensing the transparent anger and recognising that violent emotions had to be appeased, rescinded Spynie's warrant replacing it with one authorising the immediate trial of Gordon. The trial was held at once. Gordon was condemned out of hand, and on same day beheaded in Edinburgh, protesting to the last that he had no part in the killing of Moray. He had been brought ignorantly into the business 'but confessed the Lord had brought him to his shameful end for his many other great offences.' He did not implicate the King or the Chancellor. He was dispatched at the Cross, and his 'running footman' hanged. Their deaths were the least sacrifice that James could offer on the altar of public outrage.[11]

James could put a halt to an irate old woman at the gates of his capital but he could not stifle the powerful forces seeking to bring down his favourite. He had to sanction a debate in council on how to punish Huntly. Huntly was denounced for 'hamesucken' and treason under trust, both capital offences.[12] 'Hamesucken' was the premeditated hunting down and invasion of a person in his home with intent to assault. To kill a man in passion on the street, or even to waylay him on the highway, was one thing, but to invade the sanctity of his own home and there despatch him at ease and unprepared was beyond the pale. This, it was thundered, Huntly had done. Murder 'under trust' was deemed treason by an Act of 1587. The guilty party in addition to losing his life would forfeit his lands and property.[13] The deeply affected and enraged Ochiltree 'prayed the king in some rough language to show his forwardness therein, otherwise the king's self should be holden suspect herein.' Other than himself, Ochiltree declared, only the King and the Chancellor knew of Moray's residence at Donnibristle. Ochiltree had not betrayed him. The implication was obvious. The King could only angrily deny it and silence the traducer. Ochiltree had overstepped the mark and was briefly committed to ward.

But his insinuations were not so easily contained and the King had to employ all his forcefulness and powers of persuasion to convince both his nobility and the Kirk of his innocence. 'His part [was]... like David's, when

Abner was slain by Joab: "I and my kingdom are guiltless before the Lord for ever from the blood of Abner, the son of Ner'"(II Samuel 3.28).[14] James was not alone in quoting scripture for his purpose. A few days after the murder, Patrick Simpson, preaching before James on the text Genesis chapter 4 verse 9 ('The Lord said to Cain, where is Abel thy brother?'), spoke directly to the King before the whole congregation: 'Sir, I assure you in God's name, the Lord will ask at you where is the Earl of Moray your brother?' The King replied, 'Mr Patrick, my chamber door was never steeked upon you; ye might have told me anything ye thought in secret.' He retorted, 'Sir, the scandal is public.' After such a sermon he was invited to lodge awhile in Edinburgh Castle, an invitation he could not refuse, going up with 'the bible under his ochster [armpit] affirming that would plead for him.'[15]

At the same time as publicly washing his hands of all responsibility for this action of his unruly subject, the King extended his protection to the Countess of Huntly, keeping her at court. Huntly meanwhile made his apology by proxy, the master of Elphinstone justifying his actions on the grounds of the commission of lieutenancy granted him by the King. Moray disobeyed him and he was thus driven to assault him in his house. Huntly's assertion coupled by the King's delay in taking action against him and giving succour to his wife merely generated the mill of rumour and speculation. The King, it seemed, was more eager to proclaim his own innocence than pursue the guilty. A decree of council deprived Huntly of all his commissions of lieutenancy, a sanction scarcely adequate to the moment.[16]

Denied entry into Edinburgh, Moray's body – along with that of his sheriff – lay at the parish church of Leith for all to see and note. The wait, it was anticipated, would be lengthy. Thus, at a cost of £100, the body was embalmed by James Henderson, an Edinburgh surgeon whose father had performed the same service for the fourth Earl of Huntly. A further £100 and £65 respectively were spent on two lead coffins, the former for the Earl, the latter for his sheriff.[17]

In her efforts to get her son's death avenged, Lady Margaret refused to let either the citizenry or the King forget what had happened. She herself paraded the city streets, from which her son's corpse had been prohibited, with his bloodstained shirt as her banner. Later, in the north, 'Lord Forbes, an attached friend of Moray, carried his bloody shirt on a spear's head; and marching with the ghastly banner through his territories incited his followers to revenge.'[18] In this he was following a family tradition since the most dramatic and provocative use of a 'bloody serk' had taken place in August 1488 when Alexander, the then Lord Forbes, carried the shirt of the murdered King James III, 'stained with blood and torn with the marks of his wounds, suspended on a spear, through Aberdeen and the chief towns of the adjacent counties and by public proclamation called on all men to avenge the horrid deed.'[19] This 'bloody serk' was later used as the rebels' banner when they went into battle against the forces of James IV. This 'presentation of blood' was a common means both of demanding justice and of presenting proof, and in barony courts people who had been assaulted brought bloodstained clothes to the judge.[20] On an earlier occasion the Revd Mr Craig preaching in the presence of the King rebuked him for having 'lightly regarded the many bloody shirts presented to him by his subjects craving justice.'[21] The same tactic was to be employed the following year by some poor women of Nithsdale who, frustrated by the inaction of royal justice, went to the capital with the bloody shirts of their husbands, sons and servants who had been killed by the Johnstones. They paraded them through the streets, exposing the King's inadequacy in providing protection or justice.[22]

Dame Margaret would do whatever she could to ensure that her son's fate would resound throughout the kingdom despite the King. With her own hands 'she took three bullets out of her son's body and delivered them to the keeping of several and especial friends who solemnly have vowed to bestow the same bullets and others into the bodies of some principal executioners of this slaughter, for the taking of this revenge it appears that many of good quality will hazard themselves and lives, howsoever their enterprise therein shall be afterwards punished.'[23] Calderwood states that the King himself was a recipient of one of the bullets. She had proffered and he had refused every other memento mori, perhaps at last he gave way to this smallest and least odious souvenir. Another bullet, Calderwood says, she saved for herself, saying 'I shall not part with this till it be bestowed on him that hindreth justice.'[24]

The formidable matriarch was not finished yet. She 'caused draw her son's picture, as he was demained.' The life-size portrait of the corpse known as the Moray Memorial is crudely but effectively done. The body itself is rather corpulent with thick thighs and heavy torso, but whether this is owing to riotous living, the bloating effects of death, or lack of artistry is not certain. The young Earl is beardless, shorthaired, and with an elongated nose. His right leg bears a gaping gash and two deep parallel dagger strokes mar his face. Three bullet holes are apparent on his torso. So much for realism. Out of his mouth issues a scroll bearing the usual inscription 'GOD REVENGE MY CAUS.' To the left of the scroll is the date '1591 Febr 7' and to the right 'Aeta 24.' Above the body in the right-hand corner of the picture is a depiction of the scene of the murder. The buildings of Donnibristle are all alight. The shoreline forms a horseshoe before them and there on the strand lies the body of the bonnie Earl. The message of the picture is unequivocal, a mixture of symbol and graffiti, serving as crude but effective propaganda. It is likely that this Memorial was painted while the corpse lay at Leith by a jobbing artisan whose services could be speedily deployed and whose work while lacking sophistication would serve its purpose. Lady Doune intended it to be shown at the Cross in Edinburgh and she herself brought it to the king enclosed in a piece a fine lawn cloth 'with lamentations and earnest suite for justice.' But the king, we are told, 'liked not to look upon his corpse.'[25]

Apart from this macabre lying in state, Melville mentioned 'common rymes and sangs' as keeping 'the horror of Dinnibirsall in recent [fresh] detestation.'[26] The basis of the 'Ballad of the Bonnie Earl of Moray' may well have been composed at this time, helping to keep the memory of the murder alive, and perpetuating – if not creating – many unsubstantiated but damaging speculations and fabrications about it. While exonerating the King from wishing Moray's death, it negates this by asserting that Moray not only was 'the Queen's true love' but 'might hae been the king.' According to the sixteenth-century historian, Sir James Balfour of Kinnaird,

> It was given out and publicly talked, that the Earl of Huntly was only the instrument of perpetrating this fact, to satisfy the King's jealousy of Moray, whom the Queen more rashly than wisely, some days before had commended in the King's hearing, with too many epithets of a proper and gallant man.[27]

Even if Balfour is right and such a slander was noised abroad it was as improbable as it was unsubstantiated. James never seemed to evince sexual jealousy, least of all over a woman, and in particular over one as young, silly, and meddlesome as Anne.[28] On the other hand she was the Queen and as such an important and protected piece of property. Paranoid – or justifiably worried – as James could be over Bothwell's action and ambitions there is nothing to suggest Moray any more than irritated him by his sulkiness or annoyed him by his associations. He was no king in waiting. The frustrated ambition of the Regent Moray is here being attributed to his successor to the earldom. Although neither assertion has the least plausibility, they nonetheless suggest a popular perception that the King had good reason for wanting rid of the Earl of Moray. The ballad as a whole – if not in every detail – is likely to be near contemporary to the events it laments, and as such constitutes a 'trenchant piece of propaganda in favour of the Presbyterian party.'[29] It would have further traduced James in the eyes of the people.

On all sides the King was pressed to act. Many members of the nobility along with the clergy and burgesses of Edinburgh joined in the popular clamour for justice and revenge. The Earls of Mar and Morton were to the fore in this and the Duke of Lennox was 'as earnest as any.'[30] James did take some canny measures to appease popular pressure. Ochiltree was commissioned to burn and destroy the homes of those Gordons who were thought to have participated in the murder; and Lennox received the wardship of the young Earl of Moray. The perceptive Bowes read the royal mind exactly, observing that by means of the Duke the feud between the houses of Huntly and Moray would in time be appeased, that Huntly's life would be spared, 'albeit that he shall be chastised for a season, and that sundry of his friends and surname present at Moray's slaughter shall suffer death for the same.'[31] So it was to turn out and such was to be their sacrifice.

James knew that, given time, popular passions would be assuaged. He was the master of delay. The secret was to take firm action, slowly. It was soon announced that he himself would lead a punitive expedition to the north to apprehend the errant Earl who walked unscathed on the streets of Aberdeen and dwelt secure in his great Castle of Strathbogie. The date set was 11 February. It was the first of many such deadlines that promised much and yet somehow were never met. This time the journey was postponed for a month on the grounds that the necessary forces could not be levied in so short a time.

James, understandably, was in fact far more eager to apprehend Bothwell than Huntly. The treasonous Stewart, unlike the wayward Gordon, was a direct threat to the throne. The King soon left for Glasgow in pursuit of the former, conveniently distancing himself from the unwelcome pressures being placed upon him in Edinburgh by all and sundry to pursue and punish the latter. Roger Aston murmured that the journey westward was 'not so much for the pursuing of Bothwell as it was to avoid the fury of the people upon the death of Moray.'[32] Bothwell they could not apprehend, but an associate of his, one John Naismith, they did. According to Calderwood, he was threatened with torture to confess that the Earl of Moray had been present at the Holyrood raid. Naismith offered defiance in place of confession, answering that 'he would not damn his own soul with speaking untruth for any bodily pain.'[33] Unable to catch its prey the royal contingent moved to Dumbarton where it spent four days searching for the renegade Earl. He was thought to have got to his home in the Borders, his movements unimpeded by a populace disgruntled by the Moray murder. Aston feared that Bothwell might 'go where he pleases for no man will "ster" him.'[34] On the run he continued to stir up trouble for James and his Chancellor, penning defamatory letters to the Edinburgh presbytery blaming Maitland for being behind his persecution and for hounding Huntly to murder Moray.

Wild rumour did little to still the passions of the Edinburgh populace. 'Spiteful libels' were 'daily cast in the streets.' The cause of Moray, Bothwell, Argyll and the Kirk were more or less clearly identified on the one side; the cause of the King, Chancellor and Huntly on the other; while the shifting sands of personal jealousies and private animosities were an incalculable force. Mr Patrick Galloway, one of James' chaplains, and as tactless as his master, went so far as to give voice to the rumour that James himself was complicit in the murder of his Earl. It is quite possible that the King and his wayward Earl were in direct communication all the while.[35] Calderwood preserves a conspiratorial letter between the two in which James openly talks of his dissembling to the people and of his devotion to the Earl:

> Since your passing herefrom, I have been in such danger and peril of my life, as since I was borne I was never in the like, partly by the grudging and tumults of the people, and partly by the exclamation of the ministry, whereby I was moved to dissemble. Always I shall remain constant. When ye come down here, come not by the ferries; and if ye doe, accompany yourself, as ye respect your own preservation. Ye shall write to the principal ministers that are here, for thereby their anger will be greatly pacified.[36]

If genuine, and if its date and attribution are correct, this letter leaves no doubt as to the King's loyalty and affection and the lengths to which he will go to protect those he loves from the machinations of those he detests. It does not, however, in itself make him party to murder.

Huntly was blamed as being behind other recent atrocities: the murder of the thane of Cawdor in Argyll and the hanging of the eldest sons of Macintosh by the Earl of Caithness, Huntly's brother-in-law. In the capital it was assumed that civil war would again break out and Bowes informed his masters that 'most men arm and set themselves ready for the troubles.' Groups of men patrolled the streets, neighbour fell under suspicion from neighbour and 'great and hasty troubles' were 'feared to arise in the realm.' The people's 'murmur and rage increases daily, drawing many into factions and devices to encompass their desires.'[37] Argyll, Ochiltree, Athol and other of Moray's friends were reported to be leaguing together. Things were getting dangerously out of control and the troubles and turmoil of the regency years which had so terrorised the King in his youth, so recently buried, were in danger of being resurrected. Moray's murder was having repercussions none would have expected, least of all the King who in his determination to bring Bothwell to justice while letting Huntly alone found himself to be completely out of kilter with popular sentiment.

The Privy Council and the 'well affected' were concerned enough to meet the King in Linlithgow and urge him to hold a convention in Edinburgh to reform the government and punish offenders. James acceded to this. Canny political operator as he was, he always knew the time when he must be seen to concede. That time had arrived. A convention was ordered. He was prepared to make one further concession to public clamour and that was to order Huntly for trial at Linlithgow. A concession, as he was well aware, was not the same as its implementation.

In the meanwhile Huntly was to ward himself in the royal Castle of Blackness on the West Lothian coast. The fortress stood – and still stands – on a rocky promontory projecting into the Firth of Forth, surrounded on three sides by sea or salt marsh, about three and a half miles from Bo'ness and the same distance from the town of Linlithgow of which it had once been the port. Comprising a long oblong keep with a circular staircase tower at the north-east, massively fortified to withstand artillery assault, in the mid-sixteenth century it was regarded as the most secure castle in Scotland and virtually impregnable.[38] It was the state prison, the Scots equivalent of the Tower. Barely a dozen miles from Edinburgh it was near enough the King, far enough from the popular fury, and secure enough from any attempts at revenge. In Blackness Huntly could comply with the law and be safer than anywhere else in Scotland. He was not intending to stay long, and while he did so his was to be a token confinement. For prisoners of the importance of Huntly nothing would be too much trouble for the keeper, Sir James Sandilands. The Earl's own retainers could remain with him, his apartments would be spacious and well provisioned.[39] 'He had so many servants there that he is thought to be master thereof and that he rather takes his pastimes than endures any punishment.'[40] There Huntly would remain safe in royal custody, secure from any reprisals or assassination attempts. There he could live in relative opulence, and yet he would be seen to be imprisoned awaiting trial.

The 3 March 1591/2 was the day set both for the trial of Huntly at Linlithgow and for the funeral of his victim in Edinburgh. The unhappy but deliberate conjunction of the two was dangerously provocative. A dramatic public funeral, where the Memorial would be displayed, and calls for vengeance made, was designed to ensure that after the inevitable verdict was delivered the severest punishment would be imposed. The King accordingly deferred the former, and in consequence the Moray family postponed the latter.[41]

Postponement was to grow into permanence. Any burial at all, in Edinburgh or otherwise was frustrated for a further six years, owing to the reluctance of the dead Earl's supporters to inter his corpse until 'the slaughter was punished.' Exposed, it cried out to heaven and to the King in the most dramatic way. Preparations, we know, were made in April and May for a funeral, John Workman being commissioned to 'make and deliver the ceremonies and furniture.' A speedy trial and a dramatic funeral were still anticipated to coincide. After 20 May such hopes were finally to fade to extinction. The treasurer's accounts record a payment of '40s to Archibald Douglas, Masser, with letters to command and charge the Provost, Baillies and Council of Edinburgh to convene all and sundry the Inhabitants within the said burgh upon the twenty day of this instant month of May, and to pass and bury the corpse of umqujhile [sometime] James Earl of Moray in sik place as should be set down be his friends, under the pain of rebellion, &c., after the form and tenor of the said letters.'[42] Nothing, however, was to be done; no trial was to be held; no funeral was to take place until many years had passed. It was not to be until 16 February 1597/8, when all hope of justice was past, that his son and brother were charged by the Privy Council to inter the body, and at last they were to do so.

Meanwhile, Huntly was released on parole. But not for long. On the 9 March 1591/2 commissions were given to the Earl Marischal to arrest Huntly, Errol, Sir Patrick Gordon of Auchindoun and various other accomplices, and to the Earl of Athol to assist the Earl Marischal in the north.[43] Huntly himself would prove no problem, warding himself the following day in Blackness. There he continued to justify himself and pass the responsibility for the death of Moray onto his King and kin. The pursuit of Moray, he claimed, was done under royal commission, while the actual slaughter had been carried out against Huntly's will by his friends, the lairds of Cluny, Gight and Innermarky all of whom had a personal feud with Moray and whose rage and violence Huntly could not restrain.[44] Wisely these friends – less confident in the compass of royal protection – had declined the offer of imprisonment and returned home. In their absence they provided him with useful scapegoats and their flight – in contrast to their lord's surrender – lent substance to his assertions. The very next day moves were afoot to set Huntly at liberty again under caution provided that Moray's faction agreed not to pursue him.

Such a concession was not readily forthcoming. Some malcontents had solemnly sworn to 'kuf' [exchange] lives with Huntly. He nearly suffered this fate when Robert Stewart, a servant of Moray and brother of the laird of Innermeath, entered his house in Perth disguised in Highland clothes and armed with a pistol. But before he could do anything he was shown the door. Unable to get at Huntly himself, Robert and Innermeath took out their frustrations by harrying him where they could. A courier bearing 6,000 merks destined for Huntly was waylaid on the road from Perth to Queen's Ferry and robbed of his trunk.[45] Huntly, therefore, remained in protective confinement a while longer than he had anticipated until the King issued a proclamation restraining Moray from pursuing Huntly 'for his father's slaughter, in respect he, being wardit in the Castle of Blackness, was willing to abide his trial.' While there abiding, he was not inactive, seeking to strengthen his position by tying in as many retainers to his person as he could.[46]

The Privy Council met and proposals for dealing with the trial of those involved were discussed. One trial had already come to nought, and more and more problems seemed to be arising. For murder the law provided that a man be judged by a jury of his peers. Scotland did not boast eight earls who were not so closely related to either Huntly or Moray as to qualify them for serving on a jury, 'so that in that point he knows his life to be in no danger.' Next he had many friends, chiefly Lord Spynie and Sir George Home, who have shown themselves 'plain party' for him.[47] There was growing unease among Moray's supporters that much was being said but little done, and that the King by prevaricating was hoping that both he and Huntly could weather the storm unscathed. On this point they were undoubtedly near the mark. When his accusers failed to materialise at the Privy Council Huntly gave surety to present himself when summoned to judgement and on the 20 March was again released from Blackness. He stayed in Crawford's house until the time was ripe for his departure north.

In the capital there was manoeuvring on behalf of both the clergy and the courtiers. The main casualty of this was Maitland. Angry at the aspersions being cast on him, he thought it politic to distance himself from Huntly and indeed openly sided against him. But his position was precarious, and at the end of March at royal command he left the court to await his master's summons. His departure was another sacrifice to popular demand. He had to be distanced from the King. Yet James did just as much as was necessary to appease public opinion and no more. Maitland lost neither his chancellorship nor his access to the King who regularly visited him in Lethington.

Ironically, the main beneficiary of the murder was Bothwell, since 'the grudge of Moray's slaughter so works in the hearts of most men, and in the well affected, that they will not give their endeavours to touch Bothwell or prevent any matter threatening alteration in this state, in regard they think that by the welter of the state the evil councillors and instruments in the king's chamber shall be defeated and removed.'[48] The Edinburgh presbytery proposed that Huntly and his accomplices be excommunicated, a sanction they had never suggested for Bothwell. The King, incensed by this discrimination, caustically remarked that 'it would not be well till noblemen and gentlemen got licence to break ministers' heads.'[49] This sort of injudicious comment merely had the effect of making the clergy more hostile to James and more favourably disposed towards Bothwell, who thus gained a respectability he did not deserve and whose final eradication was further delayed.[50] In such circumstances the King needed his loyal friend Huntly all the more. In a conversation with the Stewart prior of Blantyre, James stipulated that the Stewarts must renounce Bothwell before he would remove Huntly.[51] Was James really prepared to be so Machiavellian towards his favourite? It is much more likely he was hoping to isolate Bothwell without jeopardising Huntly. He was playing for time, hoping for something to turn up. It did.

Lady Doune died in late March 1592.[52] Her demise so soon after that of her son may be attributable to injuries occasioned in the firing of Donnibristle, or – less likely – to 'the passion.... of her griefs conceived that she was denied to bury her son honourably in Edinburgh.' Whatever its cause, her death provided just the change in political temperature that James was waiting for. Dame Margaret had been responsible for the most trenchant and dramatic demands for the apprehension of her son's murderers, and made one further dying plea – or threat: 'in her testament and in her own hand [she] left an especial note to the king to do justice to preserve himself from violence.'[53] Her deathbed malediction on the King, and her son's cadaver lying yet unburied in its lead coffin in Leith, caused renewed murmuring.[54] This was, however, more than compensated for by her now permanent silence on the matter. The greatest danger for Huntly was over. He and his wife returned home to Strathbogie, living in relative safety and without fear, secure in their northern domain.

15

THE FIRST PUFF OF A HAGGIS[1]
1592–1594

Now wae be to thee, Huntly!
And wherefore did ye sae?
I bade ye bring him wi' you,
And forbad ye him to slay.

The Bonnie Earl of Moray

Rest not, until ye root out these barbarous feuds that their effects may be
as well smoared down [suffocated], as their barbarous name is unknown to
any other nation ... and for your easier abolishing of them put sharply to
execution my laws made against Guns and traitorous Pistolets; thinking in
your heart, tearming in your speech, and using by your punishments, all
such as wear and use them, as brigands and cut-throats.

James VI[2]

With increasing desperation the Moray family continued to petition
King and parliament for relief. The young third Earl complained that
the murder was committed 'so openly in the sight of all ... and so near
unto your majesty's own present principal residence and seat of justice
that the like was never heard of within this realm nor in any other
Christian kingdom before.' If he meant what he said he seems to have
led a very sheltered life. He continued that therefore it deserved 'to be
met and punished and revenged with the most severe, extraordinary, and
most resolute manner of justice and punishment for removing of God's
heavy plaints threatened in law and hanging above this realm and all its
inhabitants if this barbarous cruelty be not speedily revenged.'[3]

This vengeful chorus continued to be backed by a recalcitrant clergy.
On 21 May the General Assembly convened and a delegation was sent
to the King to pressure him into action. The temerity of the sanctimo-
nious and partisan ministers infuriated James, but more problematic was
the fact that the English seemed equally insistent. At his regular
audiences the English ambassador, Sir Robert Bowes would urge James
to take action against Huntly. The King, whose mastery of the art of
prevarication was as adept as that of Elizabeth herself and equally infu-
riating, sought to circumvent responsibility by disingenuously blaming

the Moray faction for the continuing delay both in burying the dead Earl and in the execution of justice against Huntly and others. In contrast to their prevarication, the King promised Bowes that the problem of Huntly's stalled trial could be resolved. If 'three wise and fit persons of Moray's friends' requested it, 'he would readily give them ordinary justice. If ordinary justice and trial could not proceed in regard that Huntly had such great alliance in blood with the nobility that no assize could be got, or by any other impediment, then he would deliberate with them for provision of some other remedy.' He was increasingly confident that no trial would take place, and that 'other remedies' might be contemplated.[4]

Huntly's stock at court remained high and, despite complaints, he still exercised the office of Lord Lieutenant in the North. 'Nothing can bite him,' observed Bowes, laconically. Even reports, fanned by the English, that Huntly and the other Catholic earls were planning to seize the king's person on his projected tour of Fife left James unmoved as did an anonymous libel pinned to his door warning him 'to beware lest he be used as King Richard II was in England.'[5] He trusted more to his own judgement than to unsubstantiated rumour or anonymous notes. In July Bowes again expressed English dismay at James' inaction.

> I let the king know that her majesty marvelled that he had not prosecuted and punished Huntly and other offenders for the murder of Moray, in regard that the same heavily burdened his own honour in the eye of the world and mightily grieved his people at home; and I showed him that this late conspiracy and attempt to have been executed at Falkland was deeply grounded and much stirred by want of expedition of justice in this cause of Moray. He readily blamed Moray's friends and denied the Falkland matter was related to this cause.[6]

The King tried to avoid Bowes for a while and Huntly never forgave his hostile interventions.

More worrying than missives from the family, sermons from the clergy and even entreaties from the ambassador, were the overtures made by Moray's supporters in the direction of Bothwell. Argyll, Athol, Ochiltree and others met together at Dunkeld to devise and forge an alliance to revenge themselves on Huntly. It was reported to James that Bothwell had attended. On being confronted with this allegation, Ochiltree denied parleying with Bothwell but stoutly retorted that he would band with anyone to be avenged on Huntly. On the other hand, he promised that if James acted swiftly against Huntly he would seek to bring Bothwell dead or alive to the King. James was not convinced.

Ochiltree was placed under house arrest and Athol was confined to his own lands. Huntly's most powerful enemies were thus inhibited by royal intervention, since the King, isolated in his struggle with Bothwell, needed Huntly almost as much as Huntly needed him.

James realised he had to end his isolation and try to split the opposition. With the encouragement of Maitland, whom he had recently restored to active office, the King attempted to win the hearts of Kirk and people by granting to the former most of its demands. Passed by parliament in June 1592, 'The Golden Act' ratified all the Kirk's liberties and privileges, granted it the right to call general assemblies, abolished episcopal jurisdiction, and gave new powers to the presbyteries. This was an especially bitter pill for James to swallow, and he spent the next few years clawing back what he had been forced to give. Little benefit did the concessions bring him. He was never allowed to forget the unavenged Moray. When he expressed his amazement that the clergy and people were still more clamorous about the murder of 'the son of the abbot of St Colme' than about that of the Earl of Eglington – his social superior – he was bluntly answered by a minister that Eglington was killed in a feud after being met by chance and that his killers were forfeited and banished. Moray, by contrast had been 'slain in the king's sight in odious manner and with no little touch to the king's honour,' and yet Huntly and his accomplices went unscathed.[7]

The King was not the only one to make pacific overtures to the Kirk. The Countess of Huntly, Alexander Duff, the laird of Petlargo, and other friends and servants of Huntly began a charm offensive to persuade the clergy to receive the submission and repentance of Huntly and to intercede with King and council on his behalf. The clergy saw through this ploy, knew Huntly for the Catholic he was, and did not abate their calls for his punishment.

Faced with this intractable opposition, Huntly now sought to leave the country for three years until passions died down. A comfortable exile for the protagonist and protection for his supporters at home was not what Moray's supporters had in mind as punishment. Nor were Huntly's friends keen on the idea since in his absence another would be appointed Lieutenant of the North, exposing them to retribution. There was a certain 'dryness' between Huntly, who had remained so firmly in royal favour, and his followers and friends who had been put to the horn. The lairds of Cluny, Gight, Innermeath and others met with him and complained that he had let them all be put to the horn for the slaughter of Moray, done for him, and he continued still in the King's grace. He answered that while he was not at the horn he was able to protect them and that hitherto they had lost neither goods nor gear. His voluntary exile, he conceded, would leave them, unaided, to the vengeance of his enemies. He decided not to go. He would brave it out, stoutly defending both himself and the Gordons.[8]

When Athol allied with Lachlan Mackintosh, chief of Clan Chattan, and the Grants, to take advantage of the uncertainty and apparent weakness of Huntly's control in the north, they merely demonstrated once again that his position was unassailable and his local alliances were secure. Cameron of Lochiel, Keppoch, Clanranald, the MacPhersons and lairds of Morayshire all remained loyal to Huntly. William Macintosh, a son of the chief, with a raiding party of 800 men marched onto the lands nearest to Strathbogie to lie in wait for Huntly at the head of the River Dovern. Huntly and his uncle, Patrick Gordon of Auchindoun, with a party of only thirty-six horsemen surprised the unwary raiders at Cabroch upon the height of Staple Hill, charged and defeated them, killing more than sixty and wounding many others. Meanwhile Angus Macintosh, William's brother, and a brigand like the rest, broke into Mar, despoiled Huntly's lands in Strathdee and Glenmuick, and killed several of his kin, including, on 1 November 1592, one old man in clear breach of hospitality and under trust. This was the notorious murder of Alexander Gordon of Brachly, 'a gentleman much commended for his hospitality, whose house was always open to strangers.' He had opened his house to Angus and his men and entertained them civilly. He was slaughtered for his pains, along with his children and servants.[9] Greedy for more booty, Angus next attempted to capture the castle at Riffen in Badenoch which had but a small garrison. Prominent in the 'yellow war coat' of a chief he was shot and killed, and the attempt failed.[10] Reprisals were swift and brutal against a clan which Huntly considered little better than vermin. He despatched Alan Macdonald on a punitive expedition against the Clan Chattan in Badenoch, resulting in a skirmish in which over fifty of the latter were slain, and Macranald with his Lochaber men against their allies, the Grants of Strathspey. They killed eighteen and wasted all the Ballandalloch lands. Huntly then descended in person on Petty Castle near Inverness. The castle belonged to Moray, its surrounds were fertile in corn and cattle, and its inhabitants were for the most part Mackintoshes. Taken by surprise, many were killed as they slept, their houses burnt and their cattle and sheep carried away. No quarter was given. Huntly had come 'with an open host and displayed banner ... and used the greatest cruelty that ever we heard was ever used on Scottish people, with fire and sword, slaughter of men, wives and bairns to the number of nine score persons ... and also consumed and dissolved by fire many buildings, places and houses.'[11] Brutality was part of the very nature of this sort of rapine. Satiated, he returned home through Moray without doing harm to any other person.

Another story, more like propaganda than fact, had a Mackintosh laird of Irish descent fleeing for his life while a guest at Strathbogie and taking refuge with Moray's friend, the Earl of Athol. Athol and Mackintosh then invaded Huntly's territory with fire and sword, killing 120 men, women and children. In retaliation the Gordons intercepted two cooks who had been sent ahead by Athol and burnt them both, 'sending the Earls word he had left two roasts for them.'[12] In the fighting that ensued Huntly captured and hanged one Pedder, another of Athol's servants. In the Earl's presence, so the English report goes, the body was dismembered at Strathbogie and the limbs displayed.[13] Whether or not the incidents of violence in the north were quite as gory as these tales suggest, there was undoubtedly major disorder and considerable bloodshed. The smoke of war billowed from Lochaber and Badenoch to the Braes of Glenlivet, Strathdee and Glenmuick. 'The heather was on fire.'[14]

The Privy Council took these disturbances seriously. They considered that this 'commotion' was more than a mere outbreak of some of the Highland clans for ordinary rapine and was in fact an organised rising on the part of the Earl of Athol, Lord Ochiltree, the lairds of Grant and Mackintosh and others.[15] On 9 November 1592 William Douglas, tenth Earl of Angus, a secret confederate of Huntly, was given a commission of lieutenancy and justiciary 'for repressing the disorders in the Highlands.' He was to act specifically against 'the lawless, broken Highlandmen of the Clan Chattan, Clan Cameron, Clan Ranald, and others pretending their dependence upon the Earls of Huntly and Athol.' He was ordered first to restrain Huntly and his forces from further revenge, next to order Athol to retire. Angus was even instructed to use Huntly's resources while he was campaigning against the wayward clans, and to delegate responsibility for peacekeeping to Huntly when he withdrew.[16] Troubles fomented by Huntly were thus to result in Huntly's rehabilitation as the only viable peacekeeper in the north.

Having re-established his authority and crushed his enemies Huntly was quite content to submit to Angus and enter into ward in Aberdeen. Athol was equally ready to come to his ward in Perth, but Mackintosh was not willing to submit. Huntly was emollient, promising no reprisals for 'auld feid or new,' and offering to give caution for all his friends provided that those presently at the horn for the murder of Moray be released. This was done by act of council.[17] It was the effective end of all attempts at retribution.

Elizabeth was not amused. Like the maiden aunt she was, she continually berated James for his failure to take action against this dissident Earl. When her warnings failed to elicit the necessary response, a most happy confirmation of Huntly's scheming came to light. In January 1592/3 the English ambassador, turning yet another screw, revealed Huntly's alleged complicity in the 'Spanish Blanks' conspiracy. 'Eight clean sheets of fair and gilded paper whereon nothing is seen written save only that some are subscribed solely by William, Earl of Angus, some by George, Earl of Huntly, some by Francis, Earl of Errol, some jointly by all three, some by the three Earls and the laird of Auchindoun' and 'addressed to a king or person of high estate' had been seized on the person of George Kerr as he tried to take passage to the continent on 27 December.[18] With them went wax stamps with the seals of the respective Earls. These 'blanks' and the consequent confessions extracted under torture from Kerr and his confederates seemed to demonstrate that Huntly and the two other Catholic Earls were again plotting with Spain to enable Spanish troops to land in Scotland to reimpose Catholicism and invade England to avenge the death of Mary. Under the influence of Jesuit priests, and in particular of the persistent and peripatetic Father William Crichton, it seems that Huntly was inveigled into putting his name and seal to this hare-brained plan which was posited on the erroneous conviction that James was ripe for conversion to the faith of his parents and that he would immediately declare himself on their side if the Scottish Catholics successfully rose. There was no chance of such a development. James was tolerant ahead of his time. He ruled a kingdom more split than unified by the Reformation. He juggled both sides of the sectarian divide making concessions to the Protestants without allowing those concessions to impinge too much on the daily lives of his Catholic subjects. He relied on his Catholic earls to counterbalance the Presbyterian ascendancy, but he tried to ensure that they themselves did not get out of hand. But he was brought up and remained a Protestant by conviction. He disliked the presumptions of the Papacy as much as those of the General Assembly. And he would resist anything that would endanger his succession to the English throne.[19]

Initially James refused to take too seriously an accusation which he dismissed as either another English fabrication designed to discredit and destroy his favourite or – even if true – as a quixotic and minor matter. If the earls had entered into treasonable negotiations with Spain this was merely a misguided attempt to bring about the downfall of the Presbyterian ministry and humiliate their English backers. It was not to overthrow the Stewart dynasty. James was quite confident that the object of enmity for the Catholic earls was the Queen of England and not the King of Scots.[20] In this they stood in marked contrast to the one man he did fear, the genuinely dangerous and usually Protestant Earl of Bothwell. Their plotting was naive, even silly, but not to be accorded a reaction befitting a real threat to the King or kingdom.

Diplomatic pressure by his 'most affectionate Sister and Cousin,' exhorting him to beware the Spanish faction and not 'accord with a discord,'[21] eventually compelled the King, against his better judgement, to take some action – but not too much. The rebel Catholic lords were commanded to ward themselves at St Andrews, and failing so to do, on 5 February 1592/3 were denounced as rebels. Armed levies were ordered to attend the King and he himself led a small token army unopposed into Aberdeen. He ensured that those against whom he progressed were well warned in advance. Huntly and the rest merely disappeared into the countryside of Caithness and Sutherland. In their absence they were put to the horn. Their estates were seized and placed in the keeping of those friendly to the owners. Strathbogie was given into the charge of Archibald Carmichael with a garrison of sixteen of the royal guard, but the Countess of Huntly was allowed to retain as her winter residence the Bog of Gight, the Gordon's greatest castle and estate.[22] Athol was made lieutenant-general beyond Spey to keep that territory out of the hands of the rebels. He received the rest of the Huntly lands, not in gift but to hold as factor for the crown. In this capacity he put to the sword fifty of Huntly's men.[23] Despite such minor reverses by the time the King was back in Edinburgh the rebel earls had emerged from their fastnesses and taken repossession of their properties.

Once again the English were faced with the incomprehensible reality that no visitation of royal justice was going to befall either Huntly or his minions, despite the repeated assurances to the contrary. The hardened English agents were not deceived and reported that, while pretending severity in confiscating the rebels' property, the King was careful to leave their strength unimpaired. Their masters in London took the same view. The reports sent south are increasingly peppered with cynical marginal notes. In the Spring of 1593 Bowes reported that James had been at pains to make 'known to me his diligence to find out the prac- tisers and practices with Spain wherein he has discovered, as he says, that the blanks subscribed by Huntly, Angus, Errol and Auchindoun are done by them' and that 'he promised to have within fourteen days a true and perfect note of the names of the other confederates not yet revealed, with which note he will shortly acquaint her Majesty.' In the margin the recipient comments: 'A fair offer, if the effects may follow.' James further denied that he had issued a warrant to dispense with the prohi- bition on those indicted for the murder of Moray from entering Aberdeen in safety.[24] Yet within weeks Huntly was released from the horn, and within months from the other restrictions and prohibitions declared in Aberdeen. He was even reported as attending a mass presided over by an Englishman at Sir Walter Lindsay's house at Balgavie. He continued to raid the territory of Moray, killing some of the inhabitants and burning 'Collord, the Mains of Mackintosh and the house of Angus Williamson.'[25] He could get away with murder. In English eyes James was a weak monarch who would agree to everything but do nothing, who would issue edicts but not enforce them. What eluded the English was that this was policy not inadequacy. In James' estimation any attempt to take really effective measures against Huntly would only have inflamed a dangerous situation further. He would not destroy his lynchpin in the north, nor would he willingly destroy a close friend. Ultimately he was vindicated, his inaction allowing 'a crisis to dissolve into an anti-climax.'[26] Huntly was preserved and Bothwell destroyed. In the interim, however, his duplicity endangered relations both with England, which began to favour Bothwell, and with the Kirk.

Exiled in the north though he was, Huntly's influence at court was maintained by intermittent clandestine visits and the continuing presence of his wife, Lady Huntly, Esmé's daughter. Both King and Queen were openly affectionate towards her and nothing the English or others could do would diminish this. Every time the ambassador urged the King to remove the Countess of Huntly from court he appeared to yield. 'Yet,' he complained, 'she is not removed and remains in good grace.' Nothing, it seemed, could dent the good odour in which the King kept his two-faced minion – 'Chanus' or 'Janus' as the English had taken to dubbing him.[27]

Nothing but Bothwell. Both the English and the Moray faction realised that inconstant as the King was in relation to Huntly he was always 'resolute against Bothwell,'[28] To undermine the former they could utilise the latter. They spawned rumours that Huntly had 'bound up' with Bothwell. The King, losing his critical acumen, was outraged at this ungrateful duplicity. He railed against him, 'calling Huntly the first traitor in the world, one to whom he will show no favour.' Yet Huntly's agent, Captain Kerr, managed to reassure James where his loyalties lay and even used the King's paranoia about Bothwell to turn the tables on the Moray faction, insinuating that it was they who were the false traitors and had poisoned the King against his true subject. It was the commendator of St Colme, the tutor and uncle of the young Earl of Moray, and the laird of Cluny who had given harbour to the fugitive Bothwell, not Huntly. James could believe it. Cluny was committed to the tolbooth and St Colme was put to the horn and lost the keeping of Castle Doune to the young Earl of Argyll, despite the fact that Athol had ward of the young Moray to whom the custody of the castle belonged.[29] This was the first sign that James was looking to the substantial House of Argyll to be his Protestant counterweight in the north rather than relying on the upstart and infant Moray and his dubious friends and associates. At a dinner hosted by a staunch co-religionist Huntly met with the King in secret conclave.[30]

On 24 July 1593 Bothwell, with the secret backing of England, insinuated himself into Holyrood Palace and successfully seized the King. James was to remain in 'protective custody' until after Bothwell's trial for witchcraft. The following month the Earl was acquitted by his peers, the only evidence against him being the testimony of 'Richy' Graham, a proven liar, who 'was enticed to accuse the Earl with hope of his life.'[31] Newly vindicated, Bothwell went to see the King. There followed a notorious repartee. He told James that he would remain under the 'protection' of Bothwell and his associates until they were relaxed from the horn, restored to their lands and offices, and the murder of Moray was punished. He pressed not only for the speedy punishment of those who wielded the weapons but also of those who had subscribed the warrant. They should all hang. Bothwell declared that 'they who slew him are known; they too who signed the warrant for the slaughter, the Chancellor Maitland, Sir George Home, and Sir Robert Melvil.' – 'Tush, tush', said the king, 'a better man than you shall answer for Sir Robert.' – 'I deny that,' retorted Bothwell, 'unless the man you mean is your Majesty himself.'[32] This was an insolent and unsubtle reference to the rumour that James was himself behind the Earl's murder. James was furious but largely impotent. He refused to appoint Bothwell and Athol lieutenants in the south and north respectively, the latter with power to prosecute Huntly. Bowes persuaded the earls to moderate their demands and an uneasy accord was reached. To buy time James consented to pardon them.

Time was all he needed. Scottish politics was a tapestry of infinite variety. Today's brother is tomorrow's enemy. Alliances swirled like mist around the protagonists. The young Duke of Lennox began to waver and within a month a powerful reaction was setting in. This played into the hands of Huntly since the King was looking for support from any source so long as it could be ranged against Bothwell. Huntly was an experienced general with a large following and was supreme in the north. In proof of this he had recently seen off an attempt by his enemies to attack him in his own lands. He had mustered a larger force than theirs and on their withdrawal had ravaged Moray, forcing the young Earl's tenants to flee leaving their possessions behind. It was reported that the King had agreed to a secret meeting with him at Falkland. The English despaired of a King 'addict and inclined' to Huntly and his 'Papist' faction. Huntly, it was feared, would soon be reappointed Lieutenant of the North. Their fears were justified but so were the King's actions. He needed to find reliable supporters against Bothwell and his faction and the Catholic earls were the most trustworthy and eager. The King was soon strong enough to emancipate himself from Bothwell and his Border thugs. On 15 September another notable military leader from the Borders, the Roman Catholic Lord Home, arrived in force to aid the King at the convention he was holding in Stirling. For some time he had been a staunch ally of Huntly. He was made captain of the royal guard. A day or two later Maitland also managed to get there with a further 200 horsemen.[33] The King marched from Stirling to Doune of Menteith where Bothwell's associates – Athol, Gowrie and Montrose – had assembled with 500 horse. The latter two were seized, the former fled into his own territory.

James was as anxious as ever to put the Moray affair, which had been the cause of so much trouble and danger behind him. At one point he was reported as even contemplating taking the blame for the murder upon himself if such a public confession would induce Huntly and Moray to reconcile. Seeing their chance the Catholic lords prostrated themselves before the King on the road near Fala in Midlothian, protesting their innocence of the Spanish Blanks or of any conspiracy to bring in foreign forces but asserting their fidelity to their creed. They were in short, good Catholics and loyal subjects. They petitioned the King for a speedy trial. They were confident of clearing their names and regaining their positions. James responded to their pleas. At a convention held in November James announced in his 'Act of Abolition' that he would readily pardon them if they would abjure Catholicism or go into exile until they did. Meanwhile they would keep their estates unscathed. They had until 1 February the following year to decide. By contrast, at the same convention Bothwell was exiled without hope of redemption and his friends, including St Colme, were hunted down and imprisoned. The ministers of the Kirk were loud in their condemnation of this resolution. Elizabeth berated James as a 'seduced king' who corrected miscreants with benefits. The peremptory and patronising tone of Elizabeth's letters to her fellow monarch is extraordinary. One can but wonder at her reaction if James had responded in kind or presumed to interfere in her management of England.[34]

Bothwell reacted to his sentence by raising his forces to attempt a second seizure of the King's person. On 3 April 1594 he rode with 600 men to Leith in the hope of meeting up with Athol and Argyll whom he expected would cross the Forth with their northern troops. The King's resolution in raising his own forces and marching against him before any allies might arrive forced his rapid retreat to Kelso. There he disbanded his troops and took refuge in England yet again. When Bothwell had been approaching Leith the King had protested in St Giles Kirk: 'If the Lord give me victory over Bothwell I shall never rest till I pass upon Huntly and the excommunicated lords.' He now resolved to move against the intransigent and ungrateful Huntly, Angus, and Errol who had finally spurned his 'Act of Abolition' as a compromise less than the full restitution they had expected and thought they deserved. At the same time as the King's resolve began to harden other factors further steeled him to action. Disturbing confessions were being made by Ardkinglas, one of those arrested over the murder of the laird of Cawdor, confessions which further implicated Huntly. Despite his later retraction, Ardkinglas' allegations increased the royal resolve to act against the northern rebels. This time he meant it, and when James meant something he was resolute in implementing it.

On 30 May the Catholic earls had been declared traitors, forfeited, stripped of their estates and a commission against them given to the

Earl of Argyll. The Countess of Huntly, so long a cherished favourite, was dismissed from the court. Nonetheless it was rumoured that James had secretly despatched Lord Home to borrow £2,000-3,000 sterling from none other than Huntly. However, the King's determination to curb his northern miscreants was further strengthened by their impudent action in July when they 'liberated' a Spanish ship held at Aberdeen with the papal nuncio on board. Under threat of their town being fired, the magistrates delivered up the prisoners and their goods. The King declared that, after his son's baptism on 30 August, he would march in person with the whole strength of the realm against the Catholic insurgents.[35]

James had proposed to lead the forces himself but to await a full muster. Wary of his resolve as a result of frustrated expectations in the past, and eager to move against the Catholics at long last, the leaders of the Kirk urged precipitate action. Thus on 25 July 1594, Huntly's most determined enemies – Argyll and Athol – were proclaimed the King's lieutenants and justices in the north with powers to act against the rebels. Huntly would resort to more or less anything – from the murder of a fellow peer to open rebellion against the King – to secure his position in the north. It was this that Moray had threatened; it was this that Argyll was now threatening, his northwards expansion clashing with Huntly's westwards.

Nevertheless, Huntly made strenuous efforts to avoid conflict. He agreed that his allies, the Earls of Errol and Angus, should make their peace with the Moray faction.[36] He himself sent the laird of Kilfauns to the King with an offer. Huntly, Errol and Angus would leave the realm under royal warrant provided that their wives and children were left in their possessions and that no reprisals were taken against their friends and followers. He tried to reassure the King – on a particularly sensitive point – that there was nothing amiss with his recent meeting with Bothwell, which was to apportion blame for the killing of Moray and not for any band between Bothwell and the other forfeited earls. He offered to hand over Bothwell if that was what James desired. The King answered more in sorrow than in anger that he had 'many times and with great care sought to preserve Huntly from ruin, and by the same had greatly hazarded himself, his life, estate and honour: whereof Huntly had no regard, but always abused him with fair words and pretenses.' Further Bothwell had made the same offer to hand over Huntly. Associating himself with Bothwell was the one act that could ultimately jeopardise Huntly's position with the King. His insubordinate Earl could be excused almost anything but not another dalliance with the fugitive Bothwell. The King ordered Kilfauns to tell Huntly flatly that he could not 'condition' or capitulate with him in any sort but would prosecute him and Bothwell by all means in his power, and with this he dismissed Kilfauns 'much discontented.'[37]

George Gordon was an outlaw and rebel. Only once before had a Huntly crossed a monarch – when the fourth Earl raised arms against Mary – with disastrous consequences. This act of defiant arms would be no replay of Corrichie. Whereas the sixth Earl of Huntly would ally with the devil and take up arms against the royal lieutenants, when it came to the pass he would not resist the King himself, and would return a penitent, the prodigal son, to the ever open arms of his forbearing and forgiving father, James.

16

A GOWK'S STORM[1]
September–October 1594

Immediately ... we kneeled down on the top of the mountain and
gave thanks to God; singing that celebrated hymn of St Ambrose and
Augustine, Te Deum laudamus. Then we buried our dead.[2]

With Huntly's overtures rejected, preparations for a punitive campaign to
the north began. Archibald Campbell, the seventh Earl of Argyll,
commander of the royal forces, was only nineteen years old. So youthful
and inexperienced a general may not have been the King's first choice, but
if reservations he had they were overruled by his ministers. If not the first
nor the ideal choice, Argyll at least was the natural one. He was the head
of the most powerful clan in Scotland. He was Huntly's only real challenger
in the north. He was of far greater substance than his step-nephew, Moray,
had ever been. He could with ease raise a substantial and well armed force
and do so largely at his own expense.[3] By making Argyll his commander
James was sending the neighbouring western Highlands and islands to
police the northern Lowlands while he could gather his own retinue on the
south. It was war by proxy. Argyll also had his personal agenda: to avenge
the murders of the laird of Cawdor and the Earl of Moray and the resultant
death of Lady Doune, all three of which he laid at the door of Huntly.

From the Hebrides Argyll summoned musketeers, spearmen, and
archers under Lauchlin McLean of Duart, an eminent chief well versed in
war. Angus Macdonald promised 500 bowmen. To these were joined
retainers and vassals, and the usual eager and ever-envious neighbours of
Huntly: Mackintosh, Grant and Mackenzie. Argyll himself raised some
5,000 men, 3,000 of whom were 'well provided with muskets, bows,
arrows, and twa-handit swords; of the quhilk number there were fifteen
hundreth musketeers and hagbutters,' the rest with swords and other mixed
weapons after the fashion of Highlanders. The English ambassador and the
historian of the Gordons estimate the total number that Argyll had at his
disposal as 8,000 foot, the author of *The Account* puts it at 12,000. The
latter figure is probably inflated by the exaggeration of distance on the one
hand or partisanship on the other, on the premise that the greater the
number of the enemy the greater the glory in destroying them.[4] Whatever
the precise strength he had mustered, Argyll's main weakness – other than

his youth and immaturity – was that he had no artillery and very few horse. In the rough terrain of the Highlands or Ireland this was often an advantage but in Lowland country it was a serious weakness. Argyll was too inexperienced to realise the full significance of this omission. Nor would he, despite Mar's entreaties to await the King's arrival, brook any further delay. He had gathered his forces twice before and been restrained. If disbanded they could not be reconstituted. He would march forward by easy marches and meet the King at Inverness. On the march he hoped to recruit some horse when Lord Forbes, Huntly's old enemy eager to avenge many a past outrage, and the lairds of Towie, Macintosh, Dunbarres, and others joined him.

And so on 21 September 1594 he set off without horse, 'much scorned in court and thought easy to be overthrown by Huntly.' To his boast that he would sleep at Strathbogie within three days Huntly retorted that he would be welcome, but that he himself would be the porter, open the gates to his young friend and rub his cloak against Argyll's plaid ere they parted. Despite this mutual bravado, Huntly made commendable efforts to avoid unnecessary innocent bloodshed, sending Cameron of Lochiel to plead for peace and 'spare the spoil and slaughter of his poor tenants.'[5] The King could adjudicate between them. Argyll would not be placated, and interpreted this disinclination to bloodshed on his adversary's part as a sign of weakness.

Huntly had gathered about 1,000 men to welcome Argyll to Strathbogie. Recognising the paramountcy of horse especially in the local terrain, and no doubt counting on Argyll's deficiency in that respect, he laboured to fortify, himself with horsemen offering 40 merks[6] a month to every common horseman and £40 Scots to every well furnished one. This liberal pay tempted many Borderers and even some who had served in the royal guard. In all Huntly and his confederates between them raised between 2,000 and 4,000 well-equipped men, including a strong contingent of cavalry and six pieces of field artillery, the latter in the very capable charge of Captain Andrew Gray of Skelton. This fast, small and mobile force could be rapidly deployed in country they knew well. The war could be taken to the enemy. It was to Huntly's advantage to initiate the fight with Argyll before he was joined by Forbes and the rest of his Lowland troops.

Having received a misleading intelligence that Argyll was approaching Moray, the Catholic earls marched to the town of Elgin in the hope of encountering him. They waited three days but heard and saw nothing of Argyll. Hardly surprising since he had been nowhere near Elgin, but had invaded Badenoch and laid siege to Riffen Castle, held for Huntly by the Macphersons. Refusing to be bogged down in a siege with a stubborn garrison in a well-defended stronghold, Argyll soon let it be and proceeded through the hills towards Strathbogie. His intention was to carry fire and sword through Huntly's lands and then to join up with Forbes who was on his way to meet him. Marching on foot, besieging Riffen, and pillaging as they went had fatally slowed the invading force. Argyll had had an enormous and unlooked for strategic advantage and had frittered it away.

With fortuitous prescience the rebel forces moved south. A cavalry detachment under Sir Patrick Gordon of Auchindoun, Huntly's uncle, was despatched to scour the country for the enemy. The main force returned at speed to Strathbogie. It arrived in the nick of time. On the very day the rebels got back to Strathbogie, Forbes and Leslie of Buquan had intended joining Argyll there with a numerous body of horse, but retired on seeing Huntly's arrival and Argyll's absence. Argyll had foolishly forfeited his much-needed cavalry. The following day Errol marched to Turref in Buchan for provisions; and having remained a few days returned to Strathbogie augmenting his forces with a further eighty to 100 horse.[7]

Soon the Catholic noblemen received positive information that the enemy was scarce twenty miles from them, laying waste the country with fire and sword. According to a propagandist in Huntly's army 'the enemy's piety was excessive, murdering children and women as they marched.' They even took with them 'a noted witch on purpose to discover the hidden property of the terrified inhabitants by her incantations.' Associating witches with the enemy was a commonplace of sixteenth-century diatribe. The north was being raped by Lowlanders from the south and Highlanders from the west. The rebels were no longer fighting for themselves but for their native soil. There was no time to lose. Huntly bade farewell to his family, heartened by the confidence of his four-year-old son who assured him that 'the victory would not be got without strokes, but that assuredly Lord Daidy would prevail.'[8]

On 1 October the rebels marched to Carnburrow where their army camped for the night. In the glow of the cooking fires 'each earl drew his sword, and swore a solemn oath to the other, that it should not be sheathed till the enemy was vanquished, or he died in the attempt.' The following morning they marched five miles with lines extended through rugged difficult roads to Auchindoun, the castle of Sir Patrick Gordon, an excellent vantage point built on a high hill overlooking a river and the rich countryside far beyond. There they encamped and waited positive news of Argyll's whereabouts and disposition. It was soon in coming. Spies reported Argyll in the vicinity. A little before dawn on Thursday 3 October, an eyewitness related,

We assembled and the Catholics in the army went into the castle to celebrate mass, after which each person's arms were blessed and consecrated, as were the standards of the noblemen. Huntly's were the arms of his family but on Errol's along with his bloody yoke which his ancestors had borne for 600 years, was painted a man bearing a cross on his shoulders, with the motto, serva iugum.[9]

They left Auchindoun and by noon had marched only a further six miles, again hindered by the difficulty of transporting baggage and particularly the cannon over rugged broken mountains. They could only guess at the whereabouts of Argyll, until Auchindoun and Captain Kerr returned with news that Argyll had spent the night at the Castle of Drimmin in Strathavon and had then moved off to meet up with the promised horse of Forbes and Leslie. The precise direction of his movements was unclear since a heavy fog – attributed to Argyll's familiar – had lain all the morning, but at least Huntly had some intelligence of his adversaries' whereabouts and disposition and Argyll had none. Their respective spies had clashed and Argyll's had been chased and killed. Huntly took this encounter as a presage of an ensuing victory.[10] Both forces stumbled on through difficult terrain, Argyll's Highlanders trying always to keep to high ground for fear of the cavalry; Huntly's horse being impeded by traversing boggy ground pitted with stones and made slippery with moss, and his cannon constantly slowing down the progress of his force.

Almost by chance the two opposing armies stumbled upon each other six miles above Auchindoun and three-quarters of a mile from Glenlivet. Despite strong advice from more experienced commanders to await Forbes and his men, the headstrong young Argyll had not avoided combat. Now he could not. He did, nonetheless, take up a strong defensive position, deploying his army in three divisions on the top of a steep and rough hill, Ben Rinnes, whose slopes were covered with high heather and stones and at whose foot was mossy ground riddled with 'peit pots,' rendering it virtually impassable for cavalry. To get at the enemy forces, Huntly's horse would have to try to canter up that potholed, heathery slope. The wind and sun also favoured Argyll.[11] The van was led by McLean of Duart, Macintosh and Auchinbreck Campbell and consisted of 3,000–4,000 footmen including the 2,000 hagbuteers. The rest were equipped with bows or Lochaber axes and swords. Argyll and Murray of Tullibardine took up the rear with the rest of the army: some 2,000.

The opposing van of some 200–300 men was led by the Earl of Errol, with Patrick Gordon, the laird of Gight, James Wood of Bonington and Thomas Kerr as his captains. Huntly followed with Gordon of Cluny on the left flank and Gordon of Abergeldy on the right, a force variously estimated at 700–1,200 men.[12] The six cannon were so placed as to be masked and protected by the cavalry and could be dragged unnoticed into a position within firing range of the enemy. This force was augmented by an unknown number of Highland irregulars from Clan Cameron and Clan Ranald of Lochaber, and by some Macphersons. The total rebel force at Glenlivet was probably in the region of 1,500–2,000 men, between a quarter and a third of the royal army.

Argyll's was essentially a Highland army of foot encountering a predom-inantly Lowland and largely cavalry force. Although outnumbered three or four to one, the latter were men determined to serve their faith and save their lands, homes and families from invasion and despoliation by savage Highlanders. Glenlivet was the opposite of Corrichie where Lowland royal troops equipped with artillery and supported by cavalry had overwhelmed a largely Highland force. The winners on each occasion were the Lowlanders, but the sides were reversed.

Argyll's army had deployed and with drums and trumpets seven standards were displayed, the King's and Argyll's both in the rear. An eyewitness in Huntly's army recorded what happened next:

> We ... formed our van opposite to the enemy's first hill, the colours were brought to the centre and we immediately began to form the rear. But the delay from the cannon and the inequality of the ground prevented us from advancing in order of battle. The pieces were placed, so as to bear with most effect on the enemy ...

Counsel was taken, some cautioned delay, others wanted to engage since cavalry were greatly superior to foot. Huntly ordered Captain Andrew Gray to shoot three field pieces while the heretic enemy was at prayer with the Bishop of Argyll. Although the destruction wrought by this first fusillade was not great, its effect was staggering. Aimed accurately at the yellow standard of Argyll, it dispatched both James Campbell and his brother, Archibald Campbell of Lochnell, the standard bearer. One of the shots also brutally decapitated a local hero, 'Neil Macnares of the Hebrides, a most valiant man but a noted plunderer.' This embodiment of the bravado of the Highlanders was extinguished in an instant and in full view of his companions by the unnerving technology of their Lowland foes.[13] 300 of Argyll's Highlanders, unused to the sight, sound and effect of artillery, made an ineffectual charge at the enemy horse, but receiving another round of shot at close range, they fled and fell flat on their faces to avoid further carnage in their ranks. Argyll himself ranged among his men, beating them to their feet with the flat of his sword. The main and the rear added to the confusion by pressing forward into the van.

Captain Kerr, an experienced soldier, saw the advantage in their foes' disconcertion, but Errol was unwilling to charge until informed that if he did not Huntly would. Fortifying himself with the sign of the cross and crying aloud 'The Virgin Mary,' Errol rushed into the midst of the enemy. The ground was so unforgiving and the opposition so fierce that he could not break through. On Kerr's advice he made a circle round the hill and attacked from the rear. As his troops did so they were exposed to fire, several horse were killed, men injured and Errol badly wounded by arrows in the left foot and in the arm. He lost his pennon to McLean of Duart.

As Argyll's van turned away to pursue Errol, Huntly saw his chance and charged. His men were forced to veer to the right by the steepness of the hill and the shot of the enemy. Huntly's uncle, Patrick Gordon of Auchindoun, with his men galloped straight up the hill towards McLean who withstood him from a strong position. An eyewitness attributed his suicidal gallop to an unmanageable horse, which ran off with him into the thickest of the enemy. He and his men were bogged down in the mossy ground and subjected to a blistering fire. Gordon was unhorsed by a shot and dirked to death by the Highlanders. They severed his head and displayed it in taunting triumph. The remnants of Errol's horse reeled back into the main body of Huntly's army and there was a pause while both sides regrouped.

Argyll had finally deployed the main body of his army and took up a strong position on the rough and high hillside of Carn Tighearn. The Highlanders now had the advantage of ground, sun and wind. Fighting resumed at three o'clock in the afternoon and raged for another two hours. The matter was almost settled by McLean of Duart who asked Argyll for 500 men to capture Huntly.[14] With this force McLean tried to enclose Huntly's van in a pincer movement between his own men and Argyll's. They were in danger of being cut to pieces and suffered their most severe losses of the day at the hands of Duart's men. Gordon of Gight was badly wounded by three bullets which hit his mail coat with such ferocity that they imbedded two plates of it in his body.[15] The situation was desperate.

Huntly had to act decisively to save the day or all was lost. Fortuitously, at that very moment the elements, which had conspired against the rebels, turned traitor to the King. The wind changed, blowing the smog of gun-smoke into the eyes of Argyll's men and the October afternoon sun, which had been dazzling the rebels, was obscured by clouds for the duration of the battle. Seizing the opportunity Huntly engaged the light horse of his rear guard. Galloping ahead of his men he charged into the close columns of the enemy. In the thick of them he singled out the most prominent opponent and bestowed upon him the last thrust of his spear. It was an act of intrepid heroics that nearly finished him. Having overstretched himself, he came under attack. Drawing his sword, Huntly managed to parry a blow at his side forcing it from his thighs and legs. The thrust was so powerful, however, that the blade cut an inch into the Earl's broadsword and struck the plates in his boot. His horse was shot from under him and he was only saved from being hacked to death in the manner of Gordon of Auchindoun by the intervention of Innermarky who extricated and re-horsed him.

By this time the rest of Huntly's cavalry had managed to engage the enemy at close quarters. The royal forces were at a disastrous disadvantage. Only the first two or three ranks of the infantry could aim accurately at their assailants. Those behind, unable to manoeuvre or take aim, shot upwards and chanced to luck. In desperation they fired volley after volley into the air so that survivors of the battle were of the staunch belief that for a full quarter of an hour the daylight was eclipsed with the continual cloud of darts and arrows that hung over the place. Most landed harmlessly behind the ever nearing foe. The few men and horse they hit were at the rear of Huntly's force and not those directly before them. Infantry unable to deploy their ranks in a hedgehog formation are extremely vulnerable to cavalry attack even by a much smaller force, as the Scots had discovered to their cost at Solway Moss. Huntly had remembered a lesson Argyll had yet to learn. Weaving in and out of ranks of men stumbling and pushing each other to defend themselves or escape their attackers, hacking away at will, horsemen make swathes like reapers in a cornfield.

Panic ensued. *Sauve qui peut*. Argyll's main force broke and fled, in desperation casting aside their weapons, shields and plaids, being driven down the far side of the hill as much by their own fear, as by Huntly's furies. They ran 'so confusedly like a herd of swine as every man proved a hinderer to his neighbour and all disabled from offending the pursuers.'[16] They died in droves as they were cut down in their flight. Only when they reached the Aven burn did some pause in their retreat and wounded many of their pursuers shooting arrows from the trees. McLean of Duart who had done most and suffered least was again foremost in the rear action. Time and again he risked his life rescuing his men, surrounded and outnumbered. They in turn, stout islanders all, would die rather than ask quarter. McLean in a daring dash hacked his way through to Huntly's standard, embedded the spike end of his axe in the mount, sliced the bearer in two, and made off with the trophy. Enough time was gained to allow Argyll to get 'so far up upon the hill as no horse could follow.'[17] However inadequate as a commander he may have been, Argyll was no coward and he had stayed in the fray too long for his own safety. Moray of Tullibardine seized his bridle and forced him off the field. He was led away in tears, still imploring his men to stand and fight.

Sir Robert Fraser, the Lyon Herald of Scotland, bearing the royal standard, was not so fortunate. He stood out conspicuously and insolently, dressed in his tabard with the red lion emblazoned on it, the emblem of his office and his safeguard. On this occasion it served less as a protection than as an incentive. With a shout of 'Have at the Lion' a contingent of Gordon horse surrounded him and speared him to death on the spot. The royal ensign he bore was taken with other spoil to Strathbogie and placed triumphantly on the top of the great tower.

In gratitude for this rare victory of a Catholic earl over a Protestant the Gordons knelt down on the hillside and sang a triumphant *Te Deum*, their voices echoing in the glen, their solemn chant soaring over a field strewn with the dead and dying. Then they buried their dead. Later a public mass was said in the semi-derelict cathedral at Elgin. The hills of the north rejoiced.

The royal army had been decimated. Two cousins of Argyll were killed, Archibald Campbell of Lochnell and his brother James, the Lyon Herald, and fifteen other men of note. The estimate of his total losses varied from 200-700 men. In contrast the eyewitness recorded that Huntly had lost only twelve men, while the *Historie* put it at sixty men and 200 horse. Whatever it was, his losses were trifling in comparison with those suffered by Argyll's poor bloody infantry. James Melville, blinded by his partisanship, called it an 'uncertain victory,' or draw, 'but greatest loss was to Huntly.'[18] By this he meant that a high proportion of the rebels killed were men of some note. The English ambassador similarly consoled himself with the knowledge that 'the chief slaughter had fallen on the chief gentleman of the Gordons, fourteen landed men of good quality being slain, and of these eleven were guilty of Moray's murder' including Patrick Gordon of Auchindoun, Huntly's uncle.[19] Greater were the number of the wounded, the most prominent of whom were the Earl of Errol and Gordon of Gight (the latter of whom had taken three bullets) who were thought unlikely to survive. Secret messages sent to Edinburgh summoned surgeons and salves to their aid. Surprisingly both lived.

Argyll could do nothing for his slain on the battlefield. His tent was cut in pieces and divided among the boys to cover their horses. His witch had been right in her prediction that both the harp and bagpipe would sound in Strathbogie and Turef. Argyll, however, had been wrong in assuming that he would be there to enjoy their most agreeable music. Nor could her sorcery foresee the death that awaited her after the victory.[20]

Weeping with shame, Argyll withdrew into Athol's lands to await the King's coming. He had to put an end to the suspense and was soon down south wandering first to Stirling and then to Dundee looking for the King. When he entered the royal presence with his small train, the King pretended not to recognise him. On being told it was the Earl of Argyll he said 'Fair fall thee, Geordie sending him home like a subject.'[21] Argyll made his excuses. He had few experienced leaders and a great part of his army had fled without good cause. The King seemed little affected by Argyll's discomfiture and in his presence often spoke of the battle with derision. Compared with the rest of his nobility Huntly was at least experienced and capable, a man whom it seemed only a king could subdue.

But it was no laughing matter. Not only had Huntly taken on the royal lieutenant and shamed him in battle, he had even slain the Lyon Herald who was wearing the King's coat. James swore to avenge this affront to his dignity. An intercepted letter from Huntly to Angus, further incensed the King by its scornful tone, referring to the projected royal campaign as likely to turn out a 'gowk's storm.' Rumours also persisted that Huntly was involved in a bond to kill him. James is unlikely to have believed this last report, but it may have steeled him the more. Huntly had overreached himself with the King this time. Bowes was overjoyed that finally 'Huntly would have a fall and perish.'[22]

James moved north to Aberdeen where he levied fines on the commons who had followed Huntly and exacted new cautions for the future in considerable numbers. In return they were pardoned. In the formula of these cautions mention was always made of the treasonable burning of Donnibristle and murder of Moray, as part and parcel of the as yet unatoned guilt of Huntly and his immediate adherents. This was another concession to the popular Presbyterian feeling, which recollected that bloody deed as standing in the indictment against the great Catholic Earl and his Gordons. As a further sop to this feeling the King was accompanied, at his own request, by prominent members of the reformed clergy, including both Andrew Melville and his nephew James, who were there to testify publicly to the sincerity and extent of his efforts to proceed against Huntly and so reassure the public who were still 'jealous over the king for his knawin and kythit [manifested] favour to the Erle.'[23]

Thus spiritually fortified, the King personally went forward with his forces to Strathbogie. The castle was well provisioned for a siege but Huntly had made off to Sutherland and the keeper fled. James swithered between razing and garrisoning it. Argyll, Lord Lindsay, and in particular the irascible Andrew Melville all pressed hard for the destruction of this soaring symbol of Huntly's pride.[24] James yielded to their powerful lust for revenge. It was some task for the pioneers, but the castle which had taken fourteen years to build was 'cast down and made equal with the ground in two days, and all men are made free to the spoyle thereof.' Their labours had been eased by the prayers of the pious and by the active participation of Melville in the demolition. The devastation was not as complete as suggested. The great tower was pulled down on 29 October but damage to the house itself was limited. Further orders were given for the demolition of other Catholic houses and strongholds in the north: Errol's castle at Slains, the laird of Newton-Gordon's house at Culsammond, Sir Walter Lindsay's at Balgavie, and Sir John Ogilvie's at Craig, both in Angus. 'Thus,' the English Deputy March Warden observed, 'he has deceived the expectations of all, who never thought he would have done so much.'[25] This typical comment demonstrates just how shallow was the English understanding of the ways of this wily King of Scots, who did things so very differently but just as effectively as their own dear Queen.

Castles had fallen, fines had been levied, but the rebels themselves were still at large. It was also reported that Huntly was keeping forces in pay even though they were dispersed. James was running out of money, that usual bugbear of Stewart kings, and could do no more than leave 200 cavalry and 100 foot to keep the peace, a token force buttressed by the threat of the King's immediate personal return should Huntly trouble the country more. On 14 November the King disbanded his force and returned to Stirling.

With the King gone, Huntly and Errol lingered in the north, awaiting an upturn in their fortunes. Huntly's house might be in ruins but his position was secure in the long term. Of his rivals in the north, Moray was dead and Argyll repulsed and humiliated. Of his allies, Errol, badly wounded, withdrew from the limelight, and Bothwell was to go into exile. The King had left the Duke of Lennox as lieutenant in the north. The Duke was Huntly's brother-in-law. He protected rather than prosecuted Huntly's followers. Where Bothwell's forfeited property was seized and dispersed, that of the Catholic earls had been allotted to their wives, a clear signal of eventual and full restoration. All Huntly had to achieve was to ingratiate himself once more with the King and with the passing of time his position would be restored. He would knock at an open door.[26]

17

THE BRIGHTEST JEWEL
1595–1597

This is what I had feared; and it is a great misfortune for the Catholic cause. Huntly listened to the blandishments of the king and his heretical friends; and was persuaded to confer with the ministers; then went to their temples to hear their sermons, and ended by openly, at least in words, if not sincerely, renouncing the Catholic religion, for which he had so gloriously combated.

Fr James Gordon[1]

In his youth a prodigal spender; in his elder age more wise and worldly.

John Spalding on Huntly[2]

Any hope of an early restitution departed with the arrest of a papal emissary, Father Morton, who revealed the objects of his mission, implicating the Catholic lords in further treasonable dealings with Spain. Despite the entreaties of Father Gordon, Huntly's uncle, not to desert the Catholic cause, both the Earls of Errol and Huntly deemed that the safest course was to remove themselves from the jurisdiction. On 17 March 1594/5 Errol embarked at Peterhead, and two days later, after hearing Mass, Huntly, accompanied by his uncle and sixteen retainers, took ship at Aberdeen for Denmark. From there he intended to pass by a circuitous route through Poland and on to Italy.[3] Going to Italy could be seen as a pilgrimage to the Catholics; going into exile could be viewed as a period of purgation in the wilderness by the Protestants. Time and absence were both great healers. The country was quiet.

He left his best ambassadors behind – his wife and his king. He had the good fortune to have a wife who was the closest friend of the Queen. The Countess of Huntly was her confidante and mainstay and attended on all the royal births. They often slept in the same bed and 'this favoured lady had "the plurality of her majesty's kisses."'[4] She bided her time, ever ingratiating herself with the royal couple and waiting her chance. She worked on the Queen when she was at her most susceptible: in and after childbirth. Within days of the birth of Princess Elizabeth on 15 August 1596, the Queen was interceding with her husband on behalf of the exiled Earl.[5] He was wavering. Huntly's wife, after all, was to be godmother of their new daughter. In October the Countess brought her eldest son to court as a pledge for his father. She herself spoke of his changed character. In exile he had not consorted with enemies of the Reformed Faith. He was willing to banish all seminary priests and known papists from his company. He would willingly engage in discussion with the ministers of the Kirk and was prepared to accept religious instruction. He would employ a pastor as his chaplain and asked only for time to wrestle with his conscience and for absolution from the sentence of excommunication imposed upon him. James was receptive; the Kirk was not.[6] Huntly and his ilk were idolaters and should be done to death. Against this 'Christian' sentiment the King countered that the truly penitent should receive forgiveness and mercy, 'the brightest jewel in his prerogative.'[7] The King was as much alienated by the vindictiveness of the Kirk as he was won over by the contrition of the courtier.

As usual James took the initiative. He wrote to Huntly more in sorrow than in anger, reminding him of how his actions had caused his King 'skaith and hazard' in his cause. This was a reproach by an injured friend rather than a reproof by an absolute ruler. Reconciliation was on offer but at a price. It would involve submission to the Kirk and an abject public apology for his part in Moray's murder to the satisfaction of the Kirk. Failing this, exile would be his lot and he would never be a Scotsman again. James could see through his old friend. He was soft but not silly. He told Huntly that the game was up: 'Deceive not yourself, to think that by lingering of time your wife and your allies shall ever get you better conditions.'[8] It was a price worth paying. Huntly had a flexible faith, one quite capable of bending with the political wind. For form's sake he was quite prepared to forsake the Roman for the Reformed persuasion. In this he was a very different man from his grandfather and from a very different age. Now that Lady Huntly had made overtures which had been well received, and James had responded according to type, Huntly decided to win his own way back into favour. In December he landed illicitly in Scotland and wrote to the King, seeking his forgiveness and favour. He protested that he had dedicated himself to follow the King in all respects, and expressed the hope that 'the prince's part to his subjects is that of a father to his children not seeking their utter ruin but by humiliation accepting their amendment.' He sought permission to come to James himself.[9] On his return from exile, as he had hoped, it was generally felt he had given satisfaction. His rehabilitation was complete.

Now it was Moray's friends who were wrong-footed. In March 1597 the Council ordered them to concord with Huntly or suffer royal displeasure. In June Huntly was pardoned and received into the Kirk, assenting to the eleven articles it had drawn up dealing with his confession of faith. Article 7 dictated that he 'declare his grief and repentance' for the slaughter of Moray and that he do so publicly on his restoration into the Kirk. Before his absolution the General Assembly declared that he was to ask God's mercy for the slaughter. The Kirk got most but not all of this. After further 'long conference and ripe advertisement,' he agreed to acknowledge the reformed Kirk, to banish Jesuits out of his company, and express unfeigned grief – but not repentance – for the slaughter of Moray.[10] It is the well-known tactic of evasion – regret for the pain caused rather than sorrow for the act done. But it proved enough.

After a day of fasting, during which Huntly and Errol made up all deadly quarrels and shook hands with Lord Forbes and their other enemies, on Sunday 26 June 1597 the Auld Kirk of Aberdeen was filled to capacity with earls, barons, gentlemen and commoners, come to witness the submission of the erstwhile Catholic earls. The ceremony of reconciliation was presided over by the Bishop of Aberdeen. In the main aisle a table was set for the sacrament of the Lord's Supper. Immediately before the episcopal sermon the three earls rose from their places and subscribed the Confession of Faith. After the sermon the earls, in carefully worded protestations, made their public peace. They confessed their apostasy and professed their newfound commitment to the true faith. In addition Huntly declared before God, the King and the Kirk his deep sorrow for the murder of Moray and sought the intercession of the ministers with Moray's friends to bring about reconciliation for his death. This done, the bishop absolved them from excommunication and they were received by the whole ministry into the bosom of the Kirk. As this liturgy was proceeding the laird of Gight sank to his knees before the pulpit and asked pardon of God, the King and the Kirk for his support for Bothwell. Gight too was absolved. Then forgivers and forgiven together took the sacrament.

Monday was given over to a day long party in Aberdeen, an orgy of forgiveness. Huntly and Errol, basking in the approbation of all, sat at the Cross, with the royal commissioner and the clergy. To the sound of trumpets Gilbert Guthrie, the Marchmount Herald, proclaimed their pacification and peace. Patrick Moray, the King's commissioner, delivered to them the wand of peace, and received them in his majesty's name. Next the ministry embraced them, and then the provost, baillies and magistrates. This was very much the sort of elaborate ceremony of repentance and reconciliation, which James loved and invested with such significance. The magistrates and city council gathered to enjoy the festivity, the quality of which may be gauged from the fact that eighty young men with hagbuts were there as musicians. The day ended with much food, more wine and innumerable broken glasses. Perhaps not quite the penitence the presbytery had envisaged.[11]

Rome, worried that the apostasy of their leaders would have a dire impact on the Scots Catholics, sent James Gordon, Huntly's uncle and a Jesuit priest, to 'divert him from giving obedience.' He found Huntly 'much changed since last they met. The Earl's confusion was very great, for he could not but feel the disgrace which his abandonment of his faith and treacherous desertion of religion had brought upon him in the eyes of the Catholics. Huntly, as royal lieutenant, was bound to arrest any Jesuits arriving in the north. He had tried to stave off the problem by writing to his uncle telling him not to come. Either the letter failed to reach him or he ignored it. Huntly's whole rehabilitation could be thrown into question by the arrival on his shores of a Jesuit sent deliberately to win him back to the Old Faith. Huntly's long-standing friendship with his uncle and their blood relationship made it impossible for him to hand him over to the ministers, but he refused to see him and ordered him to leave the country.[12] Thus Huntly preserved his new-found righteousness by rejecting his erstwhile faith and family. His true allegiance, however, may be gleaned from the aggressively Roman frontispiece, which he placed over the lintel of the restored Strathbogie. Here his faith was written in a form that would endure down the centuries.

The earls act of repentance brought immediate rewards. The following February saw another gathering, this time in Edinburgh's market-place when Huntly, Errol and Angus were restored to their honours before the Lyon King of Arms in his royal livery and witnessed 'with a great noise of trumpets.' The Queen went with the Countesses of Huntly and Errol to watch the ceremony.[13] The King may have brought reconciliation, the Kirk forgiven, the people forgotten, but the Moray family itself would neither forgive nor forget. The teenage Earl was too young to act, but his uncle, Harry, commendator of St Colme, posed more of a threat. He remained an avenging angel whose mission was to track down and bring to justice those who had killed his brother. On 19 July 1595 Robert Birrell recorded in his diary the cryptic notice that 'James, laird of Innermarky' and his servant were beheaded as partakers in the murder of the Earl of Moray and Patrick Dunbar.[14] Huntly had previously implicated them in the killing. They had set out from the Bog of Gight for Edinburgh. Following them was St Colme who arrested them on the outskirts of the capital. They were summarily tried and executed in the market place. Minions were paying for the sins of their master. The years did not lesson his resolve. As late as December 1597, despite Huntly's offer of lands and marriage as a means of ending the quarrel, St Colme was in Edinburgh plotting to assassinate the Earl, probably by engineering a street brawl. He was ordered to quit the capital and return to Fife, while Huntly was sent to the safety of Dundee.

It was quite clear to James that until the body of the dead Earl was buried the feud arising from his murder could not be laid to rest. No amount of persuasion worked. Royal command would be needed. On 16 February 1597/8, days after the sixth anniversary of the murder, the Privy Council ordered James, Earl of Moray, his uncle, and his tutors and curators to bury the body of the second Earl 'in the accustomed burial place of his predecessors within twenty days next after they be charged thereto, under the pain of rebellion and putting of them to the horn.' The preamble to the instruction indicated that pressure had come from 'certain of the ministry' in complaints to the King about the abuse which had lately crept in of keeping bodies 'so many years unburied to the offence of God and slander of his word.'[15] The body of Lord Maxwell was also ordered for burial. His corpse had remained uninterred since 1593 as a reminder of the mortal feud between the Maxwells and the Johnstones. The action of the Morays was being copied by others. The clergy who for so long had kept the memory of Moray's murder alive had been satisfied by Huntly's submission and were sanctioning the end of the feud. It is another indication that whatever 'popular' disquiet had been aroused by his murder it had little to do with his own intrinsic popularity but far more with Protestant propaganda. The murder of a Protestant aristocrat by a Catholic one played into the hands of the Protestant party and they roused what rabble they could for as long as it served their ends. When his usefulness was passed, Moray could be buried and forgotten.

'The accustomed burial place of his predecessors' where his body was to be placed must have been obvious to Moray's family at the time of the order but remains uncertain to this day. The second Earl's predecessors must mean his father's line, and their accustomed burial place suggests the Stewart family crypt at the old, isolated and dilapidated Kilmaddock cemetery near Buchany, a mile or two from Doune. Doune had been associated with his family since 1528, Moray's parents were buried there and probably his grandparents. He had been born there and had grown up in its environs. Other possibilities are Dalgety, the scene of his murder and not far from Leith, or the Moray family plot in Dyke churchyard near Elgin where the third, fourth and fifth Earls are buried but not, according to family tradition, the second Earl. Darnaway is a most unlikely last resting-place, far further distant than Doune, and having far fewer happy associations for a largely absentee second Earl. He had inherited it only by marriage and none of his ancestors was buried there. Despite some assertions, St Giles Crypt where his father-in-law, the 'Good Regent' was buried, was always most improbable and can now be discounted. Calderwood recounts that when Moray's corpse was brought over the Forth by his mother it was 'to be buried in the style of the Great Kirk of Edinburgh in the Good Regent's tombe'.[16] This was her intention immediately after his murder, but it was thwarted by the King's prohibition. On several occasions the Regent's vault has been searched in the hope of finding the second Earl's bones.[17] In vain! The most likely reason for them not being found there is the most obvious: that they were never there in the first place. Lord James was the second Earl's 'predecessor' only in the sense of being the prior holder of his title, not in terms of family. His interment in what was in effect the state chapel was owing to his status as

Regent and Protestant martyr, not by virtue of his being the first Earl of Moray. Whatever iconic status may have briefly accrued to his son-in-law as a result of his murder it was of a different order to, and lacked the permanency of that of the Regent Moray. The second Earl's origins were lowly, his intrinsic significance was never great, and the earlier refusal of the King to allow his body either to lie in St Giles or to be buried there makes it very unlikely that provision would have been made for its later internment in the High Kirk. By burying him, James hoped he was burying the feud; by burying him in St Giles he could have perpetuated it by sanctifying him as a martyr worthy to lie near the hallowed Regent and by making his grave a focus of pilgrimage. Consequently, although it must remain true that 'no man knoweth where the second Earl's sepulchre is unto this day,' Kilmaddock remains the most likely resting-place for the second Earl's longsuffering corpse, and St Giles the least.[18]

On 25 February 1597/8, about the time of his burial, an eclipse of the sun caused considerable apprehension among the populace and introspection among the clergy but no one related it to Moray's interment. He had ceased to move the firmament.[19]

18

BEQUEST OF HATRED
1598-1638

Better bairns greet than bearded men.

Sir Thomas Lyon, the master of Glamis[1]

Ye'll stay and sup wi' us tonight,
And tomorrow we shall dine;
'Twill be a token of richt goodwill,
Atween your hoose and mine.

The Ballad of the Fire of Frendraught

The interment of Moray's corpse was but a small part of the King's wider endeavour to rein in belligerent aristocrats and to reconcile feuding families. In 1598 an 'Act anent [concerning] removing and extinguishing of deadly feuds' was passed to ensure that parties at feud should be subject to the royal courts. It divided feuds into three sorts: those where no killing had taken place; those where killing had been on one side; and those where there had been fatalities on both. The provisions relating to the first and third type of feud were nothing new and took up only one third of the Act: friends of the aggrieved should settle the first type; the King should compel the parties in the third type to agree to mutual compensation. The other two thirds of the Act were directed at the second form – the category into which the Moray-Huntly feud fell – and insisted that in this sort redress had to be sought from the courts. The King would not countenance private accommodations or agreements nor grant remission in those cases. Huntly had been one of the last beneficiaries of the old system. The resolution of the feud in future had to be in accordance with law, not by royal interference, diktat or indulgence. The nobility acquiesced, however, reassured that the King had no desire to impinge on their control of their estates and areas, but merely to curb the endless cycle of violence, and impose some notion of legal process.

This was something radically new. The thinking of the King, the lawyers and the Kirk was at one in this. Scotland and its ways were being sanitised in preparation for union with the more sophisticated society to the south. As Wormald asserts, it was also being prepared for the absence of its King and 'government by the pen.' In future independent

Edinburgh lawyers, not partisan and powerful friends, would conduct the negotiations and conclude the settlement. It was the beginning of the end. Once the lawyers and judges got a foothold there would be no backsliding to earlier ways.'[2] Feuding, that staple of Scottish social history was mortally wounded and would gradually die out during the seventeenth century. By its end, feuds in Scotland, like castles, had become unfashionable, 'the country being generally more civilised' – and more subject to condescension – 'than it was of ancient times.'[3]

With the body of the late Earl of Moray finally buried, there was nothing now to stand in the way of Huntly's further advancement. On 17 April 1599, on the occasion of the baptism of his goddaughter, Princess Margaret, he was rewarded for his compliance with the King's wishes by being created Marquis of Huntly, and joint Lieutenant of the North. His elevation to the marquisate – along with Lord Hamilton – caused a stir, but the King justified it on the ground that it had been long promised and would 'comfort him in that good course of loyalty and conformity in religion, which he doubt[ed] not he will continue.' This last optimistic phrase was inserted in the King's own hand in the margin of the document.[4] In the same year when James published his political treatise, *Basilikon Doron*, he gave one of the only seven copies printed to Huntly. The English ambassador observed that the new marquis was 'in special favour with the king ... and is in better estate than ever any Earl of Huntly was.'[5] Huntly's continuing intimacy with James and his assertion of precedence over other mere Earls led to much contention, most of all with Moray whose jealousy thereby increased.[6]

Once more the King intervened to calm the passions of his feuding senior nobility: Huntly on the one hand and Moray and Argyll on the other. In 1601 he summoned the parties to Edinburgh and entreated Moray 'by the glory of his ancestors to pardon and forget his father's slaughter for the general good of the kingdom, lest otherwise by his private resentments he should hinder the public advantage, diminish the royal dignity and disturb the common wealth.' Moray, pressed so by his King, finally seemed to yield. Arbitrators were named for composing the differences. Yet the Privy Council reported in September that the assurances between Huntly, Argyll and Moray had almost expired and the variance between them was unmoved.[7] The greatest barrier to rapprochement was not Moray's son, the third Earl, but remained the third Earl's uncle, Henry Stewart. He had pursued his brother's murderer with unremitting fury, and his fury had not slackened with time.

The King continued to try to get the opposing parties to submit to his attempts at reconciliation. The three earls were commanded under pain of rebellion to subscribe to new forms of mutual assurance which were optimistically to endure until 1 January 1603.[8] Invariably one party would not turn up, or would ask for a further adjournment. Moray and his uncle even put out feelers to England to get safe passes should they decide to leave the country to avoid the royal pressure on them.[9] Yet the King persisted. It was in his nature but it was also in his interest. With a throne soon to be vacant in the south he wanted no distractions or dissensions to harm the chance of him occupying it. Despite his distaste for Argyll personally (nicknamed 'the grim,' and whom he thought looked like the treacherous Earl of Gowrie who the previous year had tried to murder him) he made much of him 'persuading him both privately and openly at his table to be friends with the marquis of Huntly. James could not understand how these two peers could either do their king good service or their nation credit 'being ready to cut one another's throat.' If they submitted, however, on his inheriting the English throne, he would make both of them dukes.[10] This was enough for Argyll and he even agreed to be godfather, along with Huntly, to the infant prince Robert. The child, however, died in May.

It took another year of persistent hard work on the King's part before Moray could be finally reconciled. Dynastic marriage, that old and noble glue, was at the heart of the submission. In due time, Huntly's eldest son, Lord George Gordon, was to marry Lady Anna Campbell, Argyll's eldest daughter, in return for £20,000 Scots. The twenty-year-old Moray, on the other hand, was to marry Lady Anne Gordon, Huntly's eldest daughter in a few months hence.[11] James and his Queen were to attend that wedding in Strathbogie in April. The Queen was so enthusiastic about the reconciling power of marriage that she went even further proposing a double tryst between the old enemies: Huntly's son should marry Moray's sister. But two weddings were deemed enough. A love feast, laid on by the King, was the final reconciliatory gesture. The nobility got on so well at table – 'as lovingly as brethren' – that Huntly was invited to Stirling to feast with Argyll, Moray and Mar there. The King was to join them. Thus they 'all took leave with many hearty and loving farewells and drinks amongst them' all united in one loving bond for the surety and service of the King. Commenting on the ending of the great feud between the houses of Moray and Huntly, which had riven the country for forty years, George Nicolson, the English agent, marvelled that nothing was now heard at court 'but kind familiarity.' So extraordinary was the transformation that 'all men wondered.'[12]

The nuptials were deferred because of pressing royal business, and the accession of James to the English throne in 1603 brought further delay. The actual weddings in fact took several years to come about. It was not until 2 October 1607 that Moray finally married Anne Gordon. The wait was worthwhile; it was a marriage that lasted. It is perhaps to this period that a manuscript in Huntly's hand to the young Earl of Moray

is to be dated. In it he swears that the murder of the Earl's father was
not intended by him and 'that unlucky accident befell out far against his
will.' Notwithstanding his denial of guilt he offered to make amends to
Moray 'for the same.'[13] Moray further benefited from the King's pleasure
at the rapprochement by being finally granted good title to his earldom:
in 1611 he was granted a charter of novadamus of the lands and earldom
of Moray to himself and heirs–male. He had resigned the earldom of
Moray into the King's hands owing to the fact that the deeds had all
been destroyed when Donnibristle was fired. Others plausibly suggest
that such deeds never existed, and that this charter was to legitimate the
Moray line. If so it was a just reward for the peace he had complied
with. In the same year his uncle, Henry, was made Lord St Colme, the
former abbey's lands having been made into a secular lordship. He too
was placated.

   The reconciliation complete, Huntly came under renewed censure for
his adherence to the Old Faith. He had continued to disregard the sensi-
tivities of the Kirk of which he had ostensibly become a devout
adherent. Soon after his elevation to the marquisate, he had held a very
public Mass in his house in Edinburgh to which many resorted, secure
under his lofty protection. The wrath of the presbytery was aroused, and
a preacher denounced Huntly in front of the King, exclaiming in his
sermon that Huntly was 'a murderer and a sacrilegious person and that
he never read Revelation but he found him there!'[14] Huntly had
misjudged. The anger of the Kirk was sufficiently strong as to induce the
Marquis to leave the court. His fluidity in the faith was to lead to regular
spats with the ministry for the rest of his life. In 1608, despite putting
him in mild ward at Elgin, James was unable to prevent his old friend's
excommunication. He was transferred to Stirling Castle. James would
not let him languish too long. He added his pleas to those of the clergy
sent into the castle to persuade the Marquis of the error of his ways. He
even sent him a brief summary of Protestant doctrine, which the
Marquis returned with his signature attached, indicating a willingness to
accept it. He seems to have failed to follow this indication through,
since in June 1610 after almost two years' incarceration there was still no
recommendation for his release. The fact that Huntly was prepared to
endure such treatment for his faith is an indication of the depth of
commitment he latterly had for it. In his later years he was decidedly less
malleable than in his youth. He was eventually released in January 1611
and despatched to his own estates with strict instructions to stay there
and receive instruction from orthodox presbyterian clergy, a chilling
fate. He was finally discharged from this confinement in May 1613.
Allowed to travel to England to see the King, he submitted entirely, and
underwent yet another conversion, being received into the Anglican
Communion by the Archbishop of Canterbury on 8 July 1616. The

archbishop, before communicating the Marquis, absolved him from his lengthy excommunication, an action which caused consternation among the ecclesiastical hierarchy in Scotland whose powers had been usurped. James and the Archbishop of Canterbury were forced to write to the Archbishop of St Andrews justifying the absolution as a 'Christian necessity,' pursuant to the pliant Marquis renouncing his erstwhile adherence to the doctrine of transubstantiation. They had felt constrained 'to strike the iron whilst it was hot.' The letters had the desired affect. The Kirk was mollified, but before it could be fully satisfied of the course taken Huntly had to appear before its General Assembly. There he publicly acknowledged his offences in despising the admonitions of the Church, and promised to adhere to the true Faith himself and to educate his children in it.[15]

Huntly had been James' most faithful if most wilful subject. Whatever Huntly's intrigues and escapades the King had always known where his ultimate loyalty lay. On the occasion of his last visit to London, James told his son Charles, the Prince of Wales, to take Huntly by the hand 'as the most faithful subject that ever served a prince, assuring him that so long as he should cherish and keep Huntly on his side, he need not be very apprehensive of great danger from seditious and turbulent heads in Scotland.'[16] It was good advice, but being good advice Charles chose to ignore it. With James' death in 1625 and the accession of Charles I the pendulum swung against Huntly. The new King was decidedly cool towards him, perhaps resenting the older man's casual intimacy with his father. Not for the first time a Huntly discovered to his cost that a special relationship with one sovereign does not transfer to the next.

Huntly went into semi-retirement, resolving 'to live at home free from the factions and vexations of the court.' He turned his mind to posterity, rebuilding Riffen after it was accidentally burnt down, repairing at great expense the derelict Strathbogie (upon which in giant letters he inscribed his name) and his town houses in Elgin and Old Aberdeen, building new houses at Aboyne and Plewlands in Moray and a hunting lodge at Kean Kaill, and further enlarging and decorating Bog of Gight.[17] It was religion that once again got him into trouble. The government was becoming increasingly uneasy about resurgent Catholicism. Protestantism was under threat throughout Europe and the menace from Catholic dissidents to the stability of the state was felt keenly throughout the two kingdoms of Scotland and England. Reports began to reach Edinburgh of an upsurge of Popery in the north. Particularly unsettling was the evidence of how many Catholics were holding public office in express disregard of the law. Roman Catholic servants or tenants of Huntly and under his protection went about armed and arrogant, poisoning others with heresy, corrupting them from obedience to the King, and flouting the laws 'to the high contempt of His Majesty's authority.' The sheriffs of Aberdeen and Inverness could not or dared not apprehend them. Huntly, as the King's 'special man of power, friendship, authority and commandement' in the north was commissioned and ordered to do so and to put the 'excommunicate rebels' on trial.[18] He was authorised to enter homes and to do everything necessary to execute his orders. He was to remove all dissidents from public office. It was asking more than the Marquis was willing to do. These 'heretics' included men whom he had appointed and promoted and with whose views and beliefs he sympathised. In 1629 he was himself put to the horn for failing in his commission. Huntly went over the heads of the Council and directly appealed to the King. He and his son agreed to hand over their hereditary sheriffdoms of Inverness and Aberdeen – a jurisdiction that had lasted 160 years – in return for £5,000 sterling, hoping that by so relinquishing legal jurisdiction they would be freed from the disagreeable necessity of persecuting their friends and retainers.[19] He was freed from the horn and allowed to go back to his domains in the north. The renunciation was for nothing. As a landlord Huntly was still held responsible for the 'Papists' on his lands. His power in the north and at court was curtailed. In 1630, his son-in-law, Moray, was at last granted the prized lieutenancy along with a commission to subjugate Clan Chattan. Huntly was no longer even a member of the Privy Council. Perhaps as a sop, his personal physician, William Leslie, was allowed to remain in the realm provided he restricted his attentions to his aristocratic patron.[20] The Marquis was now an old and ailing man whose friends had long since died, and whose powers – personal and dynastic – were waning. His last years saw a sad decline from his former glory. Now in old age he understandably 'loved rest and quietness with all his heart,' but rest and quietness were not to be.

A terrible misfortune, which echoed the fate of the second Earl of Moray, was to befall the ailing Marquis: the untimely death of his youngest son, John Gordon, Lord Melgum and Aboyne. Like Moray, Melgum was twenty-four when he died; like Moray he died away from home and as a result of a house being fired; as with Moray the background to his death is feuding over fishing rights. There was one difference: Moray died and became a Protestant martyr; Melgum was piously portrayed as publicly professing the Catholic faith as the flames took him.

James Crichton, laird of Frendraught had had a long running dispute with William Gordon of Rothiemay over salmon fishing rights in the Deveron, the river running north of Frendraught towards Huntly Castle. Such disputes frequently led to bloodshed and this was no exception. In one violent encounter, on New Year's day 1630, Crichton had been responsible for killing Rothiemay and George Gordon, the laird of

Lesmoir's brother. On that occasion John Meldrum of Reidshill had sided with Crichton. Later, however, he considered that he had not been recompensed sufficiently and stole two of Crichton's horses. In an attempt to recapture his horses on 27 September 1630 Crichton's men attacked Meldrum and his brother-in- law, John Leslie, younger of Pitcaple, who had been shot through the arm by Robert Crichton of Condland. The aggrieved parties sought to embroil the local magnates in their dispute. On 5 October Frendraught had a conference with Moray in Elgin, while the following day Leslie of Pitcaple went to Huntly at Bog of Gight for redress for his son. In an effort to resolve the dispute, which was on the verge of getting out of hand, the Marquis summoned Frendraught to Strathbogie to answer for this attack and injury. John Gordon of Rothiemay, the son of the deceased William, also attended, and a reconciliation upon payment of fifty merks was arranged between the two gentry, a reconciliation that did not include the injured man, John Leslie. His father was not satisfied with the response and made his dissatisfaction clear.

Suspecting that the Leslies were waiting in ambush, Huntly asked Rothiemay and his own son to escort Frendraught as he rode in the evening of 8 October through hostile country to his home seven miles away. When they arrived it was dark and Melgum agreed to stay the night. It was to be his last, since during the night the lower floor of the tower in which he was sleeping caught fire and killed all those in it, Melgum, Rothiemay and their six companions. There could be no escape since all the windows had thick bars imbedded in them. When the terrible news reached him, Huntly was 'broken-hearted for his son.'[21] To the ends of his days the Frendraught case was to obsess him to the exclusion of all else.

Just as many cases of food poisoning were assumed to be deliberate, so fires, another commonplace, were often assumed to be arson. Contemporaries were quick to draw a parallel between the fate of Huntly's son and of his earlier victim. 'The general comment is that the said Marquis burnt the Earl of Moray's father's house upon him, and Rothiemay's father was a chief actor in the business. It should seem that the old feuds are not quite forgotten in those parts.'[22] The crime wrought on the 'Bonnie Earl' had been repaid in full. There is, however, absolutely no evidence that Moray was in any way involved in what transpired at Frendraught nor did Huntly ever suggest he was. If there were a certain sense of justice in what happened the vengeful hand behind it was that of Divine Providence not that of a mere earl. Perhaps sensing this, Huntly would not leave punishment to the omniscient but partisan deity. Suspicion fell on several contenders, Meldrum and Pitcaple being the most likely culprits. The former was eventually hanged for it in 1633, protesting his innocence until all protest was strangled out of him.

Huntly and Lady Rothiemay, whose son had also died in the conflagration, put the ultimate blame on the laird of Frendraught himself. In
consort with this formidable lady, the Marquis persecuted the Crichtons
thereafter 'for the burning of the haus, and was cold in any other
pursuit.'[23] To the end of his days his brigands ravaged the Crichton lands.

This vigilantism embroiled him in a succession of inconclusive
lawsuits necessitating many journeys to the capital. When he failed to
appear, as several times he did, he was put to the horn; then he
compered and was released from the horn. This litigation probably
hastened his end and certainly dictated that it would be far from the
bosom of his family. As a family chronicler put it, 'now at last in his
latter days, by means of Frendraught he is so persecuted by the laws that
he is compelled to travel without pity so often to Edinburgh and now
ends his days out of his own house, without trial of the fire of
Frendraught, which doubtless was an help to his death.'[24]

On one occasion, under threat of treason the ailing Marquis was
forced to travel south in January 1635 'in ane great storm' in order to
appear before a meeting of the Privy Council at St Andrews. His
journey took fully five weeks to accomplish, the tardiness of his progress
being explained by the state of the roads, the inclemency of the weather
and his own poor health. Having given his answer to the Council and
pledged action against the 'broken men of the name of Gordon' he was
allowed to go home, a destination he reached after another long and
arduous circuit.[25] He was forced to re-appear before the Council in July,
and again allowed home. Then in September, their patience finally
expiring, Huntly was warded in Edinburgh Castle on a charge of
resetting William Ross, 'one of the principal rebels and disobedient
persons in the north.' He spent the winter alone in an unlighted room,
with only a Christmas visit from his wife to relieve the solitude. In
March 1636 'in regard of his old age and weakness of body,' he was
allowed to move to his own house in the Canongate, with liberty to
walk in the grounds of nearby Holyrood Palace but no further.[26] It was
not until late May, his health fast failing, that he finally achieved a
compassionate licence to return home. It was to be his last journey. He
made it back to Strathbogie but in a hearse not on a horse.

The circumstances of the death of this old man were to prove to be
as undignified as that of his more short-lived predecessors. Accompanied
by his faithful spouse, he was too ill to ride and had to be carried in 'a
wand bed within his chariot.' On 13 June 1636 the first Marquis of
Huntly died in Dundee. On his deathbed, and with his last breath, to be
on the safe side, he declared himself a Catholic. The corpse was placed
in a chest covered in black taffeta and there it lay until provision could
be made to move it north. On 25 June, still accompanied by his wife,
his body was brought by horse litter to the chapel at Strathbogie. The

following day his body was taken to the kirk of Belly, and the following day in the early hours it was carried to his house in Elgin. There it lay in state until the arrangements for an extravagant and exceptional funeral had been made. He would go out in the style befitting the Cock o' the North.

Finally everything was ready. On 30 August 1636 the sixth Earl and first Marquis of Huntly made his last grand procession through the streets of his town to his cathedral, the resting-place of his ancestors. It all took place at night. His coffin was placed on a funerary carriage draped with 'a rich mortcloth of black velvet whereon were wrought two white crosses.' It was escorted on its long slow procession by 300 of his friends and local gentry each carrying a lighted torch. His son, Adam, led the way; his son-in-law, the Earl of Moray, and behind him the Earl of Sutherland, walked on the right, the Earl of Seaforth and Sir Robert Gordon on the left. Thus he was 'carried to the east Kirk stile of the College Kirk, in at the south Kirk door, and buried in his own isle with much mourning and lamentation.' The chronicler comments that 'the like form of burial with torch light was seldom seen here before.'[27] In a final ironical twist to this tale the elaborate painting of the Marquis of Huntly's funeral procession was probably done by James Workman, the son of the strongest candidate for the execution of the Moray Memorial.

His rival's son outlived his father's killer by only two years. On 6 August 1638 the third Earl of Moray died at Darnaway. By contrast to his vainglorious father-in-law he was buried modestly at the church of Dyke the next day 'without pomp, or worldly glory' according to his own specific instructions.[28] His widow, and Huntly's daughter, Anne Gordon, was not to be as long-lived as her father. She died at Elgin on 19 January 1640. Gordon of Buckie, reputedly the prime assassin of the 'Bonny Earl,' outlived even the long-lived Huntly, expressing on his deathbed remorse for his part in the crime. With his passing all the players in this celebrated performance were dead. The family feud was as dead as the principals were.

19

PACIFICUS

Beati sunt Pacifici ['Blessed are the peacemakers for they shall be called the sons of God:' Matthew 5.9.]

Motto of James VI

Teach your nobility to keep your laws as precisely as the meanest.... And for their barbarous feuds, put the laws to due execution made by me there-anent [concerning them]; beginning ever rathest [soonest] at him that ye love best, and is most oblished [obliged] unto you; to make him an example to the rest. For ye shall make all your reformation to begin at your elbow.[1]

There were many similarities between the Moray murder and that of Darnley. In both the monarchs provided the lure. Mary had coaxed Darnley into leaving the security of his father's seat in the west for a house within the walls of the city of Edinburgh but not a lodging within the walls of the castle. James arranged for Moray to be enticed from the safety of his castle and lands in the north to the outskirts of Edinburgh where he would be vulnerable to his enemies. In both popular sentiment implicated the monarch by tacit encouragement if not more active involvement. In both the instrument of the murder was a leading rival among the nobility. In neither case did the monarch seem over eager to bring the guilty to justice. Bothwell and Huntly, the chief assassins in their respective plots, were protected rather than pursued by the monarch, and each had a uniquely close relationship with that monarch.[2] The huge difference is that Mary compounded her complicity by later folly while her son defused the danger by his deft handling of affairs.

But to what extent was King James directly involved in the murder of Moray? The King undoubtedly harboured ill will towards the second Earl, not because of any alleged dalliance with the Queen but because of his undoubted alliance with Bothwell, James's main bugbear and Moray's cousin germane. The fact that a few days after the murder John Naismith was threatened with torture to confess that Moray had been with Bothwell on the night of his raid on Holyrood suggests an attempt to discredit the dead man.[3] It certainly reveals the King's concern that other of his nobles were openly siding with or secretly supporting Bothwell. The notorious commission of fire and sword, which James issued to Huntly on 7 February, was directed against Bothwell and these presumed accomplices. The exact provisions are obscure since the commission itself is no longer extant, in itself a suspicious circumstance. If acting within its remit, Huntly would surely have preserved it, unless, to save embarrassment to the King, he destroyed it. The King would normally have kept a copy of so important a document among the state papers, but none has been found. Later Moray's supporters alleged that the commission was blank, allowing Huntly to interpret his orders as he saw fit, and take Moray dead or alive. The matter of the missing commission is one piece of evidence that suggests a greater complicity between Huntly and the King than either would later acknowledge.

Yet it remains inherently unlikely that James would involve himself directly or even indirectly in the squalid and bloody killing of a peer of the realm and a kinsman by marriage. A few years later, according to the official account, the treacherous Gowrie brothers were killed when they lured the King to an upper room and James frantically summoned help to prevent his own murder, help which had to batter down stout doors and ascend flights of narrow stairs and yet which arrived in time to save their sovereign and dispatch his traducers. But then the King's person was in immediate danger. Treason was being committed on the royal person and the traitors were dispatched. James was bothered by Moray but not immediately or nearly threatened. It is more likely that James merely wanted Moray's volatility reined in, his immaturity disciplined, and his associations severed. James was on the whole a man of considerable forbearance and forgiveness. He wanted the wayward Earl brought before the Council to answer for his dalliance with Bothwell. Huntly was only too pleased to act as the arresting policeman. Unbeknown to the King, his Chancellor, Maitland, may have been the one to tip Huntly off as to the whereabouts of his unwary rival. Even if Huntly were so informed with the King's acquiescence, the lines 'I bade you bring him to me, But forbade you him to slay,' may well reflect the truth and extent of the royal intention. Others may have gone much further.

For slay him Huntly did. He may not initially have compassed his irksome rival's death but once at Donnibristle, with Moray again defiant and one of his own kinsmen injured, his mood or that of his followers may have changed. He was acting within his remit when he used fire to flush out the recalcitrant Earl. In a fair fight the killing of his sheriff was also permissible. The murder of a fugitive Earl was not. Yet even then it was not Huntly who struck the fatal blow but his minions. In the heat of the moment and by the hand of his servant he was implicated in murder. However, while this scenario is quite possible, there are factors that suggest that Huntly took ruthless advantage of the opportunity provided by the temporary paranoia of the King, and the wide remit of his commission. To some extent he aimed at and engineered the death of his irksome foe. He acted in a clandestine manner, purporting to pursue a Holyrood raider, John Colven, and arousing no immediate suspicions of his larger intentions. He stole secretly to Donnibristle for a terrifying raid on unsuspecting prey. He did so as darkness fell, cloaking the precise movements and actions of his followers and friends. And he chose to take along with him notoriously violent men such as, William Gordon of Gight and James Gordon of Lesmour, as well as a man at bitter bloodfeud with Moray, Thomas Gordon of Cluny, with a longstanding debt to collect for the killing of his brother two years before. Thus, while it is equally likely that the sixth Earl of Huntly is guilty of the premeditated murder of the second Earl of Moray, on all the evidence available the historical verdict must be 'Not Proven.'

Conversely, the time and place of the killing suggests no active involvement on the King's part. The trouble with the Moray murder was that it was on the doorstep. And more, it looked as though Moray had been lured by the King from the safety of Darnaway or Doune to the insecurity of his pied a terre near Edinburgh. Ochiltree maintained that none but he, the Chancellor and the King knew that James had sent him to get Moray down south. Further, James had commissioned Huntly, and had closed the Queen's Ferry behind him. Had Huntly killed Moray in a dispute far off, in the north perhaps, a brawl in Elgin or in a gunfight at Darnaway, it would have been all the more convenient. Accurate accounts of what happened in the provinces were hard to come by, there would be opportunity for Huntly to get in his side of the story first, and the incident was far removed from the presence of the King.

In terms of his handling of the affair, the King was vilified at the time and thereafter for his failure to punish those involved. A senior member of his nobility was butchered on his doorstep and he did no more than imprison the suspects comfortably and exonerate the penitents eagerly. This inaction against Huntly does not, of course, prove that James was himself implicated in a murder plot, merely that he was reluctant to punish the murderer. Part of the explanation for this was James' sense of *realpolitik*. He was a ruler of considerable acumen. He understood fully the dynamics of the relationships between the members of the nobility and the crown, and between each other. Moray had deliberately challenged Huntly's long-established supremacy, built up over the previous two centuries by royal support and by a network of local alliances. His attempt to attract to his own following families dependant on the House of Gordon was an act of provocation which inevitably created unrest and feuding. Moray had taken a gamble and lost and the loser paid the almost inevitable price. Moray, headstrong, overweening, empty, was readily disposable. His power was not ancient, his family not extensive, his influence a faint echo of that of the Regent from whom – by marriage only – he got his title. A man of the stature of Lord James Stewart, half-brother to the Queen, could oppose an elderly, corpulent, fourth Earl of Huntly vastly out of royal favour – could oppose and could prevail. The diminutive figure of the second Earl, with none of his father-in-law's bloodline, gravitas, authority, experience or statesmanship, could oppose the young, able and well beloved sixth Earl of Huntly – but only at his own peril. James was brought up in a society where differences between neighbours were resolved by bloodfeud. For the King in these circumstances to have yielded to pressure from kin or Kirk, to take strong measures against Huntly – who himself, in the traditional and well-understood manner, offered to express contrition and pay reparation for the murder to Moray's kin – would have been to turn a difficult local situation into a national crisis. What was done was done. He had to live with Huntly in the future. He had lost one Earl of Moray; he could not afford to lose another northern earl as well. Nothing was to be gained by trying to destroy the power of a family whose record as crown servants was virtually unequalled. Huntly might aggrandise himself, he might pull down other nobles but he would not endanger the throne. The King recognised this reality, and acted accordingly. He delayed when he could, he took the minimum amount of action he could get away with at any particular time. By his inaction – and he showed himself as much a master of this political ploy as Elizabeth of England – James prevented anything more than strong feeling and a great deal of vocal uproar. As one modern commentator admiringly puts it, 'his inaction allowed a crisis to dissolve into an anti-climax.'[4] By 1599 he was able with justification to include the former rebels, Huntly and his associates, in the group of his trustiest servants. So Huntly was to remain.

Seeing the royal lenity solely as an aspect of policy, however, would be an unnecessarily monocular view. It also reflected his personal predisposition. The King had a strong affection for Huntly dating back to his childhood. As an adolescent he had turned with adulation towards older men. Esmé Stewart was his first father figure – George Gordon his first older brother. The intensity of his feelings for Huntly altered but did not subside with the passing of time: the older brother became the little brother, and then the son. Huntly was in short an old and very special friend, and James was loyal to such friends. The fact that Huntly was his friend and Moray was not must be part of any explanation for the royal reluctance to punish the former for the death of the latter. Both the personal sympathies of James, and the political realities, ensured Huntly's ultimate rehabilitation.

Thus there is no direct evidence implicating James in a murder plot. It is inherently unlikely. At best he was indifferent to his death; at worst he may have turned a blind eye as his mentor Elizabeth had done with his mother. He signed no death warrant but perhaps disingenuously he placed the power of life or death in Huntly's hands, the hands of a man with a grudge. It is very unlikely from what we know of James that he would be so crude as to urge the killing, nor need he be. The hare was on the course; all he had to do was unleash the hound. Whether he did so unwittingly, or not, will never be known for sure.

What is true is that he was painstaking in reconciling the families thereafter. This was part of his greater endeavour to control violence throughout the kingdom by reining in and reconciling the feuding parties. Throughout his reign he had used the justice inherent in bloodfeud to bring about recompense and reconciliation. After Huntly's rebellion in 1594, the power of the leading nobility subsided in comparison to the growing financial and military might of the crown. In 1598 the King enacted that feuds should be subject to royal jurisdiction. Many of the senior nobility were opposed to this, suspecting that it was less a measure to curb violence and more a means of enlarging royal influence in their localities. When the latter threat proved groundless, and it became apparent that with the exception of murder, local means of resolving feuds would be left untouched, 'noble co-operation was secured and James travelled south in 1603 with most of the great noble feuds laid to rest.'5 The Moray-Huntly feud remained the most obviously festering sore. King James sought to heal it over the next decade. He largely succeeded. Had he lived, James would have been mightily cheered to see the dead Earl's son as chief pallbearer at his father-in-law's funeral. It was a vindication of all his pacific endeavours. 'Blessed are the Peacemakers' was a motto he took seriously, and an ethic he lived and reigned by.

APPENDIX 1
Chronology

Note: Under the Julian Calendar then in use both in Scotland and England the new year began on the Feast of the Annunciation or Lady Day, 25 March. James VI ordered conformity with the Gregorian Calendar in Scotland as of 1 January 1600. England came into line in 1752. Thus dates falling between 1 January and 24 March are given in the format 3 February 1567/8.

YEAR	MONTH	EVENT
1300		
1306–29		Robert I, the Bruce.
1314	24/6	Battle of Bannockburn.
1329–71		David I.
1333	19/7	Sir Adam Gordon killed at the Battle of Halidon Hill.
1346		Sir Alexander Gordon and 3rd Earl of Moray killed at the Battle of Neville's Cross.
1357		Sir John Gordon admitted to the Scottish nobility.
1371–90		Robert II.
1388	5/8	John Gordon killed at the Battle of Otterburn.
1390–1406		Robert III.
1400		
1402	14/9	David Gordon killed at the Battle of Homildon Hill.
1406–37		James I.
1408		Elizabeth, daughter of David Gordon, married Sir Alexander Seton (1).
1412		Foundation of St Andrews University.
1437–60		James II.
1444–45		The new title Earl of Huntly created by James II for Alexander Seton (2). Earldom of Moray created.
1451		1st Huntly made Lord Badenoch.
1452	18/5	Battle of Brechin.
1453		Foundation of Glasgow University.
c.1454		1st Huntly changed family name from Seton to Gordon.
1455	1/5	Archibald Douglas, Earl of Moray, killed at the battle of Arkinholme.

1460–88		James III.
1470		Death of 1st Huntly; George Gordon succeeded as 2nd Huntly.
1473	17/3	Birth of James Stewart, later King James IV.
1476		2nd Huntly made Lieutenant of the North, 'Cock of the North.'
1485	22/8	Accession of Henry VII of England (1485–1509).
1488	11/6	Battle of Sauchieburn. Death of James III. Accession of James IV.
1488–1513		James IV.
1500		
1500		Foundation of Aberdeen University.
1501		James Stewart (1), the bastard of James IV, created Earl of Moray.
	/6	2nd Huntly died; Alexander Gordon succeeded as 3rd Huntly.
1509	21/4	Death of Henry VII, accession of Henry VIII (1509–1547).
1513	9/9	The Battle of Flodden. Death of William Gordon and James IV. Accession of James V.
1513–1542		James V.
1514[-62]		Birth of George Gordon, 4th Earl of Huntly, Lord Gordon and Badenoch.
1514	6/8	Marriage of Queen Margaret and Archibald Douglas, 6th Earl of Angus.
1517		Death of John Gordon, heir of 3rd Huntly.
1519		Adam Gordon, brother of 3rd Huntly, married Elizabeth, heiress to the earldom of Sutherland.
1520	30/4	'Cleansing the Causeway.'
1524		Death of 3rd Huntly. George Gordon succeeded his grandfather as 4th Huntly.
c1525[-90]		Birth of James Stewart (3), Commendator of St Colme and first Lord Doune.
1528	14/7	James V granted of the captaincy of Castle Doune to Sir James Stewart (2) of Beath. 4th Huntly went into exile in England with Angus.
1530	27/3	4th Huntly betrothed to Elizabeth, daughter of Robert, Lord Keith.
1531[-70]		Birth of James Stewart (4), bastard of James V, later 1st Earl of Moray.
c1531[-76]		Birth of George Gordon, 5th Earl of Huntly.
1534/35	2/2	4th Huntly married Elizabeth Keith.
1535		4th Huntly became a Privy Councillor.

1536		4th Huntly became a Vice-Regent during the absence of James V in France.
1542	24/8	Battle of Hadden-Rig.
	24/11	Battle of Solway Moss.
	8/12	Mary Queen of Scots born.
	13/12	Death of James V. Accession of Mary Queen of Scots.
1542-1567		Mary Queen of Scots Beaton, 4th Huntly, Moray and Argyll appointed themselves regents during the minority of Mary.
	22/12	Arran appointed sole Regent.
1543		James Stewart (3) made titular abbot of St Colme.
	27/4	Abbot of St Colme granted the lands of Beath to 4th Huntly.
	1/7	Treaty of Greenwich.
	8/9	Arran's abjuration.
	9/9	Mary crowned Queen of Scots.
1544-1547		The Rough Wooing.
1544	1/5	Hertford invaded Scotland.
	12/6	Reversion of the earldom of Moray to the Crown. 4th Huntly renamed Strathbogie as Huntly.
	15/7	Battle of the Field of Shirts.
1544/5	17/2	Battle of Ancrum Moor.
1545	5/9	Hertford invaded Scotland.
		James Stewart (4) matriculated at St Andrews University.
1545/6		Sir James Stewart (3) appointed commendator of the Abbey of St Colme.
1546	28/3	Martyrdom of George Wishart at St Andrews.
	29/5	Cardinal Beaton murdered at St Andrews. The castle seized by the Protestants.
1546	5/6	4th Huntly appointed Lord Chancellor.
1547	28/1	Death of Henry VIII, accession of Edward VI (1547-1553).
	Whit	Sir James Stewart (2) of Beath killed at Dunblane.
	30/7	Surrender of St Andrews castle.
	28/8	Somerset mustered to invade Scotland.
	10/9	Battle of Pinkie Cleugh. 4th Huntly imprisoned in England.
1548	7/7	Arran made Duke of Chatelherault.
	7/8	Mary Queen of Scots sailed to France.
	5/12	4th Huntly released.
1548/9	13/2	4th Huntly given charter to hold the earldom of Moray under the Crown.
1550	24/3	Treaty of Boulogne
1553		4th Huntly imprisoned for failure to put down Camerons.
	6/7	Death of Edward VI, accession of Jane (1553)
	19/7	Deposition of Jane, accession of Mary Tudor, 'Bloody Mary,' (1553-1558).
1553/4	19/2	Chatelherault resigned regency in favour of Mary of Guise.

1557	5/8	4th Huntly restored to favour to become lieutenant general of Scotland.
	3/12	The First Band of the Lords of the Congregation of Christ.
1558		Maitland of Lethington became Secretary of State.
	24/4	Mary married the Dauphin Francis in Paris.
	17/11	Death of Mary Tudor, accession of Elizabeth (1558-1603).
1559		Lord Gordon (5th Huntly) married Lady Anne Hamilton, daughter of the Duke of Chatelherault.
1559/60	27/2	The Treaty of Berwick.
1560	10/5	The treaty of Berwick confirmed.
	10/6	Death of Mary of Guise.
	8/7	The treaty of Edinburgh.
	/8	The 'Reformation Parliament'
	5/12	Death of Francis II of France.
1560/61	27/1	The First Book of Discipline (Knox) adopted.
1561	14/4	Embassy of John Lesley to Mary Queen of Scots.
	15/4	Embassy of Lord James Stewart (4) to Mary Queen of Scots..
	19/8	Mary Queen of Scots landed in Scotland.
1561/2	30/1	Mary granted Lord James Stewart (4) the earldom of Moray.
	7/2	Mary granted Lord James Stewart (4) the earldom of Mar.
	10/2	Lord James Stewart (4) married Agnes Keith.
1562		Birth of George Gordon, later 6th Earl of Huntly.
	27/6	Sir John Gordon wounded Lord Ogilvie.
	27/8	Mary arrived in Aberdeen.
	10/9	Announcement of grant of the earldom of Moray to Lord James Stewart (4).
	12/9	Mary entered Inverness castle and hanged the warden.
	22/9	Mary returned to Aberdeen.
	29/9	Mary ordered 4th Huntly to surrender his cannon.
	9/10	The Laird of Grange sent to Strathbogie to seize 4th Huntly & John Gordon.
	11/10	John Gordon attacked Mary's men.
	17/10	4th Huntly and John Gordon put to the horn.
	27/10	1st Moray granted a commission to proceed against 4th Huntly.
	28/10	Battle of Corrichie. Death of 4th Huntly.
	2/11	John Gordon beheaded in the presence of Mary. Adam Gordon spared.
	21/11	Mary returned to Edinburgh.
	28/11	George Gordon warded in Edinburgh castle.
1562/3	8/2	George Gordon condemned for treason, returned to ward in Edinburgh castle.
	10/2	Lord James Stewart (4) entitled Earl of Moray.
	11/2	George Gordon warded at Dunbar Castle.

1563	28/5	The body of 4th Huntly declared guilty of treason, and the earldom forfeited.
1563/4	11/1	Marriage of James Stewart (3) to Argyll's sister Margaret at Castle Campbell.
	6/3	Charter of the custody of Castle Doune.
1565	29/7	Mary married Darnley at Holyrood
	/8	Birth of Elizabeth Stewart, elder daughter of 1st Moray.
	3/8	Mary pardoned George, Gordon, and released him from ward.
	6/8	1st Moray put to the horn.
	14/8	1st Moray's properties seized by the Queen.
	25/8	George Lord Gordon restored by open proclamation to the lordship of Gordon.
	26/8	Mary left Edinburgh on a campaign against 1st Moray.
	31/8-1/9	The Chase-about Raid.
	6/10	1st Moray fled to England.
	8/10	George Lord Gordon made 5th Earl of Huntly.
1565/6	/3	5th Huntly appointed Chancellor.
	9/3	Murder of David Ricchio.
1566	21/4	4th Huntly's corpse transported to Strathbogie for burial at Elgin.
	1/6	The succession to the earldom of Moray was extended to Moray's heirs.
	19/6	James VI born.
	20/11-4/12	Craigmiller Conference.
	17/12	Baptism of Prince James according to Catholic rites at Stirling Castle.
1566/7	9-10/2	Murder of Darnley.
1567-1577	/8	Minority of James VI
1567		James Stewart (5), 2nd Earl of Moray born.
	24/4	Bothwell 'abducted' Mary.
	15/5	Marriage of Mary and Bothwell at Holyrood.
	15/6	Battle of Carberry Hill.
	24/7	Mary abdicated.
	29/7	James VI crowned.
1567-1569/70		Regent Moray
	22/8	1st Moray proclaimed Regent.
1568	2/5	Mary escaped from Lochleven Castle.
	13/5	Battle of Langside.
	16/5	Mary arrived in England
1569/70	23/1	1st Moray assassinated.
	14/2	1st Moray buried in St Giles kirk.
1570-1571		Regent Lennox
1570	15/7	Lennox appointed Regent.

	21/8	Castle Doune besieged by Lennox.
1570/1/2		Marriage of Lady Agnes Keith, widow of the Regent Moray to Colin Campbell, Lord Lorne, later 6th Earl of Argyll.
1571	2/4	Dumbarton Castle captured.
	7/4	John Hamilton, Archbishop of St Andrews, executed.
	4/9	Lennox assassinated.
1571-1572		Regent Mar.
	5/9	Mar appointed Regent.
	17/10	Adam Gordon routed Forbes at Tulliangus.
	20/11	Adam Gordon routed Forbes at Crabstone.
		Burning of Corgarff Castle.
1572	24/8	St Bartholomew's Day Massacre.
	28/10	Death of Mar.
	24/11	Death of John Knox; Morton appointed Regent.
1572-1580		Regent Morton.
1572/3	23/2	Pacification of Perth.
1573	28/5	Surrender of Edinburgh Castle.
	9/6	Death of Maitland of Lethington.
	3/8	Execution of Kirkaldy of Grange.
1576	19/10	Death of 5th Huntly; 6th Huntly succeeds.
1577/8-1603		Personal Rule of James VI.
1577/8	12/3	Morton deprived of the Regency.
		Second Book of Discipline (Melville).
1579		6th Huntly took refuge in Paris.
1579/80	/3	Esmé Stewart created Earl of Lennox.
1580	10/8	Repair of Doune Castle.
	31/12	Arrest of Morton on charge of treason.
1580/1	/1	Gift of wardship of Moray's inheritance to James Stewart.
	23/1	James Stewart (5) married Elizabeth, Countess of Moray.
		James Stewart (5) entitled 2nd Earl of Moray.
		Captain James Stewart (6) made Earl of Arran.
1581	2/6	Execution of Morton.
	27/8	Esmé Stewart made Duke of Lennox.
		Sir John Maitland made Lord of Session.
	24/11	Sir James Stewart (3) created Lord Doune by charter under the Great Seal.
1582		Birth of first son of 2nd Moray. This may be James Stewart (7) but see 1587.
	22/8	Ruthven Raid.
	4/12	Abandonment of attempt to seize James in Holyrood.
1583	26/5	Lennox died.
	25/6	James VI escaped from the Ruthven Raiders.
	/6	James VI asked to baptise James Stewart (7).

1584		Dispute between 2nd Moray and 6th Huntly over pension rights from the diocese of Moray.
	3/5	Trial and execution of Earl of Gowrie.
	/6	2nd Moray's servant killed by 6th Huntly's servant.
	27/6	Marriage of Margaret Stewart, younger daughter of the Regent Moray, to Francis, 9th Earl of Errol. Maitland became Secretary of State.
	10/9	Death of Colin Campbell, 6th Earl of Argyll, at Darnaway. Archibald Campbell, aged eight, succeeded as 7th Earl.
1585		6th Huntly begins litigation against 2nd Moray and his wife over fishing in the Spey.
1586		Maitland became Vice Chancellor and Keeper of the Great Seal.
	13/5	James VI's 'Reconciliation Banquet.'
1586/7	8/2	Execution of Mary Queen of Scots at Fotheringhay Castle.
1587		Possible birth date of James Stewart (7), son and heir to 2nd Moray but see 1582.
		The 'Ronie Rood.'
	19/6	James VI entered his majority.
		Maitland became Lord Chancellor.
1588	/7	The murder of the servant of 2nd Moray by Thomas Gordon.
	16/7	Death of Agnes Keith, widow of the Regent Murray, and of Colin Campbell, 6th Earl of Argyll.
	21/7	6th Huntly married Henrietta Stewart.
	1/8	6th Huntly and 2nd Moray became Commissioners under Acts against the Spanish Armada.
	2-8/8	Defeat of Spanish Armada.
	28/11	6th Huntly became Captain of the Guard at Holyrood.
1588-9	20/2	Huntly implicated in treasonous correspondence with Spain.
	28/2	6th Huntly committed to Edinburgh Castle.
	7/3	6th Huntly released.
	8/3	6th Huntly restored as captain of the guard.
1589	7/4	Bothwell gathered forces in Kelso to 'free the King.' 6th Huntly raised, with Errol, a rebellion in the North.
	18/4	Brig o' Dee.
	24/5	6th Huntly, Bothwell and Crawford arraigned and tried.
	26/5	6th Huntly restored as captain of the guard but again deprived and sent back north.
	9/7	James VI tours Grampian, stays in Darnaway.
	20/8	James VI married Anne of Denmark by proxy.
	23/11	James VI married Anne in person.
	28/11	6th Huntly quarrelled with 2nd Moray.
		6th Huntly built Riffen in Badenoch.
1589/90	5/3	2nd Moray appointed commissioner for acts against the Jesuits.

	24/3	Bothwell attempted to band with 2nd Moray and others against 6th Huntly.
		Maitland was made Lord Thirlestane.
1590	16/4	2nd Moray had 6th Huntly put to the horn.
	1/5	James VI and Anne of Denmark arrive back in Scotland.
	17/5	Anne crowned in Holyrood.
	20/7	2nd Moray became second Lord Doune on the death of his father.
	1/11	John Gordon's servant was killed by John Grant, the Tutor of Ballindalloch.
	2/11	6th Huntly captured Ballindalloch.
	5/11	A bond between 2nd Moray, Grant, Campbell of Cawdor, Athol, Lovat, Stewart of Grantully, Sutherland of Duffus.
	24/11	6th Huntly attacked Darnaway. John Gordon killed.
1590/1	23/1	6th Huntly complained of 2nd Moray's participation with malefactors in the north.
	16/3	6th Huntly forbidden to cross west of the Spey, 2nd Moray east of the Findhorn. Both ordered to proceed to Edinburgh and sign bands to keep the peace.
		6th Huntly appointed Lord Lieutenant of the North.
1591	18/11	2nd Moray's wife, Elizabeth, died, probably giving birth to Grizell.
	22/11	Several lairds promised assistance to 6th Huntly against 2nd Moray.
	27/12	Bothwell fails to seize James VI in Holyrood. Suspected complicity of 2nd Moray.
1591/2	4/2	Murder of Sir John Campbell, 3rd Thane of Cawdor by Sir John Campbell of Ardkinglas.
	7/2	Murder of 2nd Moray at Donnibristle.
	8/2	2nd Moray's corpse and John Gordon brought to Edinburgh.
	9/2	2nd Moray's body lay at the parish church of Leith. His Memorial commissioned.
	12/2	John Gordon beheaded.
	10/3	6th Huntly warded himself in Blackness.
	20/3	6th Huntly released.
	/3	Death of Lady Doune.
1592	27/5	General Assembly Convention begins. Lady Margaret Campbell died.
	/6	The 'Golden Act'
	/12	Spanish Blanks conspiracy.
1593	26/11	The Act of Abolition
1593/4	19/2	Birth of Prince Henry.
1594	3/4	Bothwell's Raid of Leith.
	17/9	6th Huntly joined in a rebellion against James VI.

	3/10	Battle of Glenlivet.
	22/10	James VI razed Strathbogie.
1595	19/3	6th Huntly goes into exile for 16 months.
	3/10	Maitland died at Lauder.
1597	26/6	6th Huntly pardoned and received into the Kirk.
1597/8	16/2	2nd Moray's body ordered to be buried.
	25/2	Eclipse of the Sun.
1598	/6	Act that feuds be submitted to justice in the royal courts.
1599	17/4	6th Huntly created first Marquis of Huntly and King's Justiciar in the North on Baptism of Princess Elizabeth.

1600

1600	5/8	Gowrie Conspiracy.
1601		Renewal of the quarrel between 1st Marquis of Huntly and 3rd Moray.
1602		Huntly Castle restored.
1603-25		James I of England, VI of Scotland
1603	23/2	The King reconciled 1st Marquis of Huntly and 3rd Moray.
	24/3	Death of Elizabeth, accession of James VI of Scotland as James I of England.
1607	2/10	3rd Moray married 1st Marquis of Huntly's eldest daughter, Anne.
		Argyll succeeded 1st Marquis of Huntly as Justiciar in the North.
1608	/7	1st Marquis of Huntly excommunicated by General Assembly, imprisoned in Stirling Castle.
1611		Henry Stewart created Lord St Colme.
1612/13		Lords Sanquhar and Maxwell executed for feud murders.
1625	27/3	Death of James VI and I, accession of Charles I.
1625-49		Charles I
1630	6/10	Death of John Gordon at Frendraught.
1636	13/6	1st Marquis of Huntly died in Dundee.
	30/8	1st Marquis of Huntly buried in the family vault in Elgin Cathedral.
1638	6/8	3rd Moray died at Darnaway.
1640	19/1	Lady Anne Gordon, Countess of Moray died at Elgin.
1649	30/1	Execution of Charles I.

APPENDIX 2
The Ballad of the Battle of Corrichie

This ballad was composed in the eighteenth century in the dialect of Aberdeen, although it may have been based on an older version now lost. It was first published in *The Weekly Magazine* or *Edinburgh Amusement* on 30 July 1772, and was republished in book form in 1808.[1] *The Weekly Magazine* noted 'we have been favoured with the following copy of an old Scots ballad by a gentleman of taste and literature which we do not remember ever having seen in print. It is said to have been written by one Forbes, schoolmaster at Maryculter upon Deeside.' No satisfactory identification has been established but the most likely candidate is William Forbes, schoolmaster at Peterculter from 1724 to 1732, and author of 'The Dominie Deposed.' Extracts are printed below:

> Mourn ye heighlands and mourn ye leighlands,
> I trow ye hae meikle need;
> For the bonnie burn o'Corrichie,
> Has run this day wi' bleid.
> Tho hopefu' Laird of Finlater,
> Erle Huntly's gallant son,
> For the love he bare our beauteous queene,
> Has gar'd fair Scotland moan.
> He has broken his ward in Aberdeen,
> Thro' dreid of the fause Murray,
> And has gather'd the gentle Gordon clan
> And his father, auld Huntley.
>
> Then Moray cried to tak' auld Gordon,
> An' mony ane ran wi' speid;
> But Stuart o'Inchbraik had him sticket,
> An' out gush'd the fat lurdane's bleid.
>
> But now the day maist waefu' cam'
> That day the queene did greet her fill;
> For Huntly's gallant stalwart son,
> Was headed on the headin' hill.
> Five noble Gordons wi' him hangit were,
> Upon the samen fatal plaine;
> Cruel Murray gar'd the waefu' queene look out,
> And see her lover and lieges slaine.

APPENDIX 3

The Birth-date of the Second Earl of Moray

The birth-date of future second Earl of Moray is unknown other than that it was sometime between 2 April 1567 and 7 February 1567/8. The early summer of 1567 is the most likely approximation. This conclusion is based on an assessment of all the information we have about his age.

1.   8 February 1566/7 – 7 February 1567/8
       The memorial commissioned by his mother – who ought to know – indicates that he was twenty-four years old on 7 February 1591/2.
(A)   If the 8 February were his birthday and he were a day short of twenty-five on 7 February 1591/2 then he could have been born as early as 8 February 1566/7.
(B)   If 7 February were his birthday and he were twenty-four on the day of his death then he could have been born as late as 7 February 1567/8.
(C)   For his death to so coincide with his birth would have surely attracted comment. Thus it is likely that at his death he was at least a month or two past his twenty-fourth birthday and a few months before his twenty-fifth.

2.   2 April 1567 – 29 April 1568
       The Calendar of State Papers (Scotland), x, p.30, states that he was twenty-one in April 1589.
(A)   If he were a day short of twenty-two years old on 1 April 1589 then he could have been born as early as 2 April 1567, or
(B)   If he were only just twenty-one on 30 April 1589 then he could have been born as late as 29 April 1568.

3.   2 April 1567 and 7 February 1567/8.
       Thus on the bases of the two sets of data above he must have been born between these dates.

4.   The Estimate says he was seventeen in 1583 but this must be wrong since it would put the year of his birth as 1566. However, it may suggest that his date of birth was nearer April 1567 than February 1567/8.

5.   The Calendar of State Papers (Scotland), ix, p.226 gives his age as twenty-four in 1586, putting his birth in 1562, but again this too is at marked variance with the other evidence.

APPENDIX 4

The Succession to the Earldom of Moray

The succession to Lord James Stewart, first Earl of Moray, is complicated but fairly clear. *A Survey of the Province of Moray*, 1798, p.15, gives the history is as follows:

On 7 February 1561/2 Lord James had been granted the earldom of Moray.

On 22 January 1563/4 Lord James obtained another charter of the earldom, limited to himself and his heirs male, whom failing, the earldom would return to the crown.

On 1 June 1566 he obtained another charter from the queen and Darnley to himself and his heirs general.

In 1567 he obtained a ratification in Parliament of the charter of 1563, limiting the earldom to himself and his heirs male, without mention of the charter of 1566.

On his death, leaving only daughters, on the basis of the charters of 1562 and 1563 and their ratification in 1567, the estate and dignity reverted to the Crown.

In 1580, James VI gifted the ward and marriage of the daughters to James Stewart, who married Elizabeth and took the title Earl of Moray. This can only have been by means of the superceded 1566 charter. By whatever means his status was immediately accepted.

James Stewart had succeeded to title but his own succession remained in doubt because of the plethora of charters. The anomaly was resolved by later measures.

In 1592 James VI and Parliament ratified to James, third Earl of Moray, son of James Stewart, and Lady Elizabeth, the charter of 1566 'and all other charters' to the Regent and his daughter Elizabeth. This merely increased the confusion.

In 1611 to rectify this the third Earl of Moray was granted a charter of novadamus of the lands and earldom of Moray to himself and heirs–male.

APPENDIX 5:

The Moray Memorial

The Moray Memorial, as it has come to be known, is the most dramatic and brutally effective example of a 'vendetta portrait' in existence. Such pictures were commissioned by the family of the deceased to keep alive the memory of a most foul murder and to bring vengeance upon the head of the murderers. The Memorial is without parallel in England but has significant precursors in Scotland, most obviously and significantly in the various illustrations occasioned by the murder of Lord Darnley and the Regent Moray.

The first was a contemporary and crude sketch depicting Darnley's murder and his baby son in his cot crying 'Judge and Defend my cause, O Lord.' This banner was displayed in Edinburgh in a successful attempt to stir up popular support for the Lords of the Congregation against the Queen.[1] When going into battle against Mary at Carberry on 15 June 1567, Captain Andrew Lammie bore an ensign of white taffeta which had painted on it 'ye cruel murther of K. Henry,' showing Darnley's body and bearing a similar inscription: 'Judge and revenge my cause, O Lord.' This banner he 'layed doune before her Majesty at quat time she presented herself as prisoner to ye lordis; at the sight whereof there was much lamentation amongst the haill gentlemen and souldiours, to see her defend him quho wes the cruel murtherer of her awen deir husband.'[2]

This itself was incorporated as an inset to the much more elaborate and devotional 'Memorial of Lord Darnley' painted by Levinus de Vogelaare in London in January 1567-8. It had been commissioned by Darnley's parents, the Earl and Countess of Lennox so that 'if they who are already old, should be deprived of this life before the majority of their descendant, the King of Scots, he may have a memorial from them in order that he shut not out of his memory the recent atrocious murder of the King his father, until God should avenge it through him.' Before the effigy kneels the infant James praying – in Latin – for the Lord to 'arise and avenge the innocent blood of the King.' The Earl and Countess of Lennox and their son Charles utter similar sentiments, Charles praying that he may be the instrument of God's revenge. It is indeed 'a depressing commentary on the kind of civilisation that Scotland had attained in the sixteenth century that perhaps the finest product of its artistic patronage should have been created for such potentially vicious ends.'[3]

After the murder of the Regent Moray in 1570 'there was hanged forth in the open street as ensign of black satin on which was painted the King [Darnley] as he was found dead, the Regent [Moray] in his bed, as he died, with his wound open, the King [James] on his knees crying "Judge and revenge my cause."'[4]

Two further instances of this sort of mortuary propaganda post-date the second Earl of Moray's murder. In July 1595 consequent on the murder of one Forester in a factional feud, the Earl of Mar whose servant the man had been 'cawsit mak the picture of the defunct on a fayre cammes [canvas], payntit with the number of the shots and wounds, to appear the mair horrible and rewthfull to the behalders,'[5] and paraded it through the lands of the family who had killed him. Surprisingly and inaccurately the author says this form was rare and 'never usit in Scotland before.' Three years later Mar reversed the normal usage and had a picture of the Laird of Johnstone 'drawn in blood to signify a murder and hung with his heels upwards with his name set under his head and INFAMY and PERJURY written athwart his legs displayed very solemnly by trumpets and heralds of arms' at Edinburgh Cross.[6]

The death and disposal of the Laird of Bargany provide the nearest parallel to that of Moray. He was about twenty-five years old when on the 11 December 1601 he was killed in a feud with the fifth Earl of Cassilis. The two sides had clashed outside Maybole, and Bargany had been mortally wounded. His young corpse, like Moray's, was laid in a Kirk in a lead coffin for a great time while his burial was prepared. In the funeral cortege a 'banner of revenge' was paraded 'wherein was painted his portrait with all his wounds, with his son sitting at his knees, written between his hands "Judge and Revenge My Cause, O Lord."' He was thus conveyed to Ayr escorted by 1,000 horsemen and laid in his tomb.[7] Cassilis in due course produced a commission authorising the use of guns and the Privy Council upheld his actions.[8]

Another progenitor is the 'effigy' or funerary depiction placed above the coffin as focus of attention. When James V died in 1542 arrangements for his funeral were set in hand immediately but the funeral itself did not take place until the following month. Payments were made to Andrew Watson for his work on the royal effigy, specifically for the painting of the crown and sceptre.[9] Prince Henry and James VI had effigies displayed on their coffin, as did Oliver Cromwell.

Pre- and post-cursors it may have had but the Moray Memorial remains unique in it stark and realistic depiction of the near naked corpse of a murdered man. There is one very striking and near contemporary parallel in the painting of a prone and near naked dead Christ by Holbein in 1522. This was an unusually dramatic portrayal in comparison with the more conventional 'deposition' portraits. Here Christ lies dead, his mother off canvas. There lies Moray, dead and alone, his mother commissioning the canvas. It may be that this parallel is more than mere coincidence. A Scottish painter working seventy years after Holbein finished his deposition may have been influenced by it. On the other hand Moray's 'Memorial' seems to be the work of a decorative or heraldic painter, and owes little to any kind of sophisticated pictorial tradition.[10]

The principal decorative painters who were employed at court in these years were Walter Binning and James and John Workman. The last is described as a 'painter, burgees and in dweller in Edinburgh.' He was licensed as a herald painter in November 1592 and died in 1604. In addition to painting interiors, furniture and banners, he was often employed in making armorials of forfeited nobles which were then ceremoniously destroyed. The style of the Memorial suggests that a herald painter was at work.[11] He is most likely candidate. It is recorded that he was contracted on 25 April 1592 by 'Mr Harrie Stewart, Commendator of St Colme's Inch' to make and deliver the 'ceremonies and furnitour' for the funeral of the Earl.[12] He was to be paid £53 9s Scots by 3 August. But the date came, no funeral took place and he did not get his money. The following January he had to begin proceedings to get his payment, and there is no record of it ever being paid. This later commission may indicate that he had carried out an earlier one – the painting of the memorial – to the family's satisfaction.

Having served what purpose it could, the painting was rolled up and deposited with the family papers at Donnibristle. In 1765 Thomas Percy recorded that 'the present Lord Moray [the eighth Earl] hath now in his possession a picture of his ancestor naked and covered with wounds which had been carried about, according to the custom of that age, in order to inflame the populace to revenge his death.'[13] After centuries of oblivion it was found in 1912 rolled up as a scroll. The then seventeenth Earl mounted it on its present frame, made supposedly from wood of the gallows tree, which stood on the banks of the Argaty burn on the east side of Doune Castle and it now hangs in the great hall of Darnaway Castle. The canvas is 29" x 87". Its wings are usually closed so that the picture will not distress the children of the house. The Memorial is now the only known portrait of the 'Bonnie Earl,' since a painting erstwhile thought to be of him has now been given a different ascription.

APPENDIX 6
The Ballad of the Bonnie Earl of Moray

Moray's mother took her own steps to ensure her son's murder would be avenged and the indignation of the populace aroused. His body was exposed in Leith, unburied. The portrait of his corpse was displayed. The bullets that killed him were dispatched to the King. Whether commissioned or acting on their own initiative, popular balladeers were quick to capture the poignancy of a young lord slain and magnify the clamour for revenge. Their endeavours were published in broadsides and hawked in the streets. A contemporary chronicler recorded that 'common rhymes and sangs' kept 'the horror of the deid of Dinnibirsall ... in recent detestation.'[1]

Two ballads relating to the murder of Moray are extant. One is the well-known ballad of 'The Bonnie Earl o' Moray' (see A below) whose emergence in print dates back to the second quarter of the eighteenth century but which was most likely contemporary to the events it laments. The other (see B below), deservedly obscure, was first published in Finlay's *Scottish Ballads* in 1808 where it was recorded 'from recitation.' Nothing more of its genesis or history prior to this is known, although several scholars from Finlay on have suspected that it was once united with the A version.[2] This is unlikely. The A version is in different metre, the language is more telling, and the historical assertions less extravagant and less erroneous.

According to the nineteenth century ballad collector, Norval Clyne, 'The Bonnie Earl of Moray' was the one ballad whose origins were most likely to pre-date the eighteenth century. Its first appearance in print was in the first half of the eighteenth century, but the precise date is unclear. Clyne asserted that it was first published in printed form as early as 1724 in the first edition of Allan Ramsay's *Tea Table Miscellany*.[3] This first edition is nowhere extant, but the 1729 fifth edition in the British Library does not include the ballad in its three volumes. Child states that the ballad is not in the ninth edition of 1733 which he had seen, but may be in the tenth which he had not.[4] He was right in his supposition. The ballad does appear in partly anglicised form in the fourth volume of the tenth edition, which was published in 1740. It was however published prior to this date in the second edition of William Thomson's *Orpheus Caledonius* in 1733.[5]

From its first appearance in 1724 at the earliest or in 1733 at the latest, the 'Ballad of the Bonnie Earl' soon became widely know. In 1742 Francis Barsanti printed it in his *Collection*. It obtained its widest circulation in Percy's *Reliques of English Poetry* in 1765. Thomas Percy, a future bishop, was then rector of the church of St Peter and St Paul, Easton Maudit, Northamptonshire. Like many country parsons he had ample time to pursue other interests. He did not merely copy the text of the ballad from the earlier collections but relied on a separate source, expressing his debt to Sir David Dalrymple of Hailes and John McGowan of Edinburgh, two avid local collectors for much background information and for the most beautiful of the Scottish songs – including 'The Bonnie Earl' – which he had incorporated into his primarily English work.[6]

The eighteenth century was the first great age of ballad collection and preservation. Discoveries were eagerly sought and expected. Some were contrived. Just as the poems of Ossian were cleverly forged to appeal to a public eager for Celtic sentiment, so some ballads were later creations. The best known fake was that of 'Hardyknute', a rather poor pastiche which was proved to come from the hand of a Lady Wardlaw who lived most of her half century (1677-1727) in Pitreavie, in the vicinity of Aberdour, suspiciously near to where the Earl's murder took place. Eighteenth century fabrication led to nineteenth century scepticism. The ballad collector David Laing and the encyclopaedist Robert Chambers both thought Lady Wardlaw was responsible for other ballads of alleged antiquity, including 'The Bonnie Earl of Moray' and 'Young Waters' – a ballad sometimes associated with his fate.[7]

Such scepticism in relation to 'The Bonnie Earl' is now generally discounted. All ages have their music, and music from all ages survives. There is no intrinsic reason why a popular ballad should not originate at or soon after the incident it records. Ballads are by their nature part of popular culture and it is intrinsically likely that 'The Bonnie Earl' would have had an oral history far pre-dating its crystallisation in print.

Sir Walter Scott and Robert Jamieson, both energetic and enthusiastic ballad collectors, obtained copies of many ballads from a Mrs Anna Brown (née Gordon) of Falkland, wife of the Rev Andrew Brown, minister of that parish. She was said to derive her knowledge of legendary lore from her maternal aunt, Mrs Farquahar of Braemar who as a young child had been taught many ballads by her mother, and the nurses and old women of Allanaquoich.[8] At the suggestion of William Tytler of Woodhouselee, in 1783 Mrs Brown sang the ballads while her son wrote them down and sent them to Tytler. The mother of James Hogg bemoaned the 'spoiling' of her songs by Scott who in transcribing them deprived them of their 'charm'. Not only may the collector 'improve' his find as the lady suggests, but ballads will have been added to or altered in their transmission. This is not to deny their antiquity, merely their integrity.

Thus there is no reason why the origins of 'The Bonnie Earl' may not lie in the 'common rymes and sangs' dating back to the time of the murder. The ballad, if transmitted by such as the old women of Allanaquoich, can reasonably claim an oral history going back at least to the mid seventeenth century. It would have sung from one generation to another until first being crystallised in written form by the assiduous collectors of the eighteenth century.

Recently another argument for its contemporaneity with the events it laments was put by A. Garner-Medwin on the basis of a postulated influence from Danish balladry. Denmark, whose princess married James VI, had many written collections of ballads, compiled for the nobility, culminating in 1591 in the publication of *A Hundred Danish Ballads* by Vedel. In his introduction Vedel emphasised the relationship expected between king and noblemen, and this relationship, is to be found in four Scottish ballads: 'Sir Patrick Spens', 'Johnnie Armstrong', 'The Laird of Logie', and 'The Bonnie Earl of Moray'. They are all concerned in one way or another with the relationship between the King and his nobles: 'The Bonnie Earl' reflects both the King's attempt to exculpate himself and popular suspicion of royal involvement in his murder; 'Johnie Armstrong' is an angry response to the execution of Armstrong, the Border laird, by James V in 1530; The 'Laird of Logie' relates the true story of a gentleman at court who is arrested but escapes aided by a Danish Lady in Waiting whom he subsequently marries; Spens closely mirrors the theme of the Danish ballad of Sir John Rimaardsson. Garner-Medwin suggests that these four Scottish ballads were all written in the sixteenth century, more or less contemporaneous to the events they depict and form a group which support in their fashion the debate about the behaviour expected of a king, as do very many of the ballads published by Vedel.[9]

The late sixteenth century was a prolific period for popular composition.[10] Several subjects of the historical ballads were contemporaries: Bothwell, Edom o' Gordon, Moray, Archie o' Cawfield, Dick o' the Cow, James MacPherson.[11] The simple versifying and stock images of 'The Bonnie Earl' do not necessitate a long gestation. A poetiser could turn such 'rymes' out instantly and to order. They could have sprung from the independent inspiration of the balladeer himself, eager to serve a popular market. In Scotland such a market existed. Bonds of clan and kin produced an identification between commoner and peer long lost south of the border. The strength of kin ties, the appeal to the blood and the name, the bonds of vassalage and tenancy, all combined in Highlands and Lowlands alike to ensure that the interests of a Gordon or a Moray were identified with the interests of those who depended on them. However, there is no evidence prior to his murder that Moray had any popular following. He was an absentee Earl in the north, and one who showed no interest in the well fare or interests of his retainers, as the letters from his factor and father attest. It is his family that would miss him most. It is the Protestant faction that would have most to gain from his 'martyrdom.' Thus the ballad was most likely commissioned either by Dame Margaret herself, by Ochiltree, or by the Kirk. After its genesis it was preserved in the memories and family traditions of people living in Edinburgh and its environs. During the course of its transmission changes may have been made and verses added. There is a whole second version of the Ballad which strays even further from the truth than the first Stanzas 3 and 5 of the first in particular suggest a provenance later than 1592. There is no suggestion in any extant document that Moray either aspired to the monarchy or was the Queen's lover. Both suggestions are without basis. They are the sort of 'romantic' additions made long after the events when history merged with legend. The former is an attribution of the ambition of the Regent Moray to his successor. This concession does not jeopardise the basic premiss that the Ballad had a contemporary commission.

Edinburgh was the ideal place for such a commission. The capital city had long been a magnet for itinerant performers and players. In 1560 all vagabonds, fiddlers and pipers without masters were ordered to leave the city on pain of branding. In 1579 'all minstrels, singers and tale-tellers' were deemed to be 'idle beggars' unless they were attached to Lords of Parliament or burghs as their common minstrels. In 1587 the city issued another edict against 'common sangsters' especially those who sang 'bawdy and filthy sangs.'[12] Attempts to control the printing of ballads were also made. In 1552 an act prohibiting the printing of 'ballads, songs, and blasphemous rhymes without licence' was passed, followed by another in 1567 when it became a crime to fail to destroy such broadsides on sight. The first to die for their popular and seditious craft were William Trumbill and William Scot who were hanged in 1579 at the cross of Sterling 'for making certain ballads which were thought to sow discord amongst the nobility.'[13] But so profitable a business in such fertile times for composition as the reigns of Mary and James and the intervening regency of Moray could not be stopped by Parliamentary legislation or even by the persuasive power of the gallows.

The Edinburgh press of Robert Lekprevik produced a constant stream of ballads and broadsheets during this period.[14] There was at least one pretty ferocious lament on the death of Darnley, several ballads in black letter appeared in January and February 1569-70 on the death of the Regent Moray.[15] The opening line of one such ballad is reminiscent of that on the second Earl:

> Ze montaines murne, ze valayis wepe
> Ze clouds and Firmament,
> Ze fluids dry up, ze seyis so depe,
> Deploir our lait Regent.

So lines quoted by Godscroft on the slaughter of the young Earl of Douglas and his brother in 1440 when they were dining with Chancellor Crichton were 'manifestly an outburst of righteous indignation by some provincial ballad maker.'

> Edinburgh castle, toune and toure,
> God grant thou sink for sinne!
> And that even for the black dinoure,
> Erl Douglas gat therein.'[16]

Murdered earls and especially those who were also Protestant martyrs were thus hymned in the streets long before the Earl of Moray joined the pantheon as heir to the 'Good Regent' and upholder of the Reformation. Melville remarked that 'the common rhymes and sangs kept the bloody deed in detestation' as much as the fulminations of the pulpit and ensured 'the Ratification of the true Kirk.' The ballad of 'The Bonnie Earl of Moray was a propaganda weapon,' 'Kirk Inspired' for political ends.[17]

APPENDIX 7
The Ballad Annotated

A

THE BONNIE EARL O'MORAY

1. Ye Highlands and ye Lawlands,[1]
    O whare hae ye been?
They hae slain the Earle o' Moray
And hae lain him on the green.[2]

2. 'Now wae be to thee, Huntly!
    And wherefore did ye sae?
I bade you bring him wi' you
And forbade you him to slay.'

3. He was a braw gallant,[3]
    And he rid at the ring;[4]
And the bonnie Earle o' Moray,
Oh! He might hae been a king![5]

4. He was a braw gallant,
    And he play'd at the ba';[6]
And the bonnie Earle o' Moray,
Was the flower amang them a'.

5. He was a braw gallant,
    And he play'd at the gluve;[7]
And the bonnie Earle o' Moray,
He was the Queen's true luve![8]

6. Oh! lang will his Lady[9]
Look owre the Castle Doune[10],
E'er she see the Earle o' Moray
Come sounding through the toune![11]

B THE BONNIE EARL O'MORAY[12]

1. 'Open the gates,
and let him come in;
He is my brother Huntly,[13]
he'll do him nae harm.'

2. The gates were opent,
They let him come in,
But fause traitor Huntly,
He did him great harm.

3. He's ben and ben,
and ben to his bed,
And wi' a sharp rapier,
he stabbed him dead.

4. The lady cam' doon the stair
wringin' her hands;
'He has slain Lord Moray,
the flower o'Scotland.'

5. But Huntly lap on his horse,
rade to the king:
'Ye're welcome hame, Huntly,
and whaur hae ye been?

6. Whare hae ye been?
and how hae ye sped?'
'I've killed the Earl o Moray
dead in his bed.'

7. 'Foul fa' ye, Huntly!
and why did ye so?
You micht ha'e ta'en Moray,
and saved his life too.'

8. 'Her bread it's to bake,
her yill is to brew;
My sister's a widow,
and sair do I rue.

9. 'Her corn grows ripe,
her meadows grow green,
But in bonnie Dinnibristle,
I daurna be seen.'

APPENDIX 8:
The Moray Vault

On several occasions in the last 150 years diligent search has been made among the bones of the crypt of St Giles Kirk to see whether 'the Bonnie Earl' lies there.

In April 1850 the Moray vault – discovered and disturbed twenty years before during the remodelling of the church – was searched at the request of the Moray family by Mr Phillips, their commissioner. The vault was found without much difficulty from information communicated by persons who had been present during the operations twenty years before. It is situated partly below the west end of the present outer lobby of the Old Church, and partly below the west side of the pulpit, leading from the outer lobby to the body of the church, when entering from parliament square. Upon lifting some of the steps, and working down to the level of the lobby, the vault was come upon. It could be more easily opened by raising some of the flags at the west end of the outer lobby. It was in a very poor state, long and narrow, running from north to south, and not wide enough for coffins to lay east to west. Phillips found that the vault had been filled up with rubbish and old bones. Three coffins were found one on top of the other. The uppermost was made of oak, and according to a plate lying loose upon it, was that of James Stewart who died in Rheims in 1768, aged twenty-two. Immediately below was a lead coffin, the arms on a shield surmounted by a coronet and the initials of Alexander the fourth Earl of Galloway, who lived but twenty years from 1670 to 1690 and was known to have been buried in 'the Moray vault.' The lowest was also of lead, bearing marks of considerable antiquity, but having no inscription. It was known that when the Regent's body had been interred his head had been placed south, contrary to normal usage, with a plate of brass upon it.[1] The lead opposite the face was broken and revealed a part of the skull, the top of which had been sawn through, probably for the purposes of embalming, and the teeth in the upper jaw were entire. By process of elimination and deduction it was concluded that these were the remains of the Regent. He had been buried three weeks after his assassination and so embalming would have been necessary. Nothing pertaining to the second Earl was found.[2]

During a further remodelling in April 1879 a similar incursion into the vault was made by William Chambers, the provost of Edinburgh and benefactor of the cathedral. Again the three lead coffins were found but the opinion was then that two contained two young men – a Francis Stewart (who was referred to erroneously as James in 1850 but who is likely to be the younger son of the second Earl of Moray according to a document in the John MacGregor Collection),[3] and the fourth Earl of Galloway – and a middle-aged woman. A skull, picked up from a heap of discarded bones, was treated with reverence since its size and shape were thought to denote the mental superiority of the Regent himself. Chambers concluded that the tomb of the regent had been destroyed in the alterations going on in January 1830 and his bones dumped on the floor of the crypt. Nor could the remains of Montrose be found.[4] Further excavations took place in 1930 and 1981 but to no greater result. Although none of the identifiable remains in the Moray vault are those of 'the Bonnie Earl,' the state of disarray beneath the cathedral and the fate of others who were certainly buried beneath its flagstones can not preclude the possibility that the second Earl was buried with them. It remains very unlikely.

APPENDIX 9

Genealogies

THE EARLS OF HUNTLY

On Crest: BYDAND 'Abiding'
On Arms: *Animo non astutia* 'by courage not by craft'

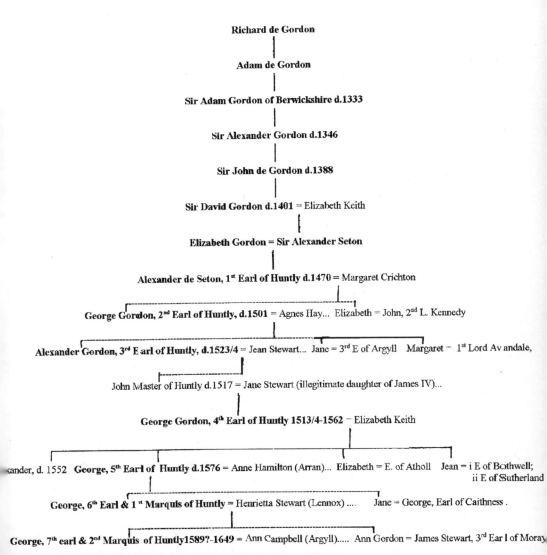

THE EARLS OF MORAY

Salus per Christum Redemptorem

I The Royal Line

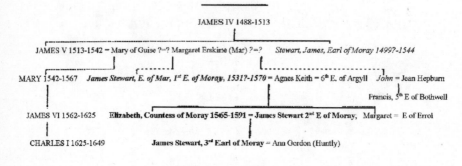

Archibald Douglas, Earl of Moray, d. 1455.

JAMES IV 1488-1513

JAMES V 1513-1542 = Mary of Guise ?=? Margaret Erskine (Mar) ?=? *Stewart, James, Earl of Moray 1499?-1544*

MARY 1542-1567   *James Stewart, E. of Mar, 1ˢᵗ E. of Moray, 1531?-1570* = Agnes Keith = 6ᵗʰ E. of Argyll   *John* = Jean Hepburn

Francis, 5ᵗʰ E of Bothwell

JAMES VI 1562-1625   **Elizabeth, Countess of Moray 1565-1591** = James Stewart 2ⁿᵈ E of Moray,   Margaret = E of Errol

CHARLES I 1625-1649   **James Stewart, 3ʳᵈ Earl of Moray** = Ann Gordon (Huntly)

II The Stewarts of Doune Line

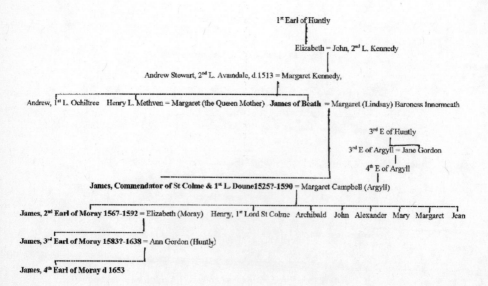

1ˢᵗ Earl of Huntly

Elizabeth = John, 2ⁿᵈ L. Kennedy

Andrew Stewart, 2ⁿᵈ L. Avandale, d. 1513 = Margaret Kennedy,

Andrew, 1ˢᵗ L. Ochiltree   Henry L. Methven = Margaret (the Queen Mother)   **James of Beath** = Margaret (Lindsay) Baroness Innermeath

3ʳᵈ E of Huntly

3ʳᵈ E of Argyll = Jane Gordon

4ᵗʰ E of Argyll

James, Commendator of St Colme & 1ˢᵗ L. Doune 1525?-1590 = Margaret Campbell (Argyll)

James, 2ⁿᵈ Earl of Moray 1567-1592 = Elizabeth (Moray)   Henry, 1ˢᵗ Lord St Colme   Archibald   John   Alexander   Mary   Margaret   Jean

James, 3ʳᵈ Earl of Moray 1583?-1638 = Ann Gordon (Huntly)

James, 4ᵗʰ Earl of Moray d 1653

HE EARLS OF ARGYLL

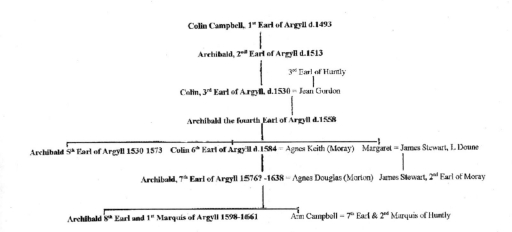

Colin Campbell, 1ˢᵗ Earl of Argyll d.1493

Archibald, 2ⁿᵈ Earl of Argyll d.1513

3ʳᵈ Earl of Huntly

Colin, 3ʳᵈ Earl of Argyll, d.1530 = Jean Gordon

Archibald the fourth Earl of Argyll d.1558

Archibald 5ᵗʰ Earl of Argyll 1530 1573   Colin 6ᵗʰ Earl of Argyll d.1584 = Agnes Keith (Moray)   Margaret = James Stewart, L Doune

Archibald, 7ᵗʰ Earl of Argyll 1576? -1638 = Agnes Douglas (Morton)   James Stewart, 2ⁿᵈ Earl of Moray

Archibald 8ᵗʰ Earl and 1ˢᵗ Marquis of Argyll 1598-1661   Ann Campbell = 7ᵗʰ Earl & 2ⁿᵈ Marquis of Huntly

HE EARLS OF ATHOLL

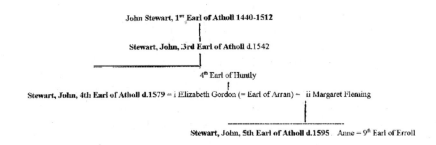

John Stewart, 1ˢᵗ Earl of Atholl 1440-1512

Stewart, John, 3rd Earl of Atholl d.1542

4ᵗʰ Earl of Huntly

Stewart, John, 4th Earl of Atholl d.1579 = i Elizabeth Gordon (= Earl of Arran) = ii Margaret Fleming

Stewart, John, 5th Earl of Atholl d.1595   Anne = 9ᵗʰ Earl of Erroll

THE EARLS OF BOTHWELL

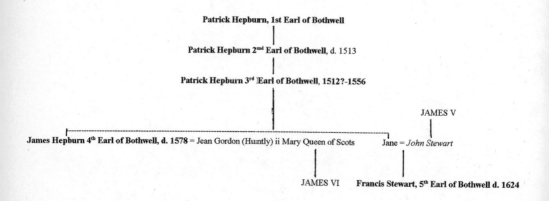

Patrick Hepburn, 1st Earl of Bothwell

Patrick Hepburn 2ⁿᵈ Earl of Bothwell, d. 1513

Patrick Hepburn 3ʳᵈ Earl of Bothwell, 1512?-1556

JAMES V

James Hepburn 4ᵗʰ Earl of Bothwell, d. 1578 = Jean Gordon (Huntly) ii Mary Queen of Scots   Jane = *John Stewart*

JAMES VI   **Francis Stewart, 5ᵗʰ Earl of Bothwell d. 1624**

THE EARLS OF ERROL

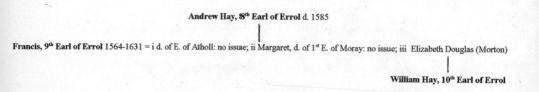

Andrew Hay, 8ᵗʰ Earl of Errol d. 1585

Francis, 9ᵗʰ Earl of Errol 1564-1631 = i d. of E. of Atholl: no issue; ii Margaret, d. of 1ˢᵗ E. of Moray: no issue; iii Elizabeth Douglas (Morton)

William Hay, 10ᵗʰ Earl of Errol

THE LORDS OCHILTREE & EARLS OF ARRAN

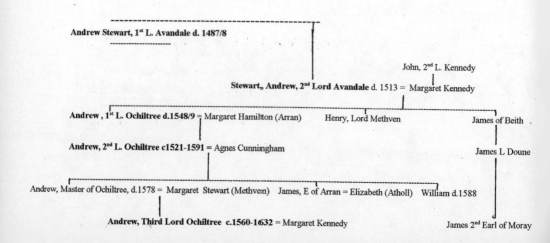

Andrew Stewart, 1ˢᵗ L. Avandale d. 1487/8

John, 2ⁿᵈ L. Kennedy

Stewart, Andrew, 2ⁿᵈ Lord Avandale d. 1513 = Margaret Kennedy

Andrew , 1ˢᵗ L. Ochiltree d.1548/9 = Margaret Hamilton (Arran)   Henry, Lord Methven   James of Beith

Andrew, 2ⁿᵈ L. Ochiltree c1521-1591 = Agnes Cunningham   James L Doune

Andrew, Master of Ochiltree, d.1578 = Margaret Stewart (Methven)   James, E of Arran = Elizabeth (Atholl)   William d.1588

Andrew, Third Lord Ochiltree c.1560-1632 = Margaret Kennedy   James 2ⁿᵈ Earl of Moray

APPENDIX 10:

Glossary

ARQUEBUS	See HARQUEBUS.
BAILIE	Chief executive officer of a barony or regality; presided over the barony court.
BARONY	Basic unit of local government in landward parts of Scotland. The chief officers of a barony were the Baillie and Chamberlain.
BATTLE	A military formation. Sixteenth century armies were divided into three battles: the vanguard, the mainward and the rearward.
BOND	Written legal obligation to repay money or perform a service. Also used of alliances between individuals for mutual protection or to perform a particular task.
CAUTION	Security.
CHAMBERLAIN	Chief financial officer of an estate, barony or regality.
CLERK REGISTER	Official responsible for state papers.
COBLE	A short flat-bottomed rowing boat.
COMMENDATOR	Person receiving the revenues of an abbey, priory, monastery or other benefice, appointed by the Pope with secular recommendation, frequently a layman.
COMPEAR	To surrender to the court.
DECREET	Decree of the final judgement or sentence of a court.
DILIGENCE	Legal procedure, usually associated with attempts to recover debt, whereby a defaulting party may have his heritable or moveable property seized.
DISCHARGE	A receipt for payment of money or the delivery of goods; the debit side of the Chamberlain's accounts.
ENTAIL	A deed whereby the normal line of succession to heritable property is cut off, and the line of heirs replacing it is specified.
ESCHEAT	Confiscation of goods in favour of the Crown.
FERME	Rent, often rent in kind.
FEU-FARM	Form of heritable tenure in return for an annual

	feu-duty in money; in the sixteenth century it replaced lease holding on many church estates, turning tenants into owners.
GEAR	Moveable goods.
GIF	If.
HACKBUTT	The English word for Arquebus.
HARQUEBUS	An early type of portable trigger operated firearm, weighing about 10lb and firing a 1/2oz lead ball, fired resting on a tripod.
HERITABLE	Lands and all rights affecting them; property which descends wholly to.
PROPERTY	An heir alone.
HORNING	Legal process of technical outlawry. To put someone 'to the horn' was to declare him a rebel to his sovereign, a procedure accompanied by three blasts on the horn or trumpet. It came to be used to enforce purely civil obligations, and especially for the extraction of payment of debts from reluctant creditors. There was no imprisonment for debt in Scotland. By putting an obstinate debtor to the horn, he was ordered, in the King's name, to pay his dues, failing which he would denounced for rebellion and imprisoned as a rebel not as a debtor and his goods escheated. The Morays demonstrated a further use, by putting Huntly to the horn for encroaching on their fishing rights.
INDWELLER	Resident of burgh who did not have burgess rights; resident of a town which was not a burgh.
INHIBITION	By 'letters of inhibition' a debtor is restrained from selling or burdening his heritable property to the prejudice of his creditors.
INTROMIT	To handle or deal with funds or property.
KINDNESS	A claim to customary inheritance of a tenancy on the basis of kinship with the previous holder.
JACK	Lightweight body armour constructed of overlapping plates of metal.
JUSTICE AYRE	The supreme criminal court on circuit.
JUSTICE CLERK	The principal clerk of justiciary; the officer of state who officiated as clerk of the justice court or justice ayre; one of the principal judges and vice-president of the court of Justiciary.
JUSTICE COURT	Court of Justiciary.
JUSTICIARY	The office or jurisdiction of a justice; The High

	Court of Justiciary was the supreme criminal court of Scotland.
KEMP	A champion who fights in single combat; a professional fighter.
LAIRD	Landowner without title of nobility but entitled to attend Parliament; a property owner; the chief of a clan eg the Laird of Grant.
LIFE RENT	Right to use a property during one's lifetime.
LORDS OF COUNCIL	Members of the sovereign's or Privy Council
LYMMER	Rogue, robber.
LYON KING OF ARMS	Royal representative, officer in charge of heraldry
MACER	Mace-bearer: 1. An officer of the Crown under the Lord Lyon King of Arms who delivered royal commands and summonses and uttered public proclamations. 2. A servant of the Court of Session, Court of Justiciary or other court, responsible for keeping order in court, executing the judge's orders and other duties.
MAILLS	Rents.
MARISCHAL	Officer with high military functions, hereditary in the Keith family since the time of Robert the Bruce.
MASSER	See MACER.
MERK	two-thirds of a £ Scots.
NOVADAMUS	A Charter of Novadamus was a means by which a superior granted certain things 'of new,' because of some defect in the former title.
POINDING	A form of diligence against a debtor's moveable property
POUND SCOTS	£4 Scots = £1 Sterling, or £1 Scots = 5 shillings
PRICKER	Light cavalryman
REGALITY	Unit of local government in which the landowner enjoyed certain exemptions form royal authority, unlike in a barony.
RELAXATION	Letters under the signet seal relaxing a debtor from the consequences of horning.
REMISSION	Royal pardon for a crime.
SEDERUNT	Lat. 'They sat:' Meeting of the Secret – or Privy Council.
SERGEANT	An inferior officer of a court.
SERVITOR	A male servant, who provided service to a noble or landed family in return for food and lodging and little else.

SHERIFF	The hereditary chief officer of a shire or county, responsible to the sovereign for peace and order, having civil and criminal jurisdiction.
SKAITH	Damage or loss in a legal sense.
SLAUGHTER	The killing of a person where the killer is known
TACK	Lease. 'In tack' was a leasehold tenancy.
TACK-DUTY	Annual payment for a tack.
TEINDS	Tithes, tenth of the produce of the land.
TENANDRY	Holding of a tenant.
TOCHER	Dowry.
TOLBOOTH	A town hall or gaol or both. The tolbooth built in Edinburgh in 1561 was to accommodate the parliament and courts of justice, and for the confinement of debtors
TOUN	A rural settlement sometimes called a farmtoun.
TUTOR	The legal representative, guardian, and administrator of the estate of a child under fourteen if male or twelve if female, who might be nominated by the child's father or, as 'tutor dative,' by the crown.
WAD	Pawned.
WADSET	To grant away land as a security for debt. The land was held by the Wadsetter until the debt was paid.
WARD	Superior's rights to the rents of lands of a deceased vassal during the minority of the heir under twenty-one.
WARDATER	The person given by the original superior the enjoyment of lands held in ward while the heir was a minor.
WHINGER	A short stabbing sword.

ABBREVIATIONS

A&D	James Melville, *Autobiography and Diary*, ed. R. Pitcairn, Edinburgh, 1842.
ABB	*Account of the Battle of Balrinnes*, 3 October 1594, in the *Spottiswoode Miscellany*, ed. James Maidment, Edinburgh, 1844.
Aboyne	*The Records of Aboyne 1230-1681*, ed. Charles, eleventh Marquis of Huntly, Aberdeen, 1894.
Accounts	*Accounts of the Lord High Treasurer of Scotland*, 12 vols, Edinburgh 1907–1970.
Birrel	Robert Birrel, *Diary 1532-1605*, in *Fragments of Scottish History*, edited by John G. Dalzell, 1798.
Brown	Keith Brown, *Bloodfeud in Scotland 1573-1625*, Edinburgh, 1985.
Buchanan	Buchanan, George, *The History of Scotland* translated from the Latin by James Aikman, 2 vols, London, 1827–1829.
Calderwood	Calderwood, David, *History of the Kirk*, 8 vols, ed.T. Thompson, The Woodrow Society, Edinburgh, 1842-9.
Cawdor	Hugh Campbell, Earl of Cawdor, *The Murders of Lord Moray and the Thane of Cawdor*, Private Mss, 1985.
CBP	*Calendar of Border Papers.*
Chronicles	*Chronicles of the Frasers*, ed. William Mackay, Edinburgh, 1905.
CP	*Complete Peerage*, 13 vols, ed. H.A. Doubleday and H.De Walden, London, 1910-1940.
CSP(I)	*Calendar of State papers Relating to Ireland.*
CSP(F)	*Calendar of State papers Relating to Foreign Affairs.*
CSP(S)	*Calendar of State Papers Relating to Scottish Affairs.*
Diurnal	*A Diurnal of Remarkable Occurents in Scotland since the Death of King James IV till the Year MDLXXV*, ed. T. Thompson, Edinburgh, 1833.
Estimate	*Estimate of the Scottish Nobility During the Minority of James VI*, edited by C. Rodgers, Grampian Club, London, 1873.
FN	'A Faithful Narrative of the Great and Miraculous Victory at Strathavon' in *Scottish Poems of the Sixteenth Century*, ed Graham Dalzell, Edinburgh, 1801.
GD	General Deposit at the SRO.
GM	*Gordon Castle Muniments.*
Grant	William Fraser, *The Chiefs of Grant,* 3 vols, Edinburgh, 1883.
Gregory	Donald Gregory, *History of the Western Highlands*, Edinburgh, 1875.
Hamilton	*The Hamilton Papers*, 2 vols, Edinburgh, 1890 and 1892.
HF	*The House of Forbes*, ed. Alistair and Henrietta Taylor, Aberdeen, 1937.
HFG	William Gordon, *History of the Family of Gordon*, 2 vols, Edinburgh, 1726-7.

HHDA	David Hume of Godscroft, *History of the Houses of Douglas and Angus*, London, 1644.
HMC	Historical Monuments Commission.
HMSO	Her Majesty's Stationery Office.
HP	*Highland Papers*, 2 vols, ed. J.R.N. McPhail, Edinburgh, 1914.
Keith	Robert Keith, *History of Affairs of Church and State to 1567*, 2 vols, ed. J.P. Lawson, Edinburgh, 1844.
Knox	John Knox, *History of the Reformation in Scotland*, 2 vols, ed. W. Croft Dickinson, Edinburgh, 1949.
Leslie	John Leslie, *Historie of Scotland*, 1596, 2 vols, ed. E.G.Cody and W. Murison, Edinburgh, 1884–5.
Lindsay	Robert Lindsay of Pitscottie, *History and Chronicles of Scotland*, 2 vols, ed. A.J.G. Mackay, Edinburgh, 1899 and 1911.
LSP	*Letters and State Papers during the Reign of James the Sixth, chiefly from the manuscript collections of Sir James Balfour of Denmyln*, Edinburgh, 1838.
Major	John Major, *History of Greater Britain*, 1521, ed. Archibald Constable, 1892.
MM	*Moray Muniments.*
Moysie	David Moysie, *Memoirs of the Affairs of Scotland from 1577 to 1603*, Edinburgh, 1830.
Narratives	*Narratives of Scottish Catholics under Mary Stewart and James VI*, ed. William Forbes-Leith, Edinburgh, 1885.
NRA(S)	National Record of Archives (Scotland).
Patten	William Patten, 'The Expedition into Scotland, 1547' in *Tudor Tracts 1532-1588,* edited by A.F. Pollard, London, 1903, pp.54-158.
Rampini	Charles Rampini, *History of Moray and Nairne*, Edinburgh, 1897.
RPC	*Register of the Privy Council of Scotland.*
RPS	*Register of the Privy Seal of Scotland*
Sadler	Sadler, Sir Ralph, *State Papers and Letters*, 3 vols, ed.Walter Scott, Edinburgh, 1809.
SCD	*Scotland before 1700 from Contemporary Documents*, ed. P.H. Brown, Edinburgh 1893.
SCML	*Scottish Correspondence of Mary of Lorraine*, ed. A. Cameron, Edinburgh, 1927.
Selve	Odet de Selve, *Correspondence Politique 1546-1549,* ed. G. Lefevre-Pontalis, Paris, 1888.
Sext	*Historie and Life of King James the Sext* ed. T.Thomson, Edinburgh, 1825.
SHR	*Scottish Historical Review.*
SHS	*Scottish History Society.*
SM	*Miscellany of the Spalding Club,* 4 vols, ed. John Stuart, Aberdeen 1842-9.
SNPG	Scottish National Portrait Gallery, Edinburgh.
SP	*The Scots Peerage*, 9 vols, ed. J.Balfour Paul, Edinburgh, 1904–1914.
Spalding	John Spalding, *History of the Troubles and Memorable Transactions in Scotland*, Aberdeen, 1829.

Spottiswood	John Spottiswood, *History of the Church of Scotland*, 1668, reprinted in 3 vols, Edinburgh, 1850.
SRO	Scottish Record Office.
Sutherland	Sir Robert Gordon, Genealogical *History of the Earldom of Sutherland*, Edinburgh, 1813.
Sutherland Book	William Fraser, *The Sutherland Book*, 3 vols, Edinburgh, 1892.
Taylor	James Taylor, *The Pictorial History of Scotland*, 2 vols, London, nd.
Tytler	Patrick Tytler, *History of Scotland*, 4 vols, enlarged edition, London, 1877.

NOTES

PREFACE

1.   Much recent research has been done on the topic, the results of which have been extensively pillaged by me. See, in particular, Jenny Wormald's 'Bloodfeud, Kindred and Government,' *Past and Present*, 87, 1980, pp.54–97; *Lords and Men in Scotland: Bonds of Manrent 1442-1603*, Edinburgh, 1985; 'The Bloodfeud,' in *The New Companion to Scottish Culture*, edited by David Daiches, Edinburgh, 1993; and Keith Brown's *Bloodfeud in Scotland*, Edinburgh, 1986.

1. THE PEOPLE OF THE NORTH

1.   Major, in SCD, p.46.
2.   Leslie, in SCD, p.143.
3.   Major, in SCD, pp.45f; 143.
4.   Major, in SCD, p.43.
5.   Buchanan, p.485
6.   Leslie, in SCD, pp.142f.
7.   Buchanan, in SCD, pp.230.
8.   Leslie, in SCD., p.144.
9.   Norman MacDougall, *James IV*, Edinburgh, 1989, pp.178ff, 190.
10.   MM 1/2/27.
11.   Lindsay, i, pp.271f.

2. COCK O' THE NORTH

1.   Hamilton, i, p.507.
2.   Knox, ii, p.62.
3.   HFG, i, p.127.
4.   *Aboyne*, p.431.
5.   Records in the Gordon Charter Chest, cited in *Aboyne*, p.432.
6.   *Acta Dominorum Concilii*, xxviii, p.402, cited in Aboyne, p.429.
7.   RPS, xxv, p.31, cited in *Aboyne*, p.435.
8.   Allan White, 'Queen Mary's Northern Province,' in *Mary Stewart, Queen in Three Kingdoms*, edited by Michael Lynch, Oxford, 1988, pp.53–70, at p.55. A bond of manrent was a contract of vassalage, pledging allegiance to a superior lord with the automatic exception of allegiance to the crown. Between 1536 and 1541 Huntly signed eight such bonds with prominent local families including the Leslies of Balquhain and the Gordons of Strahavon, together with northern clansmen like the Mackintoshes and the Mcleans of Duart. Between 1543 and 1560 he signed a further twenty mutual bonds with his cousin, the fourth Earl of Argyll, and with Lord Lovat and the Earl of Crawford, and

bonds of manrent with Grant of Freuchie and Meldrum of Fyvie (SM, iv, pp.207, 210, 205, 217-19, 214-5, 223).

9.   In Aberdeenshire, for example, the Farquharsons became the largest branch of the Clan Chattan.

10.   HF, p.67.

11.   14 July 1537. HF, p.68; *Letters and Papers of Henry VIII* (Letter of Sir Thomas Clifford to Henry VIII, 26th July 1537).

12.   Contract of marriage printed in SM, iv, pp.138ff.

13.   Their progeny were as follows:

      Alexander, Lord Gordon, died *c.*1552-3.

      George, the fifth Earl of Huntly, born *c.*1535, died 1576.

      John, executed 1562.

      William, died in Paris.

      James, a Jesuit, born *c.*1541, died in Paris 1620.

      Adam of Auchindoun, 'Edom o'Gordon,' born 1545, died at Perth, 1580.

      Patrick of Auchindoun, killed at Glenlivet, 1594.

      Robert, killed by a gun accident, 1572.

      Thomas, died *c.*1585.

      Elizabeth

      Margaret

      Jean, born, *c.*1545, died 1629.

14.   Hamilton, i, no.120.

15.   Ibid., pp.157ff (Angus and Douglas to the Privy Council, 25 August 1542); George McDonald Fraser, *The Steel Bonnets*, London, 1971, pp.248f.

16.   HFG, i, p.127.

17.   In their respective histories Knox does not mention the victor (i, p.31); Pitscottie credits Lord St John (i, pp.397f.), and Buchanan (ii, p.262) and Godscroft (p.263) credit Lord Home.

18.   Aboyne, p.437.

19.   Hamilton, i, p.285 (News from Lord Cumberland, 28 October 1542).

20.   Jamie Cameron, *James V*, East Lothian, 1998, pp.169, 304; Hamilton, i, p.lxiv (Hertford to the Council, 5 November 1542), p. lxxi ('Memorandum by a Spy,' 16 November 1542).

21.   In 1371 the crown had passed to the House of Stewart in the person of Robert II by virtue of his mother who was the daughter of Robert the Bruce.

22.   Rosalind Marshall, *Mary of Guise*, Glasgow, 1977, pp.100ff.

23.   Hamilton, i, p.471 (Lisle to Norfolk, 17 March 1542/3).

24.   Hamilton, i, pp.507 (Sadler to Henry VIII, 6 April 1543); 496 (Sadler to the Privy Council, 31 March 1543); Sadler, i, p.105 (1543).

25.   Sadler, i, p.98 (Sadler to Henry VIII, 27 March 1543). Moray, a year before his death, was responsible for a notorious and ridiculous dinner in honour of the Papal emissary to Scotland. Half way through the meal the sideboard collapsed smashing all the glass and crystal. Before the amazed guest an even more glittering array replaced what had been lost, testifying to the wealth and sophistication of Scotland, or so it was hoped (Humphrey Drummond, *Our Man in Scotland: Sir Ralph Sadler*, London, 1969, pp.107f.).

26.   Sadler, ii, p.70, 90 (1559/60).

27.   John Skelton, *Maitland of Lethington*, London, 1894; HFG, i, p.127.

28. Drummond, *Our Man in Scotland*, p.82.

29. This phrase owes its origin to a comment made by Huntly on the field of Pinkie, see below footnote 51, and Marcus Merriman, *The Rough Wooings, Mary Queen of Scots 1542-1551*, East Linton, 2000, pp.8ff.

30. William Patten, 'The Late Expedition into Scotland, 1544,' in *Tudor Tracts*, pp.39-51, at p.40.

31. 'Agreement of the principle Scots nobility to support the authority of the Queen Mother as Regent of Scotland, against the Earl of Arran, declared by this instrument to be deprived of his office, dated June 1544,' cited in Tytler, ii, p.233.

32. Also known as the battle of Lillyard's Edge, after an English woman killed in defence of her lover (so Sir Walter Scott, *Tales of a Grandfather*, Edinburgh, 1846, ch.xxix).

33. Leslie, ii, p.280.

34. Leslie, ii, p.82; Gregory, pp.159-163.

35. *Mackintosh Muniments*, p.16 (Commission, 30 October 1544).

36. Knox, i, 77.

37. RPC, i, p.55-58 (St Andrews, 26 November and 19 December 1546).

38. Scott, *Tales*, ch. xxix.

39. CSP(S), i, pp.8f ("Wait Quha" to Wharton, 28 June and 5 July 1547). His is the best estimate. Pitscottie gives its strength as 40,000, and others 36,000, estimates which are perhaps swollen by including the large retinue of camp followers in the gross figure: Caldwell, 'The Battle of Pinkie,' in *Scotland at War*, edited by Norman MacDougall, Edinburgh, 1991, pp. 61-94, at 73.

40. Patten, p.105. Patten's narrative is both first-hand and first-rate. In addition, there are several good modern accounts of the battle: Sir Charles Oman's seminal work summarised in his chapter entitled 'The Battle of Pinkie' in *The Art of War in the Sixteenth Century*, London, 1937, pp. 358-367; Sir James Fergusson, 'The Rough Wooing,' in *The White Hind*, London, 1963, pp. 11-33; Caldwell, 'The Battle of Pinkie,' pp. 61-94. The most recent analysis is that of Gervasse Phillips in *The Anglo-Scots Wars*, Woodbrodge, 1999, pp.178-200 and the revisionist account by Merriman in *The Rough Wooings*, pp.234-7.

41. Patten, pp.100ff; Drummond, *Our Man in Scotland*, p.150; Lindsay, i, xxv, pp.49, 94.

42. Patten, p.105.

43. Ibid., p.112.

44. Oman, *The Art of Warfare*, pp.364f.

45. Raphaell Holinshed, *The Chronicles of England, Scotland and Ireland*, 6 vols, edited by H. Ellis, London, 1807-8, v, p.551; Patten, p.77.

46. Selve, pp. 206, 218. Lindsay, i, xxv, p.68; Fergusson, *The White Hind*, p.32.

47. The title was bestowed on 7 July 1548.

48. Selve, p.218 (October 1547).

49. Ibid, passim, but esp. pp.223, 478.

50. CSP(S), i, p.99 (Huntly to Somerset, 20 March 1547/8), pp.104-5 (Huntly to Somerset, 29 March 1548).

51. The activities of the Earl of Huntly in England are extensively detailed in the despatches of Selve, pp. 223-7, 231-4, 240-58, 261-271, 380, 389-90, 395, 397-9, 402, 417, 421.

52. CSP(S), i, p.57 (Sir Andrew Dudley to Somerset, 3 January 1547/8).

53. CSP(S), i, p.34 (Grey of Wilton to Somerset, 31 October 1547 enclosing Cockburn's Report).

54. GM, GD 44/13/6/2/1 (Stirling Castle, 18 April 1548).

55. CSP(S), i, pp.94f. (John Brende to Somerset, 9 March 1547/8).

56. GM, GD 44/55/1/30 (indenture 5 December 1548); Hamilton, ii, p.622; Selve, p. 474.

57. GM, GD 44/14/11/1/2 (15 May 1600); *Diurnal*, p.47; Leslie, ii, pp. 318-321; Skelton, *Maitland*, p.147.

58. SCML, p.cxciv.

59. GM, GD 44/3/6/2/2 (13 February 1548/9); HHDA, p.275.

60. The English left Scotland in peace as a result of the Treaty of Boulogne, 24 March 1550.

61. *Sutherland Book*, iii, p.112.

62. *Aboyne*, p.453.

63. Margaret Mackintosh, *The Clan Mackintosh and the Clan Chattan, Edinburgh*, 1948, p.19.

64. It is this story that Scott later rather extravagantly and inaccurately embellished in his *Tales of a Grandfather*, ch.xxxix.

65. These included Glenroy, Glenspean, Glenloy, Loch Arkaig, Drumchardiny, Incolme, Cragaig, Kinnaires, Eskadaile, and Ardellan in Aird. Alexander had little time to enjoy them since he died within months of receiving them in 1552.

66. PC, i, p.107 (5 September 1550).

67. See illustrations in Ian Gow, *Scottish Country Houses 1600-1914*, Edinburgh, 1994, pp.2-5.

68. Ian Whyte, *Scotland Before the Industrial Revolution*, London, 1995, p.56.

69. Knox, i, p.62; CSP (Henry VIII), vi, p.238 (January 1543).

70. Margaret Sanderson, *Mary Stewart's People*, Edinburgh, 1987, p.36.

71. *Aboyne*, p.454.

3. THE BASTARD LORD JAMES

1. CSP(S), i, pp.354ff (Cecil to Elizabeth, 23 June 1560).

2. HHDA, p. 281.

3. *Aboyne*, p.454. SCML, pp. 348f, 364f, 381ff, 400, 430ff.

4. Lord Wharton, quoted in Tytler, ii, p.276.

5. William Camden, *The History of Elizabeth*, Chicago, 1970, p.62.

6. *Accounts*, vii, pp.163f. He matriculated under the title 'Dominus Jacobus Stewart, junior, filius quondam illustrissimi Jacobi Quinti, Scotorum Regis' in 1545, but although the average age at matriculation was fifteen, may have begun his studies prior to this: J.M.Anderson, *Early Records of the University of St Andrews*, Edinburgh, 1926, pp.xix, xxvi, 252.

7. Ted Hughes, 'The Martyrdom of Bishop Farrar,' in *Collected Poems*, p.19. The latter words are those uttered by Farrar on being chained to the stake.

8. Until they were seized and despoiled by Mary in 1562. These, it is quite possible, were the chasubles and copes that this Catholic monarch profaned to secular use in March 1567.

9. Knox, i, p.368.

10. CSP(S), i, pp.373 (Norfolk to Cecil enclosing 'Huntly's Requests' and 'The Lords Answer to Huntly,' 18 April 1560).

11. *Two Missions of Jaques de la Brosse*, edited by Gladys Dickinson, Edinburgh, 1942, p.147.

12. Her character was admired even by Buchanan, book xvi.

13. Throckmorton, the English ambassador in France, assumed that she would ally herself at home with her co-religionists, chief of whom would be Athol and Huntly (CSP(F),1561-2, pp.122f. *(Throckmorton to Cecil, 21 May 1561)*.

4. CORRICHIE

1.   CSP(S), i, p.569 (Randolph to Cecil, 11 November 1561).

2.   See Appendix 2.

3.   Leslie, ii, p.294.

4.   Buchanan, i, p.427; CSP(S), i, pp.509-511 (Maitland to Cecil, 6 February 1561).

5.   CP, vi, p.678(e).

6.   CSP(S), i, pp.555 & 563 (Randolph to Cecil, 24 September and 24 October 1561); CSP(F) 1561 pp.353f.

7.   White, 'Queen Mary's Northern Province,' p.59.

8.   CSP(F), 1562, p. 82 (Cecil to Challoner, 8 June 1562).

9.   Knox, ii, p.54.

10.   CSP(F), 1562, p.330 (Randolph to Cecil, 30 September 1562).

11.   John Hill Burton, the nineteenth century Scots lawyer and historian, quoted in Rampini, p.151.

12.   Calderwood, ii, p.194.

13.   With the overthrow of the Gordons, and the execution of John, James of Cardell was reinstated into his inheritance. As part of the re-settlement, the lands of Cardell were ceded to the Earl of Moray in 1563/4. With the restoration of the Gordons to favour, as part of a later arbitration in 1567, James Ogilvie assigned to Adam Gordon the barony of Auchindoun, in Banffshire.

14.   Randolph's letters are the main contemporary source for the events leading to the battle of Corrichie. See CSP(S), i, pp.645ff.

15.   CSP(S), i, p.645 (Randolph to Cecil, 10 August 1562). See the map in David Breeze, *A Queen's Progress*, Edinburgh, 1987, p.46.

16.   RPC, i, p.218f. (Darnaway, 10 September 1562).

17.   HHDA, p.282.

18.   CSP(S), i, pp.649 (Randolph to Cecil, 31 August 1562); 652 (Randolph to Cecil, 18 September 1562); 665 (Randolph to Cecil 2 November 1562).

19.   Leslie, SCD, p.144.

20.   Ibid.

21.   CSP(F), 1562, p.330 (Randolph to Cecil, 30 September 1562).

22.   Quoted in Rampini, p.140.

23.   RPC, i, p.218ff. (Darnaway, 10 September 1562); CSP(S), i, pp.654ff (Randolph to Cecil, 30 September 1562).

24.   The 11 September is the correct date and not the 9 September as Randolph states: see Maurice Lee, *James Stewart, Earl of Moray*, New York, 1953, p.105, footnote 80.

25.   This is the majority view, although the *Diurnal* gives his name as 'George,' p.73.

26.   MM 1/2/14 (Charter of Confirmation).

27.   Leslie, SCD, p.144; White, 'Queen Mary's Northern Province,' p.64; RMS, i, 3286.

28.   *Aboyne*, p.463; Rampini, p.152; *Chronicles*, p.148. There is an entry in the royal accounts for 11 September 1562 of 50 shillings for 'ane kinkene' of gunpowder: *Accounts*, xi, p.xlii.

29.   CSP(S), i, p.651 (Randolph to Cecil, 18 September 1562). The *Diurnal* p.73 has the execution taking place 'over the brig of Inverness,' and see also Calderwood, ii, p.196.

30.   CSP(S), i, p.655 (Randolph to Cecil, 30 September 1562). The musket does not seem to have been used to any great extent by the Scots soldiers until the mid-sixteenth century, after the power of the

handgun had been seen to disastrous effect at the battle of Pinkie. The English used an early form of musket called the arquebus. A contemporary German musket, the hackbut, was introduced to Scotland at about the same time. The Scots introduced a highly trained and well paid corps of professional shots, the harquebusiers, who were frequently foreign mercenaries. They wore only light armour consisting of a steel helmet or 'knapskull' and either a 'corslet' (a steel breast and back plate) or 'jack' (a padded jacket reinforced with steel plates). Like the later dragoons they were a mobile, mounted unit who dismounted in order to fire on the enemy. They were also trained to act in concert with pikemen whose long spears protected them from the enemy horse (Peter Marren, *Grampian Battlefields*, Edinburgh, 1990, pp.103f.).

31.   CSP(F), 1562, p.329 (Randolph to Cecil, 30 September 1562).

32.   *Aboyne*, p.465.

33.   Calderwood, ii, p.197, Knox, ii, p.58.

34.   RPC, i, p. 219 (Aberdeen, 12 October 1562); pp.220f. (Sederunt apud Edinburgh, 26 October 1562). Knox, ii, p.59; CSP(S), i, p.660 (Randolph to Cecil 23 October 1562).

35.   *Narratives*, p.88.

36.   CSP(S), i, pp.555 (Randolph to Cecil, 24 September 1561); 665 (Randolph to Cecil, 2 November 1562); Cuthbert Graham, 'Corrichie,' *Leopard Magazine*, June 1979, pp.31-33.

37.   CSP(S), i, pp.652f (Randolph to Cecil 24 September 1562); p.662 (Randolph to Cecil 28 October 1562); Donaldson, *All the Queen's Men*, p.53; White, 'Queen Mary's Northern Province,' p.62.

38.   RPC, i, p.223 (Aberdeen, 27 October 1562).

39.   *Narratives*, p.89.

40.   Graham, 'Corrichie,' p.32.

41.   CPS(S), i, p.662 (Randolph to Cecil, 28 October 1562); Knox, ii, p.59; *Diurnal*, p.74; HHDA, p.284.

42.   Calderwood, ii, p.199, 120; Knox, ii, p.61; HHDA, p. 284, estimated the Gordon losses at 120 dead and 100 captured.

43.   Marren, *Grampian Battles*, p.106.

44.   HHDA , pp.284f.

45.   CPS(S), i, 665 (Randolph to Cecil, 2 November 1562); *Diurnal*, p.74; *Aboyne*, p. 467; *Narratives*, p.90; HHDA, p.284.

46.   As James VI styled the latter's history: *Basilicon Doron*, in *Political Writings*, p.46.

47.   Knox, ii, pp.61f, reiterated in Calderwood's more temperate *History*, ii, p.199.

48.   *Accounts*, xi, pp.xliv, 245.

49.   CSP(S), i, pp.662, 668 (Randolph to Cecil 28 October and 18 November 1562)

50.   HFG, i, pp.240f.

51.   *Sutherland Book*, iii, p.141.

52.   HHDA, pp. 281f; Buchanan, i, p.430; Sutherland, p.140 (This material in this useful work is taken almost verbatim from the less accessible *History of the Feuds and Conflicts among the Clans in the Northern parts of Scotland from MXXXI-MDCXIX*, written in the reign of James VI, first published by Messrs Foulis, Glasgow, 1764);

53.   *Accounts*, xi, p.214.

54.   *Diurnal*, p.75 .

55.   *Accounts*, xi, pp.xlivf., 205, 226; *Inventories de la Royne d'Ecosse*, Edinburgh, 1863, p.xxii.

56.   *Rutland Mss* at Belvoir, cited in *Aboyne*, p.467f; CSP(S), i, pp.665,668 (Randolph to Cecil, 2 and 18 November 1562); Sutherland, p.142.

57. Sutherland, p.143; Knox, ii, p.360.

58. *Inventories*, pp.49–54. The quotation is found in Taylor's *History*, i, p. 713, but no attribution is given.

59. MM 1/2/1.

60. Knox, ii, p.62; Calderwood, ii, pp.195 & 199; see Andrew Lang, *A History of Scotland*, Edinburgh, 1907, ii, pp.118f.

61. Tytler, ii, pp.350f. Lee, Moray's most recent biographer, concurs, *James Stewart*, p.106.

62. Letter from Randolph to Cecil cited in Tytler, ii, pp.350f.

63. *Papal Negotiations*, p.163, cited in Cowan's 'The Roman Connection', in Lynch, *Mary Stewart*, p.109; Antonia Fraser, *Mary Queen of Scots*, p.203.

64. Professor Wormald makes this point forcefully and cogently in *Mary Queen of Scots: A Study in Failure*, London, 1988, p.124.

5. The Slave of Passion

1.   From a letter to Queen Elizabeth which Camden himself had seen, *History of Elizabeth*, pp. 66–7.

2.   *Narratives*, pp.80f. (Edmund Hay to Laynez, January 1563/4).

3.   Burns, J.H., 'The Political background of the Reformation, 1513–1625' in David McRoberts (ed), *Essays on the Scottish Reformation, 1513–1625*, p.19.

4.   Buchanan, ii, 468; Keith, ii, pp.307, 333; Melvil, *Memoirs*. For a detailed discussion of the veracity of these allegations see Taylor, *History*, i, pp.745–8.

5.   Keith, ii, pp.309–21 (Randolph to Cecil, 4 July 1565); p.329 (Moray, Argyll and Chatelherault to Elizabeth, 18 July 1565).

6.   On the marriage see Caroline Bingham, *Darnley*, London, 1966.

7.   *Diurnal*, pp.81 & 84, *Estimate*, p.7.

8.   White, 'Queen Mary's Northern Province,' p.65.

9.   CSP(S), ii, pp.194f. (Randolph to Cecil, 27 August 1565); 219 (Randolph to Cecil, 4 October 1565).

10. MM 10/34/bundle5/2.

11. CSP(S), ii, p.276 (Randolph to Cecil, 25 April 1566).

12. 5 November 1566: extract from the 'Detection of George Buchanan' quoted in Mahon, *The Tragedy of Kirk o' Field*, p. 245.

13. CSP(S), ii, p.278 (Randolph to Cecil, 13 May 1566).

14. Advertisement out of Scotland from the Earl of Bedford, 31 August 1566, printed in William Robertson, *History*, ii, p.p.362f.

15. 'The Protestation of the Earls of Huntly and Argyll, touching the murder of the King of Scots' (January 1569), reprinted in Tytler, ii, pp.401f; Davison, *The Casket Letters*, pp.40ff; Keith, iii, p.290–294.

16. 'Ane Answer by the Earl of Moray, Regent,' in Keith, iii, pp.294f.

17. For a very different but cogent analysis see Davison, *The Casket Letters*. He argues that it was Darnley who was planning to blow up Kirk o'Fields when Mary and her advisors were there. Moray and the Lords of the Congregation got wind of this. So too did Bothwell. He also knew that Moray was planning to kill the King after Mary's assassination by her husband. Bothwell warned Mary of the plot by Darnley, and persuaded her to stay in Edinburgh Castle while he and his men made their way to Kirk o'Fields. Thinking the entourage was that of Mary, Darnley lit the fuse and was making his escape through the garden when Moray's men, lying in wait, apprehended and strangled him.

Bothwell knowingly had sprung the trap; Moray did the killing; Mary was completely innocent of the murder.

18.   The day before Huntly's rehabilitation Moray made provision to guard himself against claims for the restitution of the jewels, furniture and chattels taken from the fourth Earl which he and his wife were enjoying. In a deed, sealed at Holyrood, the fifth Earl bound himself, his mother and siblings 'to warrand releve and keep skaithless James, Earl of Murray, and Maister John Wod, John Stewart and utheris his servands of quahatsumener gudis geir jewellis and uther grayth of quahatsumener intromettit with be thame pertaining to our unquhile fader the time of his deceis or that was then in his possession ... and never to move play call nor pursue the said Earl of Moray nor his said servandis thairfor' confessing 'that their intromission with the said gudis proceedit be our sovereign's command-ment.' HMC, MM, p.643 (Obligation by the Earl of Huntly to the Earl of Moray, 18 April, 1567).

19.   On 24 February 1566 according to Protestant rites at the Canongate church in Edinburgh. The Queen, according to Knox, wanted it solemnised according to Catholic rites in Holyrood but Bothwell would not agree (Knox, ii, p.392).

20.   Donaldson, *Mary Queen of Scots*, pp.98-9. He had lost them and his liberty for saying Mass in public.

21.   Antonia Fraser states that Lady Jean raised no objections to the ending of their marriage and her brother acquiesced (*Mary Queen of Scots*, p.319). She cites no source for this assertion other than the Ainslie Bond. Huntly's subsequent abandonment of Mary's cause seems to belie this contention. Morton, Argyll and Athol, all of whom had signed the Bond, turned against her. (Stuart, *A Lost Study*, passim).

22.   Keith, ii, pp.581f; RPC, i, 509-511 (Edinburgh, 17, 19, 21, 22 May).

23.   Her motto befitted her: 'In my end is my beginning.' It will be apparent that I entirely concur with Wormald in her welcome reappraisal of this most calamitous of Stewart monarchs.

24.   Letters from Drury to Cecil (16, 20 and 25 May, and 7 June 1567) cited in Tytler, iii, p.3.

25.   CSP(S),ii, p.354 (Throckmorton to Elizabeth, 16 July 1567).

26.   Tytler, iii, pp.5f.

6. The Twigs of Ambition

1.   *Sutherland*, p.182.

2.   Tytler, iii, pp.12 (Norris to Cecil, 16 July 1567); 13 (Heneage to Cecil, 8 July 1567).

3.   Keith, ii, 737.

4.   HHDA, p. 301.

5.   Tytler, iii, pp.24 (Moray to Cecil, 15 September 1567); 28 (Drury to Cecil, 4 January 1567/8); 18 April 1567: MM 12/43/55; HMC, MM p.643.

6.   Keith Brown, 'In Search of the Godly Magistrate in Reformation Scotland,' p.556; Buchanan, i, p.120.

7.   Tytler, iii, p.23 (Throckmorton to Cecil, 20 August 1567).

8.   Gordon Donaldson, *All the Queen's Men, Power and Politics in Mary Stewart's Scotland*, London, 1983, p.92.

9.   CSP(S), ii, p.403 (Band of Mary's Adherents signed at Hamilton, 8 May 1568). See Ian Cowan, 'The Marian Civil War' in *Scotland and War AD 79-1918*, Edinburgh, 1991, edited by MacDougall, pp.96ff.

10.   Tytler, iii, p.30.

11.   CSP(S), ii, p.407 (Battle of Langsyde, 16 May 1568).

12.   Ibid., p.406.

13.   *Mackintosh Muniments,* pp.28-30 (bond signed at Huntly 27 June 1568); Allan White, 'Queen Mary's Northern Province,' in *Mary Stewart, Queen in Three Kingdoms,* edited by Michael Lynch, pp.64-67f; CSP(F)1566-8, pp.523 (Drury to Cecil, 15 August 1568), 526-7 (Drury to Cecil, 21 August 1568). Perth is called St Johnstone, or St John's Town after the Church of St John the Baptist at its centre

14.   David Mathew, *Scotland under Charles I,* London, 1955, p.127.

15.   CSP(S), ii, pp.497 (Moray to Elizabeth, 3 September 1568); 516 (Offences by the Queen's Party, 4 October 1568); 594 (Kirkcaldy to Moray, 31 December 1568).

16.   Sir James Melvil, *Memoirs,* 3rd edn edited by George Scott, Glasgow, 1751, p.219; Sext, pp.39f.

17.   *Diurnal,* pp.144-5.

18.   CSP(S), ii, pp.658 (Moray to Elizabeth, 7 July 1569); 653 (Wood to Cecil, 4 June 1569).

19.   Buchanan, *History,* i, p.572; Dalyell, *Fragments of Scottish History,* 1798.

20.   *Diurnal,* p.156.

21.   Buchanan, i, p.485; *Correspondence Diplomatique,* iii, p.54 (La Mothe-Fénélon to Catherine de Medici, 17 February 1569/70).

22.   He so signed himself in a letter to Cecil dated 2 January 1569/70 cited in Tytler, ii, p.56.

23.   In the *Moray Muniments* is an account by John Wood of the funeral expenses of the Earl of Moray. They came to almost £58. The Account has no date or attribution. The Moray inventory states that the document is from about 1592 and relates to the 'Bonnie Earl.' This is very unlikely. A better bet is that it relates to the burial of the first Earl. Several pieces of internal evidence point to this: A John Wood of Tillidevy was secretary to the Regent Moray; while a master John Wood is referred to as one of the regent's servants (see Slave of Passion note 18) although according to Leslie he was slain in Fife' a few days after the Regent's death; the accounts list a double-sided banner and such a banner was carried in his cortege; money was distributed to the poor in the Cowgate and Canongate, both parts of Edinburgh that the Regent's funeral precession moved through or by; and in any case 1592 is not the date of the second Earl's burial (MM, 12/43/195). His 'relic,' the dome of his skull mounted in silver as a bowl, is preserved at Darnaway.

24.   CSP(S), iii, p.190 (Sussex to Cecil, 28 May 1570).

25.   CSP(S), iii, p.219 ('State of Scotland,' 19 June 1570).

26.   Atholl Murray, 'Huntly's Rebellion and the Administration of Justice in north-east Scotland, 1570-1573,' *Northern Scotland,* iv, 1981, pp. 1-6; CSP(S), iii, pp.209, 213, 216, 219, 221 (Randolph to Sussex, 13 and 16 June; to Elizabeth, 18 June; 'State of Scotland,' 1570; Sussex to Cecil, 22 June 1570); HMC, MM, pp.638 (Mary Queen of Scots to the Countess of Moray, 27 January 1570/1); p.652f (Huntly to the Countess of Moray, 9 April and 11 July 1570).

27.   *Accounts,* xii, pp.211ff; CSP(S), iii, p.291f. (Sussex to Cecil, 6 August 1570); RPC, xiv, pp.69f. (Brechin, 5 August 1570, 'Proclamation in answer to the alleged misreport by Huntly,').

28.   CSP(S), iii, pp.295-7 (letter from Lennox to Sussex received from Randolph and sent by Sussex to Cecil, 7 August 1570).

29.   CSP(S), iii, p.219 ('State of Scotland,' 19 June 1570).

30.   Keith, ii, p.236.

31.   *Diurnal,* p.245.

32.   *Sutherland Book,* i, pp.164f. HF, pp. 88-93, gives a most useful compendium of many of the sources for this dispute.

33. *Diurnal*, p.251; Lindsay, ii, pp.267-271; *Sutherland Book*, i, pp.164f; Marren, *Grampian Battles*, pp.118-123; Simpson, *The Earldom of Mar*, pp. 87f.

34. *Diurnal*, pp.253ff. Marren, *Grampian Battles*, pp.125-127.

35. Lindsay, ii, pp.272 & 289.

36. *Diurnal* p.255; *Corgarff Castle Guide*, p.4, illustration 5; Marren, *Grampian Battles,* pp.124-125.

37. Bannatyne, *Memorials of Transactions in Scotland*, p.197. The burning of Corgarff and the ballad it inspired were both precursors to an even more celebrated conflagration and even better known lament.

38. Quoted in Donaldson, *All the Queen's Men*, p.122.

39. *Mackintosh Muniments*, pp. 33f.

40. CSP(S), v, p.23 (Killigrew to Walsingham, 12 July 1574).

41. Brown, p.110.

42. *Sutherland*, pp.170f; HF, p.92.

43. RPC, ii, pp.338-9 ('Pacification of Perth,' Perth, 23 February 1572/3)

44. CSP(S), v, p.23 (Killigrew to Walsingham, 12 July 1574).

45. Allan White, 'The Regent Morton's Visitation' in The Renaissance in Scotland edited by A.A. MacDonald, Michael Lynch and Ian Cowan, pp.246-263.

46. Philip Stubbes, *Anatomie of Abuses*, 1583, cited in *The Bewitching of Anne Gunter*, by James Sharpe, p.16. Behaviour at football matches seems to have altered little with the civilising effect of the centuries. For instance, the English ambassador reported that 'some quarrel happened the other day betwixt Bothwell and the master of Marishal, upon a stroke given at football on Bothwell's leg by the master, after that the master had received a sore fall by Bothwell. They secretly appointed to meet alone in the fields the next morning; but Angus espying the appointment, travailed to pacify the matter, and seeing he could not prevail, he opened it to the King, who with some difficulty reconciled the parties, who are now well agreed.' CSP(S), vi, p.475 (Bowes to Walsingham, 29 May 1583).

47. *Memorials of Transactions in Scotland*, pp.333-338. Apparently a 'detail of the circumstances attending his sudden death' may be seen in Dalzell's *Illustrations of Scottish History*, a work I have been unable to trace.

48. *Sutherland*, p.171.

49. CSP(S), ii, p.370 (Throckmorton to Elizabeth, 31 July 1567); iv, p.131 (Hunsden to Burghley, 24 February 1571/2).

50. Brown, p.144.

7. St Colme's Son

1. Edinburgh, Waldegrave, 1597.

2. Known latterly as Sir James Stewart of Beath, after property bestowed upon him in 1543 by Richard, Abbot of St Colme.

3. MM 1/1/118; 1/1/124; 1/1/117.

4. MM 1/1/120; 122; 192; 193; 197; 198; 301.

5. Sir William Fraser, *The Red Book of Menteith*, i, p.484, ii, pp.369-400. The dispute between Edmonstoun and the Commendator of St Colme was to last until 1565/6 when Edmonstoun repented of the murder and renounced all claims to lands of James Stewart of Beath. In return he was granted a pardon for the former and £5000 for the latter: MM 1/1/146; 1/1/189; 1/1/179; 1/1/178; 1/1/150; 1/1/149; 1/1/407.

6.   James Kirk, 'Patronage and the Crown 1560-1572,' in *The Renaissance and Reformation in Scotland*, edited by Ian Cowan, pp.93-113; Peter Murray,'The Lay Administrators of Church Lands,' SHR, lxxiv, 1995, pp.26-44.

7.   The first recorded attack by an English ship was in 1315. Others are recorded, inter alia, in 1335, 1336, 1385, 1542, and 1547.

8.   *Inchcolm Abbey and Island*, HMSO, 1989, p.20.

9.   The resignation took place on 6 January 1542/3: MM 12/43/37. HMC, p.635.

10.   MM 12/43/38; 12/43/39.

11.   Patten, p.139

12.   MM 12/43/44.

13.   Keith, i, pp. 267 &.277.

14.   The religious routine of Inchcolm was ended, although the last canons were allowed to live out their days there as members of a property owning corporation. The last document bearing the signatures of canons of Inchcolm was a charter signed by Dominus John Brounhill and Dominus Andro Anguss in 1578.

15.   Keith, i, p.313.

16.   CSP(S), i, p.570 (Randolph to Cecil, 11 November 1561); Keith, ii, p.136. MM 12/43/46; HMC 636: Journal of the Journey to Paris.

17.   David Breeze, *A Queen's Progress*, p.41 and photograph.

18.   He received the charter on 6 March 1563/4. According to a charter dated 25 May 1565, 'the lands erected into the lordship of Doune were settled on the said James, his heirs and successors to be called and intitulat lords of Doune, quha shall have the honour, dignity, place and pre-eminence of our sovereign Lords Parliament;' see James Balfour Paul, SP, vii, p.188.

19.   Keith, ii, p.288.

20.   Stewart Cruden, *The Scottish Castle*, pp.84-91.

21.   See Appendix 3.

22.   He was a signatory to the bond of Mary's adherents, a bond headed by Argyll and Huntly: CSP(S), ii, p.403 (8 May 1568).

23.   RPC, ii, pp.22, 25 (Stirling, 30 August, 3 September 1569).

24.   Calderwood, iii, p.10.

25.   Hugh, Earl of Eglington, and his brother for instance were warded in 1571: RPC, ii, p.78 (Stirling, 7 September 1571).

26.   MacGibbon, *Castellated and Domestic Architecture,* iii, p.418.

27.   Fynes Morrison's Account, 1598, in *A Source Book of Scottish History*, edited by W. Croft Dickinson, second edn, 1961, p.345.

28.   James VI to the Treasurer, 10 August 1580. *Debrett's Royal Scotland*, p.71; *Doune Castle Guide*, p.7.

29.   W. Croft Dickinson, *Source Book*, ii, p.122.

30.   J.H.Hexter, 'The Education of the Aristocracy in the Renaissance' in *Reappraisals in History*, pp.45-70.

31.   Major, in SCD, p.59. There was a tendency in England for the gentry to ape their superiors, a tendency deprecated by educationalists such as Richard Mulcaster who contrasted the great nobility with those whose 'wits be as the common, their bodies oftimes worse:' Joan Simon, *Education and Society*, pp.353f.

32.   Major, in SCD, p.46.

33.   Simon, *Education and Society*, p.346 note 3.

34.   In 1562 Elizabeth was asked to grant her licence to the son of the Laird of Cawdor, a youth 'not above eighteen years, prettily learned and well travelled.' CSP(S), i , p.644 (Randolph to Cecil, 4 August 1562).

35.   *Alumni Oxonienses*, iv, pp.1422ff.

36.   John Venn, *The Book of Matriculations and Degrees: a Catalogue of those who have been matriculated or admitted to any degree in the University of Cambridge from 1544 to 1659*, Cambridge, 1913, p.64.

37.   Grose, *Dictionary of the Vulgar Tongue*, 1795.

38.   *Edinburgh University Catalogue of Graduates*, edited by D. Ian, Bannatyne Club, 1858.

39.   In 1629, in a deliberate attempt to wean them from their Faith, Roman Catholic nobles were charged to send their sons to any Scots university but Aberdeen.

40.   Although in 1672 James Stewart of Doune and his brother Charles both matriculated at King's College, Aberdeen (*Fasti Aberdoniensis 1494-1854*, p.491).

41.   A&B, p.39; Thomas McCrie, *Life of Andrew Melville*, p.33.

42.   *Munimenta Alme Universitatis Glasguensis: Records of the University of Glasgow from its Foundation till 1727*, 4 vols, edited by Cosmo Innes, Maitland Club, Glasgow, 1854.

43.   Major, in SCD, p.42.

44.   *Early Records of the University of St Andrews*, edited by James Maitland Anderson, St Andrews, 1926.

45.   HHDA, p. 284.

46.   *Accounts of the Master of Works*, i, p.307 (10 August 1580). Stone slabs for capping the wall-heads were provided by William Gibe of Stirling from the quarries of Craig of Knockhill and Burnebank, timber from the wood of Doune, and slates from the Highlands; the masonry work was done by Michael Ewing and the slating by MacQuarren: William Fraser, *Red Book of Menteith*, ii, pp.419-21; *Doune Castle Guide,* p.8; MM 1/1/300.

47.   CSP(S), v, p.611 (Randolph to Hudson, 4 February 1580/1).

48.   CSP(S), v, pp.500f. (Bowes to Burghley and Walsingham, 13 September 1580).

49.   RPS, viii, nos. 8 (5 January 1580/1); 298 (2 June); 323 (6 June); 392 (13 July). MM 1/1/275.

50.   CP, pp.183(a), 185(a). See Appendix 4.

51.   Randolph, CSP(S), v, p.611 (Randolph to Hunsdon, 4 February 1580/1). Sir Robert Bowes, the English ambassador, spoke of 'these brave triumphs solemnised by the King, Lennox, [and] Montbirneau' with contemptuous sarcasm in a letter to Walsingham (CSP(S), v, p.619 (Bowes to Walsingham, 7 February 1580/1)). The quintain, of which riding at the ring was a variant, was the sort of entertainment demanded of society weddings especially when a monarch was present. In 1575 Queen Elizabeth attended a 'solemn country bridal' at Kenilworth Castle where a quintain was set up 'for feates at arms where, in the great company of young men and lasses, the bridegroom had the first course and broke his spear very boldly:' Strut, *Sports and Pastimes*, p.119.

52.   *Acts of the Parliament of Scotland*, iii, p.230; RPC, iii, p.450 (Holyrood, 20 February 1581/2).

53.   He is first referred to by this epithet in 1765 by Percy in his introduction to the Ballad in his *Reliques*, ii, p.210.

54.   Moysie, p.183.

55.   *Estimate*, p.31.

56.   *Sext*, pp.246f.

57.   There is no other extant depiction of him. Rampini p156 mentions a picture at Darnaway as the only authentic portrait of him taken during his life, and painted shortly before his death. He has a small

head, with a long sensitive nose, prominent ears and a small mouth, pointed chin, immature moustache. His features are delicate, almost effeminate; his expression gentle. A ringlet of hair hangs from his right ear two intertwined earrings from his left. His dress is plain but rich, a crimson doublet close-buttoned down the front, a square collar, and over his right shoulder fastened behind neck with a handsome jewel is a narrow white satin embroidered scarf – the Queen's gift to him according to tradition. If this purports to describe a painting hanging today at Darnaway that portrait is now thought to be of the third rather than the second Earl. Neither the portrait nor Rampini's description bear any resemblance to the Memorial.

58. A year later – a belated wedding present – Moray and his wife were awarded a pension of £500 Scots by the King. This untoward royal generosity was cheap, however, since the pension had been that bestowed on Archibald Douglas, the bastard of Morton, by the Bishop of Aberdeen. Archibald had been denounced rebel and his pension was forfeit: RPC, iii, p.450 (Holyrood, 20 February 1581/2).

59. CSP(S), vi, p.94 (Occurrents in Scotland, 24 November 1581).

60. MM 1/1/29, 168, 328, 370, 372, 387, 390, 391, 396.

61. MM 1/1/275, 281, 297, 370.

62. MM 12/43/190 (16 October 1586); 2/3/167, 166, 168 (26 March 1588, 20 September 1588 and 11 January 1588/9). This may have been the son of Sir John Wishart of Pitarrow, the former Queen Mary's comptroller. In December 1586 Lord Doune was sent an unpaid bill for dress fabrics owed by the Earl of Moray: MM 2/3/104.

63. MM 2/3/168, 217/2/3/260-8; HFG, i, p.214; Sext, p. 246.

64. MM 2/3/262 (8 March 1581/2).

65. MM 2/3/266 (5 August 1583).

66. MM 2/3/263 (16 March 1581/2/).

67. MM 2/3/264 undated, but since Whitsun was 3 June 1582 presumably some little time before.

68. This child is generally believed to be his successor. James would be the name of his first-born son, and James was the name of the third Earl. *The Present State of the Nobility*, a document dated 1 July 1592, states that the Earl of Moray was ten at that date. However, a slight doubt about this conclusion is created by *The State of the Nobility of Scotland* which states that Moray's son and heir was two in 1589 (CSP(S), x, p.30 (10 April 1589)). If this is right the baby of 1582 must have died – a common occurrence – and there must have been no more or no living male progeny between 1582 and 1587. This cannot be so. We know that 'their eldest son' was alive in September 1586, implying that James and Francis his younger brother (later a knight of the Bath) were both born by that time, and another child was expected (MM 1/1/79 22 September 1586). The expected child would be one of the their three daughters: Margaret who married Lord Howard of Effingham; Elizabeth who married Lord Saltoun; or his last child, Grizell who married Sir Robert Innes of that Ilk. It is most unlikely to have been the last since that would imply a production rate of one child a year, not allowing for still-births and miscarriages. Moray's wife died young, on 18 November 1591, and it is probable that she did so while giving birth to Grizell. The fact that the earldom was still in ward to the Countess of Athol in October 1604 (RPC, vi, p.820 (Edinburgh, 29 March 1604); vii, pp.550 (Edinburgh, 2 May 1604, Holyrood, 3 May 1604), 572 (15 October 1604)), and that the third Earl did not marry until 1607, may suggest but certainly do not prove a later birth for him than 1582.

69. MM 1/1/79 (22 September 1585). There is a discharge for it dated 3 June 1587 (MM 1/1/53).

8. Tua Housis in the North

1.   p.246

2.   Major, in SCD, p.59; and Donaldson, *Documents*, p.101.

3.   p.31.

4.   Bannatyne, *Memorials of Transactions in Scotland*, p.338.

5.   Ibid.

6.   Spalding, p.73; Keith Brown, 'Aristocratic Finances,' p.50; Margaret Sanderson, *Scottish Rural Society*, pp.31, 177; Maureen Meikle, 'The Invisible Divide: the Greater Lairds and the Nobility of Jacobean Scotland,' SHR, LXXI, 1992, pp70-87, at pp.76f.

7.   *Narratives*, pp.137-140 (Letter of John Leslie, Bishop of Ross, June 20 1579), p.166, 171f f. (Parsons to Aquaviva, 26 September 1581).

8.   Aboyne, p.500; *Acts of the Parliament of Scotland*, iii, pp.230f.

9.   *Estimate*, p.31.

10.   *Sutherland*, pp.479f.

11.   *Estimate*, p.31; *Basilicon Doron*, in *Political Writings*, p.29; Lachlan Shaw, *History of the Province of Moray*, p.51.

12.   Tytler, iii, pp.134f.

13.   CSP(S), vi, p.159 (Lords in Favour of the Duke of Lennox and Against Him, 5 September 1582).

14.   December 1582: Tytler, iii, p.139.

15.   CSP(S), vi, pp.476f. (Bowes to Walsingham, 29 and 31 May 1583); 598 (Memorial by Walsingham, 5 September); 506 (Bowes to Walsingham, 17 June).

16.   *Aboyne*, p.501; *The Lothian Muniments*, SRO GD 40/2/ix/68; Ruth Grant, 'Politicking Jacobean Women,' p.96.

17.   CSP(S), vii, pp.24-25 (Bowes to Walsingham, 7 February 1583/4); *Aboyne*, pp.501f.

18.   CSP(S), vii, p.27 (Bowes to Walsingham, 13 February 1583-4).

9. Banging it out Bravely

1.   CSP(S), ix, p.651 (Walsingham to Fowler, 22 December 1588).

2.   *Basilikon Doron*, in *The Political Writings of King James VI and I*, p.28.

3.   Grant, iii, p. 177 (Decreet of Exemption to Athol, Grant and others from Huntly's Commission, 20 January 1590).

4.   Athol Murray, 'The Salmon Fishing of Strathnaver,' *Revue of Scottish Culture*, 8, 1993, pp.77-83; Sanderson, *Scottish Rural Society*, pp.32f; Ian Whyte, *Scotland Before the Industrial Revolution*, p.278.

5.   MM 1/15/215. *The Gordon Castle Muniments* include dozens of documents dealing with salmon fishing on the Spey: GD 44/7/11; 13; 14; 15.

6.   Major, in SCD, p.59.

7.   John Prebble, *The Lion in the North*, p.14.

8.   *Two Missions of Jaques de la Brosse*, edited by Gladys Dickinson, Scottish History Society, 1942, p.22.

9.   Brown, pp.20f.

10.   Prebble, *The Lion in the North*, p.224. On the lawless Borders in the sixteenth century see Fraser, *The Steel Bonnets*.

11.   CSP(S), vi, p.475 (Bowes to Walsingham, 29 May 1583).

12. 30 July 1588: Robert Birrell, p.24.

13. 11 December 1593: Birrel, p.31; Moysie, p.111.

14. Prebble, *The Lion in the North*, p.224.

15. Major, in SCD, p.58 and Donaldson, *Documents*, p.101.

16. A&D, p.190.

17. Major, in SCD, p. 48; Roger Mason, 'Kingship, Nobility, and Anglo-Scottish Union,' *The Innes Review*, xli, 2, 1990, p.199.

18. 15 September 1595: Birrell, p.35.

19. RPC, vii, p.509, (Edinburgh, 21 June 1607); viii, p. 271 (Edinburgh, 31 March, 1609); Brown, p.21; Jenny Wormald, 'Princes and Regions' in *Church Politics and Society*, edited by Norman MacDougall, p.77; Pitcairn, *Criminal Trials*, ii, p.532.

20. Birrell, p.13.

21. CSP(S), iii, p.305 (Randolph to Sussex, 9 August 1570).

22. CSP(S), viii, p.109 (Wotton to Walsingham, 22 September 1585)

23. SCD, pp.58-59; 'Scottish Nobility and their part in the National History, p.161; I. F. Grant, *The Social and Economic Development of Scotland,* pp.191-196.

24. RPC, iii, pp.524 (Holyrood, 3 November 1582); 751 (Dunfermline, 23 June 1585).

25. J. Wormald, 'The Bloodfeud' in *The New Companion to Scottish Culture*, edited by David Daiches, Edinburgh, 1993.

26. Grant, iii, p. 178.

27. Birrell, p.24.

28. CSP(S), viii, p.427 (Archibald Douglas to Burghley, 9 June 1586).

29. Spottiswood, ii, p.464.

30. Ibid.

31. CBP, i, p.321 (Hunsdon to Burghley, 31 March 1588).

32. Maurice Lee, *Great Britain's Solomon*, p.70.

33. Brown, p.147.

34. Lee, *Great Britain's Solomon*, p.66.

35. CSP(S), ix, pp.476 (Letter to Walsingham, 13 August 1587); 491 (Justice Clerk to Archibald Douglas, 24 October 1587); x, p.3 (Fowler to Burghley, 14 March 1588/9).

36. CBP, i, p.307 (Hunsdon to Burghley, 23 January 1587/8).

37. *Aboyne*, p.506.

38. James VI, *Poems*, ii, pp.134-145 at pp.138f; Lyall, 'James VI and the Cultural Crisis' in *The Reign of James VI*, edited by J. Goodare, pp. 55-70, at p.67.

39. Lee, *Maitland*, p.170. The bishop was forced later publicly to recant this action – among others – before the synod at St Andrews in 1591: 'Thirdly, that I married the Earl of Huntly contrar the Kirk's command, without the confession of his faith, and profession of the sincere doctrine of the Word, I repent and crave God pardon.' – A&D, pp.290f.

40. They had the following brood:

    George, 2nd Marquis of Huntly

    Francis, died in Germany in 1620.

    Adam of Auchindoun, died after 1642.

    Laurence

    John, born 1606, created Viscount Melgum and Lord Aboyne in 1627, died 1630.

Ann, married 3rd Earl of Moray.

Elizabeth, married Alexander, Lord Livingstone, 2nd Earl of Linlithgow, died 1616.

Mary, born 1611, married William, 11th Earl of Angus, died 1674.

Jean, married first Claud Hamilton, Lord Strabane, secondly Sir Phelim O'Neile.

41   *Sutherland*, p.208.

42.   HFG, ii, p.128; SM, iii, p.215.

10. A PARTICULAR FRIEND AND A GENERAL CHRISTIAN KING

1.   Luke 15.21. Akrigg, *Letters*, p.91 (James VI to Huntly, [February?] 1589).

2.   Attributed to Johnson, p.125, quoted in HFG, ii, p.42.

3.   MM 2/3/148 (1587).

4.   MM 2/3/255 (Darnaway, 26 May 1588?).

5.   MM 2/3/268 (24 November 1587).

6.   MM 2/3/132, 141, 143; 2/4/120 (8 January-3 March 1587/8)

7.   Keith Brown, 'Noble Indebtedness,' pp.261-263.

8.   MM 2/3/226 (William Douglas to the Countess of Moray, 14 March 1589/90).

9.   MM 2/3/159 (William Henryson to Moray, 9 September 1588); 273 (27 March 1590 and 11 August 1590); 298 (Discharge by Alexander Ostiane, Taylor of Edinburgh, 4 August 1590); 319 (10 February 1590/91); 315 (24 May 1591); 322 (17 July 1591); 331 (26 November 1591); 277 (Leslie to Lady Moray, 6 August 1590); 300 (Leslie to Moray, 15 August 1590); 4/120 (3 March 1587/88).

10.   MM 12/43/190 (16 October 1586); 2/3/167 (26 March 1588); 166 (20 September 1588); 168 (11 January 1588/9); 325 (Discharge for 10,000 merks in part payment, 8 December 1991).

11.   MM 2r/3/267 (26 May 1587). By August 1588 the loan had still not been repaid: MM 2/3/170 (15 August 1588).

12.   RPC, iv, p.307 (Edinburgh, 1 August 1588); HFG, ii, p.42.

13.   RPC, iv, pp.xxiv-xxviii.

14.   CBP, i, p.321 (Hunsdon to Burghley, 31 March 1588); CSP(S), ix, pp.637-8 (Ashby to Walsingham, 26 November 1588).

15.   CSP(S), ix, p.623 (Ashby to Walsingham, 13 October 1588).

16.   CSP(S), x, p.17 (Fowler to Burghley, 28 March 1589).

17.   CSP(S), ix, pp.538 (Carvell to Walsingham, 16 February 1587/8); 678 (Ashby to Walsingham, 8 February 1588/9); Aboyne, p.505.

18.   CSP(S), ix, pp.676 (Fowler to Walsingham, 6 February 1588/9); 677 (Ashby to Walsingham, 8 February 1588/9); x, p.9 (Ashby to Burghley, 18 March 1588/9).

19.   Lee, *Maitland*, p.178; CSP(S), ix, pp.622 (Selby to Walsingham, 9 October 1588); 638 (Ashby to Walsingham, 26 November 1588).

20.   CSP(S), x, p.1 (Ashby to Burghley, 14 March 1588/9).

21.   CSP(S), ix, pp.666 (Fowler to Walsingham, January 7 1588/9); 677 (Ashby to Walsingham, 8 February 1588/9).

22.   CSP(S), ix, pp.682-97 (Privy Council to English Ambassador with seven enclosures, 20 February 1588/9).

23.   Ibid.

24.   Akrigg, *Letters* pp.89-91; CSP(S), ix, p.700 (February 1588/9).

25. CSP(S), ix, p.701 (Fowler to Walsingham, 1 March 1588/9); Calderwood, v, p.36; *Sutherland*, p.213.

26. CSP(S), x, pp.4f (Fowler to Burghley, 14 March 1588/9); 9 (Ashby to Burghley 18 March 1588/9).

27. CSP(S), x, p.3 (Fowler to Burghley, 14 March 1588/9); Moysie, p.72.

28. CSP(S), x, p.3 (Fowler to Burghley, 14 March 1588/9); Ruth Grant, 'The Brig O'Dee Affair' in *The Reign of James VI*, edited by J. Goodare, p.93-109, at pp.101ff.

29. CSP(S), x, p.3 (Fowler to Burghley, 14 March 1588/9).

30. CSP(S), x, p.8 (Aston to Hudson, 15 March 1588/9).

31. Others see the plot against Huntly as having substance: see CBP, i, p.335 (Sir Henry Woddryngton to Burghley, 18 March 1588/9); Grant, 'The Brig o'Dee Affair, p.104.

32. CSP(S), x, p.10 (Fowler to Walsingham, 18 March 1588/9).

33. CSP(S), x, p.17 (Fowler to Burghley, 28 March 1589).

34. CSP(S,), x, pp.1, 5 (Ashby to Burghley, 14 March 1589); Lang, History, ii, p.344; Brown, p.148.

35. MM 2/3/227 and 230 (14 March 1589).

36. RPC, iv, p.825 (1589).

37. CSP(S), x, pp.26 (Fowler to Walsingham, 7 April 1589); 27 (Ashby to Burghley, 8 April).

38. CSP(S), x, p.38 (Fowler to Ashby, 14 April 1589).

39. Willson, King James VI and I, p.102.

40. CSP(S), x, p.62 (Fowler to Burghley, 4 May 1589).

41. Aboyne, p.511.

42. SM, iii, pp.213f. The eleventh marquis of Huntly and author of the Records of Aboyne thinks it dates from 1589 (p.511). We know that sometime before the end of May 1589 offence was caused by Lord Burleigh's letter blaming James for writing to Huntly (CSP(S), x, p.86 (Hudson to Walsingham 27 May 1589)). The letter above may be the cause of this rebuke. There are, however, other views: Francis Shearman maintains that its contents fit perfectly with a meeting between the King and Huntly on the road to Lauder on 24 October 1593 ('The Spanish Blanks,' pp.96f.), while Grant Simpson asserts without argument or evidence that it is 'an apparently secret letter of 1597' ('The Personal Letters of James VI' in *The Reign of James VI* edited by J. Goodare, pp.141-153, at pp.145f.).

43. CSP(S), x, pp.69f (Fowler to Burghley, 11 May 1589).

44. Caligula Mss D, i, fol. 392; *Aboyne*, p.512.

45. CSP(S), x, p.85 (Fowler to Burghley, 26 May 1589).

46. CSP(S), x, p.102 (Fowler to Walsingham, 14 June 1589).

47. *Sutherland*, p. 214

48. Grant was excommunicated for this 'abuse of the sacrament:' RPC, xiv, p.373 ('The names of Jesuits and Excommunicat Personis,' *c*.11 August 1590).

49. 17 September 1589: SM, ii, pp.278f.

50. On the important relationship between absentee landlords and their baillees, chamberlains, and sheriffs see Sanderson, *Scottish Rural Society in the Sixteenth Century*, chapter 3.

51. MM 2/3/226 & 227 (14 March 1589/90).

52. MM 2/3/229 (16 March 1589/90).

53. MM 2/3/232 (14 June 1589?).

54. MM 2/3/14 (Alexander Stewart, burgess of Elgin, writing to Archibald Stewart, one of Moray's servitors, complaining of injury done to him by a Scot, 'my Lord's officer.'

55. CSP(S), x, pp.196 (Ashby to Burghley and Walsingham, 18 November 1589); 259 (Bowes to Burghley, 24 March 1589/90);

56. CSP(S), x, p.839 (Bowes to Lord Treasurer and Walsingham, 3 February 1589/90).

57. MM 2/4/80.

58. *Sutherland*, p.214.

11. DISDAIN AND ENVY

1. RPC, iii, p.500 (Perth, 26 July 1582).

2. Decreet of Exemption, 20 January 1589/90, printed in Grant, iii, pp.176f.

3. MM 2/3/295 (12 April 1590).

4. MM 2/3/274 (John Grieg, 19 May 1590).

5. MM 2/3/227 (William Douglas to Moray, 14 March 1589/90); 2/3/230 (James Stewart to Moray, 14 March 1589/90).

6. RPC, iv, p.496 (Edinburgh, 24 June 1590); MM 2/3/295 (12 April 1590), 2/3/274 (19 May 1590), 2/3/287-8 (23 May 1590), 2/3/292 (23 May 1590), 2/3/57 (27 May 1590); Brown, p.151.

7. MM 2/3/249 (James VI to Moray, 30 June 1590).

8. CSP(S), x, p.300 (Bowes to Burghley, 23 May 1590).

9. CSP(S), x, p.303 (Burghley to Bowes, 30 May 1590).

10. CSP(S), x, pp.xviii, 334ff., 351 (Bowes to Burghley, 29 June, 11 July 1590).

11. CSP(S), x, p.317 (Instructions, 10 June 1590).

12. CSP(S), x, p.392 (Bowes to Burghley, 4 September 1590).

13. CSP(S), x, pp.347, 351, 443 (Bowes to Burghley, 4 and 11 July and 26 December 1590).

14. MM 2/3/304 (William Stewart to Moray, 4 August 1590).

15. *Chronicles*, p.211.

16. MM 2/3/292 (late August 1590).

17. 1 November 1590, contract in the charter chest of Grant of Monymusk: Gregory, p.248; SM, ii, pp.93f reproduces the same document but attributes it to 5 November 1590; RPC, iv, pp.569f. (Holyrood, 23 January 1590/1) gives Huntly's account.

18. Leslie, pp.246f; *Sutherland*, p.214.

19. *Chronicles*, p.212.

20. *Sutherland*, p.215.

21. RPC, iv, pp.569-70 (Holyrood, 23 January 1590/1).

22. Grant, iii, pp.176-79 at p.178.

23. Moysie, p.85; CSP(S), x, pp.428, (Bowes to Burghley, 7 December 1590); 434 (Aston to Hudson, 7 December 1590).

24. MM 2/3/296 (26 November 1590); 283 (17 December 1590).

25. CSP(S), x, p.431 (Maitland to Burghley, 7 December 1590).

26. CSP(S), x, p.428 (Bowes to Burghley, 7 December 1590).

27. RPC, iv, p.570 (Holyrood, 23 January 1590/1).

28. CBP, i, p.376 (Bowes to Hunsdon, 13 February 1590/1).

29. RPC, iv, p.570 (Holyrood, 23 January 1590/1).

30. CSP(S), x, p.437 (Bowes to Burghley, 18 December 1590).

31. CSP(S), x, p.460 (Bowes to Burghley, 13 February 1590/1).

32. CBP, i, p.376 (Bowes to Hunsdon, 13 February 1590/1).

33. CSP(S), x, p.452 (Bowes to Burghley 25 January 1590/1).

34.	CSP(S), x, pp.456-7 (Bowes to Burghley, 3 February 1590/1).

35.	Grant, iii, pp.176-9; Gregory, p.248: Ms History of Camerons.

36.	Gregory, pp.248, 250.

37.	See Chapter 13.

38.	CSP(S), x, p.469 (Bowes to Burghley, 23 February 1591).

39.	CBP, i, p.376 (Bowes to Hunsdon, 13 February 1590/1); MM 2/3/296 (26 November 1590).

40.	RPC, iv, p.597 (Edinburgh, 16 March 1590/1); CSP(S), x, p.497 (Bowes to Burghley, 6 April 1591).

41.	Lee, Great Britain's Solomon, p.73.

42.	CSP(S), x, p.574 (Advertisement, 30 September 1591).

43.	MM 2/3/251 (27 May 1591).

44.	MM 2/3/252 (18 June 1591).

45.	MM 2/3/254 (18 June 1591); Brown, p.155. Brown erroneously states that despite this he was in Edinburgh three days later when he struck Huntly's servant in the Tolbooth: but that happened in January not June.

46.	MM 2/3/327 (Leslie to Moray, 12 Instant, likely to be 12 June 1591).

47.	MM 2/3/309 (Leslie to Moray, no date but likely to be after 12 June 1591).

48.	MM 2/3/327 ('12 Instant:' in view of the succeeding letter dated 17 June 1591 it must be 12 June 1591).

49.	MM 2/3/237 (Leslie to Moray, 7 August 1591?).

50.	MM 2/3/236 (Leslie to Moray, 17 June 1591?).

51.	CSP(S), x, p.541 (Bowes to Burghley, 6 July 1591); MM 2/3/155 (3 July 1591).

52.	CSP(S), x, p.550 (Bowes to Burghley, 31 July 1591).

53.	CSP(S), x, p.547 (Bowes to Burghley, 21 July 1591).

54.	CSP(S), x, p.557 (Bowes to Burghley, 6 August 1591).

55.	CSP(S), x, pp.586-7 (Bowes to Burghley, 10 November 1591). The document mentioning this meeting comes from November 1591, but the meeting itself, from the context, must have been held in August or early September 1591, prior to the grant of the Lieutenancy.

56.	CSP(S), x, pp.573f ('Advertisement from an Englishman in Berwick,' 30 September 1591)

57.	CSP(S), x, p.572 (Bowes to Burghley, 23 September 1591); Chronicles, p.213.

58.	MM 2/3/332, 361 (12 January 1591/2).

59.	RPC, iv, p.686, (Holyrood, 3 November 1591).

60.	CSP(S), x, pp.592 (Bowes to Burghley, 4 December 1591); 601 (Bowes to Burghley, 20 December 1591).

61.	CSP(S), x, pp.601 (Bowes to Burghley, 20 December 1591); 622, 625 (Bowes to Burghley, 15 and 26 January 1591/2).

62.	Melvil, Memoirs, p.364.

63.	CSP(S), x, p.611 (Hudson to Burghley, 31 December 1591).

64.	CBP, i, pp.390f. (Forster to Burghley, 4 January 1591/2); Moysie, p.87; Spottiswood, vi, p.387. Sutherland, p.216, suggests that Moray harboured Bothwell at Donnibristle!

65.	MM 2/3/356 (James Donaldson to Moray, 25 January 1591/2)

66.	CSP(S), x, p.637 (Bowes to Burghley, 13 February 1591/2).

67.	CSP(S), x, p.635 (Aston to Bowes, 10 February 1591/2).

68.	CSP(S), x, p.632 (Bowes to Burghley, 5 February 1591/2).

69.	It is commonly said that the Ochiltree involved was the 2nd and not the 3rd Baron. The date of death of the former is not known and is variously given as 1591 and 1593. SP says 'he died about 1592,' and that it was the third Lord Ochiltree who participated in the events leading to the death of Moray. The DNB, however, states that the second was 'certainly alive until 26 December 1593,' citing the Reg.Mag.Sig.Scot 1593-1608, no.33. The overwhelming probability is that the 2nd Baron died in late 1591 and was succeeded by his thirty-one-year- old grandson before Bothwell's raid on Holyrood House. The vigour with which Ochiltree acted in the desperate days to come indicates he was a young man in the full flush of youth, not an old man of seventy, nearing death.

70.   Knox, *Works*, ii, p.320.

71.   MM 2/3/356 (Andrew Abercrombie to Moray, 25 January 1591/2).

72.   Ibid.

73.   *Sext*, p.247.

74.   MM 2/3/356 (25 January 1591/2).

12. Fashion among the Best Sort

1.   CSP(S), iii, p.305 (Randolph to Sussex, 9 August 1570).

2.   CSP(S), x, p.68 (Fowler to Burghley, 10 May 1589).

3.   Spottiswood, vi, p.387.

4.   The 'old lady, his sisters and children' are mentioned in CSP(S), x, pp.635 (Aston to Bowes, 10 February 1591/2); 641 (Bowes to Burghley, 17 February 1591/2); MM 2/4/58 (3 June 1592). According to the present Lord Moray there is a family tradition that his mother was not present and came down from Darnaway only after the murder. This is unlikely given the distance and her immediate action on her dead son's behalf. She may have been at Doune, however.

5.   M. Meickle, 'Lairds and Nobility,' pp.77f; 'Sixteenth Century Border Lairds,' pp.17f., 21, 26ff; *Atlas of Scottish History*, p.71; John Warrack, *Domestic Life in Scotland*, p.105.

6.   *Aberdour Castle Guide*, HMSO; Elizabeth Beaton, *Scotland's Traditional Houses*, pp.49-57; Nigel Tranter, *The Fortified House*, ii, p.144; On L-plan Tower Houses see J. Zeune, 'Perfecting the Tower House' in *Fortress*, 10 August 1991 pp.24-30.

7.   CSP(S), x, p. 635 (Aston to Bowes, 8 February 1591/2); MM 2/4/59.

8.   MM 2/3/356 (25 January 1591/2).

9.   CSP(S), x, p.640 (Bowes to Burghley, 17 February 1591/2).

10.   Moysie, p.89.

11.   Moysie, p.87.

12.   CSP(S), xi, pp.256f. (A Catalogue of Noblemen, 1594); RPC, v, p. 49 (Aberdeen, 9 March 1592/3). The 'Papists' included Sir Patrick Gordon of Auchindoun, Thomas Gordon of Cluny, William Gordon, the fifth laird of Gight and James Gordon the master of Lesmour. Others present were Gight's brother Captain John Gordon, and nephew Johnnie Chalmers, the son of his sister Margaret and her husband Alexander Chalmers; John Gordon of Buckie; William Gordon of the Craig of Auchindore; John Gordon the younger of Carnburrow and his brother George Gordon; Patrick Gordon of Letterfoury; Patrick Gordon of Corrachrie and his brother George Gordon; John Gordon the younger of Auchannachie; John Gordon of Altounhois; and George Gordon of Crechie. The others listed were all blood relations, retainers or servants: Norman Leslie; Robert Innes of Innermarky and his servants, James Lorymer and Alexander Chalmer; John Vans of Lochslyne; John Ross; John Drummond; Andrew Wood; John Edmonstoun; Robert Dalgleish; William Borthwick,

master stabler to Huntly; James Mowbray; James Borthwick at the Bridgend of Haillis; and William Morrison. The CSP(S), xii, p.453 adds another: Lord Moncoffer.

13. John Bulloch, *The House of Gordon*, pp.38-40.

14. MM 2/3/93 (Decreet for the trial of Robert Innes of Innermarkie, 15 July 1595). Moysie, p.88. MM 2/4/58 (Supplication to the King by James third Earl of Moray, 3 June 1592).

15. A&D, p.294.

16. HFG, ii, p. 57; Rampini, p.160.

17. HFG, ii, p.57; CSP(S), x, p.641(Bowes to Burghley, 17 February 1591/2); xi, p.179 (Bowes to Burghley, 21 September 1593).

18. CSP(S), x, p.639 (Bowes to Burghley, 13 February 1591/2); xi, p.179 (Bowes to Burghley, 21 September 1593). Leslie was later apprehended at Aberdeen.

19. CSP(S), x, pp.638, 641(Bowes to Burghley, 13 and 17 February 1591/2).

20. CSP(S), x, pp.633 (Aston to Hudson, 9 February 1591/2); 641 (Bowes to Burghley, 17 February 1591/2); Moysie, p.90; Birrell, p.26. There is some confusion as to the precise identity of this self-sacrificing official. In the numerous contemporary and near contemporary accounts he is usually referred to as the 'Sheriff of Moray,' but not always. In the Decreet of 20 January 1590, printed in Grant, iii, p.176, mention is made of 'Patrick Dunbar of Boigholl, tutor of Cumnock and sheriff wardatour of Moray.' Birrel, pp.26 and 34, refers to Patrick Dunbar as 'the sheriff of Moray,' but on the following page calls him the 'tutor to the sheriff of Moray.' To further confuse the matter, it is possible that the odd name 'Boeg' is not a separate individual but rather a corruption of the place-name Boigholl, the locality associated with Patrick Dunbar.

21. SM, ii, p.66.

22. *Sutherland*, p.214; Birrell, pp.26f; Calderwood, v, p.144. Calderwood was a student at Edinburgh University from 1590 to 1593, and so would have been in the city – it being term time – when the Earl was murdered: Alan Macdonald, 'David Calderwood: the not so hidden years, 1590-1604,' SHR, lxxiv, 1995, pp.69-74.

23. CSP(S), x, pp.633 (Aston to Hudson, 9 February 1591/2); 635 (Bowes to Burghley with enclosure from Aston to Bowes, 10 February 1591/2).

24. *Sutherland*, p.214.

25. CSP(S), x, p.655 (Bowes to Burghley, 18 March 1591/2).

26. Ian Olson in 'Just how was the Bonny Earl of Moray killed?' in *The Ballad in Scottish History*, edited by E.J.Cowan, 2000, pp.36-53, erroneously states that Buckie could not be the assassin since he had been mortally wounded by this time. The Captain John Gordon who had been so injured was not John Gordon of Buckie but the brother of Gordon of Gight.

27. Spottiswood, vi, p.387; *Sutherland*, p.214; Robert Chambers, *Life of James I*, i, p.182. Chambers in his *Domestic Annals*, i, p.134 gives an account of another murder in 1580 in which the leader of the party of assassins was compelled by his followers to stab the corpse of the victim so that he could not disclaim responsibility later on.

28. A Moray family tradition repeated in Percy's *Reliques*, ii, p.226, Scott's *Tales of Grandfather*, ch.xxxiii; and Ballingall's *The Shores of Fife*, p.39.

29. Calderwood, v, p.144.

30. Recently a medical doctor, Ian Olson, op.cit., has argued – unconvincingly – that Moray may in fact have been murdered in his bed. Such a scenario, he argues, gains support from the B version of the Ballad (see Appendix 7) and would explain the wounds as being delivered to a body curled on its side,

and unprotected by armour. However the wounds as depicted indicate a slash to the leg which would not likely be armoured, and bullet wounds which could be inflicted through a 'jack,' if in fact the Earl was wearing one. The slash wounds to the face, parallel as they are, are consistent with the contemporary account of how the dying Earl was mutilated. The time of day makes it very unlikely that the young Moray was asleep. No account supports the hypothesis that Moray was murdered in his bed, and the Memorial in an inset depicts his body lying on the beach fully clothed.

31.   CSP(S), x, p.639 (Bowes to Burghley, 13 February 1591/2).
32.   MM 2/4/93 (15 July 1595).
33.   CSP(S), x, p.635 (Bowes to Burghley, 10 February 1591/2).
34.   MM 2/4/58 (Supplication by the third Earl of Moray, 3 June 1592); CP, v, 'Doune,' p.444.
35.   *Acts of the Parliament of Scotland*, iii, p.628 ('Ratification to the Earl of Moray of his supersedere,' granted by King James, 27 May 1592).
36.   Calderwood, v, p.145.

13. EXECUTION DONE ON CAWDOR

1.   Shakespeare, *MacBeth* Act 1, scene 4. The name 'Cawdor' is sometimes written as 'Calder.' I have kept the spelling 'Cawdor' throughout.
2.   CSP(S), xi, p.338 (Bowes to Burghley, 18 May 1594).
3.   CSP(S), viii, p.109 (Wotton to Walsingham, 22 September 1585).
4.   Cawdor was born in 1541 and is buried at Ardchattan Priory.
5.   CSP(S), x, pp.633f., 642 (Bowes to Burghley, 10 February and 17 February 1591-2).
6.   CSP(S), xi, p.338 (Bowes to Burghley, 18 May 1594). Cawdor was related by marriage to Moray, having married the sister-in-law of the Good Regent.
7.   Gregory, p.246.
8.   Cawdor, p.12.
9.   Gregory, p.247.
10.   Ibid, pp.244-254.
11.   HP, i, p.180; Cawdor, p.35.
12.   CSP(S), x, p.684 (Bowes to Burghley, 6 June 1592).
13.   The confession and inquisition can be found in HP, i, pp.175-189; Cawdor, pp.31-43.
14.   HP, i, pp.175-6; Cawdor, p.31.
15.   HP, i, pp.189-193; Cawdor, pp.4, 45-48.
16.   HP, i, pp.159-175; Cawdor, p.49-60.
17.   HP, i, pp.193-4; Cawdor, p.74.
18.   On 28 March 1593 John and James Buchanan of Drumford with a band or retainers and ruffians ambushed Ardkinglas but killed Duncan Campbell mistaking him for the laird. See Cawdor, pp.28f; Pitcairn's *Criminal Trials*, i, pp.285ff., and HP, i, p.148.
19.   HP, i, pp.184f.; Maurice Lee, *Maitland*, pp.241f., adds a healthy note of scepticism.

14. 'THE HORROR OF DINNIBIRSALL'

1.   CSP(S), x, p.636. (Aston to Bowes, 8 February 1591-2).
2.   A&D, p.294.

3.   Moysie, p.89.

4.   CSP(S), x, p.637 (Bowes to Burghley, 13 February 1591/2).

5.   CSP(S), x, p.640 (Bowes to Burghley, 17 February 1591-2).

6.   Moysie, p.90.

7.   A story recounted in Scott's *Tales of a Grandfather*.

8.   CSP(S), x, p.636 (Aston to Bowes, 10 February 1591-2).

9.   CSP(S), x, p.641 (Bowes to Burghley, 17 February 1591/2); Calderwood, v, p.145; Moysie, p.90.

10.   Moysie, pp.90f.

11.   Moysie, p.90; Calderwood, v, p.146; CSP(S), x, p.641 (Bowes to Burghley, 17 February 1591/2).

12.   A&D, p.294.

13.   It was another irony in this story that John Stewart, one of Moray's younger brothers, was to be tried 1609 for the 'hamesucken and murder under trust' of John Gibb in Over Lassodie. He confessed and was sentenced to be beheaded. James VI refused to reprieve him. (SP, iii, 'Stewart, Lord Doune,' p.189).

14.   Calderwood, v, p.145.

15.   John Row, *The History of the Kirk of Scotland from the year 1558 to August 1637*, Aberdeen, 1650, p.144. The Church, the King failing, would ever more desperately take the law into its own hands so far as its ordinances could. As late as June 1592 the General Assembly meeting in Edinburgh would authorise the presbytery of Brechin, with the concurrence of the presbyteries of Angus and Mearns, to proceed against Huntly 'for the said cruel act according to the acts of the Assemblie.' (Session 22, 6 June 1592, Acts and Proceedings of the General Assemblies of the Kirk of Scotland from the year 1560, Edinburgh, 1840, pp.789ff.)

16.   CSP(S), x, pp.637 (Bowes to Burghley, 13 February 1592); 641(Bowes to Burghley, 17 February 1591/2); 648 (Aston to Bowes, 27 February 1592); RPC, iv, p.725 (Edinburgh, 8 February 1591/2).

17.   CSP(S), xi, p.165 ('State of Scotland, 1593'); MM 1/1/202 (23 March 1592/3 and 15 November 1592).

18.   Tytler, iii, p.247.

19.   Buchanan, *History*, ii, p.225. MacDougall, *James IV*, p.64.

20.   Brown,, p.29.

21.   Calderwood, v, pp.142-3.

22.   *Sext*, pp.296-7; Spottiswoode, iii, pp.445f; Calderwood, v, p.256; Brown, p.29.

23.   CSP(S), x, 641 (Bowes to Burghley, 17 February 1591/2).

24.   Calderwood, v, p.145.

25.   Ibid. See Appendix 5.

26.   A&D, p.294.

27.   Balfour, *Annals*, i, p.390.

28.   Lee, *Great Britain's Solomon*, p.74.

29.   Cowan, 'Calvinism and the Survival of Folk,' p.46; Henderson, 'The Ballad, the Folk and the Oral Tradition,' p.277; see Appendix 6.

30.   CSP(S), x, p.636 (Aston to Hudson, 11 February 1591/2).

31.   CSP(S), x, p.654 (Bowes to Burghley, 11 March 1591/2)

32.   CSP(S), x, p.648 (Bowes to Burghley, 27 February 1591/2).

33.   Calderwood, v, p.147.

34.   CSP(S), x, p.648 (Aston to Bowes, 27 February 1591/2).

35.   CSP(S), x, p.701 (Bowes to Burghley, 17 June 1592).

36.   Calderwood, v, pp.146f. This letter does read as though it were from one conspirator to another. But Calderwood gives neither date nor source, the original is not extant, nor does Huntly's name appear in what must be an extract from a longer missive.

37.   CSP(S), x, p.645 (Bowes to Burghley, 27 February 1591/2).

38.   McIvor, 'Artillery and Major Places of Strength' in *Scottish Weapons and Fortifications*, edited by David Caldwell, pp.128ff.

39.   See the reconstruction in *Blackness Castle*, HMSO, p.20.

40.   CSP(S), x, p.656 (Bowes to Burghley, 18 March 1591/2).

41.   RPC, iv, p.733 (Linlithgow, 8 March 1591/2).

42.   This passage from the Treasurer's Accounts is reproduced in David Laing's 'Notices' p.193.

43.   Text in Cawdor, pp.26f.

44.   CSP(S), x, p.655 (Bowes to Burghley, 18 March 1591/2).

45.   CSP(S), x, pp.654, 657 (Bowes to Burghley, 13 and 22 March 1591/2).

46.   For instance Sir Humphrey Colquhoune of Luss entered into a bond of manrent with Huntly, signing the bond at Blackness on 16 March 1591/2 (SM, iv, p.247).

47.   CSP(S), x, p.658 (Aston to Bowes, 22 March 1591/2).

48.   CSP(S), x, p.695 (Bowes to Burghley, 12 June 1592).

49.   Calderwood, v, p.148.

50.   Lee, *Maitland,* p.244. Lee comments that 'James's obsessive hatred of Bothwell thus betrayed him into the worst tactical blunder of his entire reign in Scotland.'

51.   CSP(S), x, p.659 (Aston to Bowes, 22 March 1591/2).

52.   So Calderwood, v, p.149. She may have died somewhat later since Bowes makes mention of her death for the first time in a letter to Burghley dated the 29 May 1592 (CSP(S), x, p.679).

53.   CSP(S), x, p.679 (Bowes to Burghley, 29 May 1592).

54.   MM 1/1/202 (15 November 1592); 12/43/195.

15. The First Puff of a Haggis

1.   'The first puff of a haggis, hottest at the first' – a contemporary insult indicating all bark and no bite.

2.   *Basilikon Doron,* in *Political Writings*, pp.28f.

3.   MM 2/4/58 (3 June 1592).

4.   CSP(S), x, p.688, 693 (Bowes to Burghley, 3 and 12 June 1592).

5.   CSP(S), x, p.700f. (Bowes to Burghley, 17 June 1592). Richard II was deposed and possibly murdered by his cousin Henry IV.

6.   CSP(S), x, p.725 (Bowes to Burghley, 16 July 1592).

7.   CSP(S), x, p.746 (Bowes to Burghley, 6 August 1592).

8.   CSP(S), x, pp.719, 741, 748, 760 (Bowes to Burghley, 4 July, 30 July, 6 August, 17 August 1592).

9.   Henry Gordon of Knock, Alexander Gordon of Toldow, and Henry Gordon of Blaircharsh: *Sutherland*, pp.217f.

10.   McClintock, *Old Irish and Highland Dress*, p.116.

11.   MM 2/4/180 (1602).

12.   CSP(S), xi, pp.165-6 (State of Scotland, *c.*August 1593).

13.   CSP(S), xi, p.91 (Bowes to Burghley, 20 May 1593).

14. *Aboyne,* pp.516f.

15. RPC, v, p.19 (Holyrood, 9 November 1592).

16. CSP(S), x, p.811(Bowes to Burghley, 11 November 1592); The Douglas Book, iii, pp.301- 9 (Commission of Lieutenancy by King James to Angus, 9 November 1592; Directions by James VI to Angus, November 1592; Memoir by the Lord Clerk Register for the Lord Lieutenant of the North, 10 November 1592; Letter by James VI to the Marchmont Herald, 9 November 1592).

17. *The Douglas Book*, iii, pp.310f (Engagement by Huntly to Athol and Mackintosh, 8 December 1592); iv pp.37f. (James VI to Angus, 28 and 30 November 1592).

18. CSP(S), x, p.828 (Bowes to Burghley, 1 January 1592/3).

19. Thomas Law, 'The Spanish Blanks and Catholic Earls, 1592-94,' in *Collected Essays and Reviews*, pp.244-276 at pp.261-268.

20. Ibid., p.248.

21. See the letters from Elizabeth I to James VI dated December 1592 and 1593 printed in *Illustrations of Scottish History*, pp.35-41.

22. CSP(S), xi, pp.72f. (Occurrents in Scotland, 19 March 1592/3).

23. CBP, i, p.462 (Carey to Burghley, 24 May 1593).

24. CSP(S), xi, pp.66 (Lord Burgh to Burghley, 6 March 1592/3); 90 (Bowes to Burghley, 20 May 1593); 172f. (Report of Bowes, *c*.15 September 1593); 179 (Bowes to Burghley, 21 September 1593).

25. On 14 May 1593. CSP(S), xi, pp.90 & 94 (Bowes to Burghley, 20 and 28 May 1993); 143 (Bowes to Burghley, 11 August, 1593).

26. Jenny Brown in A.G.R. Smith, *James VI*, p.27.

27. CSP(S), xi, pp.89, 91, 94 (Bowes to Burghley, 8, 20, and 28 May 1593).

28. CSP(S), xi, p.199 (Bowes to Burghley, 12 October 1593).

29. CSP(S), xi, pp.89 & 91 (Bowes to Burghley, 8 and 20 May 1593).

30. CBP, i, p.475 (Carey to Burghley, 18 July 1593).

31. The trial took place on 10 August 1593; 'Richy' was executed: CSP(S), xi, pp.142-3 (Bowes to Burghley, 11 August, 1593); CBP, i, pp.486ff. (Carey to Burghley, 12 August 1593).

32. Sir Robert Melvil was the brother of Sir James Melvil of Halhill, and treasurer-depute of Scotland. CSP(S), xi, p.145 (Bowes to Burghley, 16 August 1593). For this precise wording, see Tytler, iii, p. 260.

33. CBP, i, pp.489 (Carey to Burghley, 12 August 1593); 498 (Carey to Burghley, 13 September 1593); CSP(S), xi, pp.176, 180 (Bowes to Burghley, 15 and 21 September 1593).

34. CBP, i, pp.498 (Forster to Burghley, 16 September 1593); 506 (Carey to Burghley, 16 October 1593); CSP(S),xi, pp.232f, 235 (Bowes to Burghley, 30 November and 2 December 1593); Tytler, iii, p.268.; Letter from Elizabeth to James, 22 December 1593, printed in *Illustrations of Scottish History*, pp.41-45.

35. CBP, i, pp.541 (Carey to Cecil, 18 July 1594); 543 (Carey to Burghley, 10 August 1594); Law, 'The Spanish Blanks,' p.275. The Act of Secret Council, 23 July 1594 is cited in Tytler, iii, p.274. Argyll's Commission of Justiciary to pursue the earls was dated 15 July 1594.

36. SRO GCM , GD 44/13.9.2; SM, iv, p.249.

37. CSP(S), xi, p.451 (Bowes to Burghley, 24 September 1594).

16. A Gowk's Storm

1. A storm in a teacup. A gowk is a Scots word for cuckoo. A brief spring storm coinciding with the arrival of the cuckoo.

2. FN, p.150. The battle of Glenlivet, sometimes called Alltacoileachan, Strathaven or Balrinnes, and its prelude and aftermath were reported by two or three eyewitnesses:

i.   The English ambassador had in his possession a statement by John Torre, the servant boy of James Kerr, Huntly's retainer.

ii. A participant in Huntly's force also recorded the events in the anonymous, 'A Faithful Narrative of the Great and Miraculous Victory at Strathavon.'

iii. In addition the anonymous *Account of the Battle of Balrinnes* may have originated in another eyewitness account again from the perspective of Huntly.

3. ABB, p.261. On the extraordinary nature of the Campbell's power see Jane Dawson, 'The Fifth Earl of Argyll,' SHR, lxvii, April 1988, pp.1-27.

4. CSP(S), xi, p.449, 456 (Bowes to Burghley, 24 September and 7 October 1594); HFG, ii, p.82; ABB, p.270; Sext, p.338.

5. CSP(S), xi, pp.450ff (Bowes to Cecil, 24 and 28 September 1594); Tytler, iii, p.277.

6. £26 Scots.

7. FN, p.141.

8. ABB, p.269.

9. FN, p.143. Serva Iugum is the Hay family motto meaning 'Keep the Yoke.'

10. *Sutherland*, p.227.

11. *Sutherland*, p.228; Sext, p.341.

12. ABB, p.263. An eyewitness said there were 200 horse in the van, 700 in the rear (FN, p.142). Spottiswood gave a figure of 900 men, Gordon 1,200.

13. FN, pp.146f.

14. For this impudence his son afterwards, according to tradition, lost a large estate in Lochaber through the animosity of Huntly.

15. Tytler, iii, p.279.

16. ABB, pp.267-9.

17. Ibid; FN, p.148; Calderwood, v, p.350.

18. FN, p.149; Sext, pp.341f; ABB, p.270; A&D, p.318.

19. CSP(S), xi, p.458 (Bowes to Cecil, 8 October 1594).

20. FN, p.151.

21. *The Black Book of Taymouth* cited in Cawdor, p.22.

22. CSP(S), xi, p.469 (Bowes to Cecil, 29 October 1594).

23. A&D, p.318.

24. Ibid., p.319.

25. CBP, i, p.551 (Carey to Cecil, 18 November 1594).

26. William Gordon relates that Burnet in his manuscript history stated that in 1689 he had seen 'among the family papers a private remission from the King to Huntly for Glenlivet, granted the same year as it was fought and before Lennox left Aberdeen.' (HFG, ii, p.86)

17. THE BRIGHTEST JEWEL

1. Letter to Fr Claude Aquaviva in Narratives, p.231.

2. Spalding, p.73.

3. CSP(S), xii, p.570 (Advertisements from Edinburgh, 5 April 1595).

4. Tytler, iii, p.314; CSP(S), xiii, p.162 (Scottish Advices sent to Lord Scrope, 2 February 1597/8)

5. CSP(S), xii, pp.306, 387f f. (Instruction by Bowes to George Nicholson, 14 December 1596); Moysie, p.127.

6. CBP, ii, p.111 (Eure to Burghley, 28 February 1595/6); p.185 (Eure to Sir John Stanhope, 7 September 1596); CSP(S), xii, p.347 (Bowes to Burghley, 20 October 1596).

7. Tytler, iii, p.298.

8. Letter from James VI to Huntly. It is dated 2 October 1597 but as Huntly was reconciled to the Kirk in June 1597 it must be 1596. It is printed in *Illustrations of Scottish History*, pp.51-53. Tytler, iii, p.308.

9. *Analecta Scotica*, pp.102f; LSP, pp.29ff. The letter is dated the 'penult of December.' No year is given but it is attributed to 1596. Errol wrote in similar terms the following month (LSP, p.31).

10. *Acts and Proceedings of the General Assemblies of the Kirk*, 3 vols, edited by T. Thompson, Edinburgh, 1839, ii, p.897; iii, p.919. CSP(S), xii, p.550 (14 May 1597).

11. T. Mollisone's letter of 28 or 29 June 1597 to R. Paip, *Analecta Scotica, Collections illustrative of the Civil, Ecclesiastical, and Literary History of Scotland chiefly from original mss*, edited by J. Maidment, Edinburgh, 1834 p.299.

12. Fr Gordon's letter to Fr Claude Aquaviva in Narratives, pp.233f.

13. CSP(S), xiii, p.161 (Scottish Advices sent to Lord Scrope, 2 February 1597/8).

14. Birrel, p.34. The names of those involved in the murder of Moray in the Register of the Privy Council include Robert Innes of Innermarky and his servants James Lorymer and Alexander Chalmer, but there is no mention of a James Innes (RPC, v, p.49 (Aberdeen, 9 March 1592/3)). The laird is most likely Robert, the name James having been mistakenly transferred from the servant to the master. There is, however, no reason to doubt Birrel's account that some participants suffered belatedly for their role in the murder. By contrast remission was granted to James Gordon, heir of Lesmour, 'pro arte et parte proditoriae loci Dunybersill combustionsi et morthuri quondam Jacobi Comitis Moraviae:' RPS, xxxviii, no.355.

15. RPC, v, p.444 (Holyrood, 16 February 1597/8).

16. Calderwood, v, p.145. CP supports this view citing the RPC, iv, p.726 note (Edinburgh, 9 February 1591/2), but this note merely asserts the wishes of Lady Margaret and not, after her death, the fate of his body.

17. See Appendix 8.

18. Balfour, cited in Boucher, *The Kingdom of Fife*, p.99.

19. Calderwood, v, pp.681f.

18. BEQUEST OF HATRED

1. Glamis is reported to have used these words of King James when he was detained by the Ruthven raiders (Tytler, iii, p.134).

2. Jenny Wormald, 'Bloodfeud, Kindred and Government in Early Modern Scotland,' *Past and Present*, 87 [1980], pp.54-97, at pp.85f.

3. The Earl of Strathmore, quoted in Donaldson, *Scotland: James V-VII*, p.396.

4. CSP(S), xiii, p.489 ('Answers of King James VI to the Propositions submitted to him by Sir William Bowes,' 31 May 1599). The promise was made to the Duke of Lennox on the marriage of his sister to the then Earl of Huntly in 1588.

5. CSP(S), xiii, pp.450f, (Nicolson to Cecil, 20 April).

6. For instance, when, at the parliament of 1600, the new marquis demanded precedence over the Earl of Angus: CBP, ii, pp.708,712 & 718 (Willoughby to Cecil, 8 and 16 November and 12 December 1600).

7. RPC, vi, pp.290f. (Edinburgh, 2 October 1601); HFG, ii, p.97.

8. RPC, vi, p.296 (Brechin, 17 October 1601).

9. CSP(S), xiii, pp.895 & 596 (Nicolson to Cecil, 6 November 1601).

10. CSP(S), xiii, p.961 (Douglas to Cecil, 26 March 1602).

11. GM, GD 44/33/2.

12. CSP(S), xiii, pp.1106, 1110f. (Nicolson to Cecil, 1 and 9 February 1602/3).

13. William Fraser, *The House of Forbes*, pp.152f.

14. CSP(S), xiii, p.852 (Douglas to Cecil, July 1601).

15. RPC, x, pp.561-4 (Edinburgh, 9 July 1616); Calderwood, vii, p.218; Spottiswood, iii, pp.230-235.

16. 'The Portrait of True Loyalty, exposed in the family of Gordon,' MS Advocates' Library, p.417.

17. *Sutherland*, pp.231 & 480.

18. RPC, 2nd Series, ii, pp.495-507 (Holyrood, 27 November and 2 December 1628).

19. RPC, 2nd Series, iii, p.332 (Holyrood, 3 November 1629).

20. RPC, 2nd Series, iv, p.71 (Holyrood, 25 November 1630).

21. CSP(I), 1625-1632, p.582 (Rawdon to Conway, 24 October 1630).

22. Ibid.

23. *Sutherland Book*, p.467.

24. Spalding, p.37.

25. RPC, 2nd Series, v, p.507ff. (Edinburgh, 12 March 1635).

26. RPC, 2nd Series, vi, p.211f. (Edinburgh, 21 March 1536).

27. Spalding, p.39.

28. Ibid., p.54.

19. PACIFICUS

1. *James VI, Basilicon Doron,* p.28.

2. See *Darnley* by Caroline Bingham, chapter 8.

3. Calderwood, v, p.147.

4. Much of this analysis was inspired by and concurs with that of J.M. Wormald. See her Lords and Men, p.121, and 'Scottish Politics 1567-1625' *in Smith, The Reign of James VI and I*, pp.27f (under the name Jenny Brown).

5. Keith Brown, 'The Nobility of Jacobean Scotland,'in S*cotland Revisited*, edited by J.M. Wormald, London, 1991, pp.61-72, at 62.

Appendix 2 – The Ballad of the Battle of Corrichie

1.   Stephen Ree, *The Gordon Ballads*, 1907, p.40. Finlay, *Scottish Ballads*, i, 1808, p.153. Michael Brander, *Scottish and Border Battles and Ballads*, 1975.

appendix 5 – The Moray Memorial

1.   Tytler, iii, p.4.
2.   Birrell, p.10.
3.   Thompson, *Painting in Scotland,* p.19.
4.   CSP(S), iii, pp.92f (Randolph to Cecil, 1 March 1570).
5.   Sext, pp.346-7.
6.   CBP, ii, p.538 (Bowes to Burghley, 5 June 1598).
7.   Brown, p.30; 'A House Divided,' p.184; Pitcairn, Kennedy, p.68.
8.   RPC, vi, pp.346-50, 665-7, 718; Brown, 'A House Divided,' p.185.
9.   Accounts, viii, pp.141-5; Marshall, *Mary of Guise*, pp.106f; Dana Bentley-Cranch, 'Effigy and Portrait,' p.11.
10.   Bentley-Cranch, 'Effigy and Portrait,' pp.14f.
11.   Waterhouse, *Painting in Britain 1530-1790*, p.29.
12.   SRO, Register of Deeds, 1/24/9, xliii, no.104; James Holloway, *Painting in Scotland 1570-1650*, SNPG Catalogue, 'Works by Unidentified Painters 1592-1623,' p.34.
13.   Percy, *Reliques*, ii, p.210.

APPENDIX 6 – The Ballad of the Bonnie Earl of Moray

1.   A&D, p.198.
2.   John Finlay, *Scottish Historical and Romantic Ballads*, ii, pp.19ff. Finlay thinks that both ballads are coeval with the event they commemorate and may at one time have been united. Most recently but not convincingly, Ian Olson has argued the case in 'The Dreadful Death of the Bonny Earl of Murray,' 1997, and in 'Just how was the Bonny Earl of Moray killed?' in *The Ballad in Scottish History*, edited by E.J. Cowan.
3.   Allan Ramsay, *Tea Table Miscellany*, 10th edn, iv, 1740, p.356; Norval Clyne, *The Romantic Scottish Ballads*, 1859, p.27.
4.   F.J. Child, T*he English and Scottish Popular Ballads*, iii, p.447.
5.   Volume ii, song 4. *The Orpheus Caledonius* is subtitled 'A Collection of the Best Scotch Songs set to Musick' and was first published in 1725 (Stenhouse, Illustrations, p.xxviii). These editions were privately printed for the author and are not easy to find. Neither the British Library nor the Cambridge University Library has copies, and the only ones held in the United Kingdom are in the Wighton Collection of Dundee Central Library. It has both the first and second editions.
6.   Thomas Percy, *Reliques*, i, pp.xii, xxix.
7.   David Laing, *Notes to Johnson's Scots Musical Museum*, 1839; Robert Chambers, *Romantic Scottish Ballads*, 1859. Percy was the first to make the connection, in the second edition of the *Reliques*, in 1767. There is a suspicion that they may at one period have been united owing to the same peculiarity of metre and the similarity of some verses. The second stanza of Young Waters is very like the last of The Bonnie Earl:

> The queen looked over the castle wa',
>
> Beheld baith dale and down,
>
> And then she saw Young waters
>
> Come riding to the town.

8. Harvard University Library, William Tytler Brown MS, letters of 19 January 1793, and 21 April 1800, cited in extenso in Buchan, *The Ballad and the Folk* pp.63f-66. See also Robert Chambers, *Romantic Scottish Ballads*, p.34, and Norval Clyne, *The Romantic Scottish Ballads*, p.33.

9. A Garner-Medwin, 'Views of King and People in Sixteenth and Seventeenth Century Ballads' in *Bryght Lanternis* edited by J.D.McLure, pp.24-32.

10. Henderson, 'The Ballad and Popular Tradition to 1660,' in *The History of Scottish Literature*, edited by R.D.S.Jack, i, pp.263-283, especially pp.272-277.

11. Cowan, 'Calvinism and the Survival of Folk' in *The People's Past*, p.50. He also thinks that The burning of the bonnie House of Airlie while thought to refer to an incident in 1640 may refer to one in 1591.

12. James Porter, *The Ballad Image*, p.68.

13. Moysie, p.24.

14. Brother Kenneth, 'Popular Literature of the Scottish Reformation,' in *Essays On the Scottish Reformation*, edited by David McRoberts, p.180.

15. CSP(S), iii, pp.65-66 (Ballads on the Murder of the Regent Moray, January-February 1570); Froude, *History*, ix, pp.82-85n, pp.584-86.

16. HHDA , p.155; Norval Clyne, *The Romantic Ballads*, p.40.

17. So Edward Cowan, 'Calvinism and the Survival of Folk' in *The People's Past* edited by E.J.Cowan, pp.32-57, passim. Hamish Henderson, 'The Ballad and Popular Tradition to 1660,' in *The History of Scottish Literature*, edited by R.D.S.Jack, i, p. 277.

Appendix 7 – The Ballad Annotated

1. A conventional opening to many a Scots ballad. Olson believes that they are an eighteenth century creation probably by William Thomson himself since no one would willingly have linked Highlands and Lowlands in sixteenth century Scotland' ('The Dreadful Death,' p.297.) One need only look the mourning mountains and weeping valleys of the ballad lamenting the first Earl of Moray to give lie to this assertion.

2. A grassy spot. Not very accurate when he was killed on the beach, but a rhyme. In the Memorial Moray's body is lying on the ground, which when originally painted was green.

3. A brave, splendid, handsome young stud.

4. Riding at the Ring was a form of quintain or tilting in which each of a number of riders endeavoured to impale and carry off a hoop or ring of metal which was suspended from a post and held in a sheath by two springs. The force of an accurate stroke would easily draw it out on the tip of the lance. (Joseph Strut, *The Sports and Pastimes of the People of England*, London 1838, pp.112-123, Robert Fittis, *Sports and Pastimes of Scotland*, London, 1891, pp.204-207). King James was a notable and eager participant in this sport. He participated at the Earl's own wedding, when it may be that the bridegroom took first run at the target (Ibid., p.119).

5. This is without foundation and suggests that the verse is a later addition.

6. Playing at the ball was a popular pastime in the sixteenth century, so popular that it was banned at

one time for interfering with archery practice. The modern distinction between football and handball did not have had much meaning in Jacobean times. Lack of rules was not just a quirk of local 'friendly matches,' it was the norm in great set pieces. An annual contest was played on holiday either at New Year or Shrove Tuesday in most of the towns and villages on the Scottish border in which up to a 100 youths would attempt by any means to put a leather ball in their opponent's goal. Such sport still persists to this day in Kirkwall the capital of Orkney. John Robertson, observes that 'after the ba' is thrown up it can be kicked, picked up or carried, and indeed a player can do just as he likes with it providing the opposition do not stop him,' *Uppies & Doonies*, p.6). It was a game played, now as then, by all classes. The fifth Earl of Huntly had died in such sport in 1576. In 1583 the Earl of Bothwell challenged the Master of Marischal to a duel over a foul during a game of football.

7.   Another game, either tilting at a glove, gambling on horses, or fighting to challenge, or even boxing. The first is the most likely: in a masque which James composed for the wedding of Huntly as a prelude to jousting in which he mentioned both 'glove or ring or any sport with spear.'(Lusus Regis, p.6; Robert Fittis, *Sports and Pastimes of Scotland*, London, 1891, pp.206f.)

8.   This is without foundation and suggests that the verse is a later addition.

9.   This would normally be his wife but she had been dead three months by the date of his murder. The balladeer may not of know this, or it may here refer to Lady Doune, his mother.

10.   This refers to the castle given into the charge of the father of the second Earl. Many other ballads have similar verses but there 'down' is a Scots word for 'rising ground:' As in Gil Morrice:

> The lady sat on the castle wa',
>
> Beheld baith dale and down,
>
> And there she saw Gil Morrice head
>
> Come trailing to the town.

Or Young Waters. See other examples in Norval Clyne, *The Romantic Scottish Ballads*, p.24.

11.   Riding with trumpets blowing.

12.   First printed in 1808 in John Finlay, *Scottish Historical and Romantic Ballads Chiefly Ancient*, ii, pp.19ff. Recently Ian Olson has made a valiant attempt to stitch this version and the A version into one whole. I find his conclusions unconvincing since the A version emerges in print separately from the B, and the B takes even more liberties with the historical record than its predecessor. I certainly do not think it provided any reliable evidence for the supposition that Moray was killed in his bed, rather than in attempt to escape. See Ian Olson, 'Just how was the Bonny Earl of Moray killed?' in *The Ballad in Scottish History*, edited by E.J. Cowan, pp.36-53.

13.   Oddly Huntly is depicted as visiting his brother-in-law, Moray. This may be an instance of the balladeer conflating the second and third Earl of Moray since the third Earl was son-in-law to the sixth Earl and first marquis of Huntly and brother-in-law to the future second marquis.

APPENDIX 8 – THE MORAY VAULT

1.   Robert Chambers, *Traditions of Edinburgh*, Edinburgh, 1868, pp.106f.

2.   David Laing, 'Notices,' p.194; William Ross, *Aberdour and Inchcolm*, p.387.

3.   Private Notes of the Moray Family: NRA GD50/149. There is a brief reference to Francis being buried between the Regent Moray and the Marquis of Montrose.

4.   William Chambers, *The Story of St Giles Cathedral Church*, Edinburgh, 1879, pp.33f; *Historical Sketch of St Giles*, 1895, pp. li-lii.

BIBLIOGRAPHY

I MUNIMENTS

Argyll Papers, Inveraray Castle.

Fraser-Mackintosh Collection, SRO, GD 128.

Gordon Castle Muniments, SRO, GD 44.

Hamilton Papers: Letters and papers illustrating the Political Relations of England and Scotland in the XVIth Century, 2 vols, edited by Joseph Bain, Edinburgh 1890 and 1892.

Mackintosh Muniments, SRO, GD 176.

Mackintosh Muniments, edited by Henry Paton, Edinburgh, 1903.

Moray Muniments, NRA, 217. These are referred to in the text by indicating the volume number, the box number, the document number, eg. letter from the Earl of Argyll: MM [volume]1/[Box]15/[document]140.

Report of the Royal Commission on Historical Mss, vi, Moray Ms, HMC, pp.634-673.

II PRINTED PRIMARY AND EARLY HISTORICAL WORKS

Account of the Battle of Balrinnes, 3 October 1594, in the Spottiswood Society Miscellany, edited by James Maidment, Edinburgh, 1844.

Accounts of the Lord High Treasurer of Scotland,
> Vol. VII (1538-1554), edited by Sir James Balfour Paul, Edinburgh, 1907.
> Vol. XI (1559-1566), edited by Sir James Balfour Paul, Edinburgh, 1916.
> Vol. XII (1566-1574), edited by C.T. McInnes, Edinburgh, 1970.

Accounts of the Masters of Works,
> Vol. I, 1529-1615, edited by H.M. Paton, Edinburgh, 1957.

Acts of the Parliament of Scotland 1124-1707, edited by Thomas Thomson and Cosmo Innes, London, 1814-75.

Acts and Proceedings of the General Assemblies of the Kirk, 3 vols, edited by T. Thompson, Edinburgh, 1839.

Adam, R.J., *The Calendar of Fearn: Texts and Additions 1471-1667*, Edinburgh, SHS, 1991.

Alumni Oxonienses: The Members of the University of Oxford 1500-1714, 4 volumes arranged by Joseph Foster, Oxford, 1891

Analecta Scotica: Collections illustrative of the Civil, Ecclesiastical, and Literary History of Scotland chiefly from original mss, edited by J. Maidment, Edinburgh, 1834.

An Historical Atlas of Scotland, edited by Peter McNeill and Ranald Nicolson, Edinburgh, 1975.

Atlas of Scottish History to 1707, edited by Peter McNeill and Hector MacQueen, Edinburgh 1996.

Balfour, Sir James, *Annals of Scotland, Manuscripts preserved in the Library of the Faculty of Advocates*, published as *The Historical Works*, 4 vols, London 1825.

Bannatyne, Robert, *Memorials of Transactions in Scotland*, edited by R Pitcairn, 1836.

Belfour, John, *A New History of Scotland*, London, 1770.

Birrel, Robert, *Diary 1532-1605*, in *Fragments of Scottish History*, edited by John G. Dalzell, 1798.

Buchanan, George, *The History of Scotland*, 1582, translated from the Latin by James Aikman, 2 vols, London, 1827-1829.

   The Tyrannous Reign of Mary Stewart, translated and edited by W.A. Gatherer, Edinburgh, 1958.

Calderwood, David, *History of the Kirk*, 8 vols, edited by T. Thompson, The Woodrow Society, Edinburgh, 1842-9.

Calendar of Border Papers,

   Vol. I (1550-1594), edited by Joseph Bain, Edinburgh, 1894.

   Vol. II (1595-1603), edited by Joseph Bain, Edinburgh, 1896.

Calendar of State Papers relating to Scottish Affairs.

   Vol. I (1547-1563), edited by Joseph. Bain, Edinburgh, 1898.

   Vol. II (1563–1569), edited by Joseph Bain, Edinburgh, 1900.

   Vol. III (1569-1571) edited by William Boyd, Edinburgh, 1903.

   Vol. IV (1571-1574) edited by William Boyd, Edinburgh, 1905.

   Vol. V (1574-1581) edited by William Boyd, Edinburgh 1907.

   Vol. VI (1581-1583) edited by William Boyd, Edinburgh, 1910.

   Vol. VII (1584-1585) edited by William Boyd, Edinburgh, 1913.

   Vol. VIII (1585-1586) edited by William Boyd, Edinburgh, 1914.

   Vol. IX (1586-1588) edited by William Boyd, Edinburgh, 1915.

   Vol. X (1589-1593) edited by William Boyd and H. Meikle, Edinburgh, 1936.

   Vol. XI (1593-1595) edited by Annie Cameron, Edinburgh, 1936.

   Vol. XII (1595-1597) edited by M.S.Giuseppi, Edinburgh, 1936.

   Vol. XIII pts 1 and 2 (1597-1603) edited by J.D.Mackie, Edinburgh, 1969.

Calendar of State Papers relating to Foreign Affairs.

   1561, edited by Joseph Stevenson, London, 1866.

   1562, edited by Joseph Stevenson, London, 1867.

   1566-68, edited by Allan James Crosby, London, 1871.

Calendar of State Papers relating to Ireland

   1625-1632, edited by Robert Mahaffy, London 1900.

Camden, William, *History of Queen Elizabeth*, edited by W.T.MacCaffrey, Chicago, 1970.

Certayne matters concerning the realm of Scotland, dated 1597, published London, 1603.

Chronicles of the Frasers or the True Genealogy of the Frasers 916-1574 by Master James Fraser, edited by William Mackay, Edinburgh, 1905.

Criminal Trials in Scotland from 1488 to 1624, edited by R.Pitcairn, Edinburgh, 1833.

Dalzell, Sir John Graham, *Fragments of Scottish History*, Edinburgh, 1798.

   Scottish Poems of the Sixteenth Century, Edinburgh, 1801.

A Diurnal of Remarkable Occurents in Scotland since the Death of King James IV till the Year MDLXXV, from a manu-script of the Sixteenth Century, edited by T. Thompson, Edinburgh, 1833.

Early Records of the University of St Andrews, edited by James Maitland Anderson, St Andrews, 1926.

Early Travellers in Scotland, edited by Peter Hume Brown, Edinburgh, 1891.

Edinburgh University Catalogue of Graduates, edited by D. Ian, Bannatyne Club, Edinburgh, 1858

Estimate of the Scottish Nobility During the Minority of James VI, edited by C. Rodgers, Grampian Club, London, 1873.

'A Faithful Narrative of the Great and Miraculous Victory at Strathavon' in *Scottish Poems of the Sixteenth Century*, edited by Sir Graham Dalzell, Edinburgh, 1801.

Fasti Aberdoniensis 1494-1854, The Spalding Club, Aberdeen, 1854.

Fasti Ecclesiae Scoticanae: The Succession of Ministers in the Church of Scotland since the Reformation, 5 vols., edited by Hew Scott, Edinburgh, 1925.

Fraser, William, *The Chiefs of Grant*, 3 vols, Edinburgh, 1883.

    The Douglas Book, 4 vols, Edinburgh, 1885.

    The Red Book of Menteith, 2 vols, Edinburgh, 1880.

    The Lennox, 2 vols, Edinburgh, 1874.

    The Sutherland Book, 3 vols, Edinburgh, 1892.

Gordon, Sir Robert, *Genealogical History of the Earldom of Sutherland*, Edinburgh, 1813.

Gordon, William, *History of the Family of Gordon*, 2 vols, Edinburgh, 1726-1727.

Highland Papers, 2 vols, edited by J.R.N. McPhail, Edinburgh, 1914.

Historical Account of the Principal Families of the Name of Kennedy, edited by Robert Pitcairn, Edinburgh, 1830.

Historie and Life of King James the Sext edited by Thomas Thomson, Bannatyne Club, Edinburgh, 1825.

History of the Feuds and Conflicts among the Clans in the Northern parts of Scotland from MXXXI-MDCXIX, written in the reign of James VI, first published by Messrs Foulis, Glasgow, 1764.

Holinshed, Raphaell, *The Chronicles of England, Scotland and Ireland*, 6 vols, edited by H. Ellis, London, 1807-8.

House of Forbes, edited by Alistair and Henrietta Taylor, Aberdeen,1937.

Hume, David, of Godscroft, *History of the Houses of Douglas and Angus,* 2 parts, London, 1644.

Illustrations of Scottish History (Sixteenth Century): Letters and Documents of Queen Mary, Queen Elizabeth, James VI, Bothwell etc from the Originals in the possession of Sir George Warrender, edited and arranged by Margaret Warrender, Edinburgh, 1889.

Inventiaires de la Royne d'Ecosse 1556-1569, edited by J. Robertson, Edinburgh, 1863.

James VI and I, *Political Writings*, edited by J.P.Sommerville, CUP, 1994.

James I by His Contemporaries, edited by Robert Ashton, London, 1969.

Keith, Robert, *History of the Affairs of Church and State to 1567*, 2 vols, edited by J.P. Lawson, Spottiswood Society, Edinburgh, 1844.

Knox, J, *Works*, edited by D. Laing, 1846-64.

    History of the Reformation in Scotland, 1587, 2 vols, translated and edited by W Croft Dickinson, Edinburgh, 1949.

Leslie, John, *Historie of Scotland*, 1578, 2 vols, edited by E.G.Cody and William Murison, Edinburgh, 1884-5.

Letters of Elizabeth and James VI, edited by J. Bruce, 1849.

Letters of King James VI & I, edited by G.P.V. Akrigg, California, 1984.

Letters of Mary Queen of Scots, 2 vols, edited by Agnes Strickland, London, 1844.

Letters and State Papers during the Reign of James the Sixth, chiefly from the manuscript collections of Sir James Balfour of Denmyln, Edinburgh, 1838.

Lindsay, Robert of Pitscottie, *History and Chronicles of Scotland*, Scottish Text Society, 2 vols, edited by A.J.G. Mackay, Edinburgh, 1899 & 1911.

Major, John, *History of Greater Britain*, 1521, edited and translated by Archibald Constable, 1892.

Mary, Queen of Scots, *Bittersweet within my Heart*, edited by Robin Bell, London, 1992.

Melvil, Sir James of Halhill, *Memoirs*, 3rd edn edited by George Scott, Glasgow, 1751.

Melville, James, *Autobiography and Diary*, edited by R. Pitcairn, Edinburgh, Woodrow Society, 1842.

Miscellany of the Spalding Club,

    Vol. II, *The Chronicles of Aberdeen, The Erroll Papers*, edited by John Stuart, Aberdeen 1842.

Vol. III, *The Gordon Letters 1568-1742; Articles of Agreement between Huntly and Moray 1569*, edited by John Stuart, Aberdeen, 1846.

Vol. IV, *The Rentaill of the Lordship of Huntly*, edited by John Stuart, Aberdeen, 1849.

Moysie, David, *Memoirs of the Affairs of Scotland from 1577 to 1603*, Bannatyne Club, Edinburgh, 1830.

Munimenta Alme Universitatis Glasguensis: Records of the University of Glasgow from its Foundation till 1727, 4 vols, edited by Cosmo Innes, Maitland Club, Glasgow, 1854.

Narratives of Scottish Catholics under Mary Stewart and James VI, edited by William Forbes-Leith, Edinburgh, 1885.

Patten, William, 'The Late Expedition into Scotland, 1544,' in Tudor Tracts 1532-1588, edited by A.F. Pollard, London, 1903, pp.39-51.

'The Expedition into Scotland, 1547,'op.cit., pp.54-158.

Records of Aboyne 1230-1681, edited by Charles, eleventh marquis of Huntly, Earl of Aboyne, The New Spalding Club, Aberdeen, 1894.

Register of the Great Seal of Scotland

Vol VIII (1593-1608), edited by John Maitland Thomson, Edinburgh, 1890.

Register of the Privy Council of Scotland.

Vol. I (1545-1569), edited by J.H.Burton, Edinburgh, 1877.

Vol. II (1569-78), edited by J.H.Burton, Edinburgh, 1878.

Vol. III (1578-1585), edited by David Masson, Edinburgh, 1880.

Vol. IV (1585-1592), edited by David Masson, Edinburgh, 1881.

Vol. V (1592-1599), edited by David Masson, Edinburgh, 1882.

Vol. VI (1599-1604), edited by David Masson, Edinburgh, 1884.

Vol. VII (1604-1607), edited by David Masson, Edinburgh, 1885.

Vol. VIII (1607-1610), edited by David Masson, Edinburgh, 1887.

Vol. IX (1611-1612), edited by David Masson, Edinburgh, 1889.

Vol. X (1613-1616), edited by David Masson, Edinburgh, 1891.

Vol. XI (1616-1619), edited by David Masson, Edinburgh, 1894.

Vol. XII (1619-1622), edited by David Masson, Edinburgh, 1895.

Vol. XIII (1622-1625), edited by David Masson, Edinburgh, 1896.

Vol. XIV (Addenda 1545-1625), edited by David Masson, Edinburgh, 1898.

2nd Series

Vol. I (1625-1627), edited by David Masson, Edinburgh, 1899.

Vol. II (1627-1628), edited by P. Hume Brown, Edinburgh, 1900.

Vol. III (1629-1630), edited by P. Hume Brown, Edinburgh, 1901.

Vol. IV (1630-1632), edited by P. Hume Brown, Edinburgh, 1902.

Vol. V (1633-1635), edited by P. Hume Brown, Edinburgh, 1904.

Vol. VI (1635-1637), edited by P Hume Brown, Edinburgh, 1905.

Register of the Privy Seal of Scotland.

Vol. I (1488-1529), edited by Livingstone, Edinburgh 1908.

Vol II (1529-1542), edited by Fleming, Edinburgh, 1921.

Vol. III (1542-1548) edited by Fleming and Beveridge, Edinburgh, 1936.

Vol. IV (1548-1556) edited by Beveridge, Edinburgh, 1952.

Vol. Vi (1556-1567) edited by Beveridge, Edinburgh, 1957.

Vol. Vii (1556-1567) edited by Beveridge, Edinburgh, 1957.

Vol. VI (1567-1574) edited by G. Donaldson, Edinburgh, 1963.

Vol. VII (1574- 1580) edited by G. Donaldson, Edinburgh, 1966.

Vol. VIII (1581-1584), edited by G. Donaldson, Edinburgh, 1982.

Row, John, *The History of the Kirk of Scotland from the year 1558 to August 1637*, Aberdeen, 1650.

Sadler, Sir Ralph, *State Papers and Letters*, 3 vols, edited by Walter Scott, Edinburgh, 1809.

Scotland before 1700 from Contemporary Documents, edited by Peter Hume Brown , Edinburgh 1893.

Scottish Correspondence of Mary of Lorraine, edited by Annie Cameron, Edinburgh, 1927.

Scottish Historical Documents, edited by Gordon Donaldson, Edinburgh, 1970.

Selve, Odet de, *Correspondence Politique 1546-1549*, edited by G. Lefevre-Pontalis, Paris, 1888.

Source Book of Scottish History, 4 vols., 2nd edn, Dickinson, edited by W. Croft Dickinson, G. Donaldson, I.A.Milne, Edinburgh, 1958-61.

Spalding, John, *History of the Troubles and Memorable Transactions in Scotland*, Aberdeen, 1829 (originally published in 1792 from mss of John Spalding)

Spottiswood, John, *History of the Church of Scotland*, 1655, reprinted in 3 vols, Bannatyne Club, Edinburgh, 1850.

Tudor Tracts 1532-1588, edited by A.F. Pollard, London, 1903.

The Warrender Papers, 2 vols, edited by Anne Cameron, Scottish History Society, 1932.

Two Missions of Jaques de la Brosse: an Account of the Affairs of Scotland in the year 1543, and the Journal of the Siege of Leith, 1560, edited by Gladys Dickinson, Scottish History Society, Edinburgh, 1942.

III: SECONDARY WORKS

(a) Mary Queen of Scots, the 4th Earl of Huntly and 1st Earl of Moray.

Bingham, Caroline, *James V, King of Scots*, London, 1971.

    Darnley, London, 1996.

Breeze, David, *A Queen's Progress,* Edinburgh, 1987.

Brown, *Peter Hume, Scotland in the time of Mary*, Edinburgh, 1904.

Browne, Gore, *Robert, Lord Bothwell*, London, 1937.

Caldwell, David, 'The Battle of Pinkie,' in *Scotland and War AD 79-1918,* edited by Norman MacDougall, Edinburgh, 1991, pp.61-94.

Cameron, Jamie, *James V,* East Lothian, 1998.

Cowan, Ian, 'The Roman Connection: Prospects for Counter-Reformation during the Personal Reign of Mary, Queen of Scots' in *Mary Stewart, Queen in Three Kingdoms*, edited by Michael Lynch, Oxford, 1988.

'The Marian Civil War 1567-1573,' in *Scotland and War AD79-1918*, edited by Norman MacDougall, Edinburgh, 1991, pp. 95-112.

Davison, M.H. Armstrong, *The Casket Letters*, London, 1965.

Donaldson, Gordon, *Mary Queen of Scots*, Edinburgh, 1974.

    All the Queen's Men, Power and Politics in Mary Stewart's Scotland, London, 1983.

Drummond, Humphrey, *Our Man in Scotland: Sir Ralph Sadler*, London, 1969.

Duncan, T, 'Mary Stewart and the House of Huntly,' SHR, iv, 1906, pp.365-373.

    'Relations of the Earl of Moray with Mary,' SHR, vi, 1909, pp.49-57.

Fergusson, James, *The White Hind*, London, 1963.

Fleming, Hay, *Mary Queen of Scots from her Birth to her Flight into England*, London, 1898.

Fraser, Antonia, *Mary Queen of Scots*, London 1969.

Graham, Cuthbert, 'Corrichie,' *Leopard Magazine*, June 1979, pp.31-33.

Jordan, W.K., *Edward VI: The Young King*, London, 1967.

Lee, Maurice, *James Stewart, Earl of Moray*, New York, 1953.

> *John Maitland of Thirlestane and the Foundation of the Stewart Despotism in Scotland*, Princeton, 1959.

> 'The Daughter of debate: Mary Queen of Scots after 400 years,' SHR, LXVIII, April 1989, pp.70-79.

Lynch, Michael (editor), *Mary Stewart, Queen in Three Kingdoms*, Oxford, 1988.

MacKay, James, *In my End is My Beginning: A Life of Mary Queen of Scots*, Edinburgh, 1999.

Mahon, R.H., *The Tragedy of Kirk of Field*, Cambridge, 1930.

Marshall, Rosalind, *Mary of Guise*, Glasgow, 1977.

Merriman, Marcus, *The Rough Wooings, Mary Queen of Scots 1542-1551*, East Linton, 2000.

Mumby, F.A., *The Fall of Mary Stuart: A Narrative in Contemporary Letters*, London, 1921.

Oman, Charles, 'The Battle of Pinkie,' *Journal of Archaeology*, xc, 1933, pp.1-25.

> *A History of the Art of War in the Sixteenth Century*, London, 1937.

Phillips, Gervase, 'In the Shadow of Flodden: Tactics, Technology and Scottish Military Effectiveness, 1513-1550,' SHR, lxxvii, 2, October 1998, pp.162-182.

> *The Anglo-Scots Wars 1513-1550,* Woodbridge, 1999.

Sanderson, Margaret H.B., *Mary Stewart's People*, Edinburgh, 1987.

Sinclair, G.A. 'The Scots at Solway Moss,' SHR, ii, 1905, pp. 372-377.

Skelton, John, *Maitland of Lethington*, London, 1894.

Slavin, A.J, *Politics And Profit: A Study of Sir Ralph Sadler, 1507-1547*, Cambridge, 1966.

Stuart, John, *A Lost Chapter in the History of Mary Queen of Scots*, 1874.

White, Allan, 'Queen Mary's Northern Province,' in *Mary Stewart, Queen in Three Kingdoms*, edited by Michael Lynch,Oxford, 1988, pp. 53-70.

Wormald, J.M., *Mary Queen of Scots: A Study in Failure*, London, 1988.

(b) The Jacobean Regency and 5th Earl of Huntly

Hewit, George, *Scotland under Morton 1572-80*, Edinburgh, 1982.

Murray, Atholl, 'Huntly's rebellion and the administration of justice in north-east Scotland, 1570-1573,' Northern Scotland, iv, 1981, pp. 1-6.

White, Allan, 'The Regent Morton's Visitation: the Reformation of Aberdeen, 1574,' in *The Renaissance in Scotland,* edited by Macdonald, Lynch, & Cowan, Leiden, 1994, pp.246-263.

(c) James VI

Arbuckle, W.F., 'The Gowrie Conspiracy,' SHR, xxxvi, 1957, pp.1-24.

Bergeron, David, *Royal Family, Royal Lovers: King James of England and Scotland*, Missouri, 1991.

Chambers, R, *Life of James I*, 2 vols, Edinburgh, 1830.

Cowan, Edward J, 'The Darker Version of the Scottish Renaissance: the Devil and Francis Stewart' in *Renaissance and Reformation in Scotland*, edited by Ian Cowan, Edinburgh, 1983, pp.125-140.

Durston, Christopher, *James I*, London, 1993.

Fraser, Antonia, *James VI and I*, London, 1974.

Goodare, Julian, 'Scottish Politics in the Reign of James VI' in *The Reign of James VI*, edited by J. Goodare and M. Lynch, East Linton, 2000, pp.32-54.

Goodare, Julian and Michael Lynch (editors), *The Reign of James VI*, East Linton, 2000.

Grant, Ruth, 'The Brig o'Dee Affair, the sixth Earl of Huntly and the Politics of the Counter-Reformation,' in *The Reign of James VI*, edited by J. Goodare, pp. 93-109.

Houston, S.J., *James I*, 2nd edn, London, 1995.

Kirk, James, 'Royal and lay patronage in the Jacobean Kirk 1572-1600' in *Church, Politics and Society: Scotland 1408-1929*, edited by Norman MacDougall, Edinburgh, 1983, pp.127-150.

Lang, Andrew, *James VI and the Gowrie Mystery*, London, 1902.

Lee, Maurice, *James I and Henry IV*, Illinois, 1970.

   'James VI and Aristocracy,' *Scotia*, i, April 1977.

   Government by Pen: Scotland under James VI, Illinois 1980.

   'James I and the Historians: Not a Bad King After All?,' *Albion*, 16,2, summer 1984, pp.151-163.

   Great Britain's Solomon: James VI and I in his three Kingdoms, Illinois, 1990.

Lyall, Roderick, 'James VI and the sixteenth-century cultural crisis,' in *The Reign of James VI*, edited by J. Goodare and M. Lynch, Tuckwell, 2000, pp.55-70.

Lynch, Michael, 'James VI and "The Highland Problem",' in *The Reign of James VI*, edited by J. Goodare and M. Lynch, East Linton, 2000, pp.208-227.

Meikle, Maureen, 'The Invisible Divide: the Greater Lairds and the Nobility of Jacobean Scotland,' SHR, LXXI, 1992, pp70-87.

'The Sixteenth Century Border Lairs: A study of the links between Wealth and House Building,' *History of the Berwickshire Naturalist's Club*, 46(1), 1993, pp. 9-36.

Peck, L.L. *The Mental World of the Jacobean Court*, Cambridge, 1991.

Raitt, R.S. (editor) *Lusus Regis, being poems and other pieces by King James,* Westminster, 1901.

Sharpe, James, *The Bewitching of Anne Gunter*, London, 1999.

Simpson, Grant, 'The Personal letters of James VI,' in *The Reign of James VI*, edited by J. Goodare and M. Lynch, Tuckwell, 2000, pp. 141-153.

Smith, A G R (editor), *The Reign of James VI and I*, London 1973.

Willson, D.H., *King James VI and I*, Bedford Historical Series, London, 1956.

Wormald, Jenny, 'James VI: New Men for Old,' *Scotia* I(2), 1977 pp.70-76.

   'James VI: Two Kings or One?,' *History*, 68, 1983, pp.187-209.

(d) The 6th Earl of Huntly and 2nd Earl of Moray

Bingham, Mary Caperton, *Two Murders in One Act: the Bonny Earl of Moray and the Thane of Cawdor* (unpublished thesis, Harvard 1990).

Brown, Keith M., *Bloodfeud in Scotland 1573-1625*, Edinburgh, 1985.

Campbell, Hugh, Earl of Cawdor, *The Murders of Lord Moray and the Thane of Cawdor*, Private Mss, 1985.

Grant, Ruth, 'Politicking Jacobean Women: Lady Fermiehurst, the Countess of Arran and the Countess of Huntly, *c*.1580-1603,' in *Women in Scotland c.1100-c.1750*, edited by Elizabeth Ewan and Maureen Meikle, East Linton, 1999.

Ives, Edward D., *The Bonny Earl of Murray*, East Linton, 1996.

Laing, David, 'Notices of the Funeral of James, second Earl of Moray,' *Proceedings of the Society of Antiquaries of*

Scotland, i, 1855, pp.191-6.

Law, Thomas Graves, 'The Spanish Blanks and Catholic Earls, 1592-94,' *The Scottish Review,* July 1893, reprinted in *Collected Essays and Reviews,* edited by P. Hume Brown, Edinburgh, 1904.

Shearman, Francis, 'The Spanish Blanks,' *The Innes Review,* iii, 1952, pp.81-103.

(e) The Ballad of the Bonnie Earl of Moray

Aytoun, William Edmindstoune, *Ballads of Scotland,* 2 vols, Edinburgh, 1858.

Barsanti Francesco, *Collection of Old Scots Tunes,* Edinburgh, 1742.

Boucher, R, *The Kingdom of Fife, its Ballads and legends,* Edinburgh, 1899.

Brander, Michael, *Scottish Border Battles and Ballads,* London, 1975, p.95-8.

Bronson, Bertrand, *The Traditional Tunes of the Child Ballads,* 4 vols, Princeton, 1959-72.

Brown, Keith M., 'The Laird, his Daughter, her Husband and the Minister: unravelling a Popular Ballad,' in *People and Power in Scotland,* edited by Roger Mason and Norman MacDougall, Edinburgh, 1990, pp. 104-125.

Buchan, David, *The Ballad and the Folk,* London, 1972.

'The Historical ballads of the North East of Scotland,' *Lares* 4, Oct-Dec 1985, pp.443-51.

'The Historical Balladry of the North East,' *Aberdeen University Review,* 55 (1994) pp. 377-87.

Chambers, Robert, *Romantic Scottish Ballads,* Edinburgh, 1859.

Child, Francis James, *The English and Scottish Popular Ballads,* 5 volumes, New York, 1956.

Clyne, Norval, *The Romantic Scottish Ballads and the Lady Wardlaw Heresy,* Aberdeen,1859.

Cowan, Edward J, (editor) *The People's Past,* Edinburgh, 1980.

'Calvinism and the Survival of Folk,' in *The People's Past,* pp.32-57.

The Polar Twins: Scottish History and Scottish Literature, East Linton, 1998.

The Ballad in Scottish History, East Linton, 2000.

Cunningham, Allan, *The Songs of Scotland,* Edinburgh, 1825.

Dauney, William, *Ancient Scottish Melodies from a Manuscript of the Reign of King James VI,* Edinburgh, 1838.

Eyre-Todd, George, *Ancient Scots Ballads,* London, 1894.

Finlay, John, *Scottish Historical and Romantic Ballads Chiefly Ancient,* 2 vols, Edinburgh, 1808.

Gardner-Medwin, A, 'Views of King and People in Sixteenth and Seventeenth Century Ballads' in Mclure and Spiller, *Bryght Lanternis,* Aberdeen, 1989, pp. 24-32.

Glen, John, *Early Scottish Melodies,* Edinburgh, 1900.

Graham, George F, *The Songs of Scotland,* Edinburgh, 1848.

Gunnyon, William, *Illustrations of Scottish History, Life and Superstition from Song and Ballad,* London, 1877.

Henderson, Hamish, 'The Ballad, The Folk and the Oral Tradition,' in *The People's Past,* edited by E.J.Cowan, 1980, pp. 69-107.

'The Ballad and Popular Tradition to 1660', in *The History of Scottish Literature,* I, edited by R.D.S.Jack, Aberdeen, 1988, pp.263-284.

Henderson, T.F., *Scottish Vernacular Literature,* Edinburgh, 1910.

Herd, David, *Scottish Songs,* Edinburgh, 1769.

Jack R.D.S. (editor), *The History of Scottish Literature,* 4 vols, Aberdeen, 1988.

Jamieson, Robert, *Popular Ballads and Songs,* Edinburgh, 1806.

Kenneth, Brother, 'The Popular Literature of the Scottish Reformation, in *Essays On the Scottish Reformation* ed by David McRoberts, pp.169-184.

Laing, David, *Notes to Johnson's Scots Musical Museum*, 1839.

Lyle, Emily, *Scottish Ballads*, Edinburgh, 1994.

McClure, J. Derrick and Michael R.G. Spiller (editors), *Bryght Lanternis*, Aberdeen, 1989.

McDowell, William Adair, *Among the Old Scotch Minstrels*, Edinburgh, 1888.

Marshall, Nancy, *Scottish Songs and Ballads,* Edinburgh, 1990.

Martin, Burns, Allan Ramsay: *A Study of His Life and Works*, Cambridge, 1931.

Muir, Willa, *Living with Ballads*, London 1965.

Olson, Ian, 'The Dreadful Death of the Bonny Earl of Murray: Clues from the Carpenter Song Collection,'
      Folk Music Journal, 7(3), 1997, pp.281-310.
      'Just how was the Bonny Earl of Moray killed?' in *The Ballad in Scottish History,* edited by E.J.Cowan,
      2000, pp.36-53.

Percy, Thomas, *Reliques of Ancient English Poetry*, London, 1765.

Porter, James (editor), *The Ballad Image*, Los Angeles, 1983.

Ramsay, Allan, *Tea-Table Miscellany or a Collection of choice songs, Scots and English,* 1st edn, 2 vols, London, 1724;
      5th edn, 3 vols, London 1729; 10th edn, 4 vols, London 1740.
      A New Miscellany of Scots Songs, London, 1727.

Ree, Stephen (editor), *The Gordon Ballads* printed in John Bulloch, *The House of Gordon*, vol 2, Aberdeen,
      1907.

The Scots Musical Museum, 1787-1803, 2 vols, reprinted by the Scolar Press, Aldershot, 1991.

Stenhouse, William, *Illustrations of the Lyric Poetry and Music of Scotland*, Edinburgh, 1853.

Strutt, Joseph, *The Sports and Pastimes of the People of England*, London, 1838.

Thomson, William, *Orpheus Caledonius, or a Collection of Scots Songs set to Music*, 2nd edn London, 1733, printed
      for the Author at his house, reprinted by the Mercat Press, Edinburgh 1972.

Wilson, Sir James, *Old Scotch Songs and Poems*, OUP, 1927.

(f) The Moray Memorial

Bentley-Cranch, Dana, 'Effigy and Portrait in 16th Century Scotland,' *Review of Scottish Culture*, 4, 1988, pp.9-
      23.

Holloway, James, *Painting in Scotland 1570-1650*, SNPG Catalogue, Edinburgh, 1975.

Marshal, *Rosalind, Queen of Scots*, Edinburgh, HMSO, 1986.

Morton, 17th Earl of Moray, *Painting of James, 2nd Earl of Moray*, Kinfauns, Perthshire, n.pub, 19 December
      1912.

Pitcairn, R, (editor) *Historical and Genealogical Account of the Principle Families of the Name of Kennedy*, Edinburgh,
      1830, pp.48-68.

Thomson, Duncan, *Painting in Scotland 1570-1650*, SNPG Catalogue, Edinburgh, 1975.

Waterhouse, Ellis, *Painting in Britain 1530-1790*, London, 1962.

(g) Castles and Cathedrals

Apted, M.R., *Aberdour Castle*, HMSO, nd.
      Ballindalloch Castle Guide, nd.

Beaton, Elizabeth, *Scotland's Traditional Houses,* HMSO, 1997.

Bridgeland, Nick, *Hermitage Castle*, Historic Scotland, 1997.

Breeze, David J, *A Queen's Progress*, HBM, 1987.

Caldwell, David (editor), *Scottish Weapons and Fortifications 1100-1800*, Edinburgh, 1981.

Cowan I.B., and D.E. Easson, *Mediaeval Religious Houses: Scotland*, 2nd Edn, London, 1976.

Cruden, Stewart, *The Scottish Castle*, Nelson, 1960.

    St Andrews Cathedral, HMSO, nd.

Dunbar, John, *Scottish Royal Palaces*, East Linton, 1999.

    Falkland Palace Guide, National Trust, nd.

Fawcett, Richard, *Elgin Cathedral*, HMSO nd.

    Stirling Castle, Historic Scotland, 1983.

    St Andrews Castle, Historic Scotland, 1992.

    St Andrews Cathedral, Historic Scotland, 1993.

    Inchcolm Abbey and Island, HMSO, 1998.

    The Architectural History of Scotland: Scottish Architecture from the Accession of the Stewarts to the Reformation, 1371-1560, Edinburgh, 1994.

    Castle Campbell, Historic Scotland, 1999.

Fenwick, Hubert, *Scottish Baronial Houses*, London, 1986.

Foster, Sally and Alan and Ronald Mackinnes (eds), *Scottish Power Centres from the Early Middle Ages to the 20th Century*, Glasgow, 1998.

Galloway, Alexander, *Papers on Archaeological and Philological Subjects*, Glasgow, 1912.

Goodman, Jane, *Debrett's Royal Scotland,* Exeter, 1983.

Gow, Ian, and Alistair Rowan, *Scottish Country Houses 1600-1914*, Edinburgh, 1994.

Groome, F, H, *The Ordnance Gazetteer of Scotland*, 3 vols, London, 1903.

Howard, Deborah, *The Architectural History of Scotland: Scottish Architecture from the Reformation to the Restoration, 1560-1660*, Edinburgh, 1995.

MacGibben, David and Thomas Ross, *The Castellated and Domestic Architecture of Scotland*, 5 vols., Edinburgh, 1887-92.

McIvor, Ian, 'Artillery and Major Places of Strength in the Lothians and the East Border, 1513-1542,' in *Scottish Weapons and Fortifications 1100-1800*, edited by David Caldwell, Edinburgh, 1981, pp. 94-152.

    Blackness Castle, Historic Scotland, 1993.

    Corgarff Castle, Historic Scotland, 1993.

    Edinburgh Castle, Historic Scotland, 1993.

    Palace of Holyrood House, Official Guide.

Pringle, R. D., *Doune Castle*, Historic Scotland, 1987.

    Linlithgow Palace, Historic Scotland, 1989.

    Craigmillar Castle, Historic Scotland, 1996.

    Huntingtower, Historic Scotland, 1996.

    St Giles Cathedral, Edinburgh, Pitcairn, nd.

Samson, Ross, 'Tower-houses in the sixteenth century,' in *Scottish Power Centres*, pp. 133-146.

Stewart, Jeannie C, *Ancient Castles of Scotland, A Collection of Books and papers of the late Dr W.Douglas Simpson*, Edinburgh, no date.

Tabraham, Christopher, *Scottish Castles and Fortifications,* HMSO, 1986.

    Lochleven Castle, HMSO, 1994.

    Huntly Castle, HMSO, 1995.

    Kildrummy Castle, HMSO, 1995.

Aberdour Castle, Historic Scotland, 1996.

Tranter, Nigel, *The Fortified House in Scotland*, 5 vols, Edinburgh, 1986.

Zeune, Joachim, 'Perfecting the Tower House, I,' in *Fortress, The Castles and Fortifications Quarterly*, 1991, 10, pp.24-30.

(h) General

Anderson, J.M., *Early Records of the University of St Andrews*, SHS, Edinburgh, 1926.

Ballingall, William, *The Shores of Fife*, Edinburgh, 1872.

Brereton, Henry, *Gordonstoun, Ancient Estate and Modern School*, Edinburgh, 1968,

Brown, James, *A History of the Highlands and of the Highland Clans*, Glasgow, 1840.

Brown Jennifer M. (see Wormald, J.M.), 'Scottish Politics 1567-1625' in *The Reign of James VI and I*, edited by A.G.R.Smith, New York, 1973, pp.22-39.

   Bonds of Manrent in Scotland before 1603 (Glasgow University PhD), 1974.

Brown, Keith M., 'Aristocratic Finances and the Origins of the Scottish Revolution,' *English Historical Review*, civ, January 1989, pp.46-87.

   'Noble Indebtedness,' in *The Bulletin of the Institute of Historical Research*, lxii, 1989 pp.260-275.

   'In Search of the Godly Magistrate in Reformation Scotland,' *Jn Eccles History*, 40(4), October 1989, pp.553-65.

   'The Nobility of Jacobean Scotland 1567-1625,' in *Scotland Revisited*, edited by J.M.Wormald, London, 1991, pp.61-72.

   'A House Divided: Family and Feud in Carrick under John Kennedy, Fifth Earl of Cassilis,' SHR lxxv, October 1996, pp. 168-196.

   Noble Society in Scotland, Edinburgh, 2000.

Brown, Michael, 'Scotland Tamed? Kings and Magnates in Late Medieval Scotland,' *The Innes Review*, xlv (2) 1994, pp.120-146.

Brown, Peter Hume, 'The Scottish Nobility and their part in the National History,' SHR, iii, 1906, pp.157-170.

   History of Scotland, 3 vols, Cambridge, 1911.

Bulloch, John Malcolm, *The House of Gordon*, 2 vols, New Spalding Club, Aberdeen, 1907.

Burns, J.H., 'The Political background of the Reformation, 1513-1625,' in *Essays on the Scottish Reformation, 1513-1625*, edited by David McRoberts, Glasgow, 1962, pp.1-36.

Chambers, Robert, *Traditions of Edinburgh*, Edinburgh, 1868.

   Domestic Annals of Scotland, 3 vols, 3rd edn, Edinburgh, 1874.

Chambers, William, Story of St Giles Cathedral Church, Edinburgh, 1879, Edinburgh

   Historical Sketch of St Giles Cathedral, Edinburgh, 1890.

   Chronicles of the families of Atholl and Tullibardine, edited by 7th Duke of Atholl, 1908.

Complete Peerage, 13 vols, edited by H.A. Doubleday and Howard De Walden, London, 1910-1940.

Cowan, Edward J, 'Clanship, Kinship and the Campbell Acquisition of Islay,' SHR, 58, 1979, pp.132-157.

   The Polar Twins: Scottish History and Scottish Literature, East Linton, 1998.

Cowan, Ian and Duncan Shaw (editors), *The Renaissance and Reformation in Scotland*, Edinburgh, 1983.

Daiches, David (ed), *The New Companion to Scottish Culture*, Edinburgh, 1993.

Dawson, Jane, 'The Fifth Earl of Argyle, Gaelic Lordship and Political Power in Sixteenth-Century Scotland,' SHR, lxvii, April 1988, pp.1-27.

Dickinson, W Croft, *History of Scotland*, 2 vols, London, 1961.

Dictionary of National Biography, edited by Leslie Stephen, London, 1885.

Dodgshon, R.A., '"Pretense of Blude"' and "Place of their duelling": the nature of Scottish Clans, 1500-1745,' in *Scottish Society 1500-1800*, edited by R.A. Houston and I.D. Whyte, London, 1989.

Donaldson, Gordon, *The Scottish Reformation*, Edinburgh, 1960.

> *Scotland: James V to James VII*, Edinburgh, 1965.

> *Scotland: Church And Nation*, Edinburgh, 1972.

> 'The legal Profession in Scottish Society in the 16th and 17th centuries,' *Juridical Review*, 1976.

> *Scottish Church History*, Edinburgh, 1985.

Dunbar, John Telfer, *History of Highland Dress*, Edinburgh, 1962.

Durken, John, 'Education: The Laying of Fresh Foundations' in *Humanism in Renaissance Scotland*, edited by John MacQueen, Edinburgh, 1990, pp.123-160.

Ewan, Elizabeth and Maureen Meikle (editors), *Women in Scotland .1100-c.1750*, East Linton, 1999.

Eyre-Todd, George, *The Highland Clans of Scotland: Their History and Traditions*, London, 1923.

Fittis, Robert Scott, *Sports and Pastimes of Scotland*, London, 1891.

Fraser, George MacDonald, *The Steel Bonnets: The Story of the Anglo-Scottish Border Reivers*, London, 1971.

Froude, James, *History of England*, 6 vols, London, 1866.

Goodare, Julian, 'The Nobility and the Absolutist State in Scotland, 1584-1638,' *History*, lxxviii, 1993, pp.161-182.

> *State and Society in Early Modern Scotland*, Oxford, 1999.

Goodall, W, *Introduction to the History of Antiquities in Scotlan*d, 1860.

Grant, I.F., *Everyday life in Old Scotland*, 2 vols, London, 1924.

> *Social and Economic Development of Scotland before 1603*, Edinburgh, 1930.

Gregory, Donald, *History of the Western Highland*s, Edinburgh, 1875, 2nd edn., reprinted by John Donald, Edinburgh, 1975.

Grose, Francis, *The Antiquities of Scotland*, 2 vols, London, 1789 and 1791.

Hexter, J. H., 'The Education of the Aristocracy in the Renaissance' in his *Reappraisals in History*, Chicago, 1979, pp.45-70.

Hopkins, Paul, *Clans and Feudalism*, Oxford, 1995.

Houston, R.A., *Scottish Society 1500-1800*, Cambridge, 1989.

Kermack, W.R. *The Scottish Highland*s, 1957.

Kirk, James, 'Patronage and the Crown 1560-1572' in *The Renaissance and Reformation in Scotland*, edited by Ian Cowan, Edinburgh, 1983, pp.93-113.

> 'Reformation and Revolution, Kirk and Crown 1590-1690' in *Scotland Revisited*, edited by J.M.Wormald, London, 1991, pp. 82-96.

Lang, Andrew, *A History of Scotland*, 4 vols, Edinburgh, 1907.

Lynch, Michael, *Scotland: A New History*, London, 1991.

McClintock, H.F., *Old Irish and Highland Dress*, Dundalk, 1943.

M'Crie, Thomas, *Life of John Knox*, new edition, Edinburgh, 1884

> *Life of Andrew Melville*, new edition, Edinburgh, 1899.

Macdonald, Alan, 'David Calderwood: the not so hidden years, 1590-1604,' SHR, LXXIV, 197, 1995, pp.69-74.

Macdonald Alan, Lynch, M, & Cowan (editors), *The Renaissance in Scotland*, Leiden, 1994.

MacDougall, Norman (editor) Church, *Politics and Society, Scotland 1408-1927*, Edinburgh, 1983.

James IV, Edinburgh, 1989.

(editor) *Scotland and War AD 79-1918*, Edinburgh, 1991.

Mackintosh, Margaret, *The Clan Mackintosh and the Clan Chattan*, Edinburgh, 1948.

McLean-Bristol, Nicholas, *Murder Under Trust: The Crimes and Death of Sir Lachlan Mor McLean of Duart,* East Linton, 1999.

McNeill, Peter & Ranald Nicholson, *Historical Atlas of Scotland, 40-1600*, St Andrews, 1975.

MacQueen, John, (editor), *Humanism in Renaissance Scotland*, Edinburgh 1990.

McRoberts, David (editor), *Essays on the Scottish Reformation, 1513-1625*, Glasgow, 1962.

MacTaggart, R.A., 'Assault in the later Baron Courts,' *Juridical Review*, 7, 1962, pp.99-126.

Marren, Peter, *Grampian Battlefields*, Edinburgh,1990.

Mason, Roger, *Kingship and Commonwealth*, (Edinburgh PhD thesis), 1983.

'Covenant and Commonwealth: the language of Politics in Reformation Scotland' in *Church, Politics and Society: Scotland 1408-1929*, edited by Norman MacDougall, Edinburgh, 1983, pp.97-125.
'Kingship, Nobility and Anglo-Scottish Union: John Mair's History of Greater Britain (1521)', *The Innes Review*, xli, 2, 1990, pp.182-222.

Mathew, David, *Scotland under Charles I*, London, 1955.

Maxwell, Stuart, and Robin Hutchinson, *Scottish Costume 1550-1850*, London, 1958.

Murray, Atholl, L, 'The Revenues of the Bishopric of Moray in 1538,' *The Innes Review*, 19, 1968, pp. 40-56.
'The Salmon Fishings of Strathnaver, 1558-1559,' *Review of Scottish Culture*, 8, 1993 pp.77-83.

Murray, Peter J., 'The Lay Administrators of Church Lands in the Fifteenth and Sixteenth Centuries,' SHR, lxxiv, 1995, pp.26-44.

Prebble, John, *The Lion in the North: One Thousand Year s of Scotland's History*, London, 1971.

Rampini, Charles, *History of Moray and Nairne*, Edinburgh, 1897.

Robertson, John, *Uppies & Doonies: The Story of the Kirkwall Ba' Game*, Aberdeen, 1967.

Robertson, William, *The History of Scotland under Mary and James VI*, 12th edn, London, 1791.

Ross, William, *Aberdour and Inchcolm*, Edinburgh, 1885.

Sanderson, Margaret H.B., *Scottish Rural Society in the Sixteenth Century*, Edinburgh, 1982.

Cardinal of Scotland, David Beaton c.1494-1546, revised edn, Edinburgh, 2001.

Scott, W, *An Apologetical Narration of the State and Government of the Kirk of Scotland since the Reformation,* Edinburgh, 1846.

Scott, Sir Walter, *Tales of a Grandfather*, Edinburgh, 1827-9.

The Scots Peerage, edited by J.Balfour Paul, 9 vols, Edinburgh, 1904-1914.

Seton, George, *A History of the Family of Seton during eight centuries*, 2 vols, Edinburgh, 1896.

Shaw, Lachlan, *The History of the Province of Moray*, New Edition, 3 vols, edited by J.F.S.Gordon, Glasgow, 1882.

Simpson, W.D., *Earldom of Mar*, Aberdeen, 1948.

Smout, T.C., *A History of the Scottish People 1560-1830*, Glasgow, 1969.

Stringer, K.J, (editor) *Essays on the Nobility of Medieval Scotland*, Edinburgh, 1985.

Survey of the Province of Moray, Aberdeen, 1798.

Taylor, James, *The Pictorial History of Scotland*, 2 vols, London, nd.

Todd, Margo, 'Profane Pastimes and the Reformed Community: the Persistence of Popular Festivities in Early Modern Scotland,' *Journal of British Studies*, 39(2), 2000, pp.123-156.

Tytler, Patrick, *History of Scotland,* Edinburgh, 1841, new and enlarged edition in four volumes, London, 1877.

Warrack, John, *Domestic Life in Scotland 1488-1688*, London, 1920.

Watson, J & W, *Morayshire Described*, 1868.

Whittington, G and I.D. Whyte (eds), *An Historical Geography of Scotland*, London, 1983.

Whyte, Ian, D., *Scotland Before the Industrial Revolution: An Economic and Social History c1050-c1750*, London, 1995.

Williamson, A.H., 'A Patriot Nobility? Calvinism, Kin-ties and Civic Humanism,' SHR, lxxii, April 1993, pp.1-21.

Wormald, J.M., (see Jennifer M. Brown.),'Bloodfeud, Kindred and Government,' *Past and Present*, 87, 1980, pp.54-97.

Court, Kirk and Community, Edinburgh, 1981.

'Princes and the Regions in the Scottish Reformation' in *Church, Politics and Society: Scotland 1408-1929*, edited by Norman MacDougall, Edinburgh, 1983, pp.65-84.

Lords and Men in Scotland: Bonds of Manrent 1442-1603, Edinburgh, 1985.

(ed) *Scotland Revisited*, London, 1991.

'The Bloodfeud,' in *The New Companion to Scottish Culture*, edited by David Daiches, Edinburgh, 1993.

Wyness, Fenton, *Royal Valley*, Aberdeen, 1968.

Young, J.C.B, *Scottish Political parties 1573-1603* (unpublished Edinburgh PhD), 1976.

BIOGRAPHICAL INDEX

Abbott, George (1562-1633), Archbishop of Canterbury (1611), 233.

Abercrombie, Andrew, [of Pitmedden? or Pittelpie?, Aberdeenshire laird?], 143, 175.

Abercromby, Richard, last abbot of St Colme's abbey, resigned 1542, 109, 294 n.2.

Abernethy, Alexander (1537-1587), 6th Baron Saltoun (1543), 63.

Adamson, Patrick, (1537-1592), Archbishop of St Andrews (1576), 139, 299 n.39.

Albany, dukes of (see Murdoch, John and Stewart, Robert).

Angus, earls of (see Douglas).

Anne of Denmark (1574-1619), wife of James VI, Queen of Scotland (1589), 154, 156, and Bothwell, 165; and Moray, 194, and Huntly, 223-224, 226, 231, 266. Plate 8.

Arbroath, Commendator of (see Hamilton, John).

Argyll, earls of (see Campbell).

Arran, earls of (see Hamilton and Stewart).

Ashby, William, English ambassador to Scotland (1588-1590), 144.

Aston, Roger, English agent in Scotland, 175, 178, 179, 195; quotation from, 189.

Athol, earls of (see Stewart).

Balfour, Sir James, of Pittendreich (c.1525-1583), 'Blasphemous Balfour,' Clerk Register of Scotland (1566), Keeper of Edinburgh Castle, 84, 87, 95, 129.

Balfour, Sir James (1600-1657), of Kinnaird and Denmilne, Lyon king-of-arms, historian, 194.

Balliol, John (c.1250-1313), King of Scotland (1292-1296), 'Toom Tabard,' 17.

Bannatyne, Richard (d.1605), secretary to John Knox, 103.

Bargany, laird of, (see Kennedy).

Beaton, David (c.1494-1546), Cardinal (1538), Archbishop of St Andrews (1539), 31, 33, 34, 35, 36, Chancellor of St Andrews University, 51, murdered, 39, 51.

Beaton, James, (c.1480-1539), Archbishop of Glasgow (1509) and St Andrews (1522), 26, 30.

Bellenden, Sir Lewis (1553-1591), of Auchinoul, Justice Clerk (1576/7), 138.

Binning, Walter, 16th century heraldic painter, 262.

Birrell, Robert (fl. 1567-1605), burgess of Edinburgh, diarist, 226.

Borthwick, William (d.1582),7th Baron Borthwick (1566), 87.

Bothwell, Earl of, (see Hepburn, and Stewart).

Bothwell, Adam, (c.1529-1593), 11th Bishop of Orkney (1559), 88.

Bower, Walter (1385-1449), Abbot of St Colme, historian, 109.

Bowes, George,(1517-1556), English commander defeated at Ancrum Moor, 1544/5, 36.

Bowes, Sir Robert (c.1495-1554), Warden of the East March, 31, 32.

Bowes, Robert (d.1597), English ambassador (1580, 1583, 1590-1597), 156, 157, 167, 168, 169, 181, 195, 201-202, 205-206, 207, 208, 209, 213, 220, 221, 296 n.51, 308 n.52.

Boyd, Robert (c.1517-1590), 4th Baron Boyd (c.1557), a Lord of the Congregation, supporter of Moray, and latterly of Mary, 87, 90, killed by 6th Earl of Huntly, 168.

Bryan, Sir Francis (d.1550), English cavalry commander at Fawside Brae, 41.

Brown, Anna (1747-1810), née Gordon, of Falkland, ballad singer, 266.

Buchanan, George (1506-1582), scholar, historian, Reformer, tutor of James VI (1570-1578), 17, 19, 30, 46, 61, 62, 70, 72.

Burghley, Lord (see Cecil)

Burton, John Hill (1809-1881), lawyer and historian, 61, 289 n.11.

Byron, Lord George Gordon (1788-1824), 6th Baron, poet, 21, 176.

Caithness, earls of (see Sinclair).

Calder, Captain James (d.1571), murderer of the Regent Lennox (1571), 99.

Calderwood, David (1575-1650), historian, opinion of 4th Earl of Huntly, 48; Corrichie, 68-69, 74; murder of 2nd Earl of Moray, 172, 193, 196, 227, 305 n.22, 308 n.36.

Camden, William (1551-1623), English topographer and antiquary, 50.

Cameron, Alan, of Lochiel, 16th chief of the Clan Cameron, 163, 204, 214.

Cameron, Ewen (d.1545), of Lochiel, 13th chief of the Clan Cameron, executed by Huntly, 38.

Campbell, Anna, (1594-1638) daughter of 7th Earl of Argyll, 231.

Campbell, Archibald (d.1513), 2nd Earl of Argyll, 20.

Campbell, Archibald (c.1505-1558), 4th Earl of Argyll (1530-1558), cousin of the 4th Earl of Huntly; 33, 34, 35, 42, 43, 45; envy of 4th Earl of Huntly, 45; backs Huntly, 50; and the Lords of the Congregation, 52, 53; wedding of daughter to St Colme, 110.

Campbell, Archibald (1530-1573), 5th Earl of Argyll (1558), 52; 80, 81, 109; and Darnley's murder, 83, 84, 87, 89, 295 n.21; backs Mary 90, 91, 92, 94, 96, 97, 99, 295 n.22.

Campbell, Archibald, of Lochnell (d.1594), brother of John Campbell of Cabrachan, 163, 182, 183, 184; killed at Glenlivat, 217, 220.

Campbell, Archibald (1575-1638), 7th Earl of Argyll (1584), 'Gruamach' – 'the Grim' – 163, 167, 182, 184-185, 195, 196, 202, 210, 211; Glenlivet, 213-222, 230, 231. Plate 34.

Campbell, Colin (d.1530), 3rd Earl of Argyll (1513), 26.

Campbell, Colin (c.1546-1584), 6th Earl of Argyll (1573), 117, 125, 127, 129, 182.

Campbell, Colin (b. after 1575), of Lundy, brother of 7th Earl of Argyll, 183.

Campbell, Duncan (d.1593), of Auchawillan, cousin of John of Ardkinglas, 183, 306 n.18.

Campbell, Duncan (c.1554-1631), 4th laird of Glenorchy, 182-184.

Campbell, James (d.1590), of Ardkinglas, Comptroller to the King, 182.

Campbell, James, (d.1594), brother of Archibald of Lochnell, killed at Glenlivet, 217, 220.

Campbell, Lady Jean, of Ardkinglas, 185.

Campbell, John, of Ardkinglas (1590), son of James, 182-185; 210, 306 n.18.

Campbell, Sir John (1541-1592), 3rd thane of Cawdor, Morayshire, 155, 159, 160, 162, 163, 296 n.34, 306 n.4 and 6; murder of, 181-185, 196, 210, 212.

Campbell, John Oig, of Cabrachan, brother of Archibald Campbell of Lochnell, 183-185.

Campbell, John, of Auchawillan, cousin of John Campbell of Ardkinglas, 185.

Campbell, Margaret (d.1571), wife of Forbes of Towie, burnt at Corgarff Castle, 100.

Campbell, Lady Margaret (d.1592), daughter of 4th Earl of Argyll, 110; murder of son, 174, 179, 180, 190-194, 267, 304 n.4, 311 n.16; death of, 200, 212, 308 n.52.

Campbell, Neil (d.1627), Bishop of Argyll (1606-1608), 182.

Campbell, Patrick, of Auchawillan, cousin of John Campbell of Ardkinglas, 185.

Carey, Robert (c.1560-1639), Warden of the East March (1596-1598) and Middle March (1598-1603), 1st Earl of
Monmouth, 221.

Carlos, Don (1545-1568), Crown Prince of Spain, 79.

Carmichael, Archibald, of Edrom, brother of Sir John, garrisons Strathbogie (1593), 207.

Carmichael, Sir John (d.1599/1600), chief of Clan of Carmichael (1585), warden of West Marches (1588-1592),
Scottish ambassador to England, 156.

Cassilis, earls of (see Kennedy).

Cecil, William, (1520-1598), English ambassador to Scotland (1560) Secretary of State, Lord Burleigh (1571), 35
301 n.42; quotations from, 49; 75, 89, 147, 156, 161, 169.

Chambers, Robert (1832-1888), encyclopaedist, 266.

Chambers, William, Provost of Edinburgh, 271.

Charles I (1600-1649), King of Scotland and of England (1625), 233, 234.

Chisholm, Captain (d.1571), killed at Crabstane, 99.

Clinton, Edward Fiennes de (1512-1585), 9th Baron Clinton, 1st Earl of Lincoln, Admiral, 40.

Colville, John (1542-1605), former minister, participant in Holyrood raid, 176, 241.

Comyn, John (d.1300?), claimant to the Scottish throne, 17.

Craigmiller, laird of (see Fleming).

Crawford, earls of (see Lindsay).

Crawford, Captain Thomas (1530-1603), of Jordanhill, took Dumbarton Castle (1571), 98.

Crichton, Edward (d.1569), of Sanquhar, 7th Baron Crichton (1561), 90.

Crichton, James (d.c.1667), laird of Frendraught (1620), 234-236.

Crichton, Fr William (d.c.1615), Jesuit priest, 206.

Cunningham, Alexander (c.1510-1574/5), 4th Earl of Glencairn (1547), 55; 83, 87, 91, 94, 96.

Cunningham, David (1611), Bishop of Aberdeen (1577), 225, 297 n.58.

Cunningham, James (d.c.1631), 6th Earl of Glencairn (c.1580), 132.

Dacre, Sir Thomas (d.1565), commander of the English rearward at Pinkie (1547), 40.

Dalrymple, Sir David (1726-1792), of Hailes, Scottish judge, 266.

Darnley (see Stewart, Henry)

David I (c.1084-1153), King of Scotland (1124-1153), 17-18, 108.

David II (1324-1371), King of Scotland (1329-1371), 63.

Douglas, Archibald (d.1455), Earl of Moray (1445), killed at Arkinholme, 18-20, 63.

Douglas, Archibald (c.1489-1557), 6th Earl of Angus (1514), 25,26, 27, 31, 33, 36, 37; at Pinkie, 40, 42-43;
antagonism to 4th Earl of Huntly, 45-46.

Douglas, Archibald (c.1555-1588), 8th Earl of Angus (1557), 118, 132, 294 n.46.

Douglas, Sir George (c.1490-1552), of Pittendreich, brother of the 6th Earl of Angus, quotations from, 25, 31, 33,
opinion of 4th earl of Huntly 34, 35.

Douglas, George (d.1611), Bishop of Moray (1574), 131.

Douglas, James (c.1516-1581), 4th Earl of Morton (1553), 63, 68, 82, 83, 88, 297 n.58; Lords of the Congregation,
52; Ricchio murder, 82; Ainslie's bond, 85; Langside, 91, 93, 945; Moray's funeral, 96; Lennox, 97, 98; Mar,
99; Regent (1572-1577/8), 101-104; 6th Earl of Huntly, 123-124; deposed (1580), 117, 118; executed, 125.

Douglas, Margaret (1515-1578), Countess of Lennox, mother of Darnley, 80, 261.

Douglas, William (d.1452), 8th Earl of Douglas (1443), 18.

Douglas, William (c.1532-1591), 9th Earl of Angus (1588), 70, 151, 157, 163 169.

Douglas, William (c.1540-1606), of Lochleven, 6th Earl of Morton (1588), 169, 170, 194.

Douglas, William (c.1554-1611), 10th Earl of Angus (1591), 169, 170, 205, 206, 207, 211, 220, 226, 312 n.6.

Douglas, William of Earlshill, bailiff of 2nd Earl of Moray, 152-153, 155.

Drummond, John, of Blair, 137, 162, 163; at Donnibristle, 304 n.12.

Drummond, Robert of Carnock, Royal Master of Works, 116.

Dubh [or Duff, the Black], Donald (c.1480-1545), grandson of the last Lord of the Isles, 37.

Dudley, John (c.1502-1553), Earl of Warwick(1547), Duke of Northumberland (1551),40, 41.

Dudley, Robert (1533-1588), Earl of Leicester (1564), 79.

Dunbar, Elizabeth (d.1485/6), Countess of Moray, daughter and heiress of James Dunbar, 20.

Dunbar, George, sheriff of Moray, 152, 153, 166.

Dunbar, James (d.1429), of Frendraught, Earl of Moray (c.1427), 19, 20.

Dunbar, Patrick (d.1367), Earl of Moray (1346), 19.

Dunbar, Patrick (d.1591/2), of Boigholl, Sheriff of Moray, 155, 174, 178, 190, 226, 305 n.20.

Edmonstone, Sir William, laird of Duntreath, 107-108, 174, 294 n.5.

Edward I (1239-1307), King of England (1272-1307), 'Hammer of the Scots,' 17.

Edward VI (1537-1553), King of England (1547-1553), 33, 35, 36, 45.

Eglington, earls of (see Montgomerie).

Elizabeth I (1533-1603), Queen of England (1558-1603), 10, 11, 54, 58, 59, 61, 75, 79, 80, 85, 128, 201, 144, 145, 242, 296 n.34 and 51; mourns Moray, 96; 97, 98, 101; exasperation with James VI, 12, 145, 146, 150, 156-157, 205, 206, 210, 242.

Elphinstone, William (1431-1514), Bishop of Aberdeen (c.1488), founder of King's College, Aberdeen (1498), 115.

Elphinstone, Nicol (d.1578), of Shank, 124.

Elphinstone, James (1553-1612), Master of Elphinstone, 192.

Errol, earls of (see Hay).

Erskine, John (c.1510-1572), 6th Baron Erskine (1555), 1st Earl of Mar (1565), 53, 59, 61, 62, 81, 91, 94, 96; Regent (1571-1572), 99-101, death of, 100.

Erskine, John, (1562-1616), 2nd Earl of Mar (1572), 127, 132, 145, 151, 157, 170, 190, 194, 213, 231, 262.

Erskine, Margaret (d.1572), sister of John, 1st Earl of Mar, mother of Lord James (1530), 50.

Eure, Sir Ralph, (d.1544/5), English commander, killed at Ancrum Moor, 36-37.

Farnese, Alessandro (1545-1592), Duke of Parma, nephew of Philip II of Spain, 145, 147.

Fleming, John (c.1536-1572), laird of Craigmiller, Provost of Edinburgh, Lethington's brother-in-law, 5th Baron Fleming, governor of Dumbarton Castle (1567-1571), 54, 83, 87, 88, 91.

Forbes, Alexander (d.1491), 4th Baron Forbes (1463), 192.

Forbes, Arthur (1520-1571), of Balfour and Putachie, youngest son of 6th Baron Forbes, 99.

Forbes, Arthur (1550-1574), of Logie, 4th son of 7th Baron Forbes, 101.

Forbes, Duncan (d.1584), 1st laird of Monymusk, grandson of 2nd Baron Forbes, 93.

Forbes, John (1472-1547), 6th Baron Forbes (1493), third son of the 3rd Baron Forbes and the daughter of the 1st Earl of Huntly, 29.

Forbes, John (c.1511-1537), 2nd son of 6th Baron Forbes, Master of Forbes (1513), 29, 68.

Forbes, John (1542-1606), 1st son of 7th Baron Forbes, Master of Forbes, at Tulliangus, 99; at Crabstone, 100; released from Spynie, 102; 8th Baron Forbes (1594), 214, 215.

Forbes, John (d.1580) of Tollie [Towie], married firstly the daughter of John Grant of Ballindalloch, secondly

Margaret, daughter of John Campbell of Cawdor, 100, 125.

Forbes, William (1513-1594), Master of Forbes (1537), 7th Baron Forbes (1547), 68, 70, 99, 150, 192.

Forbes, William (b.1544), of Fodderbirse, 2nd son of 7th Baron Forbes, 99.

Fowler, Sir Thomas, English agent in Scotland, 146, 150, 151, 173.

Francis II (1544-1560), Dauphin, married Mary Queen of Scots (1558), King of France (1559), 43-44, 45, 52, 53, 58.

Fraser, Hugh (d.1544), 3rd Baron Lovat (1524), killed at Loch Lochy, 29, 37-38.

Fraser, Hugh (1544-1576/7), 5th Baron Lovat (1557), 64, 65.

Fraser, Simon (c.1570-1633), 6th Baron Lovat (1576/7), 155, 159.

Fraser, Robert (d.1594), Lion Herald, killed at Glenlivat, 219, 220.

Galloway, Patrick (c.1551-c.1626), Scottish divine, minister of the royal household, Moderator of the General
    Assembly (1590), 196.

Glammis, barons of (see Lyon).

Glencairn, earls of (see Cunningham).

Gordon, Sir Adam de, (d.1333), killed at Halidon Hill, 18.

Gordon, Sir Adam (d.1402), Baron Gordon (1400), killed at Homildon Hill, 18.

Gordon, Adam (c.1474-1537/8), 2nd son of 2nd Earl of Huntly, married Elizabeth, Countess of Sutherland (1500),
    became Earl of Sutherland by virtue of his wife (1515), 21, 29.

Gordon, Adam (1545-1580), 'Edom o'Gordon,' laird of Auchindoun (1567), 6th son of the 4th Earl of Huntly, 286 n.13;
    escapes execution, 71, 73; defeats Forbes at Tulliangus, 99, and Crabstane, 100; burns Corgarff Castle, 100, at Brighen,
    100, at Aberdeen, 100; 101-102; imprisoned 102, 124; and the 6th Earl of Huntly, 123, 124; death of, 124.

Gordon, Adam (d.1590), laird of Auchindoun (1580), 157.

Gordon, Adam (d. post 1642), of Aboyne and (from 1620) of Auchindoun, 3rd son of 6th Earl of Huntly, 237, 299 n.40.

Gordon, Sir Alexander (d.1346), killed at Neville's Cross, 17-18.

Gordon, Alexander (d.1523/4), 3rd Earl of Huntly (1501-1523/4), 20, 21, 25, 26, 64.

Gordon, Alexander (1501-1529/30), Master of Sutherland, 30.

Gordon, Alexander (c.1516-1575), younger brother of 4th Earl of Huntly, Bishop of Galloway (1559), Archbishop of
    Athens, 25.

Gordon, Alexander, (d.1552-3), 1st son of 4th Earl of Huntly, 47, 286 n.13, 288 n.65.

Gordon, Alexander (1552-1594), 11th Earl of Sutherland (1567), 90, 127, 163.

Gordon, Alexander, 12th Earl of Sutherland (1594), 237.

Gordon, Alexander of Bothrom (d.1562), warden of Inverness castle, 64, 289 n.25 and 29.

Gordon, Alexander (c.1538-1609), 3rd laird of Lesmour (c.1586), 135, 159, 176.

Gordon, Ann (d.1640), daughter of 1st Marquis of Huntly, married 3rd Earl of Moray, 231-232, 237, 299 n.40.

Gordon, Elizabeth (d.1438/9), daughter of Adam Gordon, married Sir Alexander Seton, 18.

Gordon, Elizabeth (d. post 1566), bastard of Adam Gordon, son of 1st Earl of Huntly, 2nd wife of Ogilvie of Findlater, 61.

Gordon, Elizabeth, eldest daughter of 4th Earl of Huntly, married 4th Earl of Atholl, 286 n.13.

Gordon, Francis (d.1620), 2nd son of 6th Earl of Huntly, 299 n.40.

Gordon, George (d.1501), 2nd Earl of Huntly (1470), married Elizabeth Dunbar, 20, 61.

Gordon, George (1514-1562), birth, 21; 4th Earl of Huntly (1524), 25; relationships with James V, 25, 27, with
    Angus, 27, with Hector Macintosh, 28; Privy Councillor (1535), 30; captain of Inverness and Inverlochy, 39;
    married Elizabeth Keith (1530), 30; offspring, 286 n.13; warden of Marches, 31; Vice Regent 33, 34; Hadden
    Rig (1542), 31; peace negotiations at York, 31; character & reputation 30, 32, 34-36, 41, 45, 48; 'Rough
    Wooing' 36, 43; Lieutenant, 37, 51; Chancellor, 39, 45, 58; Pinkie, 40-43; in England, 43-45; prospect of

dukedom, 45-46; earldom of Moray, 45, 46; killing of William Mackintosh, 46-47; accompanies Mary of Guise to France, 47; rebuilds Huntly Castle, 47; entertains French, 48; disgraced, 49-50; refuses to help Mary of Guise, 50, 55; relations with Lords of the Congregation, 52, 54, with Mary Queen of Scots, 33, 57-60, 62, 63, 64, 65, 66, 67, with Lord James, 59, 64, 242; battle of Corrichie, 67-71; death of 70-71; tried for treason, 73-74; burial 74, assessment of, 10, 11, 35.

Gordon, George, (c.1535-1576) 5th Earl of Huntly (1565), 60, 64, 67, 89, 286 n.13; marries Lady Anne Hamilton (1559), 54; condemned for treason, 73; imprisoned 73,74; restored to favour, 75, 81, 82, 85, 291 n.16; character, 81; Ainslie's Bond, 85, 86, 292 n.21; abandons Mary, 87, 89, 91; bullies Aberdeen, 92-93, 94; leads Marian party, 92, 94, 96, 97, 98, 295 n.22; and Forbes, 99-100; and Morton, 101; signs Pacification of Perth, 101; death of, 103, 294 n.47, 314 n.6; assessment of, 103-104.

Gordon, George (d.1580), 3rd laird of Gight, 125.

Gordon, George (1562-1636), 6th Earl of Huntly (1576), 1st Marquis of Huntly (1599), birth 76; youth, 123-125, 132; education 113, 114, 124-125; religious convictions, 124-125, 145, 152, 224-226, 232-233, 234, 236-237; wealth, 124; feud with Moray, 122, 125-126, 129, 131, 135, 154-172, 229; the Ballindalloch incident, 159-162; reconciled by James VI, 136, 143; relationship with James VI, 123, 126, 127, 128, 138-139, 144, 146, 150-151, 152, 167, 196, 212, 230; with Mary, 128; Ruthven Raid, 127, 128; tolerance of 'youth clubs' 134; marriage of, 128, 138-139, 315 n.7; attends Privy Council, 143; captain of the Guard, 144; animosity to Bothwell, 144, and the Armada, 143, 145; Brig O'Dee rebellion,149-150; building in the north, 126, 152, 226, 233; and Maitland, 137, 146-147, 172, 301 n.31; dispute with Athol, 137; 'Ronnie Rode' 137; protects Gight, 177; attack on Darnaway, 160; murder of Boyd, 168, commission against Bothwell, 170, 176; murder of Moray, 172, 176-180, 198, 225, 240-241, 307 n.15; murder of Cawdor, 181, 183, 184; aftermath, 190, 191, 192, 195; warded in Blackness, 197, 198, 199; aborted trial, 197, 199; returns north, 200, 201, 203, 204-205; Spanish Blanks, 205-206; dalliance with Bothwell, 211; Glenlivet, 213-220, 221-222, 310 n.26; exile, 223-224, repentance, 224; submission to Kirk, 224-225; made Marquis, 230, 312 n.6; letter to 3rd Earl of Moray, 232; and Charles I, 233; and Frendraught, 235-236, illness, 236; death, 236, funeral, 236-237. Plates 20, 21, 23-33.

Gordon, George (d.1649), 2nd Marquis of Huntly (1636), married Anna Campbell, 224, 231.

Gordon, James (c.1541-1620), son of 4th Earl of Huntly, Jesuit priest, 223, 225-226, 286 n.13.

Gordon, James (d.c.1637), Master of Lesmour, 4th laird of Lesmour (1609), and tutor of Ballindalloch, 159, 166, 177; at Donnibristle, 304 n.12; 311 n.14, 241.

Gordon, Jean or Jane (1545-1629), youngest daughter of 4th Earl of Huntly, wife of 4th Earl of Bothwell (1566-1567), Countess of Sutherland (1573), 85, 86, 87, 286 n.13, 292 n.21.

Gordon, Sir John, (d.1388), killed at Otterburn, 17.

Gordon, John (d.1517), 1st son of 3rd Earl of Huntly, Master of Huntly, married Margaret Stewart, illegitimate daughter of James IV (1510), 21.

Gordon, John (1525-1567), 10th Earl of Sutherland (1537/8), 46, 68, 81, 85.

Gordon, Sir John (d.1562), of Deskford, 3rd son of 4th Earl of Huntly, 60-61, 62, 63, 64, 65, 66, 67, 286 n.13; executed 71-73, Mary's attitude to, 71-73, 74, 75.

Gordon, John, 6th laird of Gight, 134.

Gordon, John (d.1590), brother of Thomas of Cluny, 159; killed at Darnaway, 160-162, 177.

Gordon, John, of Buckie (d.c.1640), Master of the king's household, murderer of Moray, 179; 189-190, 304 n.12; 305 n.26; death of, 237.

Gordon, John (d.1591/2), captain, son of John, 4th laird, and brother of William, 5th laird of Gight, 176, 177, 304 n.12; mortally wounded at Donnibristle 177, 180, 191, 305 n.26.

Gordon, John (1606-1630), 5th and youngest son of the 6th Earl of Huntly, viscount Melgum and lord Aboyne

(1627), death at Frendraught, 234-235, 299 n.40.

Gordon, Margaret, 2nd daughter of 4th Earl of Huntly, 99, 286 n.13.

Gordon, Patrick (d.1594), of Auchindoun (1590), 7th son of 4th Earl of Huntly, 286 n.13, 124, 204; Donnibristle, 304 n.12; Spanish Blanks, 206, 207; Glenlivet, 215, 216, 218, 220.

Gordon, Sir Robert (1580-1656), historian, pall bearer at 1st Marquis of Huntly's funeral, 237.

Gordon, Thomas, laird of Cluny, 159, 177, 179, 198, 203, 208; 216, 241, 304 n.12.

Gordon, William (d.1513), 3rd son of 2nd Earl of Huntly, ancestor of Gordons of Gight from whom Lord Byron is descended, killed at Flodden, 21.

Gordon, William (d.1577), 3rd son of 3rd Earl of Huntly, Bishop of Aberdeen (1545), 52.

Gordon, William (d.1604), 5th laird of Gight (1591/2), 176-177, murderer of 2nd Earl of Moray, 179, 198, 203, 216, 218, 220, 225, 241, 304 n.12.

Gowrie, earls of (see Ruthven).

Graham, John (1548-1608), 3rd Earl of Montrose (1571), 100, 149, 155, 209.

Graham, Robert (d.1547), Master of Graham, 42.

Graham, William (c.1500-1571), 2nd Earl of Montrose (1513), 59, 68, 90, 109.

Grant, James (1485-1553), 3rd laird of Freuchy (1528), 38.

Grant, John (d.1585), 4th laird of Freuchy (1553), 92, 124.

Grant, John (1568-1622), 5th laird of Freuchy (1585), chief of Grant, 135, 150, 155, 158-9, 160, 161, 162, 163, 164, 168, 169, 205, 213.

Grant, John, Tutor of Ballindalloch, 159, 168.

Gray, Andrew (d.c.1611), of Skelton, brother of 5th Baron Gray, 214, 217.

Gray, Elizabeth, daughter of Andrew, 2nd Baron Gray, wife of 3rd Earl of Huntly (1511), 27.

Gray, Patrick (d.1612), Master of Gray, 6th Baron Gray (1609), 157.

Gregory, Donald (d.1836), antiquary, 182.

Grey, William (d.1562), 13th Baron Grey de Wilton, 42, 54.

Guise, Charles de (1525-1574), Cardinal of Lorraine, uncle of Mary Queen of Scots, 75.

Guise, Mary of (1515-1560), Queen of Scotland (1538), 30, 33, 36, 39, 44, 45; Queen-Regent (1553/4) 49-55; Huntly, 47, 48, 50, 55, 58, 59; Lord James, 50, 51, 55; death of, 55.

Hamilton, Anne, 3rd daughter of Chatelherault, married 5th Earl of Huntly (1559), 54.

Hamilton, Claud (c.1543-1621/2), Baron Paisley (1587), 4th son of Chatelherault, 99, 132, 145, 150.

Hamilton, James (1477-1529), 2nd Baron (1479) and 1st Earl of Arran (1503), 26, 27.

Hamilton, James (c.1516-1575), 2nd Earl of Arran (1529), 33, 34 35, 36, 39, 41, 44-45, 49, 50, 53, 54, 79, 109; Duke of Chatelherault (1548), 44; and Mary, 60, 64, 67, 80, 81, 92, 94, 96, 97, 98; wealth, 120, 124.

Hamilton, James (c.1530-1609), eldest son of Chatelherault, styled 3rd Earl of Arran after 1553, 53, 89.

Hamilton, James (c.1540-1580), of Bothwell Haugh, assassin of Regent Moray, 95.

Hamilton, John (c.1511-1571), bastard of James Hamilton, 1st Earl of Arran, Commendator of Paisley, Archbishop of St Andrews (1549), 51, 85, 86, 95, 98, 99.

Hamilton, John (c.1540-1604), 2nd son of Chatelherault, commendator of Arbroath, 1st Marquis of Hamilton (1599), 97, 230.

Hay, Elizabeth (d.c.1510), daughter of William Hay, 1st Earl of Errol, sister of Nicholas Hay, 2nd Earl of Errol, 3rd wife of 2nd Earl of Huntly, 20, 27.

Hay, Francis (1564-1631), 9th Earl of Errol (1585), 132, 144, 145, 147; Brig o'Dee rebellion, 149-150, 156, 157, 198; Spanish Blanks, 206, 207, 211; Glenlivet, 215, 216, 217-218, 220; aftermath, 221, 222, 311 n.9; exile

223; submission to kirk, 225, 226.

Hay, George (d.1573/4), 7th Earl of Errol (1541), 59, 68.

Hay, William (d.c.1462), 1st Earl of Errol (1436), 20.

Hay, William (d.1576), 5th Baron Yester (1559), 65, 87, 90.

Henderson, James, surgeon of Edinburgh, embalms 2nd Earl of Moray, 192.

Henderson, Robert, surgeon of Edinburgh, embalms 4th Earl of Huntly, 73.

Henry II (1519-1559), King of France (1547-1559) 36.

Henry III, King of France (1574-1589), 124.

Henry VIII (1491-1547), King of England (1510-1547), 25, 31, 33, 34 36, 39, 40.

Hepburn, James (1536-1578), 4th Earl of Bothwell (1556), Duke of Orkney (1567), 60, 74, 82 83, 87; Darnley's
    murder, 84-85, 239, 291 n.17; marriage to Mary, 86-87, 292 n.19.

Hepburn, Patrick (c.1512-1556), 3rd Earl of Bothwell (1513), 35, 36

Hepburn, Patrick (d.1573), Bishop of Moray (1538), 90, 100.

Heriott, George (1563-1624), royal goldsmith, 142.

Herries, baron (see Maxwell).

Hertford, Earl of (see Seymour)

Home, Alexander (d.1516), 3rd Baron Home (1506), executed, 21.

Home, Alexander (c.1528-1575), 5th Baron Home (1549), 41, 87, 91, 102.

Home, Alexander (1566-1619), 6th Baron (1578) and 1st Earl of Home (1604/5), 149, 150, 151, 199, 209, 211.

Home, Sir David, of Wedderburn, 26.

Home, George (1547), 4th Baron Home (1522), 35.

Home, Sir George (d.1611), of Primroknows, Earl of Dunbar (1605-1611), 199, 209.

Howard, Thomas (1473-1554), Earl of Surrey (1514) and 3rd Duke of Norfolk (1524), 31, 32, 54.

Hume, David (c.1560-c.1630), of Godscroft, historian, 33, 49, 71, 72, 268, 286 n.17.

Huntly, earls of (see Gordon and Seton)

Innermeath, barons of, (see Stewart, John)

Innes, Robert (d.1595), laird of Innermarky, 178, 179, 198, 218, 226, 304 n.12, 311 n.14.

James II (1430-1460), King of Scotland (1437-1460), 18, 26, 109.

James III (1452-1488), King of Scotland (1460-1488), 20, 192.

James IV (1473-1513), King of Scotland (1488-1513), 19, 20, 21, 29, 33, 107, 193.

James V (1512-1542), King of Scotland (1513-1542), 25, 26, 30-33, 50, 107, 132, 262.

James VI (1566-1625), King of Scotland (1567-1625), King of England (1603-1625), motto, 239; birth, 83; baptism,
    84-85, coronation, 88; minority, 90, at Doune, 113; education, 114; religious views, 146, 151, 206; love of
    sports and hunting, 113, 118, 139, 146, 170, 176, 314 n.4; love of 6th Earl of Huntly, 12, 123, 126, 128, 138,
    144, 146, 147-148, 150-151, 156, 162, 167, 196, 199, 202, 209, 212, 230, 242; wedding of Huntly, 138-139,
    315 n.7; Ruthven raid, 127, 311 n.1; and Doune, 129; 4, 7; the virtue of forgiveness, 12, 136, 144, 146, 154,
    157, 161-162, 164, 169, 171, 210, 224, 226, 231, 243, 307 n.13; attitude to nobility, 136-137, 147, 148, 229-
    230, 242, 243; Spanish Armada, 145; Brig O'Dee rebellion, 149-150; marriage, 153-154; 2nd Earl of Moray,
    118, 296 n.51, 165, 169, 170-171, 194; fear of and loathing for Bothwell, 147, 148, 149, 151, 156, 161, 162-
    163, 164-165, 170-171, 175, 194, 196, 203, 208-209, 239, 308 n.50; murder of Moray, 175, 189, 190, 191;
    involvement in, 191-192, 203, 209, 239-240, 239-243, 308 n.36; Queen Ann, 194, 239; the art of prevarication,
    201-202, 205-208, 242; Spanish Blanks, 206-207, 210; after Glenlivet, 220, 221-222, 310 n.26; on Knox,

290 n.46; accession to English throne (1603), 231; death of 233; assessment of, 239-243; *Basilikon Doron*, 230; quotations from, 131, 136, 141, 201. Plates 6 and 7.

Jamieson, Robert (c.1780-1844), ballad collector, 266.

Keith, Agnes (d.1588), eldest daughter of William, 4th Earl Marischal, 30, married Lord James Stewart (1561/2), 59, 87, 97, 117, 120, 131.

Keith, Elizabeth, eldest daughter of Lord Robert Keith, marries 4th Earl of Huntly (1530), 30; murders Macintosh (1550), 47; and Mary Queen of Scots, 62, 65-66, 67, 71, 82-83.

Keith, George (c.1553-1623), 5th Earl Marischal (1581-1623), 99, 100, 127, 151, 198.

Keith, Robert (d.c.1514), Master of Marischal, father-in-law of 4th Earl of Huntly, 30.

Keith, Robert (1681-1757), Bishop of Fife (1733-1743), Primus, historian, 110.

Keith, William (c.1507-1581), 4th Earl Marischal (c.1527-1581), 30, 55, 59, 62.

Keith, William (d.1635), 6th Earl Marischal (1623), 132, 294 n.46.

Kennedy, Gilbert (c.1517-1558), 3rd Earl of Cassilis (1527-1558), 47, 50.

Kennedy, Gilbert (c.1541-1576), 4th Earl of Cassilis (1558-1576), 'king of Carrick,' 90, 96.

Kennedy, Gilbert (c.1576-1601), laird of Bargany, (1597), 262.

Kennedy, James (c.1406-1465), Bishop of St Andrews (1441), founder of St Salvator's College (1450), 115.

Kennedy, John (c.1574-1615), 5th Earl of Cassilis, (1576), 262.

Kennedy, Margaret, grand-daughter of 1st Earl of Huntly, 107.

Kerr, Janet (née Scott), 2nd wife of Sir Thomas Kerr of Fernihurst, 128.

Kerr, Robert (c.1570-1649), laird of Cessford, later 1st Earl of Roxburgh (1616), 132.

Kerr, Sir Thomas, (d.1585/6), laird of Fernihurst (1562), 100,101, 128, 138.

Kerr, Thomas, Captain, 208, 215, 216, 217.

Kilfauns, laird of (see Lindsay).

Kirkaldy, James (d.1573), brother of Sir William, 102.

Kirkaldy, Sir William, of Grange (c.1520-1573), Fifeshire laird, soldier, assassin of Beaton, 39; at Corrichie, 65, 66; opposes Mary, 80, 87, 91, 94; Keeper of Edinburgh Castle, 94, 96, champions Mary, 98; raids Stirling, 98-99; executed, 102.

Knox, John, Reformer (c.1514-1572), 51, 57, 60, 79, 171, 292 n.19; on the 4th Earl of Huntly, 25, 47, 286 n.17, Corrichie, 68-69, 70, 71, 74; at Moray's funeral, 96.

Kynnaird, Walter (d.1613), of Cubbin, 169.

Laing, David (1793-1878), antiquary and ballad collector, 266.

Layton, Sir Brian (d.1544/5), English commander, killed at Ancrum Moor, 36-37.

Leicester, earl of (see Dudley)

Lekprevick, Robert (fl. 1561-1588), Protestant printer, royal printer (1568-1588), 267.

Lennox, earls of (see Stewart)

Leslie, of Buquan, 215, 216.

Leslie, Andrew (d.1558), 4th Earl of Rothes, 46.

Leslie, Andrew (c.1530-1611), 5th Earl of Rothes (1558), 70, 80.

Leslie, John (c.1527-1596), Parson of Oyne, Bishop of Ross (1566), historian, quotation from 15; emissary to Mary Queen of Scots, 57; Corrichie, 69; the 'Protestation,' 84.

Leslie, John, factor of 2nd Earl of Moray, 142, 166, 167.

Leslie, Norman, at Donnibristle, 178, 304 n.12, 305 n.18.

Leslie, William, younger of Warthill, 63, 176.

Lindsay, Alexander (d.1454), 4th Earl of Crawford (1446), the 'tiger,' 18.

Lindsay, Alexander (d.1607), 1st Baron Spynie (1590), fourth son of the 10th Earl of Crawford, royal favourite, 148, 158, 166, 191, 199.

Lindsay, Sir David (1490-1555), of the Mount, poet, Lyon King of arms, 30.

Lindsay, David (1524-1574), 10th Earl of Crawford (1558), 90, 97.

Lindsay, David (c1547-1607), 11th Earl of Crawford (1574), 127, 145, 148, 149, 150, 151.

Lindsay, Henry (d.1623), brother of the 11th Earl of Crawford, laird of Kilfauns, 13th Earl of Crawford (1620), 211.

Lindsay, James (1554-1601), 7th Baron Lindsay of the Byres (1589), 221.

Lindsay, Patrick (1521-1589), 6th Baron Lindsay of the Byres (1563), 65, 66, 82, 84, 96.

Lindsay, Robert (c.1500-c.1565), of Pitscottie, historian, 286 n.17, 287 n.39.

Lindsay, Sir Walter (d.1605), of Balgavie, 207, 221.

Livingstone, William (c.1528-1592), 6th Baron Livingston (1553), 83, 90.

Lochaber, laird of, (see Cameron).

Lorraine, cardinal of (see Guise).

Lovat, barons of (see Fraser).

Lyon, John (d.1578), 8th Baron Glamis (1558-1578), 96.

Lyon, Patrick (1575-1615), 9th Baron Glamis (1578), Earl of Kinghorn (1606), 145.

Lyon, Thomas (d.1608), Master of Glamis,150, 157, 229, 311 n.1.

Macbeth (c.1005-1057), King of Scotland (1040-1057), 156.

MacDougall of Dunollie, 163, 183, 184.

Macintosh, Angus, son of Lachlan, 16th chief of Clan Chattan, 204.

Macintosh, Hector (d.1524), 14th chief of Clan Chattan, 28, 29, 38, 46.

Macintosh, Lachlan (d.1600), of Dunnachten, 16th chief of Clan Chattan (1550), 46, 68, 93, 155, 158-159, 160, 163, 164, 168, 196, 204, 205, 213, 214, 216.

Macintosh, William (d.1550), 15th Chief of Clan Chattan (1540), 37, 46-47.

McKellar, Gillimartin Oig (d.1594), 183, 184.

McKellar, Gillipatrick Oig (d.1594), 181, 183, 184, 185.

Mackenzie, Colin (d.1633), 1st Earl of Seaforth (1623), 213, 237.

McLean, Lauchlin, of Duart, 14th chief of McLean, 163, 183, 213, 216, 2 17, 218, 219, 310 n.14.

Macnares, Neil (d.1594), of the Hebrides, 217.

Maitland, Sir John,(1543-1595), of Thirlstane, younger brother of Lethington, Secretary of State (1584), Chancellor (1587-1592, 1594-1595), 102, relations with James VI, 136-137, 146-149; with Huntly, 143-144, 146-149, 151-152, 154, 157, 159, 161, 162, 169; with Bothwell, 144, 149, 154, 156, 164-165, 167, 169, 170; with Moray, 161, 162, 169, 171, 175; made 1st Baron Thirlestane (1591), 169; Cawdor, 163, 181, 182, 183, 184; implicated in murder of Moray, 172, 175, 191, 195, 199, 203, 209, 240, 241.

Maitland William (c.1525-1573), of Lethington, 'Mitchell Wylie,' Secretary of State (1558-1573), 54, 55, 59, 62, 67, 69, 75, 79, 82, 84-85, 87, 95, 102.

Major, John (1469-1550), historian, quotations from, 15, 123, 132, 133, 134.

Malcolm III (c.1031-1093), Canmore, King of Scotland (1058-1093), 64, 109.

Manners, Thomas (d.1543), 1st Earl of Rutland (1525), 31.

Mar, earls of (see Erskine).

Marischal, earl (see Keith).

Mary Tudor (1516-1558), Queen of England (1553-1558), 92.

Mary Stewart (1542-1587), Queen of Scots (1542-1587), childhood, 30, 33, 35, 43; marriage to Dauphin, 43-44,

45, 52, 53, 55, 56, 56; relations with 4th Earl of Huntly, 57-60, 288 n.13, with Elizabeth, 58, 59; the English
succession, 58, 75; John Gordon, 61, 71-73; Northern tour, 61-73; destruction of Huntly, 74-76; proposed
Spanish Marriage, 79; Darnley, 80, 82; murder of Ricchio, 82; murder of Darnley 83-85, 261, 291 n.17; 5th
Earl of Huntly, 81, 90; 1st Earl of Moray, 56, 81, 89; Bothwell, 86-87, 132, 292 n.19; Carberry, 87, 261;
abdicates, 88; Langside, 90-91; St Colme, 110; 6th Earl of Huntly, 128; 212; assessment of, 92, 239, 288 n.8,
292 n.23. Plates 2 and 6.

Matilda (1102-1167), uncrowned Queen of England during 1141, 92.

Maxwell, Sir John (c.1512-1583), of Terregles, second son of 5th Baron Maxwell, Master of Maxwell, 4th Baron
Herries (1566), 55, 91, 94.

Maxwell, John (1553-1593), 7th Baron Maxwell, Earl of Morton (1581),90, 145, 183, 184, 227.

Maxwell, Robert (d.1546), 5th Baron Maxwell (1513), 32.

Meldrum, John (d.1633), of Reidshill, 235, 236.

Melvil, Sir James (1535-1617), of Halhill, courtier, Memoirs, first published 1683, 307 n.32.

Melvil, Sir Robert, brother of Sir James of Halhill, 209, 309 n.32.

Melville, Andrew (1545-1622), educational reformer, uncle of James Melville, 115; 221.

Melville, James (1556-c.1641), nephew of Andrew Melville, diarist, author of Autobiography and Diary, 133, 189,
194, 220, 221, 265.

Melville, James, of Carnbee, murdered Cardinal Beaton, 39.

Montgomerie, Hugh (c.1531-1585), 3rd Earl of Eglington (1546), 90, 295 n.25.

Montgomerie, Hugh (1563-1586), 4th Earl of Eglington (1585), 203.

Montrose, earls of (see Graham).

Moray, earls of (see Stewart).

Morton, earls of (see Douglas).

Morton, Fr, Papal emissary, 211, 223.

Moydertach, John (d.1584), ('of Moidart'), 6th chief of Clan Ranald, 37-38, 49.

Moysie, David (ff.1582-1603), lawyer, diarist, clerk of the Privy Council, 177, 189.

Mulcaster, Richard (c.1530-1611), English educationalist, 295 n.31.

Murray, John (d.1613), of Tullibardine, Baron Murray (1604), 216, 219.

Naismith, John, associate of Bothwell, 195, 239.

Norfolk, duke of (see Howard).

Ochiltree, barons of (see Andrew Stewart).

Ogilvie, Alexander (d.1554), of Deskford and Findlater, married Elizabeth Gordon (1535), 61.

Ogilvie, James (d.c.1574), of Cardell, and Findlater, 1st son of Alexander Ogilvie of Findlater, Master of the Queen's
Household (1562-1567) 60, 61, 62, 90, 97, 289 n.13.

Ogilvie, Sir John, of Craig, 221.

Parma, duke of (see Farnese)

Patten, William (ff.1548-1580), 'judge of the Marshelsey,' receiver general of York, author of first hand account of
battle of Pinkie, 41, 43, 287 n.40.

Percy, Thomas (1729-1811), Bishop of Dromore (1782), 263, 265-266, 313 n.7.

Philip II (1527-1598), King of Spain (1556-1598), 79, 145.

Preston, Robert, of Craigmillar, captain of Dunbar castle, provost of Edinburgh, 74.

Radcliffe, Thomas (*c*.1526-1583), 2nd Earl of Sussex (1557), 97, 98, 134.

Ramsay, Allan (1686-1758), Scottish poet, 265.

Ranald Galda (d.1544), 'the stranger,'only son of Ranald Bane, 5th chief of Clan Ranald, and a daughter of Lord
     Lovat. Called 'the stranger' from being fostered by his mother's relations, the Frasers. His father died in 1541
     and Galda was usurped by his cousin John Moydertach and killed at the battle of 'the Field of Shirts,' 37-38.

Randolph, John (d.1346), 3rd Earl of Moray (1332), killed at Neville's Cross, 19.

Randolph, Thomas (d.1332), 1st Earl of Moray (1312), Regent (1329), 19, 63.

Randolph, Thomas (1523-1590), English ambassador to Scotland (1559-1566, 1570-1572, 1581, 1586), 57, 60, 62,
     63, 66, 173, 289 n.14 and 24; death of 4th Earl of Huntly, 70, 71, 75; and 1st Earl of Moray, 80, 81, 83;
     St Colme, 110; on Scots culture, 134.

Ricchio, David (*c*.1533-1566), Secretary to Mary Queen of Scots, murder of, 82, 84, 112.

Richard II (1367-1400), King of England (1377-1399), probably starved to death, 202.

Robert I (1274-1329), the Bruce, King of Scotland (1306-1329),17, 18, 19, 286 n.21.

Robert II (1316-1390), King of Scotland (1371-1390), 19, 286 n.21.

Rothes, earls of (see Leslie).

Ruthven, Patrick (*c*.1520-1566), 3rd Baron Ruthven (1552), 54; murder of Ricchio, 82, 84.

Ruthven, William (*c*.1541-1584), 4th Baron Ruthven(1566), 1st Earl of Gowrie (1581), 91, 96; Ruthven Raid, 127,
     execution, 128.

Ruthven, John (*c*.1578-1600) 3rd Earl of Gowrie (1588), 209, 231, 240.

Rutland, earl of (see Manners).

St Colme, commendator and baron of (see Stewart, James, Henry).

Sadler, Sir Ralph (1507-1587), English ambassador to Scotland (1537-45), 34-35, 42.

Saltoun, barons of (see Abernethy).

Sandilands, Sir James, Keeper of Blackness Castle, 197.

Scot, William (d.1579), Edinburgh broadside publisher, 267.

Scott, Sir Walter (1771-1832), writer, 39, 266, 288 n.64.

Seaforth, earls of (see Mackenzie).

Selve, Odet de, (d.1563), seigneur de Marignon, 2nd son of 2nd Baron Selve, French ambassador to England,
     concerns about 4th Earl of Huntly, 44-45, 287 n.51.

Seton, Sir Alexander (d.*c*.1440), 2nd son of Sir William Seton, 18.

Seton, Sir Alexander (d.1470), 1st son of Sir Alexander Seton, 1st Earl of Huntly (1445), builds Strathbogie Castle
     (1452), 47; changes name to Gordon (1458), 18, 20.

Seton, George (*c*.1530-85), 5th Baron Seton, 34, 83, 85, 87.

Seton, George, 6th Baron Seton (1585), 151.

Seymour, Edward (1506-1552), 1st Earl of Hertford (1537), Duke of Somerset and Lord Protector (1547); 36, 37,
     39, 41-43, 44, 45, 46, 109.

Sinclair, George (*c*.1520-1582), 4th Earl of Caithness (1529), 29, 90.

Sinclair, George (*c*.1566-1643), 5th Earl of Caithness (1582), 132, 196.

Sinclair, Henry (1527-1601), 5th Baron Sinclair (1570), 190.

Sinclair, Oliver (fl.537-1560), favourite of James V, 32.

Skelton, Sir John (1831-1897), historian, 35.

Somerset, Edward (1553-1628), 4th Earl of Worcester (1589), 156.

Spalding, John (fl.1650), historian, 223.

Spottiswood, John (1565-1639), Archbishop of St Andrews (1615), 137, 233, 310 n.12.

Spynie, barons of (see Lindsay, Alexander).

Stewart, Andrew (d.1513), 2nd Baron Avandale (1488), 107.

Stewart, Andrew (d.1548), 3rd Baron Avandale (1513), 1st Baron Ochiltree (1542/3), 107.

Stewart, Andrew (c.1520-c.1591), 2nd Baron Ochiltree (1548), 91, 96, 171, 303 n.69.

Stewart, Andrew (c.1560-1628), 3rd Baron Ochiltree (c.1591), 171-172, 175, 176, 178; 190, 191, 194, 196, 202, 203
    205, 241, 267, 303 n.69.

Stewart, Annabella (d.1501), daughter of James I, second wife of 2nd Earl of Huntly, 18.

Stewart, Charles (1555-1576), brother of Darnley. James VI succeeded the Regent Lennox, as 5th Earl but conveyed
    the title to Charles who became 6th Earl of Lennox (1571), 261.

Stewart, Elizabeth (1565-1591), daughter of the Regent Moray, Countess of Moray (1581), prospective marriage to
    George Gordon, 90, 122; married James Stewart, 116, 117-118, 120, 122, 141, 142; illness of, 143; feud with
    Huntly, 155; death of, 169.

Stewart, Princess Elizabeth (1596-1661/2), daughter of James VI, 223.

Stewart, Esmé (c.1542-1583), Lord d'Aubigny, 7th Earl (1579/80) and 1st Duke (1581) of Lennox, 116-117, 118;
    123, 126, 127, 138, 242.

Stewart, Francis (c.1566-1624), 5th Earl of Bothwell (1578), and Ruthven Raid, 127; violent character, 132-133,
    294 n.46; Huntly, 143, 144, 145; James VI, 133, 147, 148-151, 154, 156, 161, 162, 164-165, 170-172, 195,
    199, 202, 208-209, 210, 211, 222, 225; Moray, 118, 165, 168, 239; Maitland, 144, 149, 154, 156, 164-165, 167.

Stewart, Francis, younger son of the 2nd Earl of Moray; portrait at Darnaway as an eighteen-year-old, with Latin inscription
    'When the strength of the lion fails assume the mantle of the fox;' buried in the Regent's tomb, 271, 297 n.68, 315 n.3.

Stewart, Henrietta (1573-1642), daughter of 1st Duke of Lennox, marries 6th Earl of Huntly (1588), 138, 139, 162,
    167, 192, 203, 207-208, 210, 223-224, 226, 236-237. Plate 20.

Stewart, Henry (1495-1564), 1st Baron Methven (1528), 107.

Stewart, Henry (1545-1567), Lord Darnley, Duke of Albany, 74, 79, 80, 82, 83-84, 85, 87, 90, 92 110, 117, 125,
239,   291 n.17; the Darnley Memorials, 261, 267. Plates 15, 16 and 17.

Stewart, Henry (c.1568-1623), brother of the 2nd Earl of Moray, 2nd Baron St Colme (1611), 111, 119 177, 198,
    208, 210, 226, 230, 232, 263.

Stewart, James (c.1500-1544/5), bastard of James IV, Earl of Moray (1501), 19, 29, 31, 32, 34, 36, 37, 46, 286 n.25.

Stewart, James (d.1547) of Beath, Captain of Doune (1528), 107, 108, 294 n.2 and 5.

Stewart, James (c.1528-1590), Commendator of St Colme, 1st Baron Doune (1581), 82, 83, 91, 98, 107, 108, 109,
    110, 119, 295 n.18; character of, 109, 110, 112, 145; and Mary, 110, 112, 295 n.22; marries Margaret Campbell,
    110; Esme Stewart, 117, 118, 127; Ruthven Raid, 127-128, relations with son, 119-121, 128-129, 143, 157, 297 n.62.

Stewart, James (1531-1569/70), bastard of James V, 1st Earl of Moray, the 'Good Regent,' 30, 52, 65, 107, 169,
    character, 50-51, 58, 79, 90; St Andrews University, 51, 288 n.6; relations with Mary of Guise, 50-55, 109;
    relations with Mary, 57-60, 63-64; marries Agnes Keith (1561/2), 59; Corrichie, 69-71, 74, 79, 131; Darnley
    marriage, 80-81, 92; murder of Ricchio, 82; murder of Darnley, 83, 84, 291 n.17; Regent of Scotland (1567),
    89-96, 112; and 5th Earl of Huntly, 74, 96-97, 292 n.18; assassination, 95; Elizabeth mourns, 96; funeral, 96,
    293 n.23; debts 119, 142; tomb, 191, 227-228, 271-272; assessment, 10, 11, 242; Moray Memorial, 261, 267.
    Plates 1, 3 , 4, and 5.

Stewart, James (1567-1591/2), 2nd Earl of Moray (1580), 107, 132, childhood 113, education 113-116, 141;
    marriage, 116, 117-118, 296 n.51, 297 n.58; titled Earl of Moray, 118; physical appearance, 114, 118, 296 n.53
    and 57; character, 119-122, 142; stewardship of estates, 152-153, 157-158, 165-167, 267; children, 121,
    297 n.68; rivalry and feud with Huntly, 122, 125-126, 127, 129, 131, 132, 135, 136 141,143, 148, 154, 155-

156, 159, 160-169; financial problems, 142-143; Brig O'Dee rebellion, 149; and Cawdor, 182, 306 n.6; association with Bothwell, 144, 162-165, 167,170-172, 175, 195, 303 n.55 and 64; death of wife,169; murder of, 173-180, 221, 222, 225, 226, 305 n.30; martyr, 190, 227-228, 234, 267, 268; corpse, 192, 200, 197-198; burial of, 226-228, 230, 311 n.16; comparison with death of Melgum, 234, 235; with murder of Darnley, 239; with the Regent Moray, 12, 241-242. Plates 18 and 19.

Stewart, James (d.1595), of Bothwellmuir, 2nd son of 2nd Baron Ochiltree, Earl of Arran (1581-1586), 117, 127, 171.

Stewart, James (c.1582-1638), 3rd Earl of Moray (1591/2), birth, 121, 297 n.68, 128, 198, 201, 209, 226, 230, 231; marries Anne Gordon, 231-232; secures earldom, 232; Lieutenant in the North, 234; Frendraught, 235; funeral of Huntly, 237; death, 237.

Stewart, Jean (d.1622), sister of 2nd Earl of Moray, 111, 179.

Stewart, John (1481-1536), 4th Duke of Albany, Governor of Scotland, 26.

Stewart, John (d.1569/70), 4th Baron Innermeath (c.1530), 91.

Stewart, John (c.1518-1579), 4th Earl of Athol (1542), 46, 53, 59, 68; 81, 83, 88, 90, 94, 97, 291 n.13.

Stewart, John, (1563-1595), 5th Earl of Athol (1579), 127, 132, 137, 144, 151, 155, 159, 160, 161, 162, 163, 167, 168, 196, 198, 202, 204-205, 207, 208, 209, 210, 211.

Stewart, John (c.1562-1603), 6th Baron Innermeath (1585/6), Earl of Athol (1595/6), 198, 203.

Stewart, John, of Appin, 163, 183, 184.

Stewart, Ludovick (1574-1624), 2nd Duke of Lennox (1583), 1st Duke of Richmond (1623), 132, 148, 170, 171, 190, 194, 195, 209, 222, 312 n.4.

Stewart, Margaret, illegitimate daughter of James IV, mother of 4th Earl of Huntly, 20, 26.

Stewart, Margaret (d.1639), second daughter of Regent Moray, married the Earl of Nottingham, 117.

Stewart, Princess Margaret (1598-1600), daughter of James VI, 230.

Stewart, Matthew (1516-1571), 4th Earl of Lennox, (1526-1571), Regent of Scotland (1570), 33, 35 97-99, 112, Darnley, 80, 85; commissions memorial, 261.

Stewart, Murdoch (d.1425), 2nd Duke of Albany (1420), Regent of Scotland (1420), 111.

Stewart, Robert (1340-1420), 1st Duke of Albany (1398), Regent of Scotland (1406), 18, 111.

Stewart, Prince Robert (February-May 1602), 3rd son of James VI, died in infancy, 231.

Stewart, William (d.1588), 3rd son of 2nd Baron Ochiltree, murdered by Bothwell, 132, 171.

Surrey, earls of (see Howard).

Sussex, earls of (see Radcliffe).

Thompson, William (c.1712-c.1766), poet, 265, 313 n.5.

Throckmorton, Sir Nicholas (1515-1576), ambassador to Scotland (1565-1567), 90, 288 n.13.

Towie [or Tollie], lairds of (see Forbes).

Trumbill, William, (d.1579), Edinburgh broadside publisher, hanged, 267.

Tudor, Margaret (1489-1541), Queen of Scotland (1504-1513), 25, 26, 80, 107.

Tytler, Patrick Fraser ((1791-1849), historian, grandson of William, 75.

Tytler, William (1711-1792), of Woodhouselee, historian, 266.

Vane, Sir Ralph (d.1552), 43.

Walsingham, Francis, (c.1530-1590), ambassador to Scotland (1583), 127, 131, 138, 145.

Wardlaw, Lady (1677-1727), of Pitreavie, Aberdour, poet, 266.

Warwick, earl of (see Dudley).

Wharton, Thomas (*c*.1495-1568), 1st Baron Wharton (1544), 32.

Winter, Sir William (d.1589), Admiral (1549), 54.

Wishart, George (*c*.1513-1546), of Pitarro, Protestant martyr, burnt at St Andrews, 39, 51.

Wishart, John, of Pitarro, son of the Comptroller under Queen Mary, 119, 142, 297 n.62.

Wood, John, of Tillidevy, secretary to the Regent Moray, 292 n.18; 293 n.23.

Worcester, earls of (see Somerset).

Workman, James, funerary artist, son of John, 237, 262.

Workman, John (d.1604), funerary artist, father of James 197, 237, 262-263.

Wotton, Edward, English agent, 181.

Yester, baron (see Hay, William).

GENERAL INDEX

Aberdeen, 52, 57, 62, 65, 71, 93-94, 102-103, 115, 131, 225, 296 n. 39 and 40.

Aberdour Castle, Fife, 108, 118, 119, 174, 178. Plate 14.

'Act of Abolition' (1594), 210.

Ainslie Bond (1567), 85.

Ancrum Moor, battle of (1544/5), 37, 287 n.32.

Arkinholme, Battle of (1455), on the Esk near Langholm, 19.

Auld Alliance (1295-1567) between Scotland and France, 26, 36.

Badenoch, Inverness-shire, upper strath of river Spey from Laggan to Aviemore, 18, 21, 28, 38, 39, 46, 67, 152, 158, 204, 205, 214.

Ballads, of 'Corrichie,' 255-256; 'Edom o'Gordon,' 100, 294 n.37; 'the Bonnie Earl of Moray', 194, 265-268, 313 n.1-315 n.13; 'Frendraught,' 229; 'Young Waters,' 313 n.7; 'Gil Maurice,' 315 n.10; Black letter ballads, 96.

Ballindalloch Castle, Banffshire, 159.

Berwick, Treaty of (1560) between England and the Lords of the Congregation, 54, 109.

Black Douglases, defeat of, 19.

Blackness Castle, West Lothian, state prison, 155, description of, 197. Plate 33.

Bloodfeud, 132-135, 201, 229-230; Act against (1598), 229, 242, 243, 285 n.1.

Bog of Gight, 28, 38, 46, 152, 155, 207.

Book of Discipline, 57.

Boulogne, Treaty of (1550), 288 n.60.

Brechin, Battle of (1452), in Angus, 18.

Brig O'Dee rebellion (1589), 149-150, 157, 167. So called after the great granite bridge over the Dee, built 1520-1527 as a link to the south.

Brighen, battle of (1572), 100.

Cabroch, battle of (1592), 204.

Cambridge University, Queen's College, 114.

Cameron, Clan, 28, 37, 38, 168, 205, 216.

Carberry Hill, 'battle' of (1567), near Mussleborough, Midlothian, 86, 87, 261.

Castle Gloom (Castle Campbell), 110, 120.

Catholics and Catholicism, 16, 30, 52, 57-58, 62-63, 65-66, 80, 82, 93, 102-103, 124-125, 145, 206, 233-234, 296 n.39.

'Chaseabout Raid' (1565), 81.

Chattan, Clan, (see Mackintosh), 28, 37-38, 46-47, 158, 159, 163, 204, 205, 234, 286 n.9.

Civil War, Marian, 89-103, 111, 112.

'Cleansing the Causeway' (1520), 26.

Commendators, 16, 108-109.

Confederate Lords, 87, 89.

Congregation, Lords of the (1557), 52-55, 109, 261, 291 n.17.

Corgarff Castle, burning of (1571), 100, 294 n.37.

Corrichie, battle of, (1562), 67-71, 212, 217, 289 n.14, 290 n.42.

Crabstone, battle of (1571),100.

Craigmiller Conference (1566), 84.

'Creeping Parliament' (1571), 98.

Darnaway Castle, Moray, 20, 21, 28, 37, 63, 142, 160, 164, 167, 171, 177, 263.

Donnibristle House, Fife, 108, 112, 118, 171; description of, 117, 173-175, 193; attack on 177-180; burning of, 174, 178, 179-180, 190, 221. Plate 13.

Doune Castle, 98, 110, 114, 116, 208, 296 n.46; description of, 111-113. Plate 11.

Drybrugh Abbey, sacking of (1545), 37.

Dumbarton Castle, surrender of to Arran (1546), 39 91, Crawford (1571), 98, 118, 195.

Dunbar Castle, 40, 53, 74, 87, 89, 91.

Dunkinty, battle of (1452), 19.

Edinburgh, 26, 36, 52, balladry in, 268; Treaty of (1560), 55, 57; convention at, 94; university of, 115; Castle, 19, 43, 52, 53, 60, 81, 87, 89; under Kirkaldy, 98-99, 102. Plate 9.

Education, 15, 113-116, 133-134.

Elgin, Moray, 19, 63, 161, 163, 214, 219, 237.

England and the English, 15, 25, 31-33, 35, 36-37, 39-45, 49, 50, 51, 52, 54, 55, 57, 58, 60, 97-98, 108-109, 114, 124.

Falkland, Palace, Fife, 33, 127, 167.

Farming, 16.

Fawside Bray (1547), cavalry actions at, 41.

'Field of Shirts,' (1544), 38.

Fishing, value of, 16,17, 19; feuds over, 131, 154; 155-156, 166-167, 234.

Flodden, battle of (1513), 21, 25, 33.

Football, 103, 294 n.46, 314 n.6.

Forbes–Gordon feud: 29-30, 68, 99-100; 125.

French influence, 26, 30, 40, 47, 48, 49, 50, 52, 53, 54, 55, 60, 126.

Frendraught, fire at (1630), 234-236; ballad of, 229.

Glasgow, Pacification of (1569), 94; university, 115.

Glenlivet, battle of (1594), 184, 213-220, 310 n.2, 12, and 26.

'Golden Act,' (1592), 203.

Gordon, Clan, 16-17, 20, 28, 68, 97, 129.

Grant, Clan, 46, 135, 158-162, 204.

Greenwich, Treaty of (1543), 35.

Hadden-rig, Battle of (1542), 31.

Halidon Hill, Battle of (1333), 17.

Holyrood Palace, 36, 136, 138, 292 n.19; Bothwell's attack on (1591), 170-171.

Homildon Hill, Battle of (1402), 18.

Huntly Castle, (see Strathbogie).

Inchcolm Abbey 43, 108-109, 173, 295 n.7-9, 14.

Inverness Castle, 20, 21, taken by Mary (1562), 64.

Jedburgh Abbey, Roxburghshire, sack of (1544), 36.

Kelso Abbey, sack of (1542), 31, 32.

Kilmaddock Cemetery, 227, 263. Plate 12.

Kinlochlochy, battle of (1544), 'the 'Field of Shirts,' 38.

Kinneil House, Bo'ness, West Lothian, built in 1540s-1550s for Chatelherault, 120, 121.

Kirk, The, 90, 127, 128, 157, 170, 191, 195, 201, 203, 208, 210, 211, 224, 225, 226, 229, 232, 233, 268, 307 n.15.

Kirk o'Fields, (1566/7), 85.

Langside, battle of (1568), 91-92.

Leith, port of, 36, 43; occupied by French troops, 53; siege of, 54-55, 110; Mary Lands at, 58; 1st Earl of Moray's
    body taken to, 96; 2nd earl of Moray's body taken to, 190, 192, 200.

Linlithgow Palace, 35, 95, 96, 97, 196-197. Plate 3.

Lochaber, 21, 28, 38.

Lochmaben Castle, 32.

Lords of the Congregation (1557), 52, 53, 54.

Lordship of the Isles, 37.

MacDonald, Clan, 37-38, 213.

Mackintosh, Clan, part of Clan Chattan, 28, 46, 49-50, 68, 158, 168, 204.

Manrent, bonds of, 285 n.8

Marian party (see Civil War).

Melrose Abbey, sackings of (May 1544 and September 1545), 36, 37.

Moray, ballad of 'the Bonnie Earl' (see Ballads)

'Morayland,' 19-20, 93, 107. Plate 10.

Moray Memorial, 174, 179, 193-194, 261-263, 267. Plates 15, 16, 17, and 18.

Neville's Cross, Battle of (1346), 17.

Nobility, the Scots, poverty, 124; youthfulness, 132; education, 133, violence, 132-134.

Otterburn, battle of, (1388), j18.

Oxford University, 114.

Perth (St Johnston), 52, 293 n.13; Treaty of (1559), 52; Pacification of (1572/3), 101, 125.

Petty Castle, 204.

Pinkie, battle of (1547): 41-43, 44, 109, 287 n.39.

'Presentation of Blood,' 192-193.

Protestants (see Reformation, Kirk) 52, 58, 59, 102-103, 147.

Ranald, Clan, 37-38, 49, 204, 216

Ravenscraig Castle, 190.

Reformation, 10, 15, 30, 51, 52, 57.

Reformation Parliament (1560), 57, 110.

Regency Council, 33, 34, 35.

Riffen Castle, Badenoch, 158, 214.

'Ronie Rode,' (1587), 137

'Rough Wooing' (1544-1547), England's courtship with Scotland, 36, 39-44, 287 n.29.

Ruthven Raid (1582), 126-127.

St Andrews, 54, 59; Scotland's oldest university (1412), 51, 115-116.

St Andrews Castle, murder of Beaton (1546), 39; siege (1546-7), 39, 40, 51, 127.

St Bartholomew's Day Massacre of French Huguenots (1572), 101.

St Giles Kirk, Edinburgh, 96; 191, 210; tomb of Regent Moray, 227-228, 271-272. Plate 5.

St Machar's Cathedral, Aberdeen, 52.

Sauchieburn, battle of (1488), 20.

Solway Moss, battle of (1542) 32, 35, 37, 50, 219.

Spanish Armada (1588), 143.

'Spanish Blanks' (1592/3), 205-207.

Spey, river, 16, 19, 107, 131, 158.

Sports, 314 n.4 and 6, 315 n.7.

Spynie Palace, residence of the bishops of Moray, 19, 158, 163.

Stirling, raid on (1571), 96, 98-99.

Stirling Castle, 35, 36.

Strathbogie Castle, 17, 18, 38, 39, 47, 52, 66, 126, 155, 168, 169, 195, 214, 219, 221, 237; renamed Huntly (1544),
    39; rebuilt (1551-1554), 47; magnificence of, 47-48, 62-63, 65; despoiled (1562), 74; 207, 288 n.8; razed
    (1594), rebuilt, 233.

Tantallon Castle, 27, 40

Tulliangus, battle of (1571), 99.

Weapons, 132, 134, 177, 289 n.30.

Other Scottish history titles available from Tempus:

Flodden 1513
Niall Barr
'enthralling... reads as thrillingly as a novel.' *The Scots Magazine*
'an engrossing account of the battle... exemplary.' *BBC History Magazine*
'the first modern analysis... a very readable account.' *Historic Scotland*
'a very considerable achievement... fascinating and convincing.' *Military Illustrated*
160pp 65 illus. Paperback
£16.99/$32.50   ISBN 0 7524 1792 4

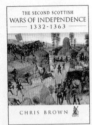

The Second Scottish War of Independence 1332–1363
Chris Brown
The least well known of Britain's medieval wars, the Second Scottish War of
Independence lasted for more than thirty years. The Scots were utterly
defeated in three major battles. So how did England lose the war?
208pp 100 illus. Paperback
£16.99/$19.99   ISBN 0 7524 2312 6

The Battle of Bannockburn 1314
Aryeh Nusbacher
'The most accessible and authoritative book on the battle' *Dr Fiona Watson,
presenter of the* BBC TV *history of Scotland*, In Search of Scotland.
'The first book on the Bannockburn campaign for almost a
century...recommended' *Historic Scotland*
176pp 73 illus. Paperback
£12.99/$18.99   ISBN 0 7524 2326 6

Scotland A History 8000 B.C. – 2000 A.D.
Fiona Watson
A *Scotsman* Bestseller
'Lavishly illustrated throughout, its trenchant views, surprising revelations and evocative
descriptions will entrance all who care about Scotland.' *BBC History Magazine*
A comprehensive history of a proud nation written by Scotland's answer to
Simon Schama, Fiona Watson, historian and presenter of *BBC* Television's
landmark history series *In Search of Scotland*.
304pp 100 illus. Paperback
£9.99/$14.99   ISBN 0 7524 2331 2

The Kings and Queens of Scotland
Richard Oram (Editor)
'the colourful, complex and frequently bloody story of Scottish rulers... an
exciting if rarely edifying tale, told in a clear and elegant format.' *BBC History
Magazine*
'remarkable' *History Today*
272pp 212 illus (29 col) Paperback
£16.99/$22.99   ISBN 0 7524 1991 9

UK ORDERING

Simply write, stating the quantity of books required and enclosing a cheque for the correct amount, to: Sales
Department, Tempus Publishing Ltd, The Mill, Brimscombe Port, Stroud, Glos. GL5 2QG, UK.
Alternatively, call the sales department on 01453 883300 to pay by Switch, Visa or Mastercard.

US ORDERING

Please call Arcadia Publishing, a division of Tempus Publishing, toll free on 1-888-313-2665